China Off Center

September 17, 2002

Jn Dennis i Debbie,

lovving China, of
volleyball, and, of course
our shared university.

With affection i appreciation

愛

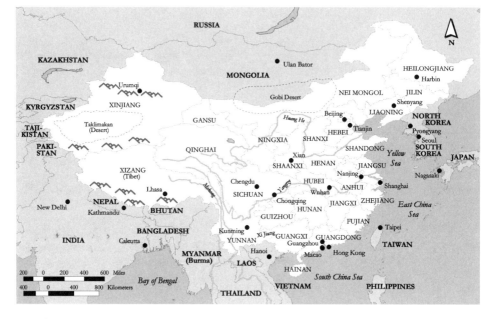

China's provinces and neighboring countries.

China
Off Center

Mapping the Margins of
the Middle Kingdom

EDITED BY **SUSAN D. BLUM**
AND **LIONEL M. JENSEN**

University of Hawai'i Press
Honolulu

Library of Congress Cataloging-in-Publication Data
China off center: mapping the margins of the middle kingdom /
edited by Susan D. Blum and Lionel M. Jensen.
p. cm.
Includes bibliographical references and index.
ISBN 0-8248-2335-4 (alk. paper)—ISBN 0-8248-2577-2 (pbk.: alk. paper)
1. China—Social conditions—1976–
I. Blum, Susan Debra. II. Jensen, Lionel M.
HN733.5 .M35 2002
306' .0951—dc21
2002002101

Maps by Carola Hiltawksy. Maps in chapter 10 adapted by Carola Hiltawsky from Mary S. Erbaugh, "The Secret History of the Hakkas," *China Quarterly* 132 (Dec. 1992).

Designed by Kaelin Chappell

Printed by The Maple-Vail Book Manufacturing Group

I heard that south of the capital city
There thrived a menagerie of mountains amassed,

East and west bordering both seas,
I struggled to delve into all, both great and small.

The Mountain Classic and other geographical works
Are confused and vague without oral traditions.

So collecting my phrases I tried writing an abstract,
But knew each point recalled meant a thousand forgotten.

I should have stopped but truthfully was unwilling,
So roughly I recount now only things I saw.

HAN YÜ (768–824)

Turning and turning in the widening gyre
The falcon cannot hear the falconer;
Things fall apart; the center cannot hold;
Mere anarchy is loosed upon the world. . . .

WILLIAM BUTLER YEATS

To our teachers and to our students,
friends and fellow travelers
in the passage from here to there

Contents

Foreword

Sovereignty and Citizenship in a Decentered China

The editors of this volume seek to demonstrate that the enduring image of China as a homogeneous society and culture—China as a distinctly "centered" society—cannot really be sustained when we look closely at the usual indicators of cultural and social integration: language, ethnicity, region, and religion, among others. The question, then, of why this image persists has as much to do with the conditions and causes of its production in China. At the same time, our expectations of what we should find in China also doubtless feed into this image.

In many ways, the idea of a centered China derives from a Western historiography that depicted imperial China in the very imperial language of centering and universalism. The official and historiographic view held that, as a universal empire, China's civilizing virtues, often embodied in "Confucian" learning, radiated out from the son of heaven, the emperor, and suffused the empire, although with declining strength the farther away one got from the center. In this sense, the ideology of civilization was seen to have both a definitive and a generative center. It was a center that not only marked off all that was civilized from that which was not but also sought to civilize (*jiaohua*) those who were not. In this conception, which we might loosely call an official view informing both Chinese and Western perceptions, China centeredness also implied sinification, and that is why, in this conception, we expect imperial China to be more or less "centered."

But, as many of the essays in this volume show us, we can scarcely think of China of having a society emerging only from a normative, political center. Differences abounded. Even where the centralized doctrines of the state were concerned, we see that, during the Qing period (1644–1911), the imperial state actually demonstrated or performed its claim to rule—its claim to sovereignty—not simply through Confucian rites and injunctions, but through a number of cosmologies that we would be hard-pressed to call *Chinese*. Thus, the Manchus located themselves, not only in the Han imperial tradition, but also as inheritors to the regional imperial tradition of the northeast associated with the Jin empire of the twelfth century. For Mongols and Tibetans, the Qing emperor was the reincarnation of the bodhi-sattva Manjusri, whose cult was performed by these emperors on Mount Wutai in Shanxi. For the smaller groups in the southwest, imperial policy was relatively loose and permitted wide variation. To be sure, sinicization or Hanification occurred through the movement of the Han population into the vast hinterlands, movement that was sometimes encouraged by the imperial state. But, as many scholars have been telling us, the Qing empire was as much a Central Asian empire as it was a Chinese one, and the center itself was hard to define, particularly in the great frontiers where myriad traditions and practices coexisted with, say, official culture.

In the twentieth century, it is said, China was no longer the universal empire but became, in the words of the great reformer Liang Qichao (1873–1929), a nation among nations. China became cosmologically decentered in that it no longer saw itself as the standard and the definer of civilization. Ironically enough, it is China as a modern nation-state that undertook the most unprecedented measures to homogenize and standardize the population—whether the minorities who occupied the vast hinterlands or the diverse peasant population in the heartland itself, both of whose practices and behavior diverged considerably from the perspective of the modernizing, nationalist elites. Consider the peripheral peoples first. Although the Guomindang (GMD, the "National People's Party," 1913–1949) regime theoretically recognized China as the Republic of Five Nationalities, its leadership and policies made it clear that the government sought to assimilate the minorities into the Han nationality. The problem with the GMD was that it was too weak politically to succeed in the assimilation project while, at the same time, its top-down administrative and, later, military measures often alienated the minority peoples. This alienation was rapidly translated into a call for a national self-determination—the mobilizing consciousness of the twentieth century—or autonomous nationhood theoretically equal to that of the Han Chinese. Ethnic and nationality rebellions were endemic from the mid-nineteenth century until the establishment of firm control by the Chinese Communist Party (CCP). In the first half of the twentieth century, secessionist movements in Mongolia, Xinjiang, and Tibet as well as many small-scale rebellions among indigenous peoples in the southwest and other parts revealed the difficulties encountered by the policies of assimilation and homogenization.

In this context, sovereignty and citizenship took on new meanings in new nation-states like China. Whereas we are led to believe that sovereignty derives from a prior right to represent a certain group of people, historically the process has often been reversed. Nation-states have presumed the right to represent many of the people in the territories over which they claimed sovereignty—whether or not the people desired such representation. The historically "successful" nation-states were able subsequently to produce, through education and other means, an identification in these people with the territorial nation-state. In the era of anti-imperialist nationalism during the twentieth century, such a brazen presumption was harder to sustain, especially where the various peoples, cultures, and regions saw themselves as the subjects of their own history. Here, the dominant nationalists frequently presented these peoples with an implicit or explicit deal whereby the latter would be compensated for surrendering their independence with the nation-state's grant of its most valued product: the right to equality and progress and the benefits of citizenship. It was this tacit compact that was, for instance, behind the declaration of the 1911 republic as the Republic of the Five Nationalities. This declaration implicitly recognized the hinterland territories as the homelands of the Tibetans, Mongols, Muslims, and others, even as they became a part of the Chinese nation-state. However, neither in its practice nor often in its doctrinal pronouncements did the GMD state actually abide by this principle of self-determination *within the nation-state.* It basically pursued a policy of assimilation and sinification of the minorities, and President Chiang Kai-shek (1887–1975) often sought to minimize the differences among the five nationalities as insignificant ones that could be overcome under Han leadership. The policies of the succeeding Communist regime were much more substantial. Not only did that regime grant citizenship rights to the peoples of the peripheries, but it also implemented a policy of affirmative action to compensate for their historical disadvantages. To be sure, discrimination has persisted in practice, and relative disparities continue between Han and non-Han even today (see Blum, chap. 8 in this volume).

Within the heartland, nationalists also sought to homogenize the immense variety of cultural life and practices in the process of making the rural and urban peoples into a modern citizenry loyal to the nation-state above all else. This was not uncommonly a violent process as GMD activists sought to commandeer temple property and lands used for various community functions in the name of fighting superstition and ignorance. In many places, the people resisted these seizures, presumably because they both valued their communal and spiritual life and because they mistrusted the ways in which the new, intrusive state apparatus would allocate these resources. After the early 1930s, the regime enacted legislation protecting "religions" and outlawing "superstition," but, by the way in which it defined and officially licensed religion, it excluded or outlawed many hundreds of religious or religiously oriented societies that commanded followings of tens, if not hundreds, of millions of rural and urban Chinese. Some of the more well-known of these societies were the Yiguandao, the Dao Yuan, and the White Lotus Society. The Communist regime regarded these religious societies in the 1940s and early 1950s as a major enemy and executed hundreds of thousands of believers. The recent resurgence of similar religious societies that was brought to world attention by the Falun Gong demonstrations and the subsequent outlawing of the group in 1999 indicates that alternative beliefs and practices are alive and well in China. It is interesting that, in the twentieth century, the power of these societies was detected by the academic radar of neither Chinese nor Western scholarship, in perfect obedience to the centered nation-state ideology advanced by the GMD and the CCP alike.

One of the great strengths of a volume such as this is that it brings to light the many alternative lives of Chinese buried under the phantom of "centeredness." A second and related advantage is its focus on a prominent global movement—transnationalism. Part of the reason for the greater visibility of suppressed and obscured forces like the Falun Gong today is the growth of transnationalism—the increasing power of global capitalism, international media, and nongovernment organizations. Within China, this has been accompanied by the weakening of the ideological legitimacy of the Communist state. Faith in alternative and transcendent sources of meaning has historically been a part of Chinese life, and a century of nationalist and Communist homogenizing discipline has not managed to eliminate these sources of difference.

To be sure, we never step into the same river twice, and the new transnational forces are already beginning to offer new means of communication—via the Internet, for instance—and, thus, new forms of support and survival for the religious groups, many of which lie beyond the boundaries of the Chinese nation. For instance, Illinois governor George H. Ryan has officially endorsed the Falun Gong, and Chicago mayor Richard M. Daley declared 25 June 1999 to be Master Li Hongzhi (founder and leader of the Falun Gong) Day in Chicago. The vision and interests of the overseas Chinese community—another transnational force—may diverge considerably from those of the nation-state. Transnational forces have also registered an impact on the peripheries of the nation (see Barnett, chap. 5 in this volume; and Gladney, chap. 6 in this volume). Mongols and Muslims are attracted to Mongol and Muslim nation-states across the Chinese border. Diasporic Tibetan nationalism and international media support for Tibetan nationalism is a matter of concern to Beijing. The border between Southeast Asia and Yunnan has once again become culturally porous, and, in northeast China, or Manchuria, a transnational economic region along the Tumen river is being developed.

Of course, it would be most foolhardy to underestimate the continued power of nationalism within China as witnessed in the vituperative and violent protests of the Belgrade embassy bombings in the spring and summer of 1999. Yet we also saw that this centering nationalist impulse was simply one part of a more complex picture, one dimension of a people who could be enraged with the U.S. government one day and sacrifice all to go to the United States the next. This is hardly unique to China. The impulse to center and decenter in the contemporary world reflects the multiple contradictory forces to which we are all subjected. What it will do to the notion of the center in the twenty-first century is worth following closely, and *China Off Center* will improve the acuity of our observation.

SUSAN D. BLUM AND
LIONEL M. JENSEN

Preface

China Off Center takes as its fundamental assumption that contemporary China can be understood only as a complex, increasingly decentralized place, where the view from above, from Beijing, and from tourist buses or conference rooms is a skewed one. Instead of generalizing about *China,* we demonstrate that this vast place is better conceived as a set of *many Chinas,* with clear similarities between yet many differences among the parts. To that end, we focus on the particular, the local, and the puzzling. We have compiled a collection of varied readings that are a reflection of the diversity of China's many faces, or at least those many, previously unrepresented faces that we have chosen to portray. In an era of the balkanization of Chinese studies, many of these faces may be seen only in specialized collections or in technical professional journals, read only by scholars of that discipline. Yet, when these many images are put together, they convey a rather different impression than when each selection appears with others like it. Like the celebrated Indian parable of the blind men and the elephant, the identity of the whole is sacrificed to the specificity of each man's perspective. We seek to collect each viewer's report into the complex elephantine whole of China, without silencing any of their voices. The readings are held together by the question, What are some little-known but significant aspects of China that keen observers have noted in the 1990s? These selections and their contextualizing introductions provide a foundation that will enable students, with the assistance of their professors, to embark on a journey to the edges of a kingdom called *middle,* where clear answers are sure to be misleading and where flux is the only constant.

We initially assembled many of these chapters for a course that we offered on contemporary Chinese society at Yunnan University in Kunming, in southwest China. Our students were all Americans from the University of Colorado, with an extremely wide range of backgrounds: some had studied the Chinese language for several years; some had an enduring focus on China; and others were merely curious. Our aim was to introduce a variety of topics both from a fairly conventional perspective (from books) and from an unusual perspective (from many of the articles included here) and ask students to compare their reading to their own observations. In the process, they had to account for differences among the various versions.

Some of these articles were written especially for this book; others derive from papers delivered at recent conferences or published in journals or books. (It should be noted that previously published material has been edited to conform to the University of Hawai'i Press house style for consistency in such matters as spelling, capitalization, italicization, and punctuation.) All share a perspective that begins "on the ground"; hence, a large number of articles are by anthropologists, people trained to find "heaven in the details." The success of the enterprise of introducing China's overwhelming localism depends on the ability of these selections to situate the reader in the Chinese experience. *China Off Center* may easily be used in conjunction with any more conventional account of the sweep of Chinese history and society.

The three parts of the book ("The Center and the Noncenter," "Geographic Margins," "Social and Cultural Margins") can be read in any order. Each of the sections has several subsections, showing one way in which this diversity can be organized. The variant everydayness that we have been able to represent is not exhaustive, but it is meant to suggest a way of framing one's inquiry. Instead of generalizing about China at the outset, with exceptions mentioned as an afterword, these accounts suggest the perils of generalization. If we turn the enterprise of understanding China on its head, we might find that common platitudes are displaced by an assortment of particular observations that *cannot* be reduced to single statements. A common claim is that "less is more." May we suggest that, with respect to a proper understanding of China, "more is more"?

Our first thanks go to our many teachers from many schools: the late Gao Gongyi at Stanford; Chester Cheng at San Francisco State; Bill Baxter, Pete Becker, James Crump, Ken DeWoskin, Norma Diamond, Paul Dresch, Sergei Kan, Shuen-fu Lin, Bruce Mannheim, Harriet Mills, Donald Munro, the late Skip Rappaport, and Aram Yengoyan at Michigan; the late Frank Markwriter of New Orleans; Peter Frost and Jay Ogilvy at Williams College; George Hatch and Mark Selden at Washington University; and Gerard Caspary, Martin Jay, David Keightley, Donald Price, Tu Wei-ming, and Frederic Wakeman at Berkeley.

We would like to thank our students from various institutions—Oklahoma State University, the University of Oklahoma, the University of Pennsylvania, Whitman College, the University of Denver, the University of Colorado at Boulder, the University of Colorado at Denver, and the University of Notre Dame—for their enthusiasm, inquiries, and puzzlement. The pioneering eleven students who accompanied us (or did we accompany them?) to Kunming in the summer of 1994 saw the first incarnation of this project. They are Alison Beckius, Betsey Coleman, Kevin Geraghty, Darren Glynn,

Elisa Holland, Erika Kuenne, Monica Liley, Michael Kai Miller, Harold Powell, Lori Shepard, and Patrice Weddig Thoresen. We are grateful to Sara Davis for assistance tracking down articles, to Joan Rhoads and Connie Turner for scanning and general moral support, and to Carolyne Janssen for exquisite guidance in technological matters. Dr. Louis C. (Rusty) Liley Jr. was extraordinarily gracious in permitting us to use his beautiful photographs. Ms. Jeanne Barnett was prompt and generous in locating the photographs of her late husband, Doak Barnett. All the maps were prepared by Carola Hiltawsky. The index was prepared by two extraordinary Notre Dame students, Megan Murphy and Seth Hiland. Without the enthusiastic support of Patricia Crosby at the University of Hawai'i Press and Barbara Watson Andaya at the University of Hawai'i and the judicious editorial intervention of Cheri Dunn and Joseph Brown, this book would not have the form that it does and would have been a much poorer one. To the authors of the chapters of this book, many of whom wrote specifically for this particular volume, we are greatly indebted. We hope that the attention of the public to their work is adequate compensation for their efforts. The Institute for Scholarship in the Liberal Arts, in the College of Arts and Letters at the University of Notre Dame, directed by Cindy S. Bergeman with the capable assistance of Beth Bland, was extremely generous in providing funding for the cartography of Carola Hiltawsky and for permission to reprint previously published material.

As always, it was our families (Blums, Jensens, and Blum Jensens) that were the ballast and the motor for our intellectual adventures. Without our daughters, Elena and Hannah, who walked the fields and streets of Yunnan with us, the adventures that led to this work would have been far less rewarding and intolerably lonely. During the book's production we lost both of Lionel's parents, Millard and Gloria Jensen, leaving us diminished and saddened. At the same time we are grateful for the sustaining power of memory and community, which serve as center. May their memories be a blessing.

Acknowledgments

It is with profound gratitude that we acknowledge the following for permission to reprint previously published materials:

Chapter 2 appeared originally as "How Much of China Is Ruled by Beijing?" by Liu Binyan, http://www.china-net.org/ccf9612-2.html (posted 13 March 1996; accessed 10 February 1998). Reprinted by permission of the author.

Chapter 3 is a condensed version of Edward Friedman, "Reconstructing China's National Identity: A Southern Alternative to Mao-Era Anti-Imperialist Nationalism," *Journal of Asian Studies* 53, no. 1 (February 1994): 67–91. Reprinted with permission of the Association for Asian Studies, Inc.

Chapter 4 is a condensed version of S. Robert Ramsey, "The Languages of China," in *The Languages of China*, 19–30, 87–115. (Copyright © 1987 by Princeton University Press). Reprinted by permission of Princeton University Press.

Chapter 5 is a condensed version of A. Doak Barnett, "Chinese Turkestan: Xinjiang," in *China's Far West: Four Decades of Change* (Boulder, Colo.: Westview, 1993), 341–407. Reprinted by permission of the author.

Chapter 6 is a condensed version of Dru Gladney, "Ethnoreligious Resurgence in a Northwestern Sufi Community," *Muslim Chinese: Ethnic Nationalism in the People's Republic,* 2nd ed. (Cambridge, Mass.: Council on East Asian Studies, 1996), 117–169. © 1991, 1996 by the President and Fellows of Harvard College. Reprinted by permission of the Harvard University Asia Center.

Chapter 9, "The Construction of Chinese and Non-Chinese Identities," is reprinted by permission of *Daedalus,* Journal of the American Academy of Arts and Sciences, from the issue, "The Living Tree: The Changing Meaning of Being Chinese Today," *Daedalus* 120, no. 2 (spring 1991).

Chapter 10 first appeared as Mary S. Erbaugh, "The Secret History of the Hakkas: The Chinese Revolution as a Hakka Enterprise," *China Quarterly* 132

(December 1992): 937–968. Reprinted by permission of Oxford University Press.

Chapter 11 is abstracted from Dalin Liu, Man Lun Ng, Li Ping Zhou, and Erwin J. Haeberle, *Sexual Behavior in Modern China: Report on the Nationwide Survey of 20,000 Men and Women*, trans. Man Lun Ng and Erwin J. Haeberle, copyright © 1997 by Dalin Liu and Man Lun Ng (New York: Continuum, 1997), 15–28, 198–216, 219–251, 288, 351–395, 403–410. Reprinted by permission of The Continuum Publishing Company.

Chapter 12 first appeared as Vincent E. Gil, "The Cut Sleeve Revisited: A Brief Ethnographic Interview with a Male Homosexual in Mainland China," *Journal of Sex Research* 29, no. 4 (November 1992): 560–577. Reprinted by permission of the author.

Chapter 13 first appeared as James Tyson and Ann Tyson, "'The Moon Reflecting the Sunlight': The Village Woman," in *Chinese Awakenings: Life Stories from the Unofficial China* (Boulder, Colo.: Westview, 1995), 185–203. Reprinted by permission of Westview Press, a member of Perseus Books, L.L.C.

Chapter 14 is a condensed version of Dorothy J. Solinger, "The Floating Population in the Cities: Chances for Assimilation?" in *Urban Spaces in Contemporary China: The Potential for Autonomy and Community in Post-Mao China*, ed. Deborah S. Davis, Richard Kraus, Barry Naughton, and Elizabeth J. Perry (Washington, D.C.: Woodrow Wilson Center Press; Cambridge: Cambridge University Press, 1995), 113–139. Reprinted by permission of the Woodrow Wilson Center Press.

Chapter 15 first appeared as Andrew F. Jones, "The Politics of Popular Music in Post-Tiananmen China," in *Popular Protest and Political Culture in Modern China* (2d ed.), ed. Elizabeth J. Perry and Jeffrey N. Wasserstrom (Boulder, Colo.: Westview, 1994), 148–165. Reprinted by permission of Jeffrey Wasserstrom.

Chapter 17 is a condensed version of Diane Dorfman, "The Spirit of Reform: The Power of Belief in Northern China," *positions: east asia cultures critique* 4, no. 2 (fall 1996): 253–289. Copyright 1996, Duke University Press. Reprinted with permission.

SUSAN D. BLUM AND
LIONEL M. JENSEN

I
Introduction

Reconsidering the Middle Kingdom

When Americans think of China, a familiar set of images tends to come to mind: the Great Wall, chopsticks, Guilin's dramatic stone and mist landscape, peasants toiling timelessly in rice paddies (see fig. 1.1), long silk dresses with slits up the side, mysterious writing, the Forbidden City, communism. Perhaps a set of more abstract issues also occurs to those who occupy themselves with public affairs: human rights violations; the handover of Hong Kong; toy, sneaker, and clothing manufacturing; strict birth control; trade imbalance; the violation of international copyright laws; and a lone resister standing before a tank in the terror to which we now refer as *the Tiananmen massacre*.

None of these impressions is wrong, just as it is not wrong when envisioning the United States to think solely about the White House or apple pie, Williamsburg or the Wild West, or our high rate of divorce and substance abuse. Still, as citizens of the United States, we would probably feel that this sampling was not adequate to convey everything that we think important about our own society. What about Nobel Prizes or our most common national pastime (claimed variously to be gardening and baseball)?

In the popular Western imagination, China has for centuries been a symbol of centeredness, in large part because of our casual translation of one of China's names for itself, Zhongguo, as "Middle Kingdom" or, even more elaborately, "the Center of the World" (Elegant 1968). Westerners have assumed that the docile Chinese population inevitably follows the dictates of central authority or, failing that, of tradition. Lack of individualism has been a truism in our understanding of some generic Chinese or even Asian person, with group identification paramount and challenges to norms immediately punished. The more recent addendum to this portrait is that the fervor for modernization has gripped the populace uniformly and that all people who are able to take advantage of contemporary economic opportunities do so in identical ways. Indeed, many people in China share this goal of harmony and uniformity and foster the image received in the West.

FIGURE 1.1
Contemporary and timeless: agricultural work in southern China. *(Photograph by Dr. Louis C. Liley Jr.)*

Yet alongside, beneath, and intersecting this purported centeredness and presumed homogeneity is an immense diversity of peoples, languages, terrain, and everyday practices. Such diversity has been either unrepresented or represented only within a one-dimensional taxonomy of ethnic quaintness by official Chinese publications and presentations. While some familiarity with China is increasingly common in the United States, China's very complexity makes grasping the nuances of its interior a daunting task. Like any society, China is defined as much by its border regions as by its center—and perhaps even more so. Although China's international image is carefully cultivated, its frontiers reveal unraveling and disputation as much in terms of culture as in terms of politics. Unable to speak directly to the country's residents, Westerners often take their view of China from those who translate it for us, usually the urban intellectuals and members of an international political economy. One thing is certain: whether our understanding of China is accurate or inaccurate, the future of the West is irrevocably linked to that of China. Thus, a more nuanced understanding of this nation with which we are increasingly intertwined can only be an asset, we believe.

By acknowledging from the start the fluid quality of contemporary Chinese life—not unlike that in many other equally daunting and complex societies—this book looks beyond its central, because commonly emphasized, features in favor of representing its lesser-known aspects. Each chapter documents some behavior on the geographic, social, cultural, psychological, or linguistic margins of the Middle Kingdom in order to offer a more complete picture of what is possible at least within the physical borders of something that, for now, almost all would call *China*. Aside from the generally fascinating topics themselves (such as ethnic minorities), the whole collection supplements and calls into question commonplace understandings that generalize about a representative Chinese culture that can be observed, say, in state-run factories in Beijing or in joint ventures in the Special Economic Zone of Shenzhen. Many of the articles are based on observations or reports that have some basis in observable behavior; most cover material quite different from what the general public thinks of when it invokes the name *China*. We would like our readers to come away with a sense that it is harder than before to generalize about China and that, like their own society, China contains individuals and groups who are not necessarily typical members of the overall society. After all, Americans feel quite entitled to pick and choose elements that contribute to their own "lifestyle" and identity. Although things do not work quite the same way in China and the United States, clearly it would be wrong to envision people in China as mindless automatons following some centralized program for their lives. Although people in the aggregate follow some sort of generalized script for their lives everywhere—in the United States the script might include going to school, going through a phase of adolescent rebellion, getting a driver's license, graduating from high school, going to college, getting a job, getting married, buying a house, having children, aging—the details that vary from one life to another may provide important insight into the range of possibilities for selves in a particular society.

Not only do we wish to supplement popular U.S. media portrayals of China; we also wish to engage the ideological, patriotic version of a unified country that China increasingly offers at home and abroad. In writing about any human society, some emphases are selected at the expense of others. To tell a coherent story, even of incoherence, one cannot include everything. Hence, most introductory accounts of China present a view from the center (however defined). In history, this is often an account of dynasties and changes of regimes. In political science, it is often a recounting of leaders and policies and laws. In economics, it is usually aggregated statistics about production and consumption, prices, and supplies and demands. In sociology, it is often a general portrayal of groups and classes and their overarching tendencies.

Without disputing the usefulness of such portrayals, for our purpose here we select rather the opposite material and present the more disaggregated views of the China less known to us but intimately familiar to the Chinese. We do so in an accessible rather than a technical way, having sought as many well-written, self-contained accounts as possible.

The two editors of this book are trained in anthropology (SDB) and history (LMJ), both with specializations in China. These two disciplines have two different histories, but they converge as they seek to look at a moment in the culture of China. Historians and anthropologists know that all that we ever have is a series of moments, connected sometimes by what historians following Fernand Braudel have called the *longue durée,* but inseparable from the groundedness and particularity of moments in particular places. In recent decades, anthropologists have been turning to moments in the past yet continuing to employ anthropological methods. Simultaneously, historians have borrowed anthropological concepts for looking at the past and have looked at the present from a historical perspective. Boundaries between disciplines have been blurring; even the clear border between the social sciences and the humanities has become fuzzy.

Anthropologists have long been partisans of a local approach to the study of culture, and, as long as they studied technologically simple islands or village societies, this view sufficed. Historians formerly focused on capitals, kings, and wars, although, since the pioneering work of the Annales school, social historians too have begun to focus on the local and the everyday. Concurrently, anthropologists have begun to study state-level societies. With insights from Marxism, they have tended (along with their Chinese colleagues) to see societies as social systems and historical formations, where forces such as *capitalism* or *colonialism* or *gender inequality* can be seen to account for the structures within which individuals operate. Large numbers of anthropologists, historians, and political scientists have noted the hegemony of a central ideology in China, fueled by propagandistic efforts of a central Party-state, identifying isolated efforts at resistance.

All this is to say that disciplinary focus on particular approaches to the study of a society has become more malleable. The more approaches that one employs in studying an entity as large as China, the more it might be possible to grasp it with something approaching adequacy. *China Off Center* is guided by anthropological interest in particular locales and by historical interest in specificity, but the authors whose works we include draw on a wide range of disciplinary, temporal, geographic, and topical perspectives.

If everyday experience in one place is what is meant by *local,* and if international forces beyond the palpable experience of an individual is what is meant by *global,* our approach is to focus on the local in the context of the global. We hesitate to make generalizations but present accounts that allow the reader, perhaps in conjunction with an instructor, to do so. There has been a fascinating convergence in recent years between the Chinese experience and scholarly explanation of that experience. Recent meetings of scholars of Asian studies are filled with panels on regionalism, the sovereignty of local forces, and ethnicity. One might notice the unraveling of a scholarly assumption about central authority and observe musings about whether the center can hold. Politicians and ordinary people also discuss the future of China's central authority, worrying that it will dissolve.

China Off Center brings some of this scholarly debate to the attention of a wider public. We do so, not to celebrate a potential fragmentation of China, but to portray the complexity and contradiction of any view of that nation. We subtitle our book *Mapping the Margins of the Middle Kingdom* to call attention to the interplay between margin and center. We have chosen to present a variety of frameworks for situating individual selves in a multiplicity of smaller locales that add up to a whole called *China.*

China can be regarded, as it often is, as a unified nation-state. Centralization is one significant current in the eddying sea that is the study of China. In this context, three significant symbols of China's unity are history, language, and culture. We call them *symbols* because, in addition to whatever facts exist about the realities present on the ground, social actors select among these to represent other, larger issues. And certain dimensions of China's history, language, and culture are commonly selected to demonstrate how unified and centralized China is and has been. We will discuss below the centralizing perspective and these three symbols of unity. Following this, we present an argument for adding nuance to this common view by incorporating a decentralizing or noncentralizing viewpoint of China, using evidence from geography, ethnicity, and society and culture. The reader should keep in mind that our intention is additive, not subtractive. A big picture of the forest is important, but a more focused picture of the trees is necessary for a more complete view. Views of the center are readily available. To supplement such views, we present ours of China off center.

CENTRALIZATION IN CHINA

The anthropologist Barbara Ward wrote many years ago about the tendency of multiple ideals to coexist in China. She examined in particular the boat people in Hong Kong. They regarded their own marriage pattern (permitting widow remarriage) as the normal Chinese one, while the land-dwelling people with whom they traded regarded their own pattern (forbidding widow remarriage) as normative. Ward termed these *conscious models* and wanted to emphasize that a variety of such models exists within a society as complex as that of China:

> To talk as we commonly do of "*the* Chinese family" or "*the* traditional social structure of China" is as misleading at the level of ideal patterns as it has long been known to be misleading at the level of actual patterns of behavior. Instead, we have to postulate a number of different Chinese ideal patterns varying in time and space with varying historical development and the demands of particular occupations and environments. . . . Important though it is to correct the popular view of a changeless China, it still remains true that the most remarkable feature of Chinese civilization over its uniquely long history and wide geographical spread is its relative continuity and uniformity. (Ward 1965, 114–115)

Correctives to extremes go both ways. Too great a focus on China's fragmentation surely exaggerates; too much faith in its integration overlooks real challenges. Ward reminds her readers that, although her focus is on China's varying patterns, the country's unity still must be accounted for.

Liu Binyan (chap. 2) argues that China's contemporary lawlessness and disregard of national policies similarly present a threat to the authority of the central government. Edward Friedman (chap. 3) suggests that south China is now beginning to exert a symbolic pull, competing with north China as the real origin of Chinese civilization. Yet, despite compelling evidence of

regional and local forces that oppose national ones, especially in China's economically strong coastal cities—Guangzhou (Canton), Shanghai, Fuzhou—
we should be careful not to overstate the case. The relation between a center
and a region has been conceived in various ways throughout this century
(Fitzgerald 1994), such conceptions only rarely attempting to impose inflexi-
ble uniformity on regions and people. More common than cultural uniformity has been political centralization.

While there is a tremendous and unprecedented amount of centralization and standardization in today's China, established especially through
the vigorous efforts at national reconstruction of the People's Republic of
China (PRC) in the 1950s and 1960s, China's immense size and intrinsic
diversity provide a constant counteractive force to centralization. There is a
high degree of visual homogeneity to China's cities, each with a Jiefang Lu
(Liberation road) or a Dongfeng Jie (Eastwind street), concrete-block apart-
ment buildings of approximately six stories heated by portable gas stoves (see
fig. 1.2), old buses groaning with their load of crammed-in passengers, banks
of trash cans, Bank of China branches, and small informal markets. Indeed,
one acquaintance of ours shocked us by his claim that "all Chinese people
look and act pretty much the same"—a view held despite his many trips to
China. Yet, below the surface, there are significant differences among peoples and local cultures. These differences are regarded as extremely important
and evident by people in China, for whom the concrete uniformity provides
only a visual backdrop for more interesting nuance; regional differences provide the topic of endless discussion. Americans also experience regional difference alongside globalizing and homogenizing tendencies. Could Americans at a McDonald's in Boston ever mistake it for one in Paris, Texas—or
Paris, France? The hamburgers and fries would be the same, but the hairstyles
and speech styles would be clearly different, the gender roles might be different, and the function of the food—meal, snack, luxury, bargain—would also
be different in different contexts (see Watson 1997).

Although there has long been a tradition in China of government-level
valorization of unity, Chinese cultural nationalism—the affective and intellectual and symbolic pull of loyalties toward the nation—is, as pointed out by
Harumi Befu (1993), a recent invention. The Chinese state has struggled to
foster a sense of connection across regions in China, and its efforts have been
only partially successful. Symbols of the nation—the Great Wall, China's history, myths, athletic teams—have been used to show that a villager in the
northwest yellow earth terrain has more in common with a Shanghai entrepreneur than with anyone across the border. We suggest otherwise—or at
least suggest that this claim may be queried.

In China today as well as in many centuries past, regional identification,
especially along the north/south divide (although also province by province
and even at divisions below that), is taken for granted as inevitable and rea-
sonable. Native place associations have served myriad social welfare purposes
throughout imperial and contemporary China. Migrants would seek fellows

FIGURE 1.2.
Today's urban kitchen.
(Photograph by Dr. Louis C. Liley Jr.)

from their native place, and they would organize quasi-kinship organizations that provided temporary lodging, emergency assistance, funeral arrangements, and so forth. Embedded in this practice is the assumption that natives of a particular place share needs, characteristics, and understandings that supersede other differences and are more significant than the claims of national politics.

But the state works mightily to unify the nation in terms of centralization and homogeneity. Owing to the daunting range of national complexity, the control of symbols is an important attribute of those in power. Some of the symbols deployed in staking a claim about China's unity are history, language, and culture.

History as a Symbol of China's Unity

The traditional view of China locates its "cultural core" in the North China plain, in the bend of the Yellow river intersecting the Wei and Huai rivers in present-day Henan and Shanxi provinces. The purported continuous thread led from the loess alluvium (yellow dust in the river basins) of the Yellow river through the various dynasties, especially of north China, to the present. The fact that about half the Chinese dynasties were actually non-Chinese is usually disregarded in listing them. Further, the conventional account goes, all people who encountered the splendor of China's evidently superior civilization willingly took it as their own, like a huge wave absorbing everything in its path, including Korea, Japan, and Vietnam.

A different account is possible, however. This one suggests that China was changed by its encounter with other forms of society. New archaeological evidence shows how splendid were centers of civilization in southern and southwestern China—especially in the states of Chu and Shu-Ba, now in Hunan and in Sichuan provinces (Sage 1992; Kleeman 1998). Much of the archaeological evidence of these ancient cultures will be submerged when the Three Gorges Dam is completed on the Yangzi river. With very different iconography evident in artifacts uncovered recently—swirling images of birds, water, clouds, dragons, monsters—these centers are embraced by contemporary southern Chinese to show that an alternative to continued identification with northern Chinese culture exists and that its longevity rivals that of the north (see Friedman, chap. 3).

The discourse of China's cultural superiority inevitably conquering neighboring societies is also evident in contemporary accounts of Greater China, Cultural China, the Five Dragons (Hong Kong, Singapore, Korea, Japan, and Taiwan), and other similar formulations. These argue that China's economic success can be explained by cultural values from imperial China, specifically what they term *Confucianism*. This unifying cultural stereotype, largely a product of the Western imagination, is also promulgated by experts in the United States (such as Tu Wei-ming) as well as by the Chinese government, which enthusiastically supports such endeavors through such entities as the Confucius Institute in Beijing. We propose an alternative portrait that calls greater attention to the background than to the foreground. At least in south China, this may be found in an alternative view of history, especially through interpretations of archaeological evidence.

Language as a Symbol of China's Unity

One very strong source of this definitive regional and local identity is language. While the official language of China is Putonghua (Common Speech, i.e., Mandarin), it is the mother tongue for only about 70 percent of the people in China, and even among that 70 percent one finds significant differences—although not necessarily barriers to communication. By law, official government business and all education must be conducted in Putonghua, yet, whenever subtleties must be conveyed, people tend to revert to their more natural dialect or language. Robert Ramsey (chap. 4) describes the major language divisions within China, discussing the types and degrees of divergence among them—differences as great as those among European languages.

The political nature of language and its varieties is well-known to scholars of multilingualism. Even the "science" of linguistics and dialectology has profound political implications. In China, the different branches of the Chinese language are termed *fangyan*, usually translated as "dialect" (although Victor Mair [1991] suggests "topolects" as a more apt rendering). Many Western linguists point out the lack of mutual intelligibility among these *fangyan* and tend to treat them as separate languages. In China, they are always treated as dialects of a single language, and their unity is often demonstrated by the fact that speakers of all *fangyan* can use the same written language.

Most areas outside the central plains contain multiple linguistic varieties; local, regional, and national varieties coexist with a usually fairly obvious division of functional labor. Susan Blum (chap. 8) recounts the multiethnic and multilingual nature of Kunming (very similar to other peripheral cities), showing that notions of uniformity and homogeneity certainly do not apply to linguistic behavior. While the national language, Putonghua, is understood by most residents of Kunming since it is the language of the media and (officially) of education, it is far from the variety most commonly used. Like other areas where local linguistic varieties are spoken (see, e.g., Chiang [1995] on Hunan), Kunming has several levels of speech. Putonghua is the most prestigious and most distant, signifying elite culture rather than homey practices. *Kunminghua,* the Kunming dialect, is used by residents of Kunming almost all the time. *Yunnanhua,* the Yunnan dialects, refers to an assortment of accents and dialects spoken throughout the province. *Mapu* refers derogatively to imperfect attempts to replicate standard Putonghua. Minority languages are also spoken, as are Chinese languages other than Beifang fangyan and Xi'nan fangyan (northern and southwestern dialects, respectively). The overall impression one has is of a layer of officialdom superimposed over the ordinary bustling complexity in which "small" people—those without official duties—are free to express themselves in any variety they like. This occurs even in schools, where education is officially required to be carried out in Putonghua but in fact is often conducted in dialect. Here we can see limits to state power; the Chinese state has the power to enforce compliance with the goals of language standardization, but it has not done so, and the enduring linguistic freedom has enabled local linguistic varieties to be sustained.

Culture as a Symbol of China's Unity

We wish, not only to contrast localism and regionalism to nationalism and centralization, but also to point out other areas of dissimilitude within the nation. These include increasing disparities in income, variations in marriage practices and ideals, religious worship, ethnic variation (which is itself a catchall for other kinds of cultural differences), and gender.

China's ideology of cultural superiority and civilization focuses on a handful of features that can be compared in terms of modernization (which is seen as intrinsically desirable): literacy, monogamy, food, hygiene, and so on. The government and individuals alike have generalized about the trajectory of history, as one can see in the 1988 television series *Heshang* (River elegy). Its screenwriters, Su Xiaokang and Wang Luxiang, criticized China as an inward-looking civilization throughout most of its past, with its monumental public works such as the Great Wall cutting off the nation from its oceanic connections to the rest of the world. With modernization, China is expected to increase its communication with and become increasing influenced by the "advanced" nations of the world, such as the United States and Japan, assuming its rightful global place.

At the same time, a discourse of cultural essentialism, describing a kind of timeless essence of Chineseness, has been promoted by the government and by some ethnic Chinese who live outside China. This discourse explains

China's growing influence and wealth as inevitable outcomes of its cultural features—of such core values as the extended family supporting its members, respect for the wisdom of the elderly, admiration for education, and frugality. Terming such a constellation of features *Confucian,* this discourse seeks to restore some selected aspects of China's past practices in its race toward the future. Some scholars have argued that China's view of modernity is a hybrid result of colonialism (Anagnost 1997), borrowing many values from incompatible societies and then measuring itself by comparison. The discourse of civilization is such a hybrid conversation, but it omits reflection on many of the features that China has retained that are oblique to modernization and industrialization. Modernity is generally believed to lead to uniformity, but there may be forms of modernity (and postmodernity?) that permit the endurance of differences. Some of these features are China's very salient challenges to centralization.

SOURCES OF DECENTERING; ALTERNATIVES TO CENTERING

Geography

Without assuming that geography causes culture to be the way it is (a doctrine known as *geographic determinism*), it is important to point out how widely the geography of China varies. This includes its physical terrain and its cultural configurations. The two aspects are often related. Yet, as scholars have long noted, even nomads in deserts are not identical across societies, so we cannot assume that the terrain *forces* a particular cultural adaptation. Environment enables and constrains culture, within the historical and cultural context that always informs the human condition. We may see an example of the interaction of geography and culture in the fact that geography permits poppies to be grown everywhere in China but that culture allows them to be grown legally only on Dai autonomous land (see the discussion of autonomous regions below, on p. 12).

China's topography includes nearly every form of landscape known except tundra: arid deserts and river-fed plains, rugged subtropical mountains and pleasant tropical beaches, snowcapped mountains and sandy coastal regions, grasslands and rainforests. China has three major river systems (the Yellow [Huang] river, the Long [Yangzi or Yangtze] river, and the West [Xi] river) as well as several other important rivers (the Wei, the Red, the Huai, the Pearl, the Golden Sands, and the Yalu).

At its most simple, we can make the characterization that north China is dry and south China wet, with the monsoons providing generally predictable summer rains needed for rice growing. More technically, we can contrast rainfall, which varies from under ten inches per year in Mongolia, Xinjiang, and Tibet to over sixty inches in Yunnan and on the southeast coast.

Throughout history, deforestation, flooding, drought, erosion, and famine have been extremely common in China, but these scourges affect different areas differently.

In terms of human geography, population density varies from fewer than 10 people per square mile in large areas of Mongolia, Xinjiang, and Tibet to over 300,000 per square mile in one district in Shanghai. Certainly, urban and rural China are extremely dissimilar. China has urbanized only recently. At the time of the 1949 Revolution, only 10.6 percent of its population was considered urban. The Communist government restricted urban migration very strictly until the 1980s. In 1983, the urban population was assessed at 23.5 percent, but, in 1984, the criteria used to determine urban/rural residence were changed to include many more towns and cities; by 1989, 51.5 percent of the population was considered to be urban. A handful of China's largest cities are well-known in the West and are frequent stops on tourists' routes.

Familiar images of China tend to derive from the coasts and from "China proper," the land within the Great Wall: the southeast coast of Hong Kong, Canton, Fujian; the east coast of Shanghai; the northeast, inland off the coast of Beijing. This tends to be fairly productive agricultural territory, inhabited largely by Han Chinese. While these areas represent the population and political-economic centers of China, there are also very significant events occurring elsewhere, such as the areas inhabited traditionally by so-called ethnic minorities.

Ethnicity

In this book, we represent two generally unfamiliar areas of China that include a large number of people classified as "ethnic minorities"—*shaoshuminzu,* usually *minzu*—because of their cultural practices and alleged descent. These people were traditionally inhabitants of the marginal areas of China. China proper is matched by an equal amount of minority territory, and, although such minorities are small in number relative to China's population—only 8 percent of its 1.2 billion—they still represent a very large and diverse number of groups. Ethnic minorities in northwest and southwest China live lives quite different from the familiar ones of coastal, urban, eastern China.

Although China is officially atheist and has traditionally had a blend of indigenous religions and Buddhism, it also includes ten ethnic groups that are Muslim—for a total of 17 million. Speaking different languages and deriving from different sources, these groups nonetheless practice Islam and in many ways have more in common with Muslims elsewhere than with other Chinese in China proper. Many of these Muslim minorities are concentrated in the northwest provinces of China, where they live on the international border with other republics. China has been concerned about such ethnic minorities, especially those groups found on both sides of the international border. Examples of such groups include the Zhuang, Dai, and Wa and many of the Muslim groups.

The two articles in this collection on northwest China describe aspects of two of China's five autonomous regions—Xinjiang (Barnett, chap. 5) and Ningxia (Gladney, chap. 6). Autonomous regions are province-level administrative units acknowledged to contain traditionally large numbers of ethnic minorities. These areas are designated *autonomous areas* to emphasize that they are permitted some degree of cultural autonomy and that a large number of their political leaders are (ideally) drawn from among minority groups.

One of the largest ethnic groups in China is the Uighurs (also written Uygurs, Mandarin Wuwei'er), a border-straddling group. In this case, the border straddled is between Xinjiang Uighur Autonomous Region and Pakistan, Russia, Mongolia, Afghanistan, and the republics of Kazakhstan, Tajikistan, and Kyrgyzstan. Xinjiang contains other ethnic groups as well; most significant are the Kazakhs, Hui, Mongols, Kyrgyz, Xibe, Tajiks, Manchus, Uzbeks, Dawuer (Daur), Tatars, and Russians.

In 1997, Uighur separatists from Xinjiang set off bombs on buses in Xinjiang and Beijing, killing a handful of people, to call attention to the seriousness of their cause and to express resentment of the Chinese Communist Party and its real intolerance of minority cultures. Rallying round a notion of pan-Turkism, many Uighurs feel that Beijing's concerns are extremely remote from their own, and they are not willing to submit to Beijing's authority. Although the number of such separatists is, it seems, small, it is nonetheless worth paying attention to this area, as it exemplifies the potential for dissolution inherent in a centralized, unified China.

Xinjiang is described physically, statistically, and socially by the late political scientist Doak Barnett (chap. 5). He compares his 1940s and 1980s visits to Xinjiang, demonstrating some ways in which the area retains characteristics that long predate its association with China, its Inner Asian, Turkic features—alongside many evident connections with China. As the observations of a longtime China hand, Barnett's remarks also provide suggestions about the trajectory of change in this region—most notably increases in urbanization, industrialization, and the migration of Han Chinese as well as improvements in education, transportation, and communication.

Dru Gladney's discussion (chap. 6) of a northwest Sufi community among Chinese-speaking Muslims in the Ningxia Hui Autonomous Region focuses on what he calls *ethnoreligious resurgence*—the increase in ethnic and religious consciousness that has accompanied the relatively more tolerant policies of the 1980s and 1990s. He shows how a community given a set of "ethnonyms"—names for their ethnicity—takes this as a symbol of permission to explore and revive old practices that were anathema to the state during periods of more stringent control, such as the 1960s. One also gets an impression from Gladney's discussion of the vibrancy of alternative practices and their multidimensional nature. Not merely religious and linguistic, many aspects of everyday life including family and economic relations—not to mention eating practices such as pork abstention—are thoroughly different from the rice-eating ancestor-worshiping "typical Chinese" of China proper.

Like the northwest, southwest China is similarly little known to Westerners and even to scholars of China who focus on central China. It is known to its own inhabitants as a relatively poor land, less involved in affairs of national importance, and with great ethnic complexity. The southwest is often taken to include Yunnan, Guizhou, and Sichuan provinces. Sydney White (chap. 7) and Susan Blum (chap. 8) focus on Yunnan province, a place remote from Beijing, Hong Kong, and Shanghai, known for its twenty-four to twenty-six officially recognized *minzu*. It was difficult to select among the many high-quality works that treat the various ethnic groups, and we wish to refer interested readers to many other available treatments of these groups from a variety of perspectives. In China as a whole, there are fifty-five minority groups officially recognized, ranging in size from about fifteen hundred (Hezhe) to 17 million (Zhuang), and totaling about 96 million. Some are educated urban groups, but the majority live on China's geographic margins.

Readers accustomed to the increasing discussion of ethnic identity and multiculturalism in the United States will see that, in the Chinese context, ethnic identity is far from static and, therefore, neither easily pinned down nor significant in all contexts. In the case of the Lijiang basin in Yunnan, for instance, where most people are Naxi, identities are far from homogeneous. Sydney White describes Lijiang, the capital of an autonomous area recognized as home to many Naxi, a group often romanticized by Han Chinese because of a "branch" known as the Mosuo, who are described in Chinese sources as matriarchal. White tells of the physical and human characteristics of the Lijiang basin. Although the Naxi are the predominant group in this area, there are also substantial numbers of people from other groups, including Han, Yi, Tibetans, and Bai. The economic, agricultural, and social interactions among them are extremely complex. Yet, even within the Naxi community, people are careful to distinguish between *town* and *village,* suggesting additional levels of meaning regarding identity in this particular context. It is safe to say that the urban/rural divide is one that resonates throughout China, but, in this case, it is made even more multifaceted by its intersection with ethnic identity. Here, we can also see that, in a setting where ethnic identities are largely uniform, other differences in identity become more salient.

In contrast to southwest China, the southeast is broadly known for its economic development. This is the land of joint ventures, stock markets, overnight millionaires, and overseas investment. But the southeast too is multiple, and one little-known aspect of its multiplicity is the prominence of members of the Hakka subethnicity in political affairs, especially in the Chinese Revolution that ended with the founding of the People's Republic in 1949. Mary Erbaugh (chap. 10) shows how overrepresented the Hakka are in biographies of revolutionaries, explaining this fact by means of cultural characteristics unique to the Hakka. The Hakka are called *guest people* (*kejiaren* in Mandarin) because they are believed to have migrated south when north China was conquered by Jurchens and became too crowded in the Song dynasty (the twelfth century C.E.) (see also Constable 1994, 1996). Although they live in many areas of China, the county of Guangdong province known as Meixian is a predominantly Hakka area. Tracing the origins of people listed as prominent revolutionaries, Erbaugh was able to show the extreme overrepresentation of the Hakka, even if their Hakka identity was not explicitly mentioned. Officially, Hakka are considered a subethnic variety of the Han; the Hakka language is one of the eight major Chinese languages (dialects), with a historical relation to Mandarin (see also Ramsey's chapter). Yet much of their culture is quite different from that of the Han around them, and some argue that they should be considered a genuine minority ethnic group. There is value in being different, and Hakka have acquired a commoditized revolutionary status. Whether one learns about them as one example of diversity among the Han or as an example of the unacknowledged groups that exist in China, one can see that generalizations about Chineseness apply only to certain people in that vast nation-state. *Chineseness* itself is dynamic and up for grabs.

Society and Culture

It is not just geography that produces a sense of marginality. On the margins of mainstream society one may find a range of sexual, economic, religious, and spiritual practices that may be entirely unknown or distasteful to the majority.

While official statements declare that China has no homosexuality, many observers have noted quite a different state of affairs. Sexuality and identification on the basis of sexuality certainly vary across cultures; behavior identified as homosexual and, by implication, deviant, in one society may simply lie within a spectrum of ordinary practices in another. Self-identification as exclusively preferring sexual relations with members of one's own gender may, indeed, be rare in China, as it was in the West until fairly recently. Chapter 11, an excerpt from China's first official survey of sexual behavior, demonstrates a wide range of practices, including homosexual encounters, that do not conform to the expectation of heterosexual, monogamous, patrilocal, universal marriage. The survey inquires into such matters as premarital sexual relations, mechanisms for meeting marriage partners (arranged or otherwise), and prevalence of and attitudes toward infidelity. Vincent Gil (chap. 12) describes his conversation with an admittedly gay man in the PRC, belying the claims about the absence of homosexuality in China. But Gil's informant has clearly had to weigh the evident external pressure toward normative sexuality against his own inclinations toward a stigmatized sexuality.

The range of reproductive behavior and kinship relations found in today's PRC is quite broad, but it is not unprecedented. Perhaps what has changed, as Michel Foucault (1980) has shown for Europe, is the explicit moralizing about a single model of propriety in which the system of patrilocal, patrilineal marriage was hegemonic. In the past, exceptions existed and were not always stigmatized. For instance, in a work on historical exceptions to normative marriage practices, Janice Stockard (1989) demonstrated that alternatives to universal marriage existed in China, at least in particular times and places. Some young women in the Canton delta of south China between 1860 and 1930 swore to one another to remain spinsters. To avoid the economic consequences that would place unmarried women outside a household (especially after the deaths of their own parents), without a husband or son to provide for them, they established houses for themselves and other sworn spinsters.

A similar desire to avoid marriage was found in Hunan at roughly the same time, and marriages were lamented in *nüshu,* "women's script" (Chiang 1995). This recently uncovered script uses a greatly simplified version of traditional Chinese characters that allowed otherwise illiterate women to sound out the words and, thus, represent their private feelings to each other.

Before the Revolution in 1949, many relations among men and women were "irregular" because the poor could not afford marriage; after 1949, standards for sexual behavior became more strict. Even in traditional, imperial times, marriage was far from a monolithic institution. Relations among husbands and wives have varied tremendously over time and place. This suggests that even the generalizations about marriage and kinship that some anthropological works are wont to make must be tempered with a more intimate knowledge of the range of such "systems," as Barbara Ward (1965) urged.

In many ways, women's lives are marginal to the dominant story of China's economic modernization, affected adversely by a simultaneous increase in opportunities and burdens. Yet, at the same time, they are critical to its upward trajectory in that they are a substantial part of the rural workforce. Indeed, a common sight in rural China today is of women laboring in fields with infants strapped to their backs. James Tyson and Ann Tyson (chap. 13) provide a description of a middle-aged rural woman who has become responsible for agricultural work. Rarely represented in the recorded course of China's history, agricultural work has in contemporary China largely been turned over to middle-aged women. While their husbands and sons seek more lucrative factory employment or jobs in semiskilled urban labor such as construction, women are left to maintain the household, field, and parenting responsibilities for months or years at a stretch.

The contemporary growth in divorce, young women working at factories far from their homes, late marriage, widow remarriage, and so forth may in part be related to other social and economic changes. One increasingly significant change is that millions of unemployed young people, mostly men, are roaming China in search of a livelihood, most migrating from the countryside to the city. With China's increasing urbanization, many feel that rural life is too constraining, dull, or unrewarding; to become part of the consumer cohort that has emerged since the economic liberalization of the 1980s, migrant workers swarm to all cities, creating new social problems along the way. Dorothy Solinger (chap. 14) analyzes the motives and demographics of these workers, sketching out a portrait of their lives and the extreme hardship that most encounter while pursuing wealth. This "floating population" (*liudong renkou*) may well increase dramatically in the years to come as a result of the government's program to privatize and downsize state-owned enterprises, which, as late as 1997, employed nearly 80 percent of the urban population.

China is not only a land of economic activity. Aesthetic and artistic pursuits have always flourished as well, but their forms have changed. While the Peking Opera and the dignity of *taijiquan* (tai chi) are familiar to many in the West, in recent years other forms of music, performance, and spiritual practices have flourished. Among these is rock and roll, as Andrew Jones points out (chap. 15). Rock and roll (*yaogun yinyue*), especially the music of Cui Jian, was to the Tiananmen democracy movement of 1989 what rock and roll was to Woodstock—central, political, and frowned on by elders who nonetheless were willing to profit from record sales. Jones also shows how some groups were eager to support the economic value of this popular music and how performers were aware of the delicate path that they needed to tread in order to continue working in a society where severe restrictions are placed on music production. Nonetheless, performers were outspoken about their insistence on following their artistic and moral visions as they understood them, even if it meant rejecting nationalistic limitations.

We see here a struggle that is visible in many domains, a struggle to determine what best expresses people's views of their lives. Whether artistic, commercial, or spiritual, people are drawing on many different sources to create a new way to negotiate their lives in a confusing and quickly changing world—especially one in which the state becomes less and less prominent. National identity is one concern among many. Cui Jian, among others, is looking globally at available artistic forms, arguing that national limitations are unduly restricting, and, in saying this, he follows closely on the heels of Fang Lizhi, the expatriate astrophysicist who has long criticized the notion that nationalism is an ethos sufficient to unify the Chinese and to enable them to join the rest of the world as a political equal. Yet nationalism and even nativism persist among China's growing middle class and its college students, as demonstrated so graphically in the popular protests against the NATO bombing of the Chinese embassy in Belgrade in May 1999 and in the uproar surrounding China's downing of a U.S. spy plane in the spring of 2001.

China's identity is of concern at a high level, but, in everyday life, spiritual matters are significant. Two chapters concern the role of science, religion, and modernity in people's endeavor to come to terms with lives that are not always predictable. China officially regards science and materialism, not idealism, as the single accurate way to explain the world—so science has become the instrument of ideology. In recent years, a fascinating merging of the language of science with the languages of mysticism and nationalism has been evident in the growing popularity of the sets of practices known as *qigong,* conveyed startlingly to Western audiences by the silent protest of the government by the Falun Gong in April 1999. The intention of Falun Gong and a host of other New Age religions or cults of human betterment in China is to explain the world entirely by means of purportedly traditional Chinese beliefs and, even more important, to demonstrate how scientific those beliefs are.

Eric Karchmer (chap. 16) connects *qigong* to magic and science, showing how the state has chosen to embrace curative and mystical *qigong* for its own nationalistic purposes. This is a fascinating intersection between individually held beliefs about causation and the state sponsorship of certain beliefs. Again, *tradition* is used as a symbol of Chinese unity through time and space.

While *qigong* is a "modern" explanatory system supported at state institutes, in rural China other unsupported spiritual activities are developing. Diane Dorfman (chap. 17) shows what contemporary spiritual and ritual practices look like in the countryside in north China. The illegality of superstition (*mixin*) had been strenuously enforced for several decades, but such practices have clearly been revived recently—although not without substantial transformation. These practices are not identical with those that were common in rural China prior to the Revolution; the principles of the post-Mao reforms have been incorporated into activities that appear purely irrational. This development stands on its head the idea of economic modernization as inherently rational and universal. Here, we see how fully dependent on culture modernization is and how the marriage between superstition and economics is a match made in heaven. Indeed, with the decline of the state's presence and the liberalization of the national economy, religious faith has become widespread. All forms of religious belief—from such officially acknowledged religions as Daoism, Catholicism, and Protestantism, to popular charismatic cults, to such traditional practices as fortune-telling and studying the Book of Changes—have been attracting growing numbers of adherents in recent years. China is flourishing, not only materially, but spiritually as well.

CONCLUSION

Considering what all this adds up to—the conflicting claims of a diverse population and its many practices and a singular Party-state—we are faced with questions: Can China's centers hold? How many centers are there? What is the proper unit to contrast with *center?* How can we understand that enormously complex society in a way that does more justice than violence to it?

Without simplifying too much, can we say anything at all about *China?* Geographically, China's territory now includes more area formerly outside "China proper" than inside. How has this sheer physical fact affected *China?* Some claim that it is best to consider something called *Greater China,* an amalgamation of societies unified by certain traits that are culturally Chinese (but usually encompassing urban Han alone). Others argue that China itself could come apart in obedience to growing regional claims of separateness and even secession. Readers of this book must decide for themselves what the prognosis is in the shorter and longer terms. Some of these issues are ones with which China has grappled for millennia. Others are new and unique. Few, if any, have escaped the notice of China's political and intellectual leaders, who, despite an outward appearance of certainty, are themselves uncertain which way the winds of change are blowing, as was made evident in their inability to manage the May 1999 anti-American protests.

The idea of *center* is an artifact of China's modern nationhood and, thus, like China today, has been transformed. It is difficult to propose any particular representation of a central China. The crowded hurrying China of Beijing, Shanghai, and Guangzhou must not be seen as representative of China as a whole. The many Chinas introduced one by one, patiently, in detail, in *China Off Center* might not be recognizable to inhabitants of other Chinas. The China of rock-and-roll musicians is a real China—to many urban young people. The China of mosques and ablutions is a real China—to Hui in the dry oases of Ningxia. The China of migrant workers adrift in the cities is a real China—to the men who have abandoned the countryside in search of work. The China of dance clubs is a real China—to its fashionable patrons both gay and straight.

Rather than argue for a sense of timeless, Chinese commonality, as do some anthropologists and historians, we suggest that China might better be understood by mastering the local details. Policies and intellectuals' reports provide one macroscopic view of China, but, in the end, such a view is as remote as the court was in imperial times, a distance registered in the common adage, The sky is high, and the emperor is far away (*tian gao di yuan*). What will make China more real to Westerners are those things that resonate with what we know to be true about our own lives. In other words, the local is meaningful. Regional concerns outweigh national or international concerns the world over.

The articles collected in this volume give the impression of a China where almost anything can be found but where many nonnormative behaviors are simply private, or rural, or the province of the powerless. The powerful spokespeople of China's identity might consider some of this just "dirty laundry," as one petty official once told one of us; some of China's problems are not appropriate for outsiders to know about. We do not agree. Nor do we agree that outsiders should remain unaware of the multiplicity of China's selves. Arrests in the spring and summer of 2001 of China-born scholars working in the United States attest to the sensitivity of the Chinese government to any airing of the realities of life on the ground, even if contrary to the image portrayed through management of impressions. We believe that only when outsiders can see China as a fully human place, with good guys and bad guys, with people we consider just like us struggling to figure out how to live a good-enough life in a morally neutral universe; only when we can see China as a country with a government at one level and human beings at another; only when we can see the magnitude of the challenges confronting a government that must take care of Muslims in Xinjiang as well as Catholics in Shanghai—only then can we claim to know enough to make judgments about China. This could, of course, be equally true for other nations as well. But China's size and complexity provide an ideal lesson from which to learn about the vast complexity of the Middle Kingdom and even about ourselves as seekers of intercultural understanding.

APPENDIX

Terminology

Certain terms are used throughout this book in ways that may be perplexing:

> *Cadre:* An official, usually a member of the Communist Party.
>
> *Yuan:* Unit of Chinese currency. Also referred to as RMB (*renminbi,* "people's money") and sometimes as FEC (foreign-exchange coupon or certificate). The exchange rate is approximately 8.3 yuan per U.S.$1.00.

Administrative Units

China has *provinces* (like states in the United States), *municipalities* (like Washington, D.C.), and *autonomous regions* (like provinces). Below these large levels are other units, listed here in decreasing size: *prefecture; county; county town* or *county seat; town; village.*

Autonomous areas: These are administrative areas that have been designated as governed primarily by people from ethnic minorities because of those minorities' historic predominance. Some laws and policies in autonomous areas differ from those in effect elsewhere, but there is no actual autonomy; ultimate control still lies with the central government. The names of autonomous areas usually include the names of the ethnic groups typically concentrated there. Such areas may be found in three different sizes (see also chap. 8): *autonomous regions; autonomous prefectures;* and *autonomous counties.* Autonomous regions are the size of provinces. There are five of these in China: Tibet autonomous region; Mongolia autonomous region; Ningxia Hui autonomous region; Guangxi Zhuang autonomous region; and Xinjiang Uighur autonomous region.

Historical Periods

Although this book is not primarily historical, mention of recent history is common in the chapters. Reference to the following names and events may be found: the Ming dynasty, 1368–1644; the Qing dynasty, 1644–1911; the 1911 Revolution, which ended imperial China; the Anti-Japanese War, 1937–1945; the Chinese Revolution, also called *Liberation*, 1949; the Cultural Revolution, 1966–1976; the (economic) Reforms, from 1978.

Language

The linguistic situation in China is very complex. There are many ways to refer to the language known as *Chinese*, in Chinese as well as in English, but each one is usually calling attention to some aspect of the language (see also chap. 8):

> *Mandarin:* This term is usually used to contrast with other Chinese languages such as Cantonese. In Chinese this is often *Beifang fangyan*, "northern dialect."
>
> *Putonghua:* This term, usually used to emphasize the proper pronunciation of the spoken language, means "common language." It may also be used to contrast with other dialects of Mandarin.
>
> *Chinese:* This term is usually used to contrast with another language, such as English.
>
> *Hanyu:* This term means "language of the Han." It usually emphasizes the written form of the language, sometimes in contrast with that of other ethnic groups.
>
> *Hanhua:* This is a regional term meaning "the spoken language of the Han," contrasting with the languages of other ethnic groups. It is usually used in places like Yunnan where it is likely that people are aware daily of interactions with people speaking many different languages.

The often-confusing symbols employed in transliterating Chinese will be more easily pronounced if the following tips are kept in mind:

> *j*   (pronounced like *dg* in *judge*): Beijing (bay-dging);
>
> *q*   (pronounced like *ch,* with lots of air): qi (chee);
>
> *x*   (pronounced a little like *sh* but also like *sy*): xiang (between shheeang and syang);
>
> *shi* (pronounced almost like *sure*);
>
> *z*   (pronounced like the *dz* in *adze*): zeng (dzung);
>
> *c*   (pronounced like the *ts* in *its*): cao (tsao);
>
> *zh*   (pronounced like the *dg* in *judge*): zhou (Joe).

PART I

The Center and the Noncenter

Center (*zhongyang*) is a word used frequently in China to refer to the central administration; it also figures into the name for China (*Zhonghua, Zhongguo*). The sinograph or character for *zhong*, 中, (center, middle) has long been considered an image of an arrow piercing a target, yet this pictographic etymology makes little sense unless the viewer takes it as a cross section. According to Cecilia Lindqvist (1991, 324–325), in the earliest Chinese written texts (ca. 1200–700 B.C.E.) the graphic predecessor of *zhong* appears as a drum mounted on a pole in this manner: 𣎳. To be sure, *zhong* is a symbol of centralization, of unity, of harmony and balance and homogeneity. In traditional Chinese political thought, the center has often been contrasted with the periphery, with chaos, with challenges to the control of a governing authority. Nonetheless, the great majority of China's population has always lived outside this administrative center, outside the metropolis, in the vast hinterlands, governed to a far greater extent by a sovereignty of the local. Mao Zedong (1893–1976) attempted to bring the inhabitants of the usually forgotten countryside into the larger Communist nation, but it was the peasants who were to transform themselves, governed as they were by the sovereignty of the local.

The diverse ways of life of the many peoples arrayed under the heading *China* have timelessly absorbed the attentions of the masses as they tended to the rhythms of planting and harvest, irrigating, and caring for family, especially ancestors. There is no one center here but a vast scattering of sites of local practice. Indeed, the most enduring feature of China's political history has been the tension between an aggrandizing administrative center and the plural cultures of the districts, provinces, and regions. This tension and the difficulty of discerning a center in contemporary China is a theme common to the readings with which this first part of the book opens. Liu Binyan (chap. 2) and Edward Friedman (chap. 3) demonstrate the untenable quality of a unitary state administered by a Party bureaucracy in the north, while Robert Ramsey (chap. 4) suggests that the great variety of languages in use in China today confounds any attempt to imagine the country as unified linguistically. Perhaps it is best to begin with the somewhat disconcerting presumption that the particular esteem lavished on the center in Chinese history reflects an age-old desire to achieve reconciliation of its cultural and linguistic contrariety with uniform political authority: a hope that power can overcome plasticity. The absence of such reconciliation is especially evident today as the Chinese people are in thrall to the captains of commerce rather than to the vanguard of communism. However, as these first readings as well as those of part II ("Geographic Margins") show, the friction produced by the commerce/communism conflict may be sufficient to ignite novel political complexes, respectful of pluralism, without centers and without chaos.—Eds.

2

How Much of China Is Ruled by Beijing?

In this brief chapter, originally posted on the Internet, Liu Binyan asks a question frequently posed throughout this book: How much of China is ruled by Beijing? His query is political and administrative; ours extends to the cultural and psychological domains. But he recounts instance after instance in which local thugs, local governments, and individuals acting in their own interest flout demands made by the center. Some of this interest is criminal—people committing acts of violence and rapacity that cannot be contained by law-enforcement personnel. Some of this interest is material selfishness—people refusing to hand over the taxes demanded by their local or provincial authorities. Some of this interest is defensive—individuals coming together to form virtual armies to protect themselves from roving bands of organized strongmen. For readers familiar with the past century of China's history, this lawless contemporary chaos will immediately call to mind the warlord period of the 1920s and 1930s, when large areas of China were under the control of local authorities, some of whom went so far as to issue their own currency and passports. The predatory reality that Liu Binyan describes is strongly at odds with the common Western perception of the Chinese government as all-powerful and of its economy as "under control." Liu does not speculate here about likely trajectories for such a fragmented China, but he makes quite clear that, at the present time at least, China's leaders lack moral and practical authority and that public contempt for them has been increasing step by step with China's economic growth and modernization. Moreover, his impressionistic portrait of violence and excess does much to convey why corruption is the nation's number one problem.

Liu Binyan is one of China's best-known journalists, famous for his unblinkered accounts of official corruption. His muckraking has come at a cost, beginning in April 1956 with the publication of his pathbreaking piece of reportage literature "At the Bridge Construction Site" (Liu [1956] 1980), which chronicled such local outrages of political corruption as incompetence and misallocation of funds that, when perpetrated under the guise of strict adherence to Party doctrine, were applauded by the central government. Labeled a

"Rightist" and sentenced to internal exile and hard labor in 1957, he lived as a political prisoner for more than two decades. Rehabilitated in 1979, Liu resumed his journalistic career, becoming the chief investigative reporter for the *Renmin ribao* (People's daily) and publishing his most celebrated piece of reportage literature, "People or Monsters?" (Liu [1979] 1983)—a horrifying account of widespread corruption in a model commune in northeastern China. In 1987, when student protests broke out in Hefei, he was again denounced as a public enemy and expelled from the Communist Party, this time for his "bourgeois liberalization." Now living in the United States, Liu Binyan has continued to write about Chinese affairs with insight and frankness, editing the journal *China Focus*, which monitors the daily political excesses of the government.—Eds.

The separatist warlord regimes that dominated China during the first half of this century have not yet reappeared. And, for the foreseeable future, the danger of nationwide civil war seems slim. However, other forms of disintegration—felt by many as only a "social security" problem—are really various social forces slowly undermining the control of the central government. This process began only in the mid-1980s, but it has already made the Beijing regime more anxious and terrified than ever.

On 14 October of last year, the China News Agency reported that, because thirty thousand peasants had poured into a remote mountain region in Qinghai province to prospect for gold, the government decided, as of 1 January 1998, to close down the two gold mines in the Kekexili mountain range of western Qinghai province.

But whether the local government is capable of forcing these peasants to leave the area is quite doubtful. About the same time that the above news was reported, another report about Linglong, China's largest gold mine (in Zhaoyuan, Shanxi province), stated that, when law-enforcement personnel tried to ban illegal gold miners from entering the mine, the miners threatened the police with violence. During another conflict there two months earlier, fifty thugs armed with handguns and rods had encircled the local cadres and mine workers, and a confrontation ensued that lasted four hours. The armed clashes between the two sides—state mines and illegal miners—are quite common in the gold mines of Qinghai province. The self-proclaimed "Gold Lords" controlling the illegal miners consider themselves unassailable, saying, "Our forces are stronger than the public-security bureaus, and our handguns are much better than theirs." But both sides suffer casualties since handguns, machine guns, as well as homemade cannons are commonly used during these confrontations.

The Chinese government is now capable of building miles of railroads and highways, but it cannot protect them from guerrilla forces. A new criminal profession appeared in the late 1980s: highwaymen and train bandits.

These people proudly, although ironically, call themselves the "Railroad Guerrilla Force"—named after the armed organization founded [in the 1930s and 1940s] by the Chinese Communist Party within the Japanese- and Guomindang-occupied regions that specialized in attacking and destroying the invaders' transportation and railway facilities. The total number of such criminals operating from north to south in China today greatly surpasses the Railroad Guerrilla Force of earlier years—which limited its activities to several regions in the north. In addition, the bandits now repeatedly appear on highways and inland navigation lines, mainly robbing passengers and looting cargo. In some southern provinces, the bandits operate so frequently on railways that one passenger has reported being robbed six times during one single trip! People call such regions *enemy-occupied regions.* In some villages, almost all the households are engaged in these kinds of criminal activities. These villages have become "base areas" that resist the jurisdiction of the regime. Because of the threat to public security, every year since 1990 the government has launched a clean-up operation meant to put these bandits out of business.

On the highways, there is another force that confronts the government. It consists of petty local authorities and thugs who pose as government officials. They set up frequent outposts on the roads to force passing vehicles to stop and pay various tolls.

The so-called three arbitraries (arbitrarily setting up posts, collecting tolls, and imposing fines) have already seriously hampered the transportation sector of the national economy. The three arbitraries and the confrontations that have ensued have reduced average travel times by 50 percent. For example, some pig-raising regions now make no profits from transporting their pigs to the city markets because the transport vehicles are frequently intercepted and their drivers made to pay usurious tolls. Shipping vegetables from vegetable-producing areas in Shandong province to Beijing was once an effective way, not only to provide fresh and affordable vegetables to city residents, but also to increase the peasants' income. Now, it is difficult to continue this because the transport routes are so often obstructed and the costs have increased so dramatically. In yet another example, the three roadways that connect the Jilin petroleum fields in the northeast to the outside have been broken up by local outposts, averaging one every ten kilometers. Over the last year, the various highway and bridge tolls for the Jilin petroleum enterprise's five thousand vehicles have cost 30 million yuan above and beyond the 50 million yuan paid as the annual road-maintenance fee. The result is that many units in this oil field are now incurring losses where they previously made profits. Because these units do not have enough cash in circulation, the enterprise still owes 4 million yuan reimbursement to its drivers, who have had to pay the illegal tolls.

More and more primary-level organizations of the Chinese Communist Party and administrative units under its control have become paralyzed.

Communist Party decrees are ignored in numerous villages that are dominated by clans, various cults and sects, as well as criminals. In effect, these villages have become independent kingdoms.

In the Dongting and Hongze lake regions, large areas have become completely segregated from the rest of the regime. Historically, people who were fed up with repression or economic exploitation escaped with their families to these lake areas, where for years they lived on boats among the weeds in the water. Now, these areas have also become hiding places for various criminals. They are very much like the so-called liberated areas during the period of the civil war between the Communist Party and the Guomindang regime. The only difference is that there is no political party to control the local powers or any armed struggle for a unified goal.

The third kind of decentralized area consists of villages that have organized spontaneously, refusing to sell grain at low prices or to pay heavy taxes to the state. The local Communist Party power in these areas either sides with the peasants or is ignored by the people. In either case, local Party officials can no longer function effectively. Of course, the majority of the regions are still under the control of the Chinese Communist Party. However, local interests often lead to resistance by the local Party organizations to the upper-level administration of the Party. For instance, when court officials try to carry out verdicts, to seize criminals who cross provincial boundaries, to rescue hostages, or to demand reparations, they are more and more often coming under attack from all sides. Nothing the political center does can stop the nationwide marketing of counterfeit medicines, liquor, and cigarettes despite the central government's determined efforts to inspect and to crack down on the perpetrators month after month, year after year. The villages, enterprises, towns, and cities that have specialized in the manufacturing and retailing of these counterfeit products have already created their own networks and connections to survive. Under the protection of the local governments, they are in effect engaged in a permanent guerrilla war with the central government. In several districts and towns where nationally known counterfeit-medicine markets are located, whenever the upper levels of the government send in inspection teams, the phony medicine-trading markets vanish at once; but, the minute the inspectors leave, the lively business immediately resumes.

In reality, the map of crime in the People's Republic of China is covered with complex networks connecting countless dots: commodity smuggling; various imitations of established products; the manufacture and trade of illegal guns, drugs, pornographic books and videotapes, and fake currencies; prostitution under many different covers; and the abduction and selling of women and children. The scope and influence of the criminal organizations (known locally as "black societies") and the black markets involved in these illegal activities have grown rapidly, to such a degree that this mafia even holds its own national conference.

It is true that the Chinese government enjoys all the privileges of being the only legal political power, controlling the military forces and the armed police. But its control is actually not any stronger than that of its opponents, as it has lost one battle after another. Although the government can carry out larger- and larger-scale arrests and executions, it has not succeeded in frightening the criminals. The power of the criminals has clearly expanded as their gains outweigh their losses. The criminals have also become more experienced and less fearful, and now their weapons, equipment, and vehicles are usually of better quality than that of the official police force. In 1995, over 100,000 illegal guns were captured nationwide, while, in the first seven months of 1996, according to an incomplete estimate from fourteen provinces, 300,000 illegal guns were confiscated.

In the last few years, private, provincial armies and police forces have surfaced in various parts of the country. This has become an enormous satire on the "proletarian dictatorship" of the state apparatus, which is the only effective repressive tool held tightly by the Chinese Communist Party. According to the few published sources available, Shanxi and Yunnan provinces both have their own armies, each with six hundred to eight hundred officers and soldiers; each army also has its own military designations, uniforms, equipment, and munitions factories. They even have their own police stations and police forces. Quite possibly, these armies may represent the embryos of future warlord regimes, and the millions of unemployed vagrants will be their natural reserve forces.

The popularizing of violent behavior is now making a psychological foundation for future turmoil. Restaurants and hotels extort high prices from their guests; if they show any resistance, they are beaten or detained. This has become a common occurrence in China. In business operations, the abducting of hostages, the threatening of one's opponents with bodily injury, and the use of force to ensure the fulfillment of contracts have all become common practices. Local tyrants now employ violence to commit all types of crimes, to monopolize villages, or to dominate a trade market.

Without the corruption of the state apparatus—in the military, judicial, and law-enforcement spheres—all the above-mentioned developments would naturally be impossible. A legal verdict can be altered from guilt to innocence, and a death sentence can turn into a not-guilty verdict depending on the amount of the bribes. Reductions in the lengths of prison terms can be bought. Police stations can open covert brothels or gambling houses, or they can provide protection for them. The military routinely employs naval vessels and airplanes for smuggling activities. The police utilize the mafia (black societies) or criminal gangs to subdue other criminals—the so-called combat-poison-with-poison policy has in fact legitimated the existing "police-bandit collaboration."

After all, the answer to the question, How much of China is still ruled by the Chinese Communist Party? is to be found, not on a map, but in the hearts of the Chinese people. Even those who are completely convinced of the political authority and power of the Chinese Communist Party leave only a small corner in their hearts for the Party. And this small corner is not for the Party itself but rather for worries about the collapse of the regime and the consequences of China's loss of stability. In the hearts of the majority of Chinese, there is growing resentment and hatred toward the Party. One reason that a large-scale confrontation has not yet occurred is the lack of political freedom. But the incurable corruption of the Party instead gives the Chinese people another kind of freedom: the freedom to feel justified in engaging in antisocial behavior to fulfill one's own selfish desires—this will be the most harmful legacy of this regime for China.

3
Symbols of Southern Identity
Rivaling Unitary Nationalism

The political scientist Edward Friedman inquires here into the possibilities for nationalism in different moments in modern China. Inspired by Benedict Anderson's *Imagined Communities* ([1989] 1991), in which one of the origins of nationalism is traced to the development of a common literature, an "administrative vernacular," Friedman discusses literature, language, history, and "mythos" and the way they serve—or fail to serve—to unify the nation. He draws a contrast between the kind of nationalism that Mao-era (1949–1976) China attempted to establish ("Leninist," anti-imperialist, closed to the outside world, unitary, focused on north China, on Mandarin, and on the ancient autocratic state of Qin) and the post-Mao alternatives that appear to him to be prevalent in the 1990s and today (popular, open to the outside world, focused on south China, on southern dialects, on pluralism and federalism, and on the ancient state of Chu). The complexity of the article derives from the complexity of the phenomena being united by Friedman.

Friedman's striking depiction of Chu culture, a Warring States era (479–220 B.C.E.) state located in what is now Hunan province, in south China, as a symbol from which southern Chinese derive pride and identity may be very much at odds with familiar treatments of China's history as deriving from a northern "cradle" of civilization around the Yellow river basin to the north. Chu's culture was quite distinctive and very different from the adjacent cultures now usually considered ancestral to that of China. Southern Chinese have been embracing the recent archaeological excavations of Chu, which demonstrate a clearly flourishing culture just as "advanced" as that in North China. This symbol of a rival antiquity serves as justification for southern pride and resistance to the domination of northern symbols and claims.

Moreover, since 1997, this north/south tension has taken on a more aggressive cast as the Communist Party has financed an elaborate archaeological project to date the early historic eras of northern Chinese antiquity, the Xia, Shang, Zhou (Sandai) Chronology Project. Complicating this nativist rivalry even more is the ongoing Three Gorges Dam project, which, if completed, will result in the inundation and permanent loss of numerous ancient sites of the southern Dai culture, perhaps older than those chronicled under the Sandai project. One nation, many peoples, with a decidedly troubling future trajectory of intense regional conflict, is the China that we glimpse through Friedman and the China that we confront today where southern intellectuals and Party operatives toast the greatness of China by recalling the superiority of Chu antiquity.—Eds.

THE ECLIPSE OF ANTI-IMPERIALIST NATIONALISM

The People's Republic of China in the Mao era (1949–1976) presented itself as the heir of a Han people who had come together millennia earlier in the north China plain of the Yellow river valley, built a great civilization, fought to preserve it, and expanded over the centuries by civilizing barbarian invaders. Mao's anti-imperialist revolution was the culmination of this Chinese national history. The Museum of History displayed this nationalist history as an ascent from Peking man through an expansionist, amalgamating, and unifying Han culture to the founding of the People's Republic.

An anthropologist of China, Robert Thorp, explained, "The ascendancy of the Communist Party and creation of New China are both understood as the inevitable outcome of China's historical process. . . . [T]he antiquity and continuity of Chinese culture . . . give China a respectable status. . . . Creating a sense of national cultural identity requires persuading all of the non-Han peoples that they have a stake in the fate of the Han majority. If ethnic groups always place their 'Chinese' citizenship behind their own ethnicity, the state will fragment" (Thorp 1992, 18–19).

By the 1990s, however, Chinese teachers forced to repeat this story of a singular north China origin to Chinese civilization, which was recapitulated and advanced in Mao's north China peasant movement, described it as a lie: "An essentially unilinear evolutionary model . . . no longer enjoys universal acceptance in China. . . . [T]he old, hyper-simplistic notion that increasing social complexity during the north China Neolithic period is best explained as an inevitable evolutionary process by which a highly localized early Neolithic Yangshao culture spawned a late Neolithic Longshan culture forming the foundation for the genesis of Chinese Bronze Age civilization is no longer tenable. Most Chinese archaeologists now agree that the late Neolithic and Bronze Age of China were a rich amalgam of influences from many areas, including those outside the middle Yellow River valley itself" (Olsen 1993, 4).

As soon as reforms began in the post-Mao era, archaeological and anthropological associations, journals, and conferences, aware since the mid-1960s of data for "a new conception of the Chinese past," swiftly undermined the northern, Maoist mythos of national genesis, insisting that scientific findings made impossible "the viewpoint of linear development . . . of cultural development . . . from one central point . . . radiated out." "Late Paleolithic cultures in the southern part of our country . . . represented . . . a continuation of their own type of development." Measurements today revealed "proportionate differences between the residents of the North and the South." "This type of regional differentiation can be traced back to the human fossils of the late Paleolithic."[1] In the "Neolithic Revolution," while the Yellow river basin of the North centered on "dry farming and millet," in contrast, "culture in the Yangzi River basin as far back as seven thousand years ago was already proficient in rice crop agriculture." In sum, "The Yellow River basin . . . taken to be the cradle of the most ancient civilization in China . . . would not be in conformity with the reality discovered through archaeological excavations. . . . [T]he genesis of China's civilization came not from one source, but from many . . . that were scattered throughout the different regions . . . through their mutual influence and blending." In short, "The Yangzi River valley . . . was just as much a cradle of Chinese civilization as was the Yellow." Furthermore, as Greg Guldin has pointed out, one had to look at the "importance of foreign contacts in the development of Chinese civilization and culture and the relative impact of non-Han peoples on Han" (Guldin 1990, 16, 135, 134–135, 124, 81, 77, 75, 80, 22).

The celebrated archaeologist Kwang-chih Chang observed an attitudinal change in Chinese scholarship, noting that "many Chinese archaeologists became converted to the multilinear view during the mid-1970s, when a decentralized archaeological apparatus brought about major discoveries outside the Zhongyuan cradle, and when the new carbon-14 dates showed that some of the 'marginal' cultures were as early as the Zhongyuan center" (personal communication, 31 July 1992).

Swiftly, all over the country, from Xi'an on the Silk Road to Changzhou on the south China coast, museums were reorganized or new ones were built to tell stories that contravened the notion of a northern origin.[2] More and more Chinese by the 1990s were envisioning the south as integral to the future of China, reimagining their history such that the promise of China was no longer premised on a northern-based purist history. Democrats organized in Hunan province in June 1989 described the virtue of "the people of Hunan" as a result of their "being the offspring of centuries of intermarriage between northerners and southerners" (*Anthems of Defeat* 1992, 201). The anti-imperialist regime's legitimating national myth of a pure ethnos was subverted.

THE RISE OF A SOUTHERN-ORIENTED NATIONAL IDENTITY

In the Mao era, speech in the language of the north had been rewarded. Cantonese were urged to speak Mandarin. The language of the capital region in the north was the language of status, power, and career prosperity. As Michael Frolic has written, "You have to learn Mandarin to have a good career in China" (Frolic 1980, 104). In the early years of Mao's rule, Beijing residents openly ridiculed the purported ugliness of southern speech. By the end of the 1980s, in contrast, Geremie Barmé and Linda Jaivin observed, a writer would comment, "His soft, kindly voice was clear and pleasant; he had a southern accent" (Barmé and Jaivin 1992, 377). Mandarin-speaking northerners visiting the south now felt themselves as foreigners. One said to me, he might as well be in Hanoi as in Canton. Merchants in Canton pretended not to comprehend Mandarin, humiliating northern visitors, turning them into peripheralized outsiders. Meanwhile, southerners declared, "We've no need to speak Mandarin." "We have our own language. China's like Europe, and we want to speak our own language just as in France people speak French" (*New York Times,* 23 April 1992). Southern tongues again resonated with the beauty of a better national future. In place of Mao-era, anti-imperialist nationalism that privileged poor, hinterland, Yellow river, north China peasants as the source of nation building, national success by the 1980s was identified with the market-oriented activities of southerners who joined with Chinese capital from diaspora Hong Kong, Macao, or Southeast Asia to produce world-competitive products that earned foreign exchange that could be invested in building a prosperous China.[3] In the new narrative, northern peasants—a people whose culture fostered frugality and bravery and permitted sacrifice and martyrdom for the national cause of independence from imperialist exploitation—were recategorized as backward, ignorant, superstitious, insular, and static. And, as for able northern intellectuals, southerners announced that "sixty percent of Beijing intellectuals come from the south" (*Geographical Knowledge* 1992).

The discredited myth of a salvationist north did not prefigure China's real and better future. Young Chinese began to abandon the artifacts of the ancient north and instead took honeymoon trips to the south to see the future, buy clothes, and learn about contemporary household interiors. Whereas, in the Mao era, southerners "eagerly sought out those who came from the north with more reliable information," in the post-Mao era, in contrast, a "fashionable magazine" of the south, *Nanfeng chuang* (The window to the south wind), introduced "an alluring world of style, freedom, comfort, capital, technology and experience" (Vogel 1989, 19, 63).

From the chitchat of ordinary folk to highest-level intellectual production, such as archaeology, with all linked by a new cultural discourse that challenged and subverted the Maoist discourse, Chinese experienced a transvaluation of values. The anti-imperialist mythos disintegrated, and a new national project that privileges the dynamism of the south has been constructed. This is a future-oriented political project, not an accurate scholarly explication of new discoveries in archaeology.

The pervasive presupposition that shaped popular gossip and elite analysis was that, in China, what was good originated in the south. When China's paramount leader went south at the outset of 1992 to reinvigorate policies of openness and reform, the line that spread from his talks was, "I had to go south to speak because in the north many people won't listen to me." It became presuppositional that successful change originated in the south:

> Ever since the Opium Wars, the southern and northern parts of China have evolved in different directions; in the south, Western influence has been strong and politics relatively liberal, while in the north, Western influence has been kept to a minimum and politics remained rather conservative. At his wit's end after the 1911 Revolution, Sun Yat-sen went down south to organize a revolutionary government, and . . . opened a new chapter in modern Chinese history. And before he outmaneuvered Liu Shaoqi and Lin Biao, Mao Zedong . . . headed down south. Given such precedents, it is believed that Deng Xiaoping's recent trip to the south of China is a signal of an imminent showdown with Chen Yun. (*Baixing* 1992, 17)

A cultural reconstruction transformed political discourse throughout China. I heard southerners describe their liberation, not as 1949 and the establishment of Mao's rule, but as a moment, usually in the 1980s, when "northern sent-down officials" who had (mis)ruled since 1949 or so, and made southerners the dominated objects of an imposed northern project, were finally replaced by local people, southerners, us. Nineteen forty-nine was them.

People literally heard the language of Great Wall closed-door despotism as the hated dialect of outmoded conservatives in Beijing. Perry Link reports that "in Cantonese . . . Mandarin is known colloquially as . . . 'big brother speech,' meaning the language of the big brothers who descended from the north after the Communist revolution." Given this popular reinterpretation of crucial rhetorical polarities, when antireform leader Chen Yun declared that he would play the Chinese card and ally with speakers of the Beijing dialect to defeat reform, stating, "I speak the Beijing dialect. [the reform leader] Hu Yaobang speaks a local dialect," it was obvious that, "in Chen Yun's view, 'Beijing dialect' conflicts with 'local dialect,' and, of course, 'Chinese card' is in conflict with 'openness card'" (Ruan 1992, 5). The Mandarin language of Beijing and its self-serving chauvinism had been particularized and revealed as the narrow interest of a backward-facing group situated in the northern capital. The promise of a reformed China open to the world and prospering lay elsewhere.

CHU SHALL RISE AGAIN

When the past is reimagined to preview a more hopeful future, a new national project can be legitimated. Students of nationalism find that a nation must be popularly imagined before it can be politically established. Studies of the history and archaeology of the south have become a growth industry of enormous proportions. The civilizing force in the Chinese historical imagination has migrated to the south. Scientific findings validate the project of the south. Nationhood has been reimagined to include the southern state of Chu before the ancient era of Confucius.

An inexpensive 1988 volume, *A History of Chu Culture*, with magnificent color pictures of ancient items from the state of Chu, argued in rich detail that the ancient, southern state of Chu was essential to Chinese culture; the Chu contribution made Chinese culture "higher" and permitted it therefore to spread "more broadly" (Zhang Zhengming 1987, 520). Chu culture had "exerted a lasting influence on . . . Chinese civilization." The old view that Chu culture "had been imported" from the north was denied.[4] Instead, Chu culture was seen as largely indigenous. Ancient Zhou influence was found to be particularly weak in Chu because Shang remnants held out longest as a buffer between the two. The great 1923 Henan archaeological finds were no longer judged distinctive products of the north but instead were found to have a "style [that] was formed in the state of Chu and then spread northward." By the sixth century B.C.E. according to some scholars, the distinctive Chu culture, "among the most advanced of the bronze cultures," spread north, south, and west, "unit[ing] the southern half of China" and "exerting important influences on its neighboring states" (Lawton 1991, xi, 6, 9, 10, 12, 21, 22). Even the English-language *China Daily* argued that, during the Warring States period, because of the advance of a Chu army into present-day Yunnan, "advanced culture and superior productive methods of the Chu kingdom were introduced, greatly promoting . . . economic and cultural development" (*China Daily* [suppl.], 30 August 1992).

By 1992 a "hot tide of studying Chu culture" was celebrated in national exhibitions (*People's Daily* [overseas ed.], 20 April 1992). Museums sprouted up along the south coast with exhibitions on the ancient trading culture of the south. International conferences were held. Celebrations of Chu civilization became a matter of national moment. In fact, according to the Asian art historian Milo Beach, "Monographs about virtually every possible aspect of Chu culture appear regularly" (Beach quoted in Lawton 1991, x). Non-Chinese archaeologists at a 1990 international symposium on Chu found that culture powerful and original in ways "unmatched by anything comparable in Western Zhou." The weight of shamanism and unique burial practices clearly distinguished Chu from Zhou (Lawton 1991, 186, 165, 147, 159, 156, 166).

In general, the people of the south, including the Wu people of the Yangzi region, were portrayed as cultural and commercial innovators going back many millennia.[5] Some people understood the new national narrative as Chinese culture moving from an ancient, northern hinterland origin to a modern, southern littoral future. Others note that "most archaeologists believe that China's culture did not derive from a single root or source and then slowly radiate outward . . . ; rather, even before the neolithic period, China's culture was already pluralistic. . . . In the early period of its development, Chinese culture took shape under the mutual influence and impetus of agricultural and pastoral civilizations" (Tu 1991b, 302–303). Whether focusing on a progressive move to the south, a southern creative origin, or a continuous and dynamic synthetic ecumene, the new identity had no place for a pure northern origin, with continuous northern inspiration legitimating war mobilization to keep impure forces outside of heavily guarded gates.

What was *not* bought was what the regime sold in school: "In kindergarten, I learned that Beijing was the capital of the People's Republic of China, the place where Chairman Mao lived. In primary schools I learned that it was an ancient city with a long cultural history, the cradle of China's 5,000-year-old civilization" (Luo 1990, 313).

In the Mao era, which privileged the north, an anti-imperialist discourse had stigmatized the south as the enemy of the nation. On 18 May 1966, Lin Biao legitimated his rise to power in a report to the Politburo of the Chinese Communist Party's Central Committee by claiming that his military would prevent a coup as the regimes of Nkrumah, Ben Bella, and Sukarno had not. The first major Chinese coup that served as a negative lesson involved the southern state of Chu. In Lin Biao's only reference to the south, "rebellions broke out soon after the establishment of the Zhou dynasty. . . . [W]ithin a single state, men killed one another. Shang Zhen, son of Emperor Zhen of the state of Chu, encircled the palace . . . to compel Emperor Zhen to commit suicide. . . . Emperor Zhen was forced to kill himself at once" (Kao 1975, 329–330). Invoking the south as the enemy of a strong, united state is virtually inconceivable in the new national narrative that privileges the south as China's future. Political consciousness has experienced a transvaluation of values. The force of societal imagination has resisted and reversed statist propaganda, now seen as propaganda.

By 1989 even the democratic movement actually centered in Beijing was often not credited to the north. Instead, Chinese observers noted, even in the far northern city of Shenyang during the 1989 democracy movement, that "the leader, Ji Futang . . . had originally come . . . from [the southern city of] Wuhan and the south China component was said to be strong. One student at the Northeast Engineering Institute claimed that there was no student from the Northeast on the students' steering committee or think tanks. Some student leaders dismissed people from the Northeast as being 'asleep'" (Gunn 1990, 244–245). In May 1989, Beijing democracy activists like Shen Tong found hope in the rumor "that the Shanghai branch of the Communist Party had declared itself separate . . . and that the southern provinces were thinking of breaking with the central government" (Shen and Ye 1990, 308). Michael Duke observed that student broadcasters at Beijing University falsely announced, "The Mayor of Shanghai has joined the pro-democracy demonstrations." "Liang Xiang, the provincial governor of Hainan Island, has proclaimed his disassociation from the government" (Duke 1990, 16). Movement leaders hoped the garrison in Canton would side with them.

In response to the new view that Mao's anti-imperialism was unnecessary or counterproductive, a still-fervent supporter of the now discredited anti-imperialist view noted, "I heard that some students in Jilin province said that if we still had the Japanese in Changchun, construction work would definitely be better than now." He angrily retorted, "If we still had the Japanese occupation . . . the population of Changchun would be only 20 percent Chinese because by 1945, 60 percent . . . were Japanese" (Yu 1991, 1).[6] Amazingly, a new national narrative that the old guard portrayed as national suicide won over ever more Chinese.[7]

Responding to the eclipse of northern anti-imperialism to keep out aggressors and the rise in its stead of a southern openness to international exchange as hopeful nationalism, the reactionary octogenarian General Wang Zhen acidly commented, "If the Japanese were to invade, these assistant professors would all be on the welcoming committee. . . . [T]he Party and the State will be finished" (Bodman and Wan 1991, 20). General Wang Zhen's denunciation of the promulgators of the new southern project ("You are unpatriotic; you curse your ancestors") was hopefully understood as a last gasp of reaction on its deathbed (Tu 1991b, 308). In fact, the anti-Japan rhetoric of the old guard was dismissed as a fraud to obscure the fact that the delegitimated rulers actually abandoned China's anti-Japan nationalism by not obtaining an indemnity for the losses suffered during Japan's brutal war against China so that these actually antinationalist Chinese rulers could personally have their family members benefit from private deals with the Japanese at the expense of the suffering Chinese nation. Given the new presuppositions that privilege the historical role of the south, the northern-imagined anti-imperialist nationalism was discredited as hypocritical when it claimed to be anti-Japanese. Representative of this delegitimating discourse is Zhang Jie's 1987 short story "What's Wrong with Him?" in which an enterprising Chinese importer of clothing from Hong Kong is bankrupted by the selfish collusion of corrupt and unpatriotic Chinese officials with sharp Japanese merchants. The northern narrative of having saved the Chinese from Japanese imperialists is now seen as pure fiction.

Already in the Cultural Revolution, when travel revealed that the south was relatively prosperous in comparison to a miserably poor north, it was a conscious matter to punish by dispatching people to the northern hinterlands. Increasingly, southerners presumed that nothing healthy could grow in that hinterland, while the south had long been enriched by absorbing the good of the world. The 1974 Li Yizhe big-character poster in Canton defended the south's introduction of democracy and legal rights in this language: "Exactly like someone from the well-watered south visiting the desert and realizing for the first time the preciousness of water, the broad masses during the Cultural Revolution only realized the preciousness of democratic rights when they were robbed of them."

Powerful hidden forces of change have even altered the consciousness of the ruling elite. The reporter Harrison Salisbury's narrative tying together the memoir impressions of China's ruling elite families and colleagues who spoke with him contrasts Mao and anti-Mao as the ancient northern mythos against the revolutionary south. Mao, "modern Emperor Qin . . . had unified

China and devastated its people." In contrast, Marshal Ye, the leader of the effort to end the Maoist project, "was a native of Canton. . . . Since before the time of Sun Yatsen, Canton had led its own political life, often independent of Beijing. It was the traditional base for insurrection" (Salisbury 1992, 348, 349). Even elites in Beijing shared a discourse in which "the south shall rise again."

A SOUTHERN NATIONAL NARRATIVE

In the northern anti-imperialist mythos, China's choice was dictatorship or disintegration because only a despotic center could make China strong so foreign forces could not invade and plunder the nation. The regime apologist He Xin still sings the old tune. He worries that democratization could undermine "national cohesiveness" and "destroy" prospects for development, threatening both "splitting and civil war" "whereby politicians and warlords set up their separatist regimes and fight with one another," causing a loss of "Xinjiang and Tibet," whose "rich underground and mineral resources" supposedly make speedy economic growth possible. He Xin finds that China could again "fall into great chaos and disintegration" because the nationalism of Leninist anti-imperialism has failed to forge a common Chinese identity, such that "a Beijinger and a resident from the hinterland provinces . . . can probably be as far apart as heaven and earth" (*Guangming ribao* 1990, 4). In sum, even to an apologist for the discredited regime, China remains bedeviled by the unresolved and divisive political challenges of the late nineteenth and early twentieth centuries.

The same persistent divisive tendencies are also described by a critic of China's Leninist dictatorship, the economist Liu Guoguang. The "visible phenomena" he finds in China's dynamic are "regionalism, total chaos, and the back and forth central versus local power struggle" (*Caimao jingji* 1990, 96). The Canton scholar He Bochuan notes the prospect of "chaos and division of the nation," finding that China's "unification is only superficial" and that "in the age of regional economics which lies ahead . . . it will be difficult to avoid conflict between the regions and the central government" (He 1991, 155).[8] Hence a foreign scholar like Brantley Womack who does "not see regionalism in China" and who concludes that "separatism in the core areas is not likely to become a problem" (Womack 1992, 181) is at odds with the shared perception of the widest spectrum of Chinese. Fang Lizhi, a democratic opponent of China's Leninist dictatorship, can even see the strength of centrifugal forces as a hopeful opportunity: "As soon as Deng Xiaoping dies [he predicted], central control will weaken and local forces will rise. Guangdong, Fujian, and Shanghai will ask for more democracy. . . . The strong autonomous tendency among local authorities is not entirely a bad thing. Maybe it can put an end to the oligarchy in China" (*Free China Journal*, 2 August 1990, 5).

In China, according to the Harvard professor Wei-ming Tu, "the center no longer has the ability, insight, or legitimate authority to dictate the agenda for cultural China." "Either the center will bifurcate or, as is more likely, the [coastal] periphery will come to set the economic and cultural agenda for the center, thereby undermining its political effectiveness" (Tu 1991a, 27, 28, 12). Ever more Chinese imagine a more open future as the heir of a more open past.

The Chinese scholar Chen Kun in 1981 denounced the tyrannical impositions of the Qin dynasty of 221 B.C.E. that unified a large state, slaughtered intellectuals, and built the Great Wall to keep others out. "Qin people did not have time to grieve for themselves. Their descendants did. The descendants grieved but did not learn. Later generations were made to grieve for the descendants again." For Chen, an autocratic China is not a strong nation. Rather, it is an inhuman one. Chen equates "autocracy and atrocity" (Chen quoted in Schwarcz 1986–1987, 594, 601). Mao's identification with a continuous tradition of a strong exclusionary state is thus exploded.

In the new national narrative, as described by the Chinese scholar Tang Yijie, China is not the nation of the Qin dictators, with supposed strength found by hiding behind a Great Wall. Instead "Chinese . . . vitality" lies in an "open attitude toward foreign cultural influence," as exemplified by the hybrid vigor inherent in China's millennia-long absorption of Indian Buddhism. "Therefore, all purist talk of 'native culture' or 'national essence' cannot but harm the development of national culture and reflects the withering of the vitality of a nation's culture" (Tang quoted in Schwarcz 1986–1987, 603). Hence, a project of military defense to wall out alien influences actually weakens the Chinese nation.

Anthropology, archaeology, and history have been revolutionized so that Chinese are no longer imagined as a people descended from an isolated, northern-plain culture but instead as the consequence of the southern Chu and other cultures, each involved outside of China, all merging with the others. There is no center in the north that can spread. The focus now is on the normality of decentralization, the power in local creativity, a need for confederation premised on federal divisions of power rather than military concentrations of power.

In the new cultural consciousness, the identity of Mao with the ancien régime that hid behind walls reveals both as reactionary and antipopular the antitheses of what a vital, future-oriented national community requires. According to Vera Schwarcz, Mao's anti-imperialist roots are ridiculed: "The cultural conservative Gou Hongming . . . wore a long pigtail down his back . . . and mocked May Fourth activists by calling the proponents of democracy 'demo-crazy.' That is what Mao thought about intellectuals as well: crazy and dispensable" (Schwarcz 1992, 7). Mao and his project are redefined as at one with the most reactionary, outlandish, narrow nativists, from superstitious Boxer rebels to Qing dynasty die-hards.

In contrast, a new national project seems a palpable reality in a mobile south China that reaches out through the Chinese diaspora to the world. What Chinese are increasingly conscious of is not a single northern Han people who filled an empty space but a land long peopled by plural groups, with "extreme linguistic heterogeneity . . . mainly characteristic of the southeastern coastal provinces in an area extending roughly from Shanghai, through Guangdong, and somewhat into Guangxi" (Cohen 1991, 115). Chinese are reimagining themselves as diverse, not homogeneous, not a nation that is supposedly 95 percent Han. In the eyes of the anthropologist David Wu, "The regionally defined groups . . . Cantonese, Shanghaiese, and Taiwanese, including those living overseas, have obvious ethnic differences in speech, dress, customs, religious beliefs, and so on. . . . [T]he difference between two Han groups can . . . be more pronounced than that between a Han and a so-called minority nationality group" (Wu 1991, 167). The Chinese press comments about how different regions prefer different teas or celebrate holidays differently. It is difference that catches popular attention. It is how people talk and see.

Given this Chinese reconstruction of national identity, the southern narrative could become a self-fulfilling prophecy. Chinese find that this more open south embodies "littoral vitality" and that "the coastal cities on the lower Yangtze River and the provinces of Fujian and Guangdong" will "become increasingly internationalized," a "transnational and cosmopolitan" part of the Pacific Rim (Lee 1991, 224).

So much is it a presupposition that the southern people, understood as the heirs of the state of Chu, are revitalizing China that even the official press describes the dynamism of southern people as "a history of leading change in China." "As early as in the spring and autumn period (770–476 B.C.E.), the Chu Kingdom already offered fertile soil for the 'Chu culture' whose salient features have doubtlessly influenced people in today's Hunan Province, the intellectuals in particular." (Historians accept Hunan intellectuals as quintessential true patriots.) The purported "industrious and pioneering" nature of such people was said to have been reinforced by "massive migration" that brought vigor to the area and by "the development of waterways for transportation," turning the area "into a traffic hub" (*China Daily,* 26 March 1991). The presupposition is that nonmobile, rooted northerners, toiling away on ancestral land, are obstacles to progress. A renewed Chinese nation must build on a national vision imagined in southern terms of openness, mobility, and decentralization.

Contrasting north/south experiences are interpreted as causes of two national projects, anti-imperialist centralized dictatorship and open decentralist confederation. In the twentieth century, desperate north China peasants fled to northern and western frontiers. Fixated on the misery of leaving home to dwell in poor, minority, and climatically harsh regions, northern oral culture and folk songs celebrated the virtues of staying home with the family, thus embracing Mao's conquest of state power as ending their painful dilemmas where "a poor house is hard to abandon, one's land is hard to leave."

In contrast, poor southerners were imagined as having fled overseas. Their family members who stayed home in south China experienced economic benefits from overseas remittances and openness to the world. The northerners pushed minorities off land and gave themselves good conscience for their racist chauvinism in terms of ethnonationalist superiority. Southerners, in contrast, defined patriotism to harmonize with continuous ties to a non-Chinese world. The southerner was open to a world of market, money, mobility, and other people. The conflict between north and south is imagined as a conflict between closed and open, intolerant and tolerant, the failed project of a self-wounding Leninist anti-imperialism and the rising project of a successful nation. The northern project is seen as a dead-end error.

The experience now is one of taking off blinders. Ever more Chinese see reality as do southerners. Traditionally, north China cities were built around an enclosed government or aristocratic center. The emperor's back was literally turned to the merchants' quarter. By the Tang dynasty the cities of the south, in contrast, were bustling, irregular commercial centers with numerous foreign visitors. The north-south split seems historical, profound, and obvious.

A happier future is imagined as the fruit of the southern project.[9] With its facilitating of a dynamic commodity economy of material progress, "Guangzhou could be the cradle of China's new culture," proclaimed a Cantonese analyst in 1986 (see White and Cheng 1993). The city's glory, wrote the Cantonese historian Ye Chansheng, came from its distance over the centuries from northern "feudal influences" (quoted in White and Cheng 1993). The south was popular, not elitist, democratic, not aristocratic.

By the 1990s, people in Canton were the biggest newspaper-reading audience in China. Chinese elsewhere sought out Canton newspapers. Cantonese intellectuals projected a new national culture, premised on Canton's open, plural, entrepreneurial, amalgamated, mass culture. The south has a common print culture giving voice to a shared narrative of a hopeful future, a new national consciousness in embryo.

Inside families, southern children are being taught to hate cruel northerners. The south, southerners now say, has always been more advanced than the north. In fact, southerners find, the north has lived off the earnings of the south. The grain of the south even fed the north. The south has always been open to trade and other peoples. China has been held back by northerners, who are indigent, insular, and ignorant.

In Song times (960–1279), southerners note, reform was needed. The southern reformist Wang Anshi opposed the northern reactionary Sima Guang. Unfortunately, the Song court was dominated by northerners, who sided with the reactionary Sima Guang. The south lost. Reform was blocked.

All China consequently suffered. China was conquered in the north by the Liao, Jin, and Xisha and then by the Mongols. Blood, language, and culture were intermixed in the north. Teachers of Cantonese tell students that Cantonese is closer to the original Chinese language while the tongue spoken up north is more of a foreign imposition.

When the Mongols momentarily conquered the south, they graded their subjects into four tiers. First came the Bannermen, the Mongols themselves. Next came the colored-eye (*Semu*) people of the west, seen as coming from places where eyes were not black. Third were the mixed groups of the north previously conquered by the Liao, Jin, and Xisha. These were labeled *Han*. The actual survivors of the ancient Han era, now in the south, often the descendants of Chu, were called *southerners*. They were the true Chinese, an advanced people, the hope of a revitalized China.

The resurgent Chinese Ming dynasty, based in the south, envisioning the north as an area for many centuries corrupted by non-Chinese rule, decreed that all Chinese return to the dress of the Tang dynasty and that Mongol costumes and surnames be discontinued. When the Ming capital was moved to Beijing to help sinicize alien northern territory, the north became economically dependent, culturally conservative, and politically bureaucratic, while the south monetized its economy, expanded its trade, and increased its urban component. South China benefited greatly from silver carried there through international trade. The rulers in the north never figured out how to reform to compete in that world economy and instead increased the tax burden on productive people. The Manchu conquest and the subsequent Mao era are imagined as the consequence and continuation of a politically bureaucratic, culturally conservative, economically unreformed northern rule.

Thus it seems natural that modern ideas and practices were first established in China's south: the north's conservatism led the northern people to reject modern ways. The southern reformer Tan Sitong (1864–1898), a hero of the young who identify reactionary post-Mao elders with the Empress Dowager, used an eclectic cosmopolitan ethos to attack Confucian hierarchy. Reactionaries in the government, trying to hold power in the 1990s by promoting Confucianism, opposing heterodoxy, and fearing the south's successful opening to the world economy, seem caught in a time warp that would leave the Chinese people ever further behind the rapidly developing world.

Defensive, anxious Mao-style anti-imperialist nationalism is now revealed as a false path to suit a particular and parochial political project. The recent transvaluation of values reveals some of the repressed political alternatives that the anti-imperialist myth made invisible or treasonous.

The growing presuppositional popularity of the new national history does not mean that China will democratize, or that a southern-based consciousness will establish a new national polity, or that the nation will split, or even that the anti-imperialist reactionaries legitimated by the old northern narrative will be deposed. Political culture in itself is not decisive. But a new cultural consciousness popularly legitimates political projects that are more diverse than imagined by observers still mesmerized by the old northern narrative. These possibilities include confederated democracy or an open, southern-based state. While politics will decide among numerous contending projects, the southern narrative that privileges Chu and peripheralizes Qin is ever more potent.

Scholars of national identity tend to find that people engaged in a political struggle are likely to identify with one national history or another, to choose between perceived poles in an oppositional binary. The democracy movement representative Chen Ziming wrote early in 1991 while in prison, "I cast aside . . . serving the state of Qin in the morning and Chu in the evening" (*Asia Watch,* 10 June 1992, 16). The data assembled in this article suggest that choosing Chu over Qin is not an individual idiosyncrasy but a broadly shared identity transformation that may be full of significance for China's national future.

4
The Languages of China

In this very clear yet technical chapter, Robert Ramsey describes the sorts of differences that exist among the contemporary dialects of Chinese, usually divided into seven major groups, each with a large number of subdivisions not all of which are mutually intelligible. He explains the origins of some of these differences as the result of migrations, historical events, and cultural values. Readers will note a pervasive difference between the "north" and the "south," most of the north being linguistically fairly homogeneous and the south extremely diverse. While south China has a particular character, notable for its romance and good business sense, and north China is regarded as more prosaic, the seat of government rather than revolution, conservative rather than experimental, this difference does not hold for language, with the southern dialects relatively conservative and the northern dialects relatively innovative. (This means that linguistic features that scholars believe existed in earlier periods, such as the Tang dynasty, are retained in more southern dialects but have been eliminated in the northern dialects.) Ramsey assumes that readers know that languages change and that they change in systematic ways—that is, they generally change, not a word at a time, but rather in terms of structures and patterns.

A striking difference between the languages of China and American dialects is that, while in the United States most dialect differences have to do with vowels (think of a New Yorker, a South Carolinian, and an Iowan pronouncing the word *five*), in China many of the differences have to do with consonants. For instance, in most of south China, speakers do not distinguish between the sounds written *s* and *sh*, while, in the standard form of the northern dialects, these two sounds are always different. A similar lack of distinction can also be seen between *n* and *l*, *-n* and *-ng*, and other sounds (so that, e.g., the word *Nanjing* is pronounced something like "Lanjin" by that city's inhabitants).

One of the ways that Chinese dialects, and even related languages within a single dialect group, differ is in their tones. Tones are analyzed as both *classes* and *reflexes*, that is, in terms of how many different types of tones a given dialect has and how those types actually actually sound when they are produced. Linguists have been using a five-point scale, with 5 the highest and 1 the lowest, to describe the pattern followed by the pronunciation of a given word—actually, the main vowel of each syllable. Some tones are even or level, others rise or fall, and some both rise and fall. The meanings of words differ according to their tones. Imagine an American parent confronting a defiant toddler who does not want to go to bed. The child says "No!" in a strong, falling tone, while the incredulous parent may ask "No?" in a high-rising tone. If these were Chinese words, they would have totally unrelated meanings.

You may notice that language changes reveal relationships among groups that might otherwise be difficult to trace. One of the somewhat surprising conclusions that Ramsey reaches on the basis of his linguistic analysis is that the Cantonese (Yue) languages share many features with the Tai languages, which were spoken when Chinese from the north first migrated south. Anthropologists have often speculated about a "Thai substratum" in southern China, especially in Guangdong and Guangxi, where Southeast Asian features combined with Chinese features to produce a unique hybrid culture quite distinctive from any other.

The nature of Chinese writing is often regarded as mystical by those who do not know the language, but the principles are quite simple (see De Francis 1984, 1989). An analogy may be drawn with Arabic numerals. Take the numeral 5. It is pronounced the following ways in various languages:

> English, *five* /faiv/
> Spanish, *cinco* /siŋko/
> French, *cinq* /sæŋk/
> German, *fünf* /fynf/
> Hebrew, *chamesh* /xameʃ/

Yet the meaning of the symbol remains essentially identical in all these languages. The symbol is used to remind speakers of words that they know. Similarly, the Chinese character 人, *ren*, means "person." It is read differently by speakers of different languages:

> Mandarin, /ren2/
> Cantonese, /yan2/
> Shanghainese, /nieng2/
> Japanese, /nin/ or /jin/

This demonstration suggests that reliance on a single writing system does not necessarily require—or prove—linguistic identity. Yet Western scholars who would challenge the unity of China's language(s) are seen as challenging the unity of China itself. Ramsey accepts the designation of these linguistic varieties as *dialects* and describes the specific features of each so that readers can better grasp the scale of the differences. They are often said to vary by phonology (sound system) by 80 percent, by semantics (word meaning) by 40 percent, and by syntax (word order and sentence patterns) by only 20 percent.

The result is that, if a speaker of one dialect masters the correspondence in sound system of another, more than half of what he or she hears will be intelligible. This, of course, requires motivation to do so. And, in a country where only one *fangyan* (topolect, dialect) is officially recognized (but see Erbaugh 1995), such motivation may not always exist.

One emerges from reading Ramsey's treatment of language in China with a more complex view of communication and social interaction in the vast territory of the People's Republic of China.—Eds.

CHINA, NORTH AND SOUTH

Today, in the last decades of the twentieth century, Chinese is spoken by about 1 billion people. No other language is remotely comparable. English, the next most widely spoken language, has fewer than half that many speakers.

Almost all of the Chinese people live in the densely populated eastern half of China, an area geographically about the size of the United States east of the Mississippi. Relatively few live outside this region. In modern times the Chinese have begun to colonize more intensively the immense territories in the western half of their country. Manchuria and Inner Mongolia to the north, areas forbidden to most Chinese as long as the Manchus were in power, have also begun to feel the pressures of intense immigration. But all of China's territorial possessions, both in the north and in the west, are as yet relatively sparsely settled. More than 95 percent of the Chinese still live in Inner China, the part of the country east of the Tibetan plateau and south of the Great Wall.

Inner China, the traditional homeland of the Chinese people, is divided naturally into two parts, the north and the south. North China is a treeless expanse of plain and plateau that extends south from the Great Wall over the area drained by the Yellow river and its tributaries. South China is the Yangzi river valley and the well-watered hills and valleys and rice-growing areas that lie to its south. These two regions, each of which is dominated by a great river, together form the geographic setting for Chinese civilization and history.

North China belongs climatically and geographically to the interior of the Asian continent. The entire western half of the region is a dry and dusty highland known as the Loess plateau. Here, for 100,000 square miles, the hills and mountains are covered with a powdery yellow dust, called *loess,* that in places is as much as three hundred feet thick. Loess is believed to have blown down from the deserts of Inner Asia into the western half of north China during the last Ice Age, when the north winds were unimaginably fiercer than anything known today. It erodes easily. The modern continental winds may be mild by comparison with those that blew in prehistoric times, but during the winter they are still powerful enough to raise great dust storms and fill the air with grit all the way to the Yellow sea. Sometimes the air-borne yellow powder is carried far enough east to sting eyes and faces in Korea and dust windows and gardens in Japan. To the east of the Loess plateau lies the Yellow plain. Its yellow soils, too, come from the Asian interior. This broad, flat floodplain of the Yellow river consists entirely of thick deposits of loess silt that have been built up over the ages. Where the Yellow river flows down from the mountains of the Loess plateau, it is colored bright yellow by the soil that it and its tributaries have picked up in cutting through several hundred miles of loess deposits. At this point, the solids held in suspension sometimes make up almost half of the flow of the Yellow river by weight. As the river enters the flat Yellow plain, it slows down abruptly, and the silt begins to settle, building up the floodplain at a rate exceeded by that of no other major river system in the world. This river is with justice called *China's Sorrow.* The Chinese have tried for millennia to keep the Yellow river within its banks by building elaborate systems of dikes. But, as the silt in the water settles, the bed of the river rises higher and higher, and the dikes must also be built up higher to keep pace. Some dikes are forty or more feet above the surrounding land. Eventually the river must break through these restraining walls, and then it deposits thick layers of sediment over many miles of the surrounding countryside. In this way the yellow substance from the deserts of Inner Asia is spread over north China all the way to the sea.

The loess soils of the Loess plateau and the Yellow plain are fertile but relatively dry. In good years when rainfall is adequate, fine stands of wheat, millet, and other crops that require less water than rice can be and are grown. The traditional staples of the region are therefore noodles, breads, and other foods made from these grains. But water is too scarce or unpredictable to sustain the intensive irrigation that rice requires, and the bowls of this grain that are eaten in Beijing must usually be shipped from south China.

The climate of south China is more oceanic. The colors are not brown and yellow but green. Most of the region is protected from the northern continental winds by the Qinling mountains, the range that forms the watershed between the Yellow and the Yangzi rivers, and the loess deposits of north China stop at this mountain barrier. The rivers and streams that flow from its southern slopes therefore do not pick up the characteristic yellow silt that is found in northern rivers. Here the prevailing winds are generally from the south—the so-called summer monsoons—and they bring with them moisture and warm air from the ocean. Summers in south China are hot and steamy; clothes and books mold and mildew. Winters are cooler and drier than summers, but in many areas they are still mild enough for crops to grow. South China is a region of rice fields and terraces, lakes, rivers, and canals; hilly or mountainous areas not under cultivation are often covered with trees and thick vegetation, which in the southwestern part of the country turn into the jungles of Southeast Asia.

The south has China's best farmland. Rainfall makes it a richer place than north China; population densities are higher, and the people are generally better nourished. In contrast with the north, with its harsh climatic extremes, the fresh and verdant lands of the south are almost ideal for the growing of rice. Around Canton, for example, two good rice crops are regularly grown each year. The region is also well suited to the cultivation of a variety of other warm-weather crops as well, including teas, cotton, tangerines and other fruits, and mulberry bushes for silk production.

The Chinese language, like China itself, is geographically divided into the north and the south. The northern varieties of the language, usually known in English as the *Mandarin dialects,* are spread across the Yellow plain and the Loess plateau. This dialect area also creeps south to the Yangzi river, and a long arm bends down to the extreme southwest, extending across the provinces of Sichuan and Yunnan all the way to the Thai border. This southwestern branch is for the most part recently settled territory, as are Manchuria, Inner Mongolia, and the far northwest, where Mandarin is the only kind of Chinese spoken. As a result of these accretions, the Mandarin area now covers more than three-fourths of the country. The southern varieties of the language—the so-called non-Mandarin dialects—are confined to the wedge of land formed in the southeast by the lower course of the Yangzi river and the South China sea.

There is a qualitative difference between these two areas. The Mandarin area, on the one hand, is unusually uniform; virtually all of the dialects spoken there are mutually intelligible—or very nearly so. A native of Harbin, in the extreme northeastern corner of the Mandarin range, has little trouble conversing with someone from Chongqing, a city in the extreme southwest over sixteen hundred miles away. Mandarin has no more variety than French, say, or German. But the non-Mandarin area is extremely varied, and within it sharply divergent forms of speech are often separated by only a few miles. The Xiamen dialect, for example, which is spoken on the southeastern coast opposite Taiwan, is completely unintelligible to anyone living much farther away than a hundred miles in any direction. The variety of the language in the south is so great that the dialects there can be classified into at least six groups, each of which is as varied as the entire Mandarin area.

This remarkable linguistic difference between a unified north and a fragmented south is a measure of how much life and society have been affected by geography. It is not surprising, of course, that the newly settled Mandarin territories are uniform; that is only to be expected. It usually takes time for regional differences to grow up—as we can see in recently populated areas of North America and Australia, where only the subtlest differences in speech can be detected across thousands of miles of land. What is unusual about Chinese is the difference in homogeneity between the north and the south of Inner China; both of these regions have long been inhabited by the Chinese people, and for much of that time the country has been culturally and even politically united. The correlation between the dichotomy in the language and the climatic and geographic division of the country is therefore all the more striking. The physical character of the land on which the Chinese live has apparently affected the ability to communicate.

One way the Chinese describe the contrast between the north and the south is with the catchword *nan chuan bei ma,* "in the south the boat, in the north the horse." In traditional times the horse was the best way to travel in north China. Mounted, one could generally move at will over the dry open terrain without encountering serious obstacles. Even the great Yellow river itself was in most places so shallow it could be forded. But in the south the horseman had to dismount. The lakes, rivers, and canals in the flat low-lying areas on the floodplains of the Yangzi and its tributaries could be crossed only by ferry. Still farther to the south, beyond the Yangzi plain, the rugged hills and mountains with their high terraced rice fields and dense vegetation were difficult to cross even on foot and on horseback virtually impossible. From the Yangzi on south, there were few roads of the kind that stretched across the north; in this southern half of China the highways were the rivers, streams, and canals that connected rice-growing area to market, town to town. The only efficient means of transportation in the south was by boat.

In the north there was much more freedom of movement. Water is an efficient medium of transport for bulk shipments of grain or freight, but it is less convenient for personal travel because waterways and currents do not necessarily flow in the direction one wants to go. In the open spaces of the north, communication and transportation were quicker and easier than in the south, a region finely crosshatched with natural barriers.

The linguistic homogeneity of north China shows what a difference this has made. Mandarin has dialects, of course, especially in the hillier parts of the Loess plateau. But there is nothing in the north to compare with the complex variety of the southern dialects. The open terrain made possible linguistic cohesion.

South China, by contrast, has an abundance of the linguistic variety we expect to find where there are many barriers to communication and where people have stayed put for relatively long periods of time. Over much of the south the speech of each community—commonly a group of farming villages served by the same market—has tended to diverge from that of other, neighboring communities. The amount of divergence depends largely on the degree to which it is isolated from its neighbors. In general, the greater the barriers to travel and communication, the greater will be the differences in speech. Wuzhou and Taishan, for example, are both towns in the far south that are served by Canton, the capital of Guangdong province, as a commercial and cultural center. Wuzhou is a fairly new town that lies 120 miles directly upstream from Canton on the West river, a major shipping artery into the provincial capital. It was largely settled from Canton and still maintains close contacts with that city. Taishan, on the other hand, is only about sixty miles southwest of Canton, but several rivers must be crossed to get there. Thus, in spite of the fact that Taishan is actually twice as close as Wuzhou to the provincial capital, it is much less accessible, and the dialect has diverged far more. A considerable number of linguistic changes separate Taishan from the cosmopolitan variety of Cantonese. An even sharper example of the effects of isolation can be drawn when the city of Shantou (also known as Swatow) is brought into the picture. Although Shantou is located in Guangdong province, it is separated from Canton by rows of rugged mountains. It was therefore settled from the north along the coastline and is still culturally and commercially independent of Canton. As a result, the dialect spoken there is totally unintelligible to a speaker of Cantonese.

Complicating this regional stratification, especially in the far south, are the linguistic layers left by successive waves of immigrants. The modern city of Hong Kong with its hodgepodge of people from all over China is in any case exceptional; but commercial centers along the south China coast have long been places where different linguistic groups have lived side by side for extended periods of time. Also, to a slightly lesser degree, various groups have been able to coexist fairly close to each other in the geographically fragmented hill country farther inland. The physical isolation imposed by geography has helped to keep these groups from being assimilated.

A provocative question that remains to be answered is how linguistic unity was effected in north China. It is clear that physical geography was a necessary condition—the contrast with south China is enough to show that. But, given this geographic fact, what further historical forces were then necessary to make this expanse of land cohere? Far broader plains and larger river valleys exist in the world. There have even been empires where comparable numbers of people have been brought together under one government. But nowhere before modern times has there ever been a linguistic unity like that of north China. Part of the answer, at least, must lie in the political and social institutions of traditional China. Linguistic uniformity is ample testimony to the efficiency and organizational strength of its central government. But were institutional factors alone enough?

The study of linguistic geography elsewhere in the world has shown us time and time again that homogeneity of the kind found in north China usually exists only in areas that have been settled fairly recently. One avenue that might be useful to explore, therefore, is the possibility that there has been extensive intraregional migration in the north. Could the populations of north China have moved around enough to homogenize the language? We know that there has been considerable local movement in both halves of China, but was the displacement of people in the north significantly greater than that in the south—and greater enough to reach a linguistically critical mass? There were, after all, reasons why peasant life might be more vulnerable in the north.

There was first of all greater economic stability in the south. Predictable rainfall meant that harvests could be depended on from year to year, and that made farming a less risky occupation. The south was not free from natural disasters, but floods and droughts were seldom as frequent or as intense as those that struck the north. When the Yellow river abruptly shifted its course in 1194, a series of floods swept across the entire northeast, devastating the economy and driving great numbers of peasants from their homes. The Grand Canal, an artificial waterway connecting the imperial capital in the north to the rice baskets of the Yangzi valley, was of undeniable benefit for disaster relief, especially in areas immediately adjacent to the canal. But nothing could completely make up for the enormous disparity in economic stability between the south and the north.

Another consideration was personal safety. The north was more accessible to overland trade, but it was also more vulnerable to invading armies. The border skirmishes that China now has with Soviet troops give barely a hint of the almost unending wars that the Chinese once waged on their northern borders to hold the "barbarians" at bay. A weakened Chinese state brought invasion, and invasion brought death, destruction, economic chaos, and dislocation. But, while this threat hung like a cloud over north China, the distant south lay well beyond the reach of most foreign armies. Not only was the south relatively safe because continental forces had to pass through the north first; the terrain of the south itself made the region almost impregnable. It was a stronghold for Chinese civilization. The northern invaders were cavalry, and horses were of little use in south China. How were horsemen to fight while crossing waterways and slogging through rice paddies? On his own ground, the mounted warrior was an efficient fighting machine, but, when he came to south China, he had to dismount like any other traveler—and on foot he faced Chinese infantries.

Even the invincible Mongols found the going hard in south China. In 1211 Genghis Khan and his hordes swept down into north China, and in a series of lightning campaigns that lasted only four years they crushed resistance and seized control of all of China north of the Yellow river. But the Yangzi valley, though protected by only a relatively weak Chinese state, escaped Mongol conquest for over half a century more. Long after Genghis had died, his grandson Khubilai Khan launched a series of flanking maneuvers that took his armies west and then south through the Tai kingdom of Nanzhao. Then, in 1268, after his encircling armies had already penetrated what is now Vietnam, Khubilai was able to mount his forces and attack the Song, moving down the river systems into central China. Finally, in 1279, sixty-eight years after they had first entered north China, the Mongols succeeded in destroying the Chinese government and in conquering south China. But, even then, life was disrupted less than in north China, where the Mongols could move about quickly into any area.

Did the more frequent military incursions suffered by the north displace enough people to make significant changes in the language? Could floods and droughts have had a similar effect? If enough people were forced to leave their lands, if only for short distances, then north China could effectively have been returned to the state of newly settled territory in spite of the antiquity of its civilization. Could such a thing have happened? The study of the language alone cannot answer these questions; without detailed demographic data linguistic information is more tantalizing than conclusive. It does, however, show us something about China that needs to be explained. The linguistic unity of north China is an extraordinary fact that may well require an extraordinary explanation.

THE SPREAD OF NORTHERN INFLUENCE

Many things have changed in China since the Communist Revolution, including some attitudes about the Chinese language. The writer Mao Dun, who had been one of the radical opponents of linguistic unification, became one of the most eloquent promoters of Putonghua, the Common Language. The man who in the 1930s had scorned any idea of subordinating Cantonese or other local forms of speech to a national standard—there was no such thing, he had scoffed, as a "modern Chinese common language"—later changed his public stand completely. In 1978 he wrote a pronouncement advocating that the Chinese people "firmly hold to the task of popularizing the Common Language." "The final goal of spreading the Common Language," Mao Dun concluded, "is to have all Han people speak it. At present we are still a long way from realizing that goal. We must devise methods to hasten toward it" (Mao [1978] 1979).

The standardization of Chinese is a matter of high priority in the People's Republic, and there is now almost no one who questions that goal. Discussion ended with the articulation of the official language policy in 1956. Two years later, in 1958, Premier Zhou Enlai emphasized in a speech on language reform how vital the government considered the implementation of that policy. "Spreading the use of the Common Language, which takes the Beijing pronunciation as the standard, is an important political task," he said (Zhou 1958). Through the Hundred Flowers Movement, the Cultural Revolution, the reign of the Gang of Four, and their subsequent downfall, the government has never altered this objective. The policy of standardization has moved slowly and deliberately ahead.

In north China, this policy has been of little or no consequence. Broad discrepancies from the Beijing norm are tolerated as acceptable variations in the Common Language, and people who speak natively any dialect of Mandarin have simply continued to use the same speech patterns that they have always used. But in the non-Mandarin dialect areas of south China, where speech is substantially different from that of Beijing, the effects of language standardization have been real and considerable. The lives of virtually everyone in the south have in varying degrees been touched by the policy.

Passive exposure to the standard language comes via film, radio, and television. Books, magazines, and newspapers are all written in the standard colloquial style, and dialect publications—such as the Cantonese newspapers commonly seen in Hong Kong, for example—have apparently became rare in the People's Republic. We have no word as to the fate of dialect literature, but none seems to appear in any officially sanctioned outlets. More active linguistic ability is required for such things as political rallies, meetings, and classes. Refugees in Hong Kong report that in such sessions both teachers and students often revert to their native dialect as soon as a topic becomes complicated or the debate heated. But the official medium is nevertheless the standard language, and a genuine effort is made to maintain that rule.

The school occupies a special place in this program of standardization: the government has concentrated its efforts on changing the speech habits of the very young. In 1956 it issued a State Council directive that all school instruction, from the first grade through university, be conducted in Putonghua. This step represented a radical departure from the past and one difficult to carry out because most teachers in the south were at that time almost as unfamiliar with Beijing speech as their students were. Workshops for teachers were opened, and within two years 721,000 were said to have been trained in Beijing phonetics. There was probably considerable variation in the level of skill that these teachers acquired, and the thoroughness of subsequent training programs is perhaps open to question as well. But, for the present generation of Chinese children, the cumulative results of these efforts are undeniable. For a child growing up in Canton or Shanghai, Putonghua is the language of education. Immersion might be less complete in rural areas, but in city schools today the primary medium of instruction from the end of the first year on is the standard language.

The first grade is where southern children learn this new form of speech. On the first day of school they hear only the familiar sounds of their own language (or dialect, as the Chinese would insist). But gradually, over a period of months, the teacher begins to use more and more words and phrases of the standard language, and before the end of the first year most classroom subjects are discussed in Putonghua. This is not, in the strictest sense, foreign-language instruction: we must remember that the Chinese do not think of the "dialects" as different languages, and the schools reflect this fact. Formal instruction is given only in reading and writing properly, and exposure to the spoken version of the standard language is for the most part treated as incidental to this process. The children simply "pick up" speaking skills based on the model of the teacher. Nevertheless, owing to the tender age at which they begin this process, the children become effective users of Putonghua fairly quickly. Observers report that, although they have pronounced local "accents," even pupils in the lower grades are able to converse fluently on almost any school subject.

This high level of fluency does not always last. As Mao Dun once lamented, most of these children gradually lose their ability to speak the Common Language after they leave school because the people all around them speak the local dialect. Certainly, the language of the streets in Shanghai, Fuzhou, or Canton has not become Putonghua; most southerners still speak the same dialect or dialects that their parents and grandparents did. But it would be surprising indeed if any of today's schoolchildren did not retain at least some linguistic skills into later life. Experience with the standard language during these early years is critical.

In south China today Putonghua is the language of the government, and southerners tend to use it for all activities associated with public life. For everything outside the public sphere the language is usually the local dialect. In the case of schoolchildren, the resulting formula is simple: in school use Putonghua; outside school use the home dialect. For adults the rules are more complicated; government penetrates their lives much more intricately, and the importance of the standard language to an individual depends on a wide variety of factors—obviously a young telegrapher or a tour guide or a cadre has more contact with the Common Language than an old farmer or street sweeper. But almost no one completely escapes public activity and the standard language. As the official language of China, Putonghua, the Common Language, reaches wherever the government does, and, whatever contact southerners have with public life, there they find in some measure the standard language.

Throughout the south an increasing number of ordinary people, adults as well as children, are becoming familiar with Putonghua and are even able to speak it. Recent visitors to south China have noted that it is now possible in almost any southern city to shop, buy tickets, or ask directions using only the standard language. With it, it is even possible, they say, to strike up conversations with people in the streets. As any old China hand will attest, this is a far cry from prerevolutionary China, where outsiders who did not know the local dialect could quickly find themselves hopelessly lost.

The rapid spread of Putonghua in south China does not mean that the dialects will soon die, however. Southerners do not forget all the other varieties of Chinese they know as soon as they learn the standard one. On the contrary, Putonghua complicates (or enriches) their life by adding another dimension to it. It becomes a useful tool, but at the same time it remains highly inappropriate and inconvenient in certain situations. There are many times and places where southerners must unavoidably speak their local dialect—that is, unless they want to sever their ties completely with the social groups in which they grew up. The role of the dialect may be developing into something not unlike that of Swiss German, which has coexisted alongside standard High German in Switzerland for generations.

In the linguistically complex land that south China already is, Putonghua represents yet another layer of language. This northern import cannot and will not immediately replace the many other varieties of Chinese that are already there. But even on levels farthest removed from public life its influence is already being felt. In Shanghai, which is a sophisticated southern metropolis close to the leading edge of the Mandarin dialect area, some educated families have begun to use the standard language in their homes. For children growing up in such households, Putonghua is already a second home language. In Canton, a city far down in the deep south and a stronghold of regional pride, Cantonese is reportedly still the exclusive medium of communication in the home. But even there the vocabulary and locutions of new ways of life will eventually reach the most intimate levels of language.

The kind of linguistic changes that language standardization is bringing about are not completely new, however. The promotion of Putonghua is the product of modern nationalism, and its methods are those of twentieth-century technology (without modern transportation and communication the standard could never be spread so quickly). But, in accelerated form, the spread of Putonghua is a continuation of much the same linguistic process that has been going on in China for a long time. One of the most consistent themes of Chinese history has been the flow of northern influence into the south, and the language standardization policy of the People's Republic is in some ways only the most recent surge in the process.

TODAY'S DIALECTS

The modern dialects are usually classified into seven major groups. In the list of those groups presented in table 4.1, the population estimates are based on a total Han Chinese population of 950 million.

North

Mandarin   The northern varieties of Chinese are usually known as the Mandarin dialects. They are typified by the Beijing dialect, which is the basis of the standard language and of "Mandarin" in a much narrower—and older—sense. These dialects are spoken by more than two-thirds of the Chinese people. With the total Chinese population having now passed the billion mark, this proportion means that there are around 700 million Mandarin speakers in the world—considerably more than the number of people who speak English as their first language. The area where these Mandarin dialects are spoken covers more than three-fourths of China. It extends over all of north China and Sichuan as well as the more recently sinicized territories of the northwest and southwest (see map 4.1).

This enormous dialect area is customarily divided by Chinese linguists into four subgroups: (1) Northern Mandarin, spoken in the northeast and including the Beijing dialect; (2) Northwestern Mandarin, which includes the dialects of the Loess plateau and the territories to the west of it; (3) Southwestern Mandarin, spoken in Sichuan and adjacent regions; (4) Eastern or Lower Yangzi Mandarin, represented by the dialects spoken around Nanjing. The actual linguistic differences between these groups are relatively slight and are difficult to delineate in any systematic way.

TABLE 4.1   Modern Chinese Dialects

| Dialect Group | Estimated Population | | Where Spoken |
	N	%	
North:			
Mandarin	679,250,000	71.5	All of north and southwest
South:			
Wu	80,750,000	8.5	Coastal area around Shanghai, Zhejiang
Gan	22,800,000	2.4	Jiangxi
Xiang	45,600,000	4.8	Hunan
Hakka	35,150,000	3.7	Widely scattered from Sichuan to Taiwan
Yue	47,500,000	5.0	Guangdong, Guangxi, and overseas communities
Min	38,950,000	4.1	Fujian, coastal areas of south

South

Wu   The Wu dialects are spoken in the Yangzi delta and the coastal region around Shanghai. This is an area in the most fertile and densely populated part of China. There are more than 80 million speakers of Wu, and they live in a space approximately the size of the state of Georgia (which has a population of about 5½ million).

The heart of this Wu-speaking area is Shanghai, China's largest city. Located on the flatlands of the rich Shanghai delta, this great metropolis of 11 million people serves as the economic and cultural focal point for the entire Yangzi basin. It is, above all, a city of industry and commerce. Its eight thousand factories produce everything from shoe polish and sweets to automobiles and steel and altogether account for one-eighth of China's total industrial output. Its port, which is connected to the Yangzi estuary by the muddy Huangpu river, accommodates a volume of cargo that ranks it among the twelve busiest in the world. The cultural impact of Shanghai on the rest of China is considerable. Of all the urban areas in the People's Republic, it is by far the most cosmopolitan. Of course, Communist reform long ago destroyed the wicked opulence of what was once called the *Paris of Asia*—there are no more opium dens or prostitutes, posh foreign restaurants, hotels, or bars. Shanghai's old racetrack, for example, has become People's Park. Yet, in spite of more than thirty years of reeducation and reorientation, an atmosphere of smart sophistication still remains in Shanghai. Clothing is more colorful and, by Western standards, more stylish than elsewhere in the country. After the fall of the Gang of Four, Shanghai's women took up permanent waves and makeup again more quickly than did their counterparts in other cities. Nanjing road, which runs through the heart of what was formerly the British settlement, still has its reputation for better shopping, and bureaucrats from

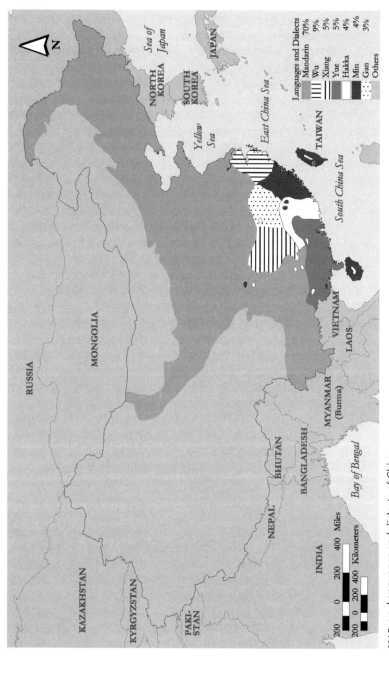

MAP 4.1. Languages and dialects of China.

elsewhere seldom leave Shanghai without a visit to its stores. The appearance of downtown Shanghai, too, has changed little since 1949, and much of it still looks like the Paris of Asia. The foreign communities may have been dis-enfranchised, but the streets and buildings where they once lived are still there, occupied by others and used for different purposes. The look of this European architecture stands in sharp contrast to that of the monumental mixture of imperial and Stalinist style to be seen in Beijing. Nothing else in China is quite like Shanghai.

By Chinese standards Shanghai is a new city. It began to be built up by foreign capital in the latter half of the nineteenth century; before that, it was an insignificant southern town. Ancient records tell us that around 200 B.C.E. it was the site of a tiny fishing village, which was part of the kingdom of Wu. (The Wu dialects are named after this ancient "barbarian" state.) Suzhou was the most important city in the area then; it was the capital of Wu. After Wu territory became Chinese, Suzhou kept its position of promi-nence in the Yangzi delta, continuing as a cultural and literary center through all the succeeding Chinese dynasties. Shanghai, meanwhile, became the port for Suzhou in about 500 C.E., and its fortunes remained tied to that other city until the mid-nineteenth century. Then, with the granting of the foreign concessions, its orientation changed, and it quickly came to eclipse Suzhou in population and money. The needs of the foreign commu-nity, which was bent on the exploitation of all of China, made it a boom town, as skilled and semiskilled labor poured in from the surrounding areas to take advantage of economic opportunity. Many of these migrants were also refugees, for the enclaves of Shanghai offered those willing to cut their roots with tradition a sanctuary against the very real physical dangers of liv-ing in a Chinese countryside that was rapidly becoming chaotic. By the end of the nineteenth century the population of Shanghai had swelled to over 4 million. Now it is three times that large.

The language of Shanghai reflects this turbulence. It comes in many varieties, depending on neighborhood and social group, and there is evi-dence of rapid generational change. Earlier missionary descriptions indicate that around the turn of the century it still had a sound system and vocabu-lary much like that of Suzhou. But increased immigration of artisans and clerks from slightly farther down the coast began to give the metropolitan area a more southern flavor, and today colloquial Shanghai speech is differ-ent from that of Suzhou, with an apparent mixture of elements from various places in the Wu dialect area. In discussing the linguistic state of affairs, one Western writer notes this mixing and refers to "the so-called Shanghai dialect," saying that it is "not a pure dialect at all, but a metropolitan hodge-podge" (George Kennedy quoted in Sherard 1972, 7).

Nevertheless, in the Wu dialect area today, Shanghai is clearly the place to be from, and anyone from anywhere near the metropolitan area will iden-tify himself or herself as "Shanghainese." The upper-class dialect of Suzhou, which was once the object of esteem and envy even in Shanghai itself, is now thought of as slightly old-fashioned or quaint. The majority speech of downtown Shanghai has become by far the most important of the Wu dialects.

Gan To the west and somewhat south of the Wu area are the Gan dialects. These little-known and little-studied varieties of Chinese are spoken mostly in Jiangxi, a province that stretches from the hills and mountain passes along the border of Guangdong northward to the great bow of the Yangzi river as it bends south to touch Boyang lake. Some Gan dialects are also spoken in the eastern part of Hunan, next to Jiangxi, and perhaps in the southeastern corner of Hubei province as well; very few details are known about the distribution of Gan dialects in these peripheral regions, however. The Gan dialect area is not clearly differentiated from the dialect areas adjacent to it. Through the center of Jiangxi flows the Gan river, the most prominent geographic feature of the region. It has given its name to the region and thus also to the dialect group.

Xiang The Xiang dialects are also a southern group in transition—even more so than Gan. They are exposed to Mandarin from several directions. Hunan, the place where they are spoken, borders Mandarin-speaking territory on its north, west, and southwest. The densely populated center of the province is easily accessible from the Yangzi via the Xiang river and its tributaries. As a result of these inroads from the north, the Xiang dialects have become complex mixtures of older southernisms and Mandarinized, newer features.

The Xiang dialects are divided into two types of speech, usually referred to as *New Xiang* and *Old Xiang*. New Xiang is spoken in the northwestern part of Hunan as well as in larger towns and cities all over the province. Old Xiang is the form of Chinese generally heard in mountain areas and farming communities. These two types of Xiang are reportedly very different. According to Chinese linguists: "The general impression is that communication between New Xiang and Southwestern Mandarin is actually not difficult, while between New Xiang and Old Xiang there is a great barrier. For this reason some people prefer to classify New Xiang as Southwestern Mandarin" (Yuan et al. 1960). In other words, the urban variety of Xiang—that is, "New Xiang"—has significantly diverged from its more conservative, rural counterpart; it has been so affected by Mandarin influence it appears to be very close to becoming Mandarin itself.

Yue (Cantonese) The Yue dialects are popularly known as the Cantonese dialects. They are spoken in Guangdong and Guangxi, in the area around the southernmost point in the curve of the south China coastline. The speech of Canton city, which is Cantonese in its narrower sense, is the best known and most generally esteemed of the Yue dialects.

These dialects are also spoken in North America. Unlike people from other parts of China, the people who speak Yue dialects—the "Cantonese"— have settled in fairly large numbers in the United States and Canada. An estimated 86 percent of Chinese Americans trace their ancestry to Guangdong province and usually to Taishan, a tiny, rural district about sixty miles southwest of Canton. Taishan was only one of the ninety-eight districts of Guangdong (which was only one of some twenty Chinese provinces), but it had the advantage of being accessible from the sea when American sailing vessels came to recruit cheap labor in the middle of the nineteenth century. Immigration from the south has given the American Chinatown a distinctive and lasting regional flavor.

The Yue-speaking people are relatively distinct from northern Chinese. Named after an ancient "barbarian" state located in the deep south, the Yue are true southerners. The word *southern,* in fact, is sometimes used as an exclusive synonym for *Yue.* (In the world of Chinese restaurants, e.g., south Chinese cooking almost always means Cantonese cooking, and anything north of Guangdong is considered northern.) If there is a well-defined subgroup of the Han Chinese today, it is the Yue. They may not be as numerous as speakers of Wu, but they have a far better developed sense of group identity. People from Shanghai know that their speech is somehow very similar to that of Suzhou or Hangzhou, but they have usually never heard of a Wu dialect area and certainly do not think of a Wu culture distinct against the greater background of China. Yue speakers, by contrast, will always identify themselves as "Cantonese." They look to Canton as the center of their local culture. They recognize Canton dialect as standard.

The Yue refer to themselves as *people of the Tang.* They call their country *Tang mountain,* their cuisine *Tang food,* and their clothing *Tang clothes.* The American Chinatown is known even in Mandarin as the "Tang People's Neighborhood" (*Tangrenjie*). The Yue have a strong tradition of reciting the classics that dates back to the Tang, and the phonological categories of their dialects derive almost entirely from those of the literary standard of that period. Apparently, the mixture of native and immigrant in Guangdong must have reached a critical mass of acculturation during the Tang dynasty.

Among the Yue people the dialect of Canton has enjoyed prestige for centuries, at least since the Ming dynasty, by which time the Pearl river delta had become the most important economic and cultural center in the deep south. From that time on, Cantonese had no local rivals. A vernacular literature grew up, including the enormously popular *yueou,* which were ballads sung to the accompaniment of the Chinese lute, the *pipa.* A kind of epic poetry, chanted to the clacking beat of two pieces of wood called *muyu,* thrived in late imperial times. *Nanyin,* or "southern melody," usually sung by a blind girl, was also popular—it survives best today in some of the airs of Cantonese opera. In addition, there was some writing of fiction and other kinds of vernacular literature. These styles of colloquial writing were relatively crude and unambitious, and they were never used for formal compositions; yet they were important enough to make Cantonese the only modern Chinese dialect (besides Mandarin) with widely recognized, nontraditional graphs for colloquial words and expressions. A few of these Cantonese characters are known to people all over China. Today such dialect writing is largely suppressed in the People's Republic, but it continues in Hong Kong and overseas Chinese communities, where Cantonese newspapers and other colloquial publications are sold on almost every newsstand. Cantonese is being challenged these days by Putonghua and the language policies of the Beijing government. But, as yet, its speakers retain their own separate traditions.

Cantonese is thus more than a widely spoken dialect. It is a genuine regional standard. In Guangdong province, even people whose home language is not Yue, including some national minorities whose home language is not even Han Chinese, use it and respect it as a model for speech. No other southern dialect, including Shanghainese, has this kind of stature.

Cantonese is said to be a conservative dialect, and to a certain extent this reputation is deserved. In its sound system it preserves with great fidelity the final consonants and tonal categories of the Tang dynasty literary standard. This means that a Tang poem read in Cantonese keeps more of its original patterns of rhyme than when read in Mandarin—or in any other dialect. Perhaps, as has sometimes been suggested, immigrants far from home were more careful about language and tradition. But, on the other hand, perhaps it was more important that the immigrants moved into a geographic area where such distinctions were likely to be preserved. The aboriginal Tai people of Guangdong with whom the Chinese mixed spoke languages with relatively large numbers of tones and final consonants. Cantonese is today the southernmost of the Chinese dialects—it is the closest both geographically and typologically to Southeast Asia.

Min   The Min-speaking part of China is Fujian province and the northeastern tip of Guangdong. The best-known dialects in the area are those of Fuzhou, Xiamen, and Shantou.

Speakers of Min are also found outside of this dialect area. Because they are seafarers and fishermen, many Min have settled along the coastal areas of Guangdong, especially around the Leizhou peninsula and the periphery of Hainan island. Other Min are found even farther south, in the various countries of Southeast Asia. Taiwan, too, is Min speaking. Lying about one hundred miles off the Fujian coast, the island was populated mainly by immigrants from southern Fujian who sailed across the Formosa strait during the late Ming period. The dialect called Taiwanese is very close to that of Xiamen, and the people who speak it still outnumber all other groups on the island, including the Mainlanders who fled to Taiwan following the Nationalist defeat at the hands of the Communists in 1950.

Fujian is relatively isolated from the interior of China. The entire province is mountainous, with few navigable rivers, and the small number of overland links it has with the rest of the country are poor. Access is easier by sea. Fujian was the last part of southeastern Inner China to be settled by Chinese, and most of the early immigrants had to travel down the coast to reach it.

This geographic isolation has kept the Min dialects somewhat out of the Chinese linguistic mainstream. Certain historical changes have not taken place in Min, leaving these dialects with some very archaic features not to be seen in other varieties of Chinese.

The Min dialects are the most heterogeneous in China. Though they all share certain broad classificatory features—such as the historical developments described above—they are also, at the same time, highly differentiated. According to one Chinese linguist (Ye Guoqing) there are at least nine mutually unintelligible groups of these dialects in Fujian (mentioned in Yuan et al. 1960, 239). To this number must be added the groups of Min dialects spoken in northeastern Guangdong. It is common practice among Chinese linguists to divide Min as a whole into a northern group, as typified by Fuzhou dialect, and a southern group, usually represented by Xiamen dialect. However, recent evidence suggests that a more basic division exists between the inland dialects in the western part of Fujian and the coastal dialects—including Fuzhou and Xiamen—that are spoken along the relatively accessible eastern seaboard. This more recent evidence makes Fujian appear to be an even more complex place than it had originally been thought to be.

Hakka Scattered over most of south China are communities of Hakka. Villages of these unusual people can be found in the countryside from Sichuan to Taiwan and are especially common in the hillier parts of Guangdong, Guangxi, and southern Fujian. The area around Meixian (Plum County), in the mountainous northeastern corner of Guangdong, and the adjoining counties of Jiangxi and Fujian is considered their homeland. In this remote part of south China, the Hakka outnumber all other groups. Everywhere else, they remain a distinct and recognizable minority.

The name *Hakka* is a word of Cantonese origin that literally means "guest" or "stranger." The Hakka were called this when they began migrating into Yue-speaking territory, and the exotic name seems to have stuck quite simply because, until fairly recently, many Cantonese and Min mistakenly thought that the Hakka were not Chinese at all but rather some kind of strange non-Han "barbarians" like the Tai or the Miao. In many parts of south China, these "guests" are still treated as outsiders and intruders even though everyone now concedes that they are Han Chinese.

The Hakka identify themselves as northern Chinese, and this contention has some basis in fact. Local genealogies and other historical records indicate that many of the ancestors of the Hakka were people originally from the northern plains who in a series of waves migrated deeper and deeper into the south. What remains to be explored, however, are the contributions made by local populations to the formation of the Hakka people and how these differed from those that made up the Yue or the Min. For, no matter what the ethnic origin of the Hakka, the group is linguistically southern Chinese. The Hakka dialects are historically allied to the other southern dialects around them. They have some unmistakably northern features, but they are actually not much more like Mandarin than Cantonese is. The Hakka dialects were formed in the south—almost surely in northeastern Guangdong—and the present widespread distribution of their speakers is the result of large-scale migrations that took place out of Meixian during the Qing dynasty.

Middle Chinese voiced consonants became aspirated consonants in Hakka. This historical development is often considered to be the most important characteristic of the dialect group. Since the Gan dialects of Jiangxi—just to the north of the Hakka-speaking area—underwent the same change, many linguists used to group Gan and Hakka together as Gan-Hakka. But, since there are no other good reasons for this grouping, it has now generally been abandoned. Gan and Hakka are nowadays usually classified separately.

PART II
Geographic Margins

The title "Geographic Margins" conveys the impression that there is a geographic center. In fact there is: China proper, including the provinces of Shandong, Hebei, Henan, Hubei, Shanxi, Shaanxi, Anhui, Jiangsu, Zhejiang, Fujian, Guangzhou, Jiangxi, Hunan, and Sichuan. This geographically tiny fraction of the contemporary Chinese nation-state has been inhabited by people whose material cultural remains suggest continuity with Han culture since approximately 3000 B.C.E. This is the densest part of China and contains most of the well-known cities and landmarks associated with imperial Chinese history. But a glance at a map will show that a far greater portion of China's territory is not China proper, raising the question of how the margins can be greater than the center. In some ways of thinking, we might compare the frontier of empires with the boundaries of nation-states (Lattimore 1940), with the former a fuzzy area of cultural exchange among diverse peoples and the latter a clear-cut line setting off distinct, named peoples. Although the twentieth century has attempted to create nothing but boundaries, in fact much of what we see is more like frontiers. (Some scholars express these exchanges as *transnational*, although in some ways they remain significantly like those of past centuries.)

In this part of the book, we call attention to some characteristics of areas considered in some sense marginal to a geographic center. Some of this marginality is a consequence of the terrain: in north, northwest, and western China, one finds the Gobi desert, the Takla Makan, the Himalayas. These areas have also been inhabited for millennia, but only sparsely, and are more difficult to explore archaeologically. Their influences have been Central Asian and South or Southeast Asian more than Chinese. Indeed, only in the last several centuries has Chinese control been anything more than symbolic. The poor fit with central China is manifest in the recent accusations of Uighur separatism by Beijing: thousands of putative separatists have been killed for treason in Xinjiang, with the government suggesting that they advocate a free country of East Turkestan. Most of the inhabitants, prior to the large resettling of Han Chinese by the government in recent decades, are Muslim or Tibetan Buddhist.

Another aspect of geographic marginality is what we might consider cultural geographic: the fact that people living in certain areas have habits of living that align them with centers other than China's. In the southwest, where there is a huge mixture of ethnic minorities, many of the people's life ways have been abhorrent to Han Chinese, whether because of marriage patterns (brides not moving to their husbands' homes until after the birth of their first child, e.g.), subsistence systems (living in high, cold mountains where it is impossible to grow rice, so people eat corn instead), religious practices and beliefs (such as belief in various nature gods that demand the sacrifice of, perhaps, bulls), or gender roles (women having strong voices in family decisions). Many of the peoples in these regions have been considered backward or primitive by the Han Chinese, and, indeed, poverty and illiteracy have characterized most of them. The general Han approach has been to sinify them, to make them like the Han, sometimes out of goodwill and the sense that the minorities must be helped become more modern. The pull of the Chinese center, however, is matched by a push away from that center by regional loyalties and by some cross-border dynamics. The southwestern minorities tend to speak languages similar to those spoken by groups in other Southeast Asian nations and to share their cultural patterns to some extent.

The China diaspora—the spread of people of Chinese background throughout the world—is in some ways another aspect of geographic marginality. Whole collections on this topic have been written, but we wish to point out merely that the image of diaspora, of the scattering of seeds, like dandelion seeds scattering in the wind, relies on a once-upon-a-time center and that that center is the heart of the Mainland.

There is a final aspect of geographic marginality, and that has to do with integration into and exclusion from the feeling of national unity. Some Western scholars have become fascinated with what they call *subethnicities*, the groups officially considered Han who nevertheless have some noteworthy differences from the Han. Some of these groups include the Hakka, who speak a Han language and have many Han customs but who are clearly distinguished in some ways from the Han. (Hakka women, e.g., never bound their feet.) The south and southeast of China have a large number of people whose practices do not feel very Chinese to others. The boat people of Hong Kong, about whom Barbara Ward (1965) has written, are often accused of being less Chinese than the land dwellers with whom they trade, in part because their life ways appear alien.

A notion of unity may be desirable for nation-states, but, in the case of China and, we suspect, most other sizable nation-states, the reality is that, however powerful the image of center may be, the actual facts show that this is but a specter refracted by the sun shining differently through the atmosphere of different climates, seen by people who name it in different languages, and symbolized by people whose myths are not shared.—Eds.

NORTHWEST

At present, China's northwest is arguably one of the most intriguing areas of the nation, for it is here that cultural tensions have recently spilled over into violence against the Chinese government. In February 1997, the Uighur minority peoples staged a demonstration in the city of Yining in northwestern Xinjiang to protest government intervention in local religious and cultural practices; police fatally shot two Uighur men. Uighurs retaliated shortly thereafter by detonating a bomb on a crowded Beijing bus. The considerable and growing presence of Hui, Chinese Muslims, in the northwest where China abuts the Muslim countries of Kazakhstan, Kyrgyzstan, Tajikistan, Afghanistan, and Pakistan makes the ethnic politics of the region thicker and potentially more ominous. The capital of the province, Urumqi, is little more than a thousand miles from the activist Muslim centers of Islamabad (Pakistan) and Kabul (Afghanistan) but fifteen hundred miles from Beijing.

As a region, the northwest is massive, representing an area in excess of 2 million square kilometers. It includes the provinces of Qinghai, Gansu, and Shaanxi plus the Xinjiang Uighur autonomous region and the Ningxia Hui autonomous region; some geographers might also include Inner Mongolia (the Mongolian autonomous region). Shaanxi and Gansu have been part of China for millennia, while the other areas have been included fairly recently. These parts of the continent connect China along the northern Silk Road to Central Asia. Their climate includes loesslands (areas of yellow dust blown from the desert), desert, arid mountains, oases, and snowcapped peaks. Much of the area has been unpopulated or has been populated only sparsely by nomadic pastoralists. The northwest, specifically Xinjiang or "New Territories," did not become part of China proper until the first decades of the eighteenth century following aggressive annexation by the imperial armies of the Qing dynasty.

Still, much like Tibet, which was also forcibly drawn into the Qing imperial orbit and has since been identified as part of China, Xinjiang and the rest of the northwest is a region rich in history both ancient and modern and remains critical (perhaps because of this meaningful past, Xinjiang's surfeit of natural resources, and its role as a testing ground for China's nuclear arsenal) to contemporary political identity. The complex cultural, religious, and political portraits offered by Barnett (chap. 5) and Gladney (chap. 6) richly depict the variety and vibrance of this remote outpost of the Chinese nation and help the reader grasp those conditions that move the Hui and Uighurs to agitate for religious and political freedoms discouraged by the Chinese government. With these readings, a substantial geographic space provides the contrastive margin for the definition of the center.—Eds.

5

Chinese Turkestan

Xinjiang

In this chapter, excerpted from the long book *China's Far West* (1993), the late Doak Barnett describes his impressions of Xinjiang Uighur autonomous region from his 1988 trip and compares them to those of a similar trip undertaken in 1948—just before the establishment of the People's Republic of China. He notes especially the substantial urbanization of the region, the increase in proportion of Han Chinese, the increase in industrialization, and improvements in education, communication, and transportation. In the course of the chapter, Barnett also mentions several uprisings in Xinjiang, most notably the 1940s Ili uprising, putting them in the context of changing relations between China and the Soviet Union. He also mentions several aspects of China's policies regarding ethnic minorities and, in passing, comments on the use of statistics in drawing conclusions about contemporary circumstances. Barnett's focus is political economy, and he relies on interviews with high-ranking officials as well as very practiced observations. The book from which this chapter derives is a unique combination of journalism, scholarship, and personal experience produced by a man who, in his day, was one of the most senior China scholars—one whose entire life was involved with the quest to understand China and all its complexity.

Xinjiang is the most northwestern of all China's province-level units (see map. 5.1). It borders many of the most sensitive countries and regions with which China's foreign relations must be considered: Mongolia, Russia, Kazakhstan, Kyrgyzstan, Tajikistan, and Pakistan as well as Tibet, Qinghai, and Gansu. Only loosely connected to China for the past two millennia, it was one of the corridors along which the Silk Road connected China with Central Asia, and its strategic importance has been long known. China's power is more consolidated there now than at any time previously—because of many of the factors that Barnett enumerates—yet the political space separating the far west from the country's administrative center is daunting.—Eds.

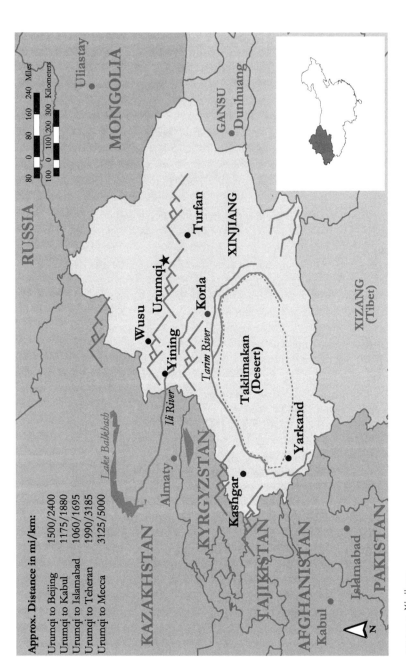

MAP 5.1. Xinjiang.

Approx. Distance in mi/km:

Urumqi to Beijing	1500/2400
Urumqi to Kabul	1175/1880
Urumqi to Islamabad	1060/1695
Urumqi to Teheran	1990/3185
Urumqi to Mecca	3125/5000

RUSSIA

MONGOLIA

Uliastay

GANSU
Dunhuang

KAZAKHSTAN

Lake Balkhash

Almaty

KYRGYZSTAN

Ili River

Wusu

Yining

Urumqi

Turfan

Korla

Tarim River

XINJIANG

Taklimakan
(Desert)

Kashgar

Yarkand

XIZANG
(Tibet)

TAJIKISTAN

AFGHANISTAN

Kabul

Islamabad

PAKISTAN

N

80 0 80 160 240 Miles
100 0 100 200 300 Kilometers

Xinjiang is often translated into English as "New Dominion" (literally, *xin* means "new," and *jiang* means "frontier" or "boundary"). However, I have always preferred *Chinese Turkestan* or *Eastern Turkestan,* the terms used for Xinjiang in many early Western writings. The last of China's outlying areas to be incorporated into the Qing dynasty's formal administrative system, Xinjiang was, historically, more associated with Central Asia than with China, and in many respects the atmosphere in parts of the region is still more Central Asian than Han Chinese. The area has had an extraordinarily colorful and turbulent history, and it is unquestionably a land of many superlatives.

It is the largest provincial-level unit in China, and its territory—almost 620,000 square miles—is greater than that of the United Kingdom, France, Italy, and the recently united Germany combined. Within its area are some of the tallest mountains in China—and the world (most of them are in the Pamir, the Tian Shan, and Kunlun ranges). It also contains the lowest point in China (Turfan, which is well below sea level) and China's largest desert (the Taklimakan). In ancient times, it was a crucial link on the Silk Road between China and the Roman world. During much of the nineteenth and twentieth centuries, it was a focal point for conflict between China and two competing imperial powers—Russia (later the Soviet Union) and Great Britain. Its position continues to be strategically very important: The region's external borders touch four states that were part of the Soviet Union (Russia, Kazakhstan, Tajikistan, and Kyrgyzstan), Outer Mongolia, Afghanistan, and Pakistan, and internally it is adjacent to Gansu, Qinghai, and Tibet.

Most of Xinjiang is virtually empty. Apart from the Ili region, in past centuries the small population was concentrated almost entirely in glacier-fed oases, where deserts meet mountains. In recent years the population has grown rapidly, although it is still small for such an enormous area. When I visited Xinjiang in 1948, local officials estimated its population at that time to be about 4 million. Between the late 1940s and the late 1980s, the population rose to roughly 14 million. (It was 13.84 million in 1986.) The population has always been a complex mixture of ethnic groups; in recent centuries Turkic Muslim peoples have been predominant. In 1948, less than 6 percent of the population consisted of Han Chinese. Now, minority groups still make up the majority (more than three-fifths), but the Han population has increased dramatically and now accounts for almost two-fifths of the region's inhabitants.

Xinjiang has always been a crossroads, swept by waves of migration and invasion. Many different Indo-European, Turkic, Mongol, and Tibetan peoples have, at different times, controlled all or parts of it. As early as the Han dynasty (206 B.C.E.–220 C.E.), however, the Han Chinese recognized the strategic importance of the region and established garrisons in key oases. From then on, the Silk Road was the main trade route linking China with the West. This continued to be true until modern times. But the power of the Chinese empire waxed and waned over the centuries, and the imperial rulers exercised effective power in the region only in the empire's greatest periods of western expansionism, during the Han, Tang, Yuan, Ming, and Qing dynasties.

Tibetans controlled major parts of the region in the seventh century and again in part of the eighth century. In the latter half of the eighth and the first half of the ninth centuries, the Uighurs, a major Turkic group, established a local kingdom that controlled the Tarim basin as well as parts of Mongolia for almost a century. Uighur political control continued into the eleventh century in certain areas, and in a few other areas it lasted until Genghis Khan's conquest in the thirteenth century. Starting in the eighth century, most of the population of the region was gradually converted to Islam, and its doctrines spread throughout Central Asia.

Although Han Chinese power waned at the end of the Ming dynasty, once the Manchus conquered China and established the Qing dynasty in the seventeenth century they rapidly reasserted control over key areas of Turkestan (although, like past rulers, they had to compromise with local leaders, and their control in many areas was fairly loose). By the nineteenth century, however, the Qing's strategic control weakened, and the strategic importance of the region began to decline—after Western maritime powers forcibly "opened" coastal China in the 1840s. What had for centuries been China's "front door" now became its "back door."

Nevertheless, Xinjiang continued to be a cockpit for political intrigue, competition, and conflict. Both the Russians, expanding eastward from Central Asia (and Siberia), and the British, looking north from India, competed actively for influence in the region. In the 1860s, a huge rebellion exploded in Xinjiang, led by a Muslim named Yakub Beg. His rebels conquered most of the region, but the Russians, taking advantage of the situation, occupied the Ili area in the northwest. It took years for the Chinese to reassert control. However, eventually Zuo Zongtang (1812–1885) defeated the rebels in the 1870s, and in the 1880s China recovered the Ili region from the Russians. Finally, in the 1880s, China converted Xinjiang into a regular province and incorporated it into the Chinese (Manchu) administrative system.

That was by no means the end of turbulence in the region, however. When China broke up after the 1911 collapse of the Qing dynasty, a succession of autonomous Chinese warlords controlled Xinjiang. Their power was threatened, however, when the post-1917 Soviet regime in Russia reasserted its influence in the 1920s. Then, in the 1930s there was another large revolt, led by Ma Zhongying, a Gansu Hui leader. Out of the resulting chaos, Sheng Shicai emerged as the leader of the province. Headquartered in Urumqi (then called Dihua), he obtained Soviet support, defeated Ma, and established a pro-Moscow regime. For some years, the Soviet Union played a very large role in the province; in fact, it stationed a mechanized regiment in Hami, at the eastern edge of the province. Then, suddenly, Sheng made a political about-face and expelled the Russians in 1942. The Russians, for their own geopolitical reasons, nevertheless continued providing military assistance to the

Nationalist regime, then headquartered in Chongqing, for the war against Japan, and Xinjiang was the main route over which Soviet aid was delivered. Finally, in 1944, the Nationalists were able to reassert direct control over Xinjiang and eased Sheng out of the governorship.

When I visited Xinjiang in 1948, the Nationalists were more or less in control of part of the region but were facing imminent defeat in their internal struggle against the Communists in north China. Xinjiang at that time was still so remote from the main battlegrounds of the civil war that it remained on the sidelines in that conflict. However, it was itself heavily militarized, and Chinese control of the local population depended fundamentally on the army. The provincial regime faced two external major military threats of its own, from the north. During 1944–1945 rebels in the Ili region, along the Soviet border with Xinjiang in the northwest, had established, with Soviet assistance, the so-called East Turkestan Republic in the Ili region. They were led mainly by Uighurs, but their forces included Kazakhs and others. These rebels controlled three of Xinjiang's ten administrative districts. An attempt was made to negotiate a settlement, and, for a brief period after the signing of a compromise peace agreement in 1946, a provincial coalition government had tried to function in Urumqi. But this government had collapsed in 1947, not long before my visit. At the time of my visit in the summer of 1948, although the Chinese and rebel forces were not actively fighting, they still confronted each other, in warlike formations, across the Manas river, northwest of Urumqi. I traveled by truck the seventy-odd miles to the river, where I could see soldiers on both sides peering at each other warily, but there were no exchanges of fire when I was there.

I also traveled by truck to Qitai, about 145 miles east of Urumqi, to visit the headquarters of the Chinese forces that confronted Mongol troops at Beidashan. In this area, a small mountain range dominated the still-undemarcated border area between Xinjiang and Outer Mongolia. Disputes over the border had led to armed clashes in 1947, and occasional military incidents were still taking place in 1948. (From Qitai, I also made a memorable trek by horseback into the nearby Tian Shan mountain range to visit Osman Bator, the preeminent Kazakh leader in Xinjiang at that time, who had only recently aligned with the Chinese in their conflicts with both the Ili rebels and the Mongols.)

Four decades later, in 1988, when I prepared to fly to Xinjiang in late April, I refreshed my memory about the area by rereading some of the things I had written at the time of my first trip. In 1948, Xinjiang was an extremely undeveloped area in almost every respect. Even in the capital, then called Dihua (now Urumqi), there were few signs of the twentieth century. It was a large, sprawling, dusty town, consisting mainly of one-story shops and residences. Some local people estimated its population at about 80,000; others claimed that it was over 100,000. No one—even the best-informed officials—seemed to be certain. Although the town was the center of Han power in the province, the people in its streets at that time were a colorful mixture of Han

Chinese, most of whom wore very traditional, premodern Chinese clothing, and Uighurs, almost all of whom were dressed in very traditional Muslim clothing—the men wearing skullcaps and the women wearing hoods. There also were quite a few colorful Kazakhs, the men riding horses with great flair, like cocky cowboys who had come down from the hills. On the unpaved streets, there were not many modern vehicles, only a few trucks. Most of the traffic consisted of horse-drawn carts, and there were quite a few people on horseback—mainly Kazakhs, most of them wearing traditional fur-lined silk hats with large earflaps. A few gravel and dirt roads—used by trucks—connected the city with the major oases scattered elsewhere throughout the province, but the only modern transportation that connected it with the outside world was an occasional airplane flying to and from other major Chinese cities in the east. (No railway had yet been built.) The atmosphere was very much that of a Central Asian city, not that of a Chinese urban center.

The population of Xinjiang province was estimated by local officials at that time to be roughly 4 million. (Official statistics published by the government in Nanjing in the early 1940s had placed it at 3.73 million.) Uighurs, who accounted for almost 75 percent of the total, were engaged mainly in agriculture. They dominated the oases in the south, where a very large proportion of the province's population (possibly as much as two-thirds of the total) was concentrated. The Kazakhs, most of whom were still nomadic, accounted for just over 10 percent of the population. They were concentrated in the northern parts of the province, on the slopes of the Tian Shan range, and in the Ili region. In the Ili region they occupied the grasslands, and the Uighurs and Chinese farmed the lowlands. Although Han Chinese were the third largest group, they accounted for less than 6 percent of the total population of the province. Some were farmers, but a large percentage of them were merchants and officials. The rest of the population was very mixed and consisted of a variety of groups: Dongan (another group of Chinese Muslims—2 percent); Taranqi (classified by some people as a subgroup of the Uighurs—2 percent); Kyrgyz (under 2 percent); Mongols (1.5 percent); Uzbeks (under 1 percent); and several even smaller groups, including the Xibe, Solon, Manchus, Tatars, Tajiks, and "White Russians." Virtually all of Xinjiang's population—almost 95 percent—consisted of Muslims who spoke some form of the Turki language.

In 1948, provincial officials whom I interviewed estimated that, although the majority of the population was engaged in agriculture, they tilled only about 1 percent of the province's whole territory. Nomadic herdsmen, who were somewhat fewer in number, used another 5 percent of the province's land. Most of the territory was entirely uninhabited. In the entire province, moreover, there were fewer than a dozen small factories. My memories of the region were of an area that was extremely backward—but also fascinating and romantic. I vividly recalled interviews with some of the most colorful leaders I had ever met anywhere. The most memorable leader, perhaps, was Osman Bator, whom I and two companions interviewed in his yurt encampment in the Tian Shan. Everything in my 1948 visit had seemed like an adventure in a faraway place in a distant era: I traveled by truck across a trackless plain, chasing gazelles en route to the towering mountain of Bogda Ola; went by truck to the Manas river and Qitai across wilderness areas at the foothills of the mountains; climbed to a Kazakh encampment and stayed in yurts at the foot of the glacier at fourteen thousand feet at Bogda Ola; and rode horseback far into the Tian Shan range to visit Osman Bator.

When I boarded a modern airplane in Beijing in late April 1988 to make my second visit to Xinjiang, the most basic question in my mind was a very simple one: How much had all of that changed in forty years?

I flew from Beijing to Urumqi on a Tupolev 154, a relatively new model of Soviet passenger plane that had been recently acquired by the Chinese. By the standards of the 1980s, it was less than comfortable. Configured to take 164 passengers, it was jam-packed. As was true of most planes in China at the time, the seats were narrow and placed so closely together that there was almost no legroom. The overhead luggage compartments were tiny—only big enough for small packages. It was more comfortable, though, than the bucket-seat military transport plane on which I had flown to Xinjiang in 1948. All of the passengers on the Tupolev were Chinese except for me and several Russian technicians, who—I was told—were traveling in China to check up on the plane's performance.

The air distance from Beijing to Urumqi was 1,864 miles—considerably further than from Beijing to Tokyo. The schedule called for our leaving Beijing at 7:00 P.M. and arriving at Urumqi roughly four hours later. Actually, we left an hour late, but, because of favorable winds, the flight took only $3^{1}/_{2}$ hours. It was an uneventful flight—and also quite uninteresting because of the high altitude at which we flew and the steadily darkening skies. I had hoped to see the countryside that we traversed, but we could see almost nothing of the terrain below us—not the agriculture areas, the grasslands, or the deserts or high mountains. Dusk descended about an hour and a half after we took off, and for the rest of the trip—right up until our arrival late at night—the sky was a peculiar mixture of twilight and nighttime. The land below was pitch black; a thin strip of bright orange marked the horizon; and above that there was a wide, light blue band of sky. Right above us, the sky was inky black. (The scene reminded me of the way dusk often appears to descend in a planetarium, except that on this trip it continued for virtually our entire time in the air.)

In recent years, flying over many parts of China I had seen electric lights in many rural areas, but on this trip we saw few signs of life below until we made our approach to Urumqi. Then, we were suddenly above an area that was extremely well lit, even late at night. We landed at 11:30 P.M., Beijing time. Officially, it was also 11:30 in Urumqi since in theory all of China was still operating on the same time as the capital. I soon discovered, however, that Urumqi operates on a double time standard. Most official schedules were given in Beijing time, but in reality everyone operated on local time, which was two hours different. Some people kept their watches on Beijing time; others set theirs by local time. This discrepancy did not seem to bother local people at all, but it was a little disconcerting for newcomers.

The airport at Urumqi was the largest and grandest of any that I saw anywhere in west China; it was comparable, in fact, to the largest ones in east China. Soviet specialists had helped to build the airfield, and its size reflected the importance of Xinjiang in Sino-Soviet relations in the 1950s, when construction of the major runways was begun, I was told. But the passenger terminal had been completed only in the 1970s. When I had flown to Xinjiang in 1948, we had landed at a tiny, primitive airstrip just outside the city. When I arrived in 1988, I asked where it was and was told that it no longer existed. The spot where it had been was now right in the middle of the city—in an area that had been totally absorbed by the city—not far from the headquarters of the regional government.

Like all of the major cities in northwest China that I revisited in 1988, Urumqi had been totally transformed in the four decades since my previous visit. No longer a mud-colored town, it had become a very modern metropolis—although its "old city" still had a distinct Middle Eastern flavor. As the capital of the autonomous region, it was really Xinjiang's only major metropolis; it was the only city in the region classified as a "prefecture-level" municipality. By 1986 (the latest year for which I could obtain definite, published statistics), Urumqi's population had grown to more than 1,203,000. Most of the population lived in six city districts, but some were scattered throughout the one county that belonged to the municipality. Altogether the municipality encompassed 4,416 square miles. Of the total population, more than 80 percent—just under a million—were urban residents and engaged in non-farming occupations. Although minorities—by far the largest number of whom were Uighurs—still made up three-fifths of the autonomous region's population in 1988, in the city of Urumqi itself Han Chinese constituted three-quarters of the municipality's population. The largest minority groups in the municipality were the Uighurs (with 12 percent of the total population), Hui Muslims (8 percent), and Kazakhs (3 percent).

The modern city of Urumqi that I saw in 1988 was much more attractive and livable than the pre-Communist city that I had visited in 1948. Near to the city center were two fairly large parks, one called "Red Mountain" (*hong shan*) and the other called "People's Park" (*renmin gongyuan*). In the former was a hill topped by a pagoda that local residents viewed as a kind of symbol or logo of the city. Both parks were obviously very popular recreation spots, and the city had recently "modernized" them by installing pool tables and video games. Not far from Red Mountain—near the center of the city—was a large office building that housed both the municipal Party headquarters and the municipal government. Two wide, tree-lined avenues, with side lanes for bicycles and pedestrians, stretched to the north. Many of the buildings in this area were of stolid Russian style. Generally, they were fairly squat—only a few stories high. Most of them were public buildings, and the majority dated to the 1950s and 1960s. One of the most impressive buildings in this section was a large, classical-style structure housing the headquarters of the Xinjiang Production and Construction Corps, the dominant economic institution in the region (which I will discuss later). Scattered among the Soviet-style edifices were some more modern high-rise buildings, which were constructed in the 1980s. To the north, the city stretched a considerable distance, and then a highway led northwest toward the nearest sizable city, Shihezi, which was roughly ninety-five miles away and located adjacent to the Manas river.

From the center of the city, several other large boulevards went toward the south, and they were lined with many tall, modern buildings—the tallest one rose over twenty stories. Among the most impressive of them was a recently built Economic Commission headquarters, a new office building for the State Security Bureau (still under construction), and a new hotel, called the Global Hotel, which was expected to be Urumqi's finest. In this area the new skyscrapers had all been built during the 1980s, and they looked much more modern—and Western—than the Soviet-style buildings of earlier years and the few remaining pre-1949 structures.

Directly to the east of People's Park was the main business district. It, too, contained numerous high-rise buildings mixed in with older buildings. To the south and east was the old city. Once walled (the wall had been torn down several years previously), this area contained many older buildings, yet even here there were a few high-rise office buildings and apartments. This was the main Uighur area, and in 1988 it still had a distinctly Muslim flavor. Numerous mosques, a few of them large but many quite small, were scattered throughout this entire area. The streets were crowded and lively, especially around the numerous bazaars, which looked much like those one can see throughout Central Asia and the Middle East. A little to the east was the regional Party headquarters. To the south, a highway stretched toward Turfan. A few miles along the route to Turfan, the city had built a large reservoir, and its wide canal (about fifteen feet wide) was a major source of the city's water. In all the areas immediately around the core of urban Urumqi, the suburbs looked semiurban, but then the city gradually tapered off into small villages, consisting mostly of one-story mud houses surrounded by farmland.

When I had visited Urumqi in 1948, there was virtually no modern industry of any sort in the city or, for that matter, anywhere in the province. Three factories operated in the city, manufacturing clothing, glass, and animal serum, and there was one factory in Khotan. The Urumqi of 1988 still could not be considered one of the major industrial centers in China, but compared to the pre-Communist period it had developed a significant base of industry. Officials I met in 1988 told me that before 1949 industry had employed only 2,653 people in the city and that the value of its output was very small (4.39 million yuan). By the mid-1980s Urumqi's industry employed 188,000 people, and its gross output value had risen to 1.875 billion yuan. The city's farms produced mainly food for local consumption—

including about twenty-five thousand tons of grain, more than three thousand tons of edible vegetable oil, and over eighty thousand sheep (which yielded close to fifteen hundred tons of mutton a year). Much of the municipality's farmland belonged to six state farms established in the 1950s and 1960s, which were inhabited by a population of almost forty-seven thousand people—about a quarter of the entire farming population in the municipality.

In general, I was really amazed by how modern Urumqi appeared in 1988 compared to 1948. All the roads I saw were now paved (there were about 125 miles in the municipality), and many of them were impressive avenues. They carried substantial traffic, including numerous cars, buses, and trucks; only in the older part of the city were there many donkey-drawn, two-wheeled carts of the kind that were standard in 1948. Buildings constructed since my previous visit contained more than ten times the space of those that existed before 1949, I was told, and about half of the new space consisted of modern "standard departments"—generally several stories high. The high-rise structures built in the 1980s had created an entirely new skyline. People in the streets were well dressed, mostly in Chinese versions of Western clothes of considerable variety and color (women clearly favored red). Only in the few older parts of the city did I see many Uighurs wearing traditional clothes, and even there I saw no Kazakhs dressed as they had been in the old days. Men in uniform (soldiers, People's Armed Police, and Public Security Police) were definitely more numerous and visible in Urumqi than in any other place that I visited in northwest China in 1988 (and I will have more to say about this later); even so, the military presence was much less obvious than it had been in 1948.

The first of my two trips outside of Urumqi was to Nanshan, the "Southern Mountains." Before I arrived in Urumqi, I had informed my host that one of my highest priorities was to revisit a major Kazakh area in some mountain area near to Urumqi; I was determined to do this to see how much the traditional Kazakh tribal way of life had changed since I observed it in 1948 (both at a Kazakh encampment at the foot of Bogda's glacier and at Osman Bator's headquarters in the Tian Shan, south of Qitai). Although it would not be possible to revisit those areas, the trip to Nanshan, I was told, would be a good opportunity to see another Kazakh area.

We left early one morning in a Toyota Land Cruiser, a very sturdy vehicle with multiple gears and a high undercarriage, with room for two to sit in front and three in the back. It was not a very long trip—roughly forty-seven miles each way. But we stopped several times, so the round-trip took a full day. En route, my Kazakh host talked at length about the organization, activities, and livelihood of the Kazakhs in Xinjiang. Although much of what he told me repeated things that I had learned forty years earlier, he did bring me up to date and informed me about some things I had not known. The largest groupings of Kazakhs, he said, consisted of three "hordes," called *jüz*. He said that one was called the Da Jüz (the large, or great, horde—sometimes called the east horde); another the Zhong Jüz (middle horde—also called north horde); and the third the Xiao Jüz (the small, or western, horde). (The terminology he used mixed Chinese and Turki words.) In 1948, the Kazakhs I met had not used the word *jüz* in describing various groups to me. I had heard the term used to describe Kyrgyz, but this was the first time I had heard it used to describe Kazakhs.

Of these various groups, my host said, the most numerous consisted of the Zhong Jüz. Each *jüz* was divided into several *buluo* (or *bulo*), or "tribes," he said. There were six of these under the Zhong Jüz, including the Kirei (Keré), the Naiman, the Auwak (Uwak), the Arghun, the Kongerat (Khongerat), and the Kupjack. Since I was not an expert on Kazakh affairs—or a linguist who knew Turki—I simply tried to translate, phonetically, the terms that he used, as I heard them; an expert might well have written them differently.

Some of the specific tribal names were ones that had been mentioned repeatedly to me in my visit in 1948. At that time, I had heard Osman Bator talk at length about the first three of these groups; he himself belonged to the Kirei, but he had talked at some length about the others. (In 1988, I was more than a little mystified to hear *Arghun* used to label a Kazakh; I had always associated this title with the Mongols.) In any case, one thing I learned in 1948 was confirmed in 1988, namely, that the most important Kazakh tribes in Chinese territory had long been—and continued to be—the Naiman and the Kirei. My Kazakh host explained that every tribe was divided into subtribes. For example, the Kirei had twelve subtribes and the Naiman had nine. Below these subtribes, he said, there were at least four lower subdivisions into which groups of yurts were divided, each of which had a designated leader. In the Nanshan area, my host said, there was a mixture of Kirei and Naiman Kazakhs.

According to my host, the largest tribal divisions—especially the *jüz*—continued to be important, but the significance of many of the subdivisions, including the *buluo,* had declined in the post-1949 period. The *awul* (*aul*), the smallest Kazakh unit (usually with five to ten households, possibly with fifteen), traditionally had consisted of families from the same *buluo,* but this had begun to change even before 1949, and now many of the smallest units were mixtures of Naiman and Kirei. Even when a particular *awul* was not mixed, there could be members of both Naiman and Kirei *awul* grouped together under higher units.

Both my host on the trip to Nanshan and several officials from the Xinjiang Nationalities Commission, whom I later interviewed in their offices, talked to me at some length about continuities and changes in the Kazakh way of life in Xinjiang. I was told that although a few Kazakhs had entered new occupations, including agriculture, the overwhelming majority—probably over 90 percent—still engaged in traditional animal husbandry. But the rhythm of their life had changed—in some cases quite radically, in some cases marginally. Before 1949, only a few Kazakhs had owned permanent houses; most of them moved constantly (an old saying was that they "moved forty times a year"). But, by the 1980s, many of them had built permanent winter residences. Although a large number of them still were nomadic for at least part of the year, an increasing number had started some farming.

Most Kazakhs in Xinjiang were organized into "cooperatives" and then into "communes" when these institutions were established throughout China in the 1950s, but these units were generally based on the old *awul,* I was told, so real change was limited. The authorities did, though, try to assign pasturelands in a definite way to particular groups, and they enforced such limits fairly strictly. However, my informants said, whereas originally the *awul* were organized mainly on the basis of blood ties, the new units were essentially administrative ones, and many of them mixed different tribal and clan groups. Traditionally, the *awul* were generally identified by the name of their leaders, but after 1949 many were given new names. Officially the traditional Kazakh titles for various groups and leaders were abandoned, but informally they were still the names used by most local people. In the 1980s, when decollectivization occurred elsewhere in China, the old Chinese terms—*xiang* (township) and *cun* (village)—replaced the old commune and brigade titles introduced in the late 1950s. The animals owned by communes were divided up, and most were again individually owned. Assigned pasturelands also were readjusted. In practice, however, my hosts said, although pastureland borders now were fairly clear and were usually observed in the wintertime, most people were tolerant about encroachments on their land by other groups if they were temporary and brief—particularly in the summertime. Some state farms (ranches) in animal-husbandry areas continued to exist, but many of these had been broken up during the decollectivization.

I found all of this informative and interesting, but I was eager to see for myself how Kazakh life had changed in a "typical" Kazakh area and to interview people there. So I looked forward with great anticipation as we drove toward Nanshan, thinking that this would be an opportunity to see things myself.

The two-lane paved road to Nanshan took us first across a long, flat plain, where we passed some farming villages that looked very poor (the houses were almost all made of mud brick; see fig. 5.1). We also passed a number of small, domed Muslim tombs, which I was told were centuries old and commemorated very famous Muslim leaders. Then we entered an area that consisted mostly of *huangmo* (wasteland), with only very scattered habitations. From the time we left Urumqi, we paralleled the beautiful snowcapped peaks of the Tian Shan, and Bogda Ola was visible much of the way. Toward the end of the trip, we entered foothills and passed occasional clusters of very poor Kazakh houses (some of which were simple log cabins plastered with mud). Yet even in this poor area I saw many television antennae! Finally, we entered the mountains, climbing to perhaps five or six thousand feet. At the end, the road petered out and became gravel; at that point, snow and ice blocked vehicular travel, so we got out and walked the final stretch to our

FIGURE 5.1.
The barn of a Kazakh home. Because they are isolated, many Kazakh families lead hard lives (the children of this family walked several miles each way to attend school in 1988). *(Photograph by A. Doak Barnett, courtesy of Jeanne B. Barnett.)*

ultimate destination. (By this time in my western travels, I was beginning to think that this was standard—that is, that most roads at some point simply petered out.)

At our final destination, I discovered, there was no Kazakh encampment. I then learned from my host that the main purpose of our trip was really to see a famous waterfall, which had become a major tourist attraction! Near the waterfall were a few Kazakhs setting up a half dozen yurts, and we stopped to visit briefly with them. They were very hospitable. Sitting on rugs, we sipped tea and ate snacks and exchanged pleasantries; inside the yurt, it was snug and warm even though it was quite cold outside. But these Kazakhs, I learned, no longer raised animals: They had become "administrative cadres" responsible for handling tourists. (This area was scheduled to be opened for the annual tourist season in a couple of weeks, but they had been asked to set up some yurts ahead of time because of my visit.) I asked where the nearest real Kazakh encampments were and was told that there were no nomadic groups in the entire local area at that time of year; to reach such groups in a pastureland area now in use one would have to go considerably further, by horseback (see fig. 5.2). Moreover, I was told by the Kazakhs I did meet at Nanshan that in April no nomadic Kazakhs were even near this area; nor would there be any until they moved back from fairly distant mountain pastures at the start of the summer. To say that I was disappointed is putting it mildly. I began to wonder whether my hosts might have been instructed not to take me to a Kazakh tribal area. Rightly or wrongly, I began to feel that I was getting a classic runaround.

My second trip in 1988 outside of Urumqi was to Turfan. This oasis city developed many centuries ago as an important stopping point on the ancient Silk Road, and it was a key strategic point, located in southern Xinjiang on the northern edge of the huge Tarim basin. Two of the principal branches of the Silk Road went through this general area. The main stopping points on the northern route were Hami, Turfan, Karashahr, Kucha (Kuqa), Aksu,

FIGURE 5.2.
A Kazakh horseman showing off his riding skill in 1988, much as Osman Bator's men had done in 1948. *(Photograph by A. Doak Barnett, courtesy of Jeanne B. Barnett.)*

Tumshuk, and finally Kashgar (Kashi). The main southern route went through Miran, Cherchen, Khotan, and Yarkand before finally reaching Kashgar. Kashgar was the largest and most important oasis city in the west. From it (as well as from the cities of Yarkand and Khotan), several routes led to what are now India, Pakistan, Afghanistan, and Central Asia, and from there the Silk Road went on to Tashkent, Samarkand, Bokhara (the first two of which I had visited on earlier travels) and then to the Middle East and to the West.

The history of Turfan has been extremely complex, mirroring the turbulence of two millennia of constant migrations and conflicts in that part of the world. Several ancient kingdoms had been established at different times in its area, and, periodically, from the first century B.C.E. on, when the military forces of the Han dynasty first conquered the area, Chinese garrison forces had been stationed there. Several times, Turfan was destroyed and then rebuilt.

Buddhism, imported along the Silk Road from India, had a very significant impact on Turfan. Later, the influences of many other religions were also extremely important. Eventually, most of the population was converted to Islam, but Manichaean believers and Nestorian Christians continued to be fairly numerous in the area for many years. About the time that the Tang rulers were ascendant in China, the Uighurs established a kingdom centered in Turfan, but its power peaked during the eighth century, and it was destroyed by the Kyrgyz in the ninth century. The Uighurs continued to occupy many influential positions in the area, though, and, when Genghis Khan conquered the region, he borrowed the Uighur alphabet and employed many Uighurs in his civil administration. Later, during the Ming and Qing periods, the Chinese regarded Turfan as one of the most important strategic oases in the entire region. Partly because of this history, Turfan has continued into the modern period to be regarded as one of Xinjiang's most important oasis cities. Together with Kashgar and other major southern oases, it continues to be viewed by many people as representative of the essence of Uighur Muslim life and culture in Xinjiang.

The old camel caravans are now long gone, and, when I made my trip to Turfan, I traveled on an excellent two-lane paved highway. Most of the road was quite smooth, but we did encounter several bumpy stretches, and in desert areas—through which we traveled most of the way—it was very dusty and windblown. The distance from Urumqi, according to our driver, was about 112 miles, although on a map that I obtained in Urumqi an arrow pointing toward Turfan noted that it was about 75 miles. I never was able to clarify which was right, but I guessed that one of them may have been measured as the crow flies. After leaving Urumqi, we first drove through rolling, brown hills where we passed a number of scattered villages and some farmland. All along this part of the route, Bogda rose out of the lowlands on our left and was a magnificent sight. Then the road entered a wide valley; here there were quite high snowcapped peaks on one side and low, barren mountains on the other. For a short way, we paralleled the main Urumqi-Lanzhou railway. We also passed three large salt lakes—the color of which was a striking milky green. Near two of the lakes were urban settlements and a few isolated farms, and next to one of them was a chemical factory and a small town, with workers' housing. Most of the territory we went through, though, was extremely sparsely populated and desertlike—a mixture of rocky *gebi* (gravel desert) and *huangmo,* with small clumps of grass, widely separated.

About halfway along our trip, we stopped at Daban, a sizable village or town inhabited mainly by Hui Muslims but with a mixture of other groups including Han Chinese, Uighurs, and Kazakhs. It was dominated by a large bazaar—enclosed and with a high ceiling—within which were many small shops, stalls, and little restaurants, most of them operated by Hui entrepreneurs. We stopped and had a very pleasant lunch, dominated—as most Hui meals are—by various mutton dishes.

After Daban, we entered a grassland area, where there were large numbers of sheep but very few villages. Before long, our road divided, with one branch going to the heart of southern Xinjiang and the other to Turfan. On the Turfan road, we immediately entered a gorge that cut through barren mountains, following a stream with small trees on its banks. When we emerged from the gorge, we entered a very wide valley, with low hills on our right and fairly high snow-covered mountains in the far distance on the left. This valley was one of the most forbidding areas of *gebi* that I had ever encountered. For, as far as the eye could see ahead, there was nothing but gray rocks, most of them about the size of large pieces of gravel. Not a single living thing could be seen, not even a bush or a blade of grass. The area looked as if a cosmic dump truck had deposited endless miles of rock on the area. In the far distance, at the edge of the mountains, we could see huge rock slides—which I presumed had been the source of the gravel that had covered this entire valley. Ahead, all we could see, as far as the horizon, was the thin ribbon of our road, stretching mile after mile, gradually narrowing in the distance into a fine line stretching toward infinity. The sun beat down fiercely and was so debilitating that at one point our dyspeptic Uighur driver simply announced that he was tired and was going to take a nap: He stopped the car, stretched out in the front seat, and was oblivious to the world for fifteen minutes—and then silently resumed his driving.

This awesome rock desert continued for the rest of the way to the Turfan oasis. The only signs of civilization anywhere along the road itself were telephone lines and, at one point, a branch rail line that connected with the main route going south toward the Tarim basin. Finally, we saw in the far distance some trees, at the foot of the mountains to our right. This was the start of the Turfan oasis, which thereafter continued for many miles. Eventually, we entered the center of the oasis and stopped at a small village. It was typical of the rural areas around Turfan. The atmosphere was totally Middle Eastern. Except for a single new, hard-brick, two-story house, all of the homes were very traditional, one-story mud structures. They were separated by narrow tree-lined lanes that wound throughout the village. Two-wheel donkey carts plodded along the dirt paths. At one point, a group of bearded elders came down a lane; they were returning home after a meeting at one of the local mosques. Following the men were a number of women and young girls, all wearing multicolored scarfs on their heads. On the outskirts of the main part of the village, there were many irrigated vineyards and melon fields, but beyond them the land was saline and uncultivable. We saw evidence of underground canals—typical of much of the Middle East—which were punctuated periodically by open wells; they provided the village's lifeblood, water. At several vineyards, there were structures built of lattice brickwork, through which breezes could blow; they were for drying grapes to make raisins. Some of the melon fields were covered with plastic sheeting, a relatively recent innovation.

Before entering the center of the city of Turfan, we made a detour to stop at Jiaohe Gucheng, the remains of a very ancient Chinese city. Built originally in the first century B.C.E. as a garrison city for Chinese troops, it was five kilometers (a little more than three miles) in circumference and was constructed on the pattern of a miniature imperial city, with an outer wall, a second wall within it, and still a third one further in—all encircling the city center. During the Tang dynasty, the city had been an extremely important center, and at one point, I was told, the Uighurs used it as their capital. It was abandoned in the fourteenth century, according to local people. I found the place to be a fascinating, ghostly relic of ancient times; its high mud wall and scattered buildings had been eroded over the centuries into very strange shapes.

FIGURE 5.3.
A street in Turfan's old city. This traditional Uighur scene looks as if it could be in the Middle East. *(Photograph by A. Doak Barnett, courtesy of Jeanne B. Barnett.)*

The only other historic site that I had time to visit in Turfan was the Imin Minaret, a very impressive brick tower more than 120 feet tall with intricate brick designs on its surface. Built in 1777, during the Qianlong era of the Qing dynasty, it was named after a local Turfan leader who had helped the Chinese suppress a rebellion in the area but who also had strongly defended Islam. Reputedly, it was the tallest minaret in Xinjiang. (Unfortunately, I had no time during my brief period in Turfan to visit any of the numerous Buddhist sites located near the city, many of which are justly famous.)

When we finally arrived in the center of Turfan, I discovered that, like many cities throughout west China, it consisted of two distinct urban areas. In Turfan's case, the "old city" was immediately adjacent to the "new city." We entered the old city first. It strongly resembled traditional Muslim towns throughout Central Asia (see fig. 5.3). Its ancient city wall had disappeared, but the streets in this part of the city were narrow and lined with tall, stately poplars. The buildings were almost all low, one-story structures. Modern transportation had only recently invaded the scene in this area, and motor vehicles passed donkey carts on the narrow streets; the result was an intriguing mixture of old and new. However, most people dressed in very traditional clothes, which gave the entire area a very Muslim atmosphere.

This old city merged quickly into the modern part of Turfan. Actually, I was told, although it was called *new city,* this area had begun to develop many years previously ("perhaps a hundred years ago") on the edge of the old city, but it had been totally rebuilt during the previous years—mainly in the 1980s. According to the senior local Muslim leader who briefed me at considerable length about the city, in the early 1980s some of the local authorities began to construct buildings that were modern but were adorned with many features of traditional Islamic architecture—features such as arches, domes, and minaretlike towers. The earliest building constructed in this new modern Islamic style was the first modern hotel in the city. Started in 1983, the Turfan Hotel was a fairly gaudy but nevertheless quite attractive example of Islamic architecture. It was no longer considered to be the best place to stay in the city, but it was still the object of considerable local pride. However, as more buildings of this kind were built, some local Han Chinese officials began to criticize this hybrid architecture, and, according to my informants, considerable controversy followed. But when Zhao Ziyang visited Turfan (in 1985, I was told), he strongly and publicly endorsed the architectural mixture of modern and traditional Islamic styles, stating that it effectively symbolized the merging of minority culture and modernization in a Chinese environment. Subsequently, there was a burst of new construction of many large buildings in this distinctive style. To beautify the center of the city, a large grape arbor was built over one of the main avenues, and local officials began to call Turfan the *grape city*. It was a touch of PR sloganeering that reminded me of Alashan's designation of Bayanhaote as *camel city*.

The core of the new part of Turfan city, where most of the modern Islamic architecture was located, consisted of only a few square blocks, but in it were many important buildings, including a new People's Congress building, the government headquarters, a local television station, a huge and extremely colorful bazaar (the front of which looked very much like that of an elegant mosque), and many other quite attractive modern/Islamic public buildings. Also in this area was the city's newest hotel (opened in 1986), called the "Oasis" (Lüzhou)—but also referred to by many as the "New Guest House" (*xin binguan*). This hotel, where I stayed, effectively captured, I thought, the varying flavors of Islam, Han China, and the modern West. Designed mainly for Western tourists, it was surprisingly modern and comfortable; in fact, it came close to meeting the standards of the best Western-style hotels in east China. Its external architecture was distinctively Islamic, as was the interior decor. But it contained all the appurtenances of a very modern hotel. The food was excellent, and it mixed Chinese and Muslim dishes (kebab, mutton, pilaf, and so on) together with typical Chinese dishes. The waitresses—half of them Uighur and half of them Han Chinese—were extremely attractive young ladies, sporting permanent waves, calf-length skirts (red or black), white blouses, and high-heeled shoes (red, black, or white). One of them, whose hair was tied in a ponytail, wore jeans, a T-shirt, and a very "mod" jacket, together with red high-heeled shoes. During my brief stay there, I encountered several other foreign tourists, including four Japanese and two young Americans. The guests in the hotel also included a half dozen Uighur cadres.

Even though my visit was in the spring, the weather in Turfan was very hot. The temperature rose to the high eighties (Fahrenheit), and it was sticky. There was good reason for the heat: Turfan lies in a deep basin, about two hundred feet below sea level. In summer the temperature rises very much higher—reportedly it is considered almost intolerable by most foreigners. However, the rooms in the new hotel were all effectively air-conditioned! In any case, I did not mind the heat. In fact, I am a genuine fan of dry, desert climate. Despite the heat, therefore, I thoroughly enjoyed wandering throughout the entire city and poking about in bazaars—and I learned a good deal about the existing situation from ordinary people as well as local officials.

Turfan, I learned, was a *diqu,* or "prefecture," one of sixteen prefecture-level units in Xinjiang. (In 1988, eleven of the sixteen were regular prefectures, and five were autonomous prefectures, *zizhi zhou.*) In much of east China, prefectures have been gradually disappearing—replaced by enlarged municipalities that have incorporated numerous adjacent counties. This did not seem likely to happen in Xinjiang, though, in part because the counties and urban settlements are too widely scattered to fit logically into economic areas centered on a few large cities.

All five of Xinjiang's autonomous prefectures were in areas where minority groups other than Uighurs predominated. The comparable units, at the same level, where Uighurs were the majority, remained as regular prefectures. No *zizhi zhou* were established in Uighur areas because the Uighurs were the majority group in the entire region. Local officials in Turfan carefully explained to me the differences between regular prefectures and the *zizhi zhou.* Regular prefectures, they pointed out, were simply "administrative" (*xingshu*) units that were "dispatched organs" (*paichu jigou*) of the regional government—that is, they functioned, in effect, simply as branches of the government in Urumqi, and their leaders were appointed by the region and operated on the basis of direct instructions from above. In theory, at least, the *zizhi zhou* had more autonomy in making local decisions: They elected their own leaders and could decide on some issues themselves. In reality, however, differences were less than they appeared on the surface. The regional government in Urumqi still had a very large say in determining the leadership and in managing all affairs in the *zizhi zhou* as well as in the regular prefectures—even though Turfan officials went out of their way to emphasize that they did have some leeway in making decisions on local issues that most regular prefectures did not have.

The inhabitants of Turfan whom I interviewed showed obvious pride in the historic strategic position of their city and the fact that, because of its key location southeast of Urumqi, it had always been an extremely important stopping place on the old Silk Road. They also maintained that it continued to be a city of special strategic importance: They asserted that everyone recognized that it was the most important city in the entire area between Urumqi and Hami—and was located extremely near the main rail route. Local people made a distinction that I had not heard earlier. They said that, whereas most of Xinjiang could be classified as either part of North Xinjiang (Bei Jiang—the heart of which is Dzungaria) or part of South Xinjiang (Nan Jiang—with the Tarim basin as its center), Turfan was unique in that it belonged to neither of those two major areas but instead was the principal city of what they called East Xinjiang (Dong Jiang).

Originally, the area of Turfan consisted of three counties, I was told. But then one of the counties—the one containing the main urban center of the oasis—was granted the status of a county-level city, and the other two units remained as counties—Shanshan in the east and Toksin in the west. Under them were seventeen townships (*xiang*) and eight towns (*zhen*). The counties encompassed not only the fertile oasis land at the foot of the mountains but also a considerable area of *gebi* desert. Turfan prefecture was one of the "smallest major administrative units" in Xinjiang, local officials said, but by the standards of other parts of China it was not small. The total territory of the prefecture, I was told, was a little more than twenty-seven thousand square miles—an area about the size of West Virginia. (Nothing in Xinjiang is really small!)

The population of the entire prefecture, according to the latest figures that local officials could give to me, was roughly 450,000. About 310,000 (or more than two-thirds of the total) were Uighurs. In addition, the inhabitants included roughly 90,000 Han Chinese, more than 40,000 Hui Muslims, and perhaps 10,000 or so Kazakhs (most of whom lived in nearby mountain areas). The majority of the Han residents of the prefecture, and a great many of the Hui, were relative newcomers. Before 1949, I was told, there were only "a few" Han Chinese in Turfan. But after 1949 they moved to the area in several different waves. One group came at the time of the Communist takeover; later waves included the young people assigned to help Xinjiang's "construction" from the 1950s on, demobilized army men, and cadres sent from the "interior" (*neidi*) at various periods. I was struck, incidentally, by the fact that when people in Turfan—and, in fact, in the rest of Xinjiang—talked about provinces further east, although at times they referred to them as *coastal provinces,* most frequently they categorized them as being in the *interior.* This practice was the exact reverse of the use of the term *interior* by Chinese in eastern areas, who invariably used it to refer to places far from the coast, those in the west.

I was told that there had been relatively little intermarriage between Han Chinese and Uighurs. "It occurs sometimes, but we do not encourage it," one person said, adding that, "when there are mixed marriages, it is important to have very clear arrangements or understanding because customs are so different." Whether male or female, Han Chinese were expected to convert to Islam when marrying Muslims in this area.

However, almost everyone I met emphasized that the local policy in selecting leaders—not only political leaders but also leaders in economic units—was to try to mix different ethnic groups; in appointing cadres, the aim was to see that the numbers were roughly proportionate to the different groups' shares in the population. The Party secretary of the prefecture was a Han Chinese, but the Standing Committee had both Han and Uighur members. The head of the Turfan prefectural government was a Uighur. (The previous prefectural head, I was told, had subsequently become the major of Urumqi.) All of the county magistrates were Uighurs, my informant said; however, under them the cadres in subordinate jobs were ethnically diverse. I was given a number of examples of how the leadership in a variety of organizations was mixed in numbers roughly proportionate to ethnic representation in the population. The examples included government bureaus such as the Municipal Foreign Affairs Office, enterprises such as a local chemical factory, the Oasis Hotel where I was staying, and various others. On the surface, I saw no obvious signs of Han-Uighur tensions (but in Turfan, as elsewhere, I assumed that there must be some potential tensions existing under the surface because of past conflicts as well as recent demographic trends).

In Turfan, as in all of China, religion had come under severe attack in earlier years, especially during the Cultural Revolution. But local people asserted—convincingly, I thought—that in the 1980s, since the adoption of a relatively conciliatory policy toward religion, there had been a genuine religious revival. During the Cultural Revolution, I was told, "many" mosques were destroyed, and almost all of the rest were taken over for use as factories, warehouses, and organizational headquarters. However, in the 1980s, not only were the mosques that had been destroyed or damaged rebuilt, but many entirely new ones were constructed. Some of these new mosques were "better" than the old ones, according to my informants, and "most had been built with local contributions, not government support." By 1988, there were "several hundred" operating mosques scattered throughout the prefecture—"more than before the Cultural Revolution."

At the time of my visit in 1988, I could see that the economy of Turfan was still basically agricultural and, in many respects, traditional, but I saw many signs that "modernization" had begun to transform it. The city had recently established numerous links with the outside world—connections of a kind that would have been almost inconceivable in the years before 1949. Most of these links had developed very recently, since 1978. Moreover, the character of Turfan had obviously begun to be changed in very important ways by the prevalence of paved roads and television and other modern communications as well as by the recently built modern buildings, obvious improvements in agricultural methods, the introduction of some modern factories, growing contacts with at least a few foreign businesses, and the burgeoning tourist industry.

The population of the prefecture remained mainly rural, however. Only seventy to eighty thousand people (about a sixth of the total population)—workers, cadres, merchants, and so on—were classified as urban. These people were concentrated in the new part of Turfan city (which contained perhaps forty thousand people) and in the county seats and the eight towns (*zhen*) under the prefecture. Roughly five-sixths of the total population were still engaged in agriculture, raising grains such as wheat and sorghum, fruits such as grapes and "Hami" melon, cotton, and vegetables. Local officials asserted that agriculture had made notable progress and that the prefecture was now self-sufficient in grain, even though, since decollectivization, there had been a major shift from grain to cash crops. Except for people working in two state farms (which concentrated on growing fruit), all farmers—I was told—now operated under the household contract responsibility system.

Some improved seeds, many new methods, and modern technology of various kinds had been introduced into agriculture. (Plastic sheets to cover fields were one very visible example.)

As a result of recent economic trends, there had been a significant increase in the per capita income of rural families; I was told that the average had been under 300 yuan before 1978 and had risen to roughly 500 yuan in 1987. The target for the rural population of the prefecture for the near future was 800 yuan. There were still some "quite poor" rural families, local officials told me, but there was also a growing number of quite affluent ones (including quite a few who earned more than 10,000 yuan a year). The general level, in any case, had clearly risen significantly.

Irrigation remained the most crucial underpinning of agriculture—as always is true in desert areas. In the entire prefecture, I was told, there were more than 1,860 miles of waterways in numerous underground canals (of varying lengths). I had first seen this type of underground canal many years previously—both in Xinjiang and in Iran and other areas in the Middle East. They are impressive feats of simple engineering. Designed to convey glacial and stream water for long distances underground, with minimal evaporation, they are testimony to the skill of local engineers dating to very ancient times. In addition to these underground canals, Turfan had six above-ground canals—which brought substantial amounts of water from the Tian Shan—as well as more than a thousand deep wells.

Animal husbandry ranked well below agriculture in its importance to the local economy, but local officials told me that there were about a half million sheep that grazed in the nearby mountains (tended mainly by Kazakhs) and almost an equal number of sheep owned by agricultural households. The prefecture's output of mutton and lamb now made it "almost self-sufficient" in the production of these meats, but Turfan still had to import a significant amount of pork (for non-Muslims) from other areas.

Modern industry was still limited in Turfan, but I was impressed that it at least had made a start. The largest local factory was a chemical plant, which used raw materials transported from Lake Aydingkol (Aiding), a salt lake not very far to the south that also provided raw materials for several smaller chemical plants and a salt-processing plant. "Several dozen" small coal mines provided fuel for the prefecture's thermal power plant as well as for other local uses, and two main hydropower stations in the mountains—plus several smaller ones elsewhere—also provided some local power. In addition, there were many wineries in the area. Growing wine had been a centuries-old occupation, but it had been expanded and somewhat modernized recently. (I asked whether the Xinjiang Production and Construction Corps ran any farms or enterprises in the Turfan area, and local officials said: "No, most of their activity is in the north." But I was not sure that this was absolutely correct; I had been told elsewhere that the Corps did operate in some eastern and southern areas.)

I was given figures by local officials for the gross value of the entire economic output of the prefecture in 1987. The total, they said, was roughly 300 million yuan. However, this was a figure that they cited from memory, and I did not have time to get them to check it and give me a precise figure. When I asked them about their budget, again they gave me a very general and rather vague answer. Local tax revenue, they said, was not sufficient to cover their expenditures, so they relied fairly heavily on subsidies from the regional government. They did not give me any specific figures.

Even though modernization in Turfan was obviously in a very early stage, it impressed me because it contrasted so much with my memories of Xinjiang in the 1940s. And I was genuinely surprised to hear about the degree to which new links had been forged with the outside world. "Foreign trade," I was told, was growing steadily and now "accounted for about 10 percent of Turfan's gross value of output" (although no one made clear to me exactly what this meant or even whether the term *foreign trade* meant only trade with foreign countries or included trade with coastal Chinese provinces). The leaders of Turfan clearly hoped to attract foreign business cooperation and investment. So far, two wineries had obtained some foreign capital and had purchased some foreign machinery—from Japan, the United States, and Switzerland. Refrigeration equipment had been imported from the United States, and some packaging technology had been purchased from Switzerland.

The most important new industry in Turfan that created significant links with other parts of China as well as with foreign countries was clearly tourism. Whereas in 1980—according to the head of the local Foreign Affairs Office—fewer than 1,000 foreign tourists had visited Turfan, in 1987 about 18,000 had come. The number of Chinese tourists had grown even more rapidly. By 1987 the total number of all tourists, including both Chinese and foreign, had risen to more than 100,000. To serve these tourists, especially the foreigners, Turfan had constructed three modern hotels, with about five hundred beds, and it had acquired thirty imported vehicles (mainly Japanese cars, vans, and buses) with approximately four hundred seats to take tourists on trips to nearby historic sites. The impact of tourism went far beyond the foreign exchange earned. Even more important, in my opinion, it greatly expanded contacts between the local population and people of all kinds from other areas, including foreigners. Moreover, the attempt to develop local services that could meet the standards expected by foreign tourists had compelled them to learn much more about the outside world than they had previously known. This inevitably had had a significant impact on the ideas, and even the values, of local people. I had no way to measure this impact, but my impression was that it was very significant. Geographically, Turfan was still a very remote place, but its sense of isolation was gradually being destroyed.

The officials I interviewed in 1988 made a great point of stressing that the present leadership in the region was strongly committed to implementing policy designed to treat minorities with real equality and, in fact, to give them special preferential treatment in many respects. (I will discuss later some of Xinjiang's "affirmative action" policies.) But, in some nonofficial conversations that I had, I received a strong impression that, although the state of Han-minority relations in most of the region was not critical (in this respect, the situation in Xinjiang in 1988 seemed to me to be very different from that in Tibet), historically based frictions continued to pose problems, even in Urumqi. One man said, for example:

> Although Han Chinese and Uighurs mix reasonably well in normal times, there are some underlying tensions that can erupt as a result of incidents. In 1986, to cite one example, there were some fairly large student demonstrations in Urumqi. Some voiced a desire for independence as well as a demand for democracy. Also, periodically, Han-Uighur disputes break out and cause friction. For example, several years ago there was an incident in which a Han shopkeeper built a structure on a neighboring Uighur's land, and this led to a dispute that ended with the Han shopkeeper shooting and killing the Uighur with a hunting gun. This led to riots. Then Wang Enmao—leader in the region at the time—handled it as follows. He first called together a group of Uighur leaders and urged them to cool their emotions, and then he did the same with a group of Han leaders. The offender was tried and convicted, and this cooled things down. Actually, Han leaders have leaned over backward to placate the Uighurs. Nevertheless, young Uighur students and intellectuals remain a source of potential instability.

There were reports in 1988, published in official Chinese journals, of several incidents of ethnic conflict in Xinjiang. Even Wang Enmao, who was no longer local Party chief but still headed the Regional Party Advisory Commission, was quoted as charging that Xinjiang faced a threat from "elements coming from outside to conduct acts of sabotage and separation." He reportedly named three subversive groups: the East Turkestan National Salvation Committee, the East Turkestan Popular Revolutionary Front, and the World Islamic Alliance. All three were accused of sending spies, instigating underground action, calling for "independence for Xinjiang," and trying to organize an East Turkestan Party. These charges were especially notable because their source was Wang Enmao, a man generally regarded by virtually all the people I met as a leader who had worked hard to promote good ethnic relations in the region. He had attempted, for example, to prevent destruction of mosques during the Cultural Revolution. On ethnic issues, he had the reputation of being a conciliatory moderate. There also were some reports in 1988 of arrests of a number of Kazakhs in the Ili region as well as some other reports of demonstrations in Urumqi in which students protested graffiti that was allegedly racially motivated.

I was unable to judge accurately how serious the underlying tensions might be or what the potential for political instability was. On the surface, Han-Uighur relations generally appeared to me to be quite "normal" in the

FIGURE 5.4.
Han Chinese and Uighurs mix at a local fair. The modern ambience is very different from that of 1948. *(Photograph by A. Doak Barnett, courtesy of Jeanne B. Barnett.)*

limited areas that I visited (see fig. 5.4). I sensed, though, rightly or wrongly, that this might be less true of Han-Kazakh relations. I had no doubt that historical and cultural differences still posed problems. Nevertheless, my overall impression was that the regime's policies during the 1980s had significantly reduced tensions at least in Urumqi and nearby areas.

One important set of questions that I tried to explore in Xinjiang, as elsewhere in China in 1988, concerned the changes in the political leadership that had occurred during the decade of the 1980s. In 1948 I had met virtually all of the most important leaders in Urumqi. In 1988 I was not able to do this, but I did have an excellent, long interview with one of the senior deputy chairmen of the Xinjiang Uighur autonomous region, a man named Mao Dehao, and I met a number of senior officials. They told me a great deal about both the leadership and the administration of the region. In 1988, leaders and officials in Xinjiang, as in the other provinces in autonomous regions that I visited, were willing to discuss such matters in considerable detail.

The region's top leaders, I was told, consisted, in 1988, of fifteen individuals on the Party Standing Committee and eight top government leaders. The ethnic balance and the career profiles of these leaders were similar to those I had learned about in other areas in the west that I had just visited. The secretary of the Party was a Han technocrat (Song Hanliang, formerly an engineer who had worked at the Karamai oil fields). His five deputies included two Han Chinese, two Uighurs, and one Kazakh. Of the nine other members of the Standing Committee, six were Han, two were Uighurs, and one was a Mongol. One of the Han members served concurrently as the political commissar of the Xinjiang military district. The chairman of the regional government (who concurrently served as the ranking deputy secretary of the Party) was a Uighur; of his six deputies (one of whom also served as a member of the Party Standing Committee), three were Han (including Deputy Chairman Mao, whom I interviewed), two were Uighurs, and one was a Kazakh. The secretary-general was a Uighur.

In the leadership of the Xinjiang People's Congress, the chairman and eight of the twelve deputy chairmen were of minority ethnic origin. If one added to all of the aforementioned leaders a few others who were classified by local people as "top leaders" (including the chairman and deputy chairman of the People's Political Consultative Conference), the total number of individuals listed as members of the "top leadership" totaled just over fifty—and more than half of these (55 percent) belonged to minority ethnic groups.

A majority of these top leaders were people who had risen to high positions very recently, during Deng Xiaoping's nationwide campaign in the mid-1980s to promote younger, better-educated, and more technically qualified leaders. Deputy Chairman Mao Dehao was a good example of the kind of individual promoted. He impressed me as being competent, pragmatic, and a thorough professional—comparable to the majority of the technocratic and professional leaders I had been encountering throughout northwest China. Mao, fifty-two years old, had been born in Jiangsu province and educated at Nanjing University, where he obtained a degree in geology. Assigned to Xinjiang right after graduation, he had spent most of his three decades there working in the Xinjiang Academy of Sciences. His research included a great deal of work on agricultural problems and rural planning but also involved investigation of glaciers. Ultimately, Mao rose to be president of the Xinjiang Academy of Sciences. Then, in late 1985, he was selected to be a deputy chairman of the region; his primary area of responsibility was culture and education, including science (the so-called *wenjiao* system). He impressed me as being a very different type of person from a majority of the provincial-level leaders that I had met either in the 1940s or during the Mao Zedong era.

In the bureaucracies and in the leadership at lower levels there also was a large representation of minority groups. For example, I was told that, at both the regional and the prefectural levels, more than 41 percent of unit heads within the bureaucracies were minority cadres. The percentage dropped at the county level to roughly 32 percent. However, in "autonomous counties," 53 percent of all cadres were said to consist of members of minority groups. In the region as a whole, the total number of minority people who were "state cadres" (*guojia ganbu*)—that is, functionaries and officials of all kinds—had risen to 210,000. One top official pointed out—and emphasized—that this was seventy times the number of people of minority origin who held any sort of official position in Xinjiang before 1949.

Of the total number of people in the province classified as "scientific and technical personnel"—around two hundred thousand—more than half were said to be members of ethnic minorities. I was also given a variety of other figures, which I will not cite here, that highlighted the great increase in the number of minority people who had achieved cadre status since the Communist takeover. (Chinese Communist officials have a great penchant—in fact an irresistible impulse—to compare "before and after," with the dividing line usually being either 1949 or the Cultural Revolution.)

All of the statistics of this sort that were given to me clearly indicated that members of minority groups were playing a much larger role than in the past in both the leadership and the bureaucracies and that they had risen steadily also in the intellectually scientific elite of the region. National laws and regulations required that they hold certain top government positions, but they obviously had been rising into many positions that no laws or regulations required. However, their representation in a good many sectors was still somewhat lower than their percentage in the region's population. Moreover, as in most of the other areas of northwest China that I visited, it was fairly clear that Han Chinese still held the most powerful positions in the most important centers of power—especially in the Party and the military. I was told, for example, that probably under ten of the top local Party leaders—that is, Party Committee secretaries in the major geographic-administrative divisions within the region—were minority cadres even though there were at least some minority cadres in all Party Standing Committees. Nonetheless, there was no doubt that the political roles and the political influence of the Uighurs, at least, were now substantial. One observer I met who impressed me as particularly knowledgeable about the local situation (he was a Han Chinese) said: "The Uighurs in high positions are by no means mere figureheads now; they do have real influence; actually, some Han Chinese increasingly complain about the discrimination in favor of minorities."

My strong impression was that the influence of minority leaders was greatest in day-to-day government affairs, particularly at subregional levels and especially in "autonomous" areas—most of all in areas that were relatively far from the capital.

Urbanization and occupational changes were only two of many important indices of the progress of modernization in Xinjiang in the years since my first visit. The development of education was another important one. I had not obtained detailed data on education in the province when I visited it in 1948, but it was clear at that time that, in general, modern forms of education had barely begun to develop and did not reach most of the Uighur and Kazakh populations. By the late 1980s modern education had been significantly expanded, and official policies gave high priority to developing further the education of minority groups.

Wherever ethnic groups are mixed in an education system, language issues generally become sensitive problems. In Xinjiang, this was obviously the case, but it was also clear that important compromises had been made to try to accommodate the linguistic diversity. In primary and middle schools (and other secondary-level schools), classes were taught, I was told, in six different languages: Uighur, Hanyu[1] (Chinese), Kazakh, Mongol, Xibe, and Kyrgyz. There were textbooks in all six of these languages. Most of them were translations of texts received from Beijing, although some minority-language texts had been prepared locally. Not all schools taught all six languages; exactly what was taught—and the textbooks used—varied by school. A few schools were "mixed," which meant that they taught in more than one language, but most were not. In effect, the system was based on different language "tracks," and my informants asserted that about 95 percent of the primary and middle school students attended schools in which the basic teaching was in their own native language track. However, from the third grade on, I was told, minority students were expected to be able to use the Chinese language (Hanyu[2] and spoken Chinese, Putonghua). Han Chinese students were required to study a foreign language—but it did not have to be one of the local nationality groups' languages, and in recent years, my informants said, the study of Western languages (especially English) had become increasingly popular, and the number of Han Chinese studying minority languages had declined.

In Xinjiang, as elsewhere in west China, the local officials I met—minority officials as well as Han Chinese—strongly stressed to me that preferential treatment was being given to minority students, and to minority languages, especially in higher education. In some institutions of higher learning the basic language was Hanyu, but in others it was Uighur (although even in these schools all students had to study Hanyu). In the Normal College in Ili, both the Uighur and Kazakh language (Turki) and Hanyu were considered to be "basic languages." Minority students were admitted to college-level institutions with scores that were lower than those required for Han Chinese students—usually one hundred points lower—and I was told that most students took entrance exams in their own languages. If they were enrolled in an institution within Xinjiang where the basic language was Hanyu, they could, if their knowledge of Hanyu was below par, either attend a special language-training course, given by the Education Commission, or spend their initial year at the college studying Hanyu (which extended their college program to five years).

A sizable number of students from Xinjiang were sent to universities elsewhere in China. I was told that roughly four thousand went each year to attend universities in other provinces. Many of these students first spent two years in basic training at one of the two main minority institutes—in Beijing or Lanzhou—where their curricula focused on learning the Chinese language, and then they went on (or at least many of them did) to other universities in Beijing, Shanghai, Guangzhou, and elsewhere.[3]

For many years there had been—and continued to be—a serious "brain drain" problem, I was told, which was especially troublesome among the Han Chinese students. My informants said that, whereas the majority of minority students from Xinjiang who attended universities elsewhere returned to the region, only about 40 percent of Han students from the region did so. Officials candidly admitted that many of the latter "do not like to live and work in the northwest"; in contrast, they said, most Uighurs and other ethnic groups (except, perhaps, the Xibe—for reasons they did not explain) "do not like to live and work in other provinces, as a rule." In early 1988, I was told, Beijing's State Council adopted a policy that required all Xinjiang students going for university education elsewhere to return to the region following graduation, but the people with whom I talked were uncertain as to how effectively this could be implemented.

From what I learned in 1988, it seemed clear that, in contrast to the pre-1949 period, the government was trying to extend basic education to most of the population. There was no doubt in my mind, though, that the quality of the education remained relatively low. Virtually all of the officials I met frankly admitted that this was the case and said that they were dissatisfied with the situation and gave high priority to improving it. I had no basis for judging exactly how low the quality was, but it was clear that Xinjiang shared this problem with most of the rest of China—perhaps in a somewhat more acute form. Nevertheless, certain basic knowledge, including literacy and mathematical skills, and some general knowledge about the society and the world were being imparted to virtually the entire younger generation.

I speculated about what the possible political effects of greatly expanded education might be in the long run. Local Chinese leaders obviously hoped that their education policies not only would raise the level of knowledge and skill of the minority ethnic groups but would also tend over time to integrate them more effectively into a unified society. They also hoped that their policies would, at the same time, satisfy the desire of ethnic groups to maintain their own languages and cultural identities. Whether these multiple goals are likely to be successfully achieved remains to be seen. It is also conceivable that, despite the preferential treatment given to minority ethnic groups, the simple fact of steadily rising education levels may, over time, create a stronger base for "local nationalism." Moreover, there is no question that, as development makes progress, education will have to be upgraded, qualitatively, and all the local leaders I met fully recognized this. Nevertheless, the quantitative development of education since the 1940s had clearly played a very major and essential role in Xinjiang's recent development and modernization.

During the four decades of modernization in Xinjiang from the late 1940s on, the region had major ups and downs—but it made significant economic progress. Several things were crucial in the process of development. One was the extension of modern transportation—especially rail transportation—into the region.

In addition to building the first railways in the area—the length of which totaled 870 miles in the entire region by 1987 and would, they said, grow to about 1,000 miles by 1990—the local regime had given priority from the 1950s on to building a network of paved roads, connecting all major urban areas in the region. By 1987, I was told, this road network totaled roughly 13,000 miles, and the most important roads were paved. Officials stated that roads now reached every county and town in the autonomous region, and public bus service connected the most important centers of population—although the main use of the roads continued to be for trucking cargo rather than for passenger traffic.

Air travel had also been significantly expanded (it was extremely primitive before 1949). Urumqi now had direct scheduled air service to seven major Chinese cities (Beijing, Tianjin, Shanghai, Xi'an, Lanzhou, Guangzhou, and Chengdu). When I flew to Urumqi in 1948, it was like making an adventurous expedition into the unknown. Now that Urumqi is well connected with virtually the entire country, air travel is routine. This has been a much more profound change than those who have never lived in places without air travel may realize. Recently a local airline company, called Dunhuang Air, established regular links between Urumqi and other major cities within the region.

Even though Xinjiang's modern transportation system is still minimal in some respects and clearly requires further development, by the late 1980s the isolation that had characterized the region in the 1940s had ended—forever. Moreover, in Xinjiang, as elsewhere in China, the great expansion of modern media that had taken place in the 1980s had created much closer communication links than had ever existed before, both within the region and with other parts of China and the entire world.

The press and other publications had expanded greatly (and newspapers were now published in all the major languages). However, because I did not have time to gather detailed information about every aspect of the modern media, I concentrated on trying to learn as much as I could about the growth of the electronic media, the prevalence of which I found so remarkable in every place that I visited in northwest China.

In the Xinjiang region as a whole, I was told, official estimates indicated that 70 percent of the entire population had access to, and listened to, the radio in 1988. (I remember seeing virtually no radios anywhere in Xinjiang when I visited it in 1948—except for a few sets owned by foreign consulates.) Apart from the major broadcasting station in Urumqi, ten counties had built their own wireless radio stations, and each of them did some programming of its own as well as rebroadcasting many national and regional radio programs. Virtually all the settled population in the region, moreover, was linked into wired radio-speaker systems (somewhat similar to "rediffusion" in the West), which had been universally developed from the 1950s on. I was told that not only did all counties have such systems but 701 townships and 1,294 villages did, too. My informants asserted that all of these could originate local programs—or at least make local announcements over the loudspeakers—as well as rebroadcast programs from Beijing and Urumqi. On my own radio, I found the airwaves, both long and short wave, filled with an extraordinary variety of programs from all over China and abroad as well as the region itself. (For some reason, however, I had considerable difficulty finding any FM stations, and frequently the shortwave reception was poorer than I expected in this region—where I thought that interference would be minimal.)

But here as elsewhere it was the penetration of television—which had occurred entirely during the decade of the 1980s—that struck me most forcefully. By 1988, I was told by informed local people, there were 1.1 million television sets in Xinjiang; this amounted to about one per every three households, regionwide. In urban areas, I was told, virtually every household owned a television set. It was estimated that about 65 percent of the entire population of the region was within geographic areas that were effectively reached by television signals. Throughout the region, in addition to regular television stations, there were 92 television relay stations, mostly rebroadcasting the output of the stations in Beijing and Urumqi. Altogether, within the region, there were twenty-three local television stations that had at least some capability to put out their own programming, but everyone stated that most of the programs were ones rebroadcast from national and provincial stations. I was told, though, that—in contrast to Inner Mongolia and Qinghai—Xinjiang had not yet actively promoted the sale and distribution of small windmill generators; as a result, many people in the grasslands, especially Kazakhs, had no source of electricity and therefore lacked television. My informants mentioned among possible reasons the fact that local fluctuations in wind were quite large. My guess was that they simply had not yet pushed the idea. They said some study had been made of simple solar generators, but they were not in wide use either.

In Urumqi itself, there were fourteen hours a day of television broadcasting in the Chinese language (Putonghua), and twelve hours a day in Uighur (Turki), but only three to four hours on a single day each week were devoted to special programs for Kazakhs. This allocation of programming obviously gave local Uighurs in the city a disproportionate amount of program time in their native language since only 12 percent of Urumqi's population was Uighur and virtually all of them spoke the Chinese language. But, in light of the fact that Urumqi programs were relayed throughout the region, the time allotted was understandable. The Han Chinese, whose population made up 82 percent of the municipality's population (and roughly two-fifths of the region's population), had slightly more air time. Even though the Kazakhs constituted only 3 percent of Urumqi's population and only 7 percent of the population of the region, and even though most of them could understand Turki programs produced for the Uighurs, it nevertheless seemed to me that they were being shortchanged in the television field—as in many others—in comparison with the Uighurs.

The mix of television programs—national news (which contained some segments of local news), entertainment, educational programs, and advertising—seemed very much like that in Beijing. The nightly national news had a very large local audience, I was told (my impression was that this was true throughout China). I was impressed by the fact that the local newscasters closely imitated their national, and international, models: The coanchors of news programs—usually one man and one woman—were smartly dressed in Western clothes and looked remarkably like their counterparts on the American networks (on whom they seemed to model their style). Political propaganda was largely absent in 1988. Television was full of images of China's most developed areas and of very modern areas in the West—especially the United States and Europe—and bombarded viewers with scenes of modern life in all of its varied aspects. Subtly, and not so subtly, both advertisements and regular programs strongly promoted consumerism—by urging everyone to buy every conceivable kind of consumer durable and many kinds of luxury consumables. A combination of all the messages being communicated by the electronic media (at least before the Tiananmen disaster in 1989) and the effects of modern transportation created powerful new forces for modernization.

Local leaders assumed that in the 1990s, as in the 1980s, the relatively relaxed international environment would encourage faster economic development. If post–cold war trends—especially Sino-Soviet détente—continued, they said, the region could enjoy one of the longest periods without conflict in its modern history. When I asked whether there was any danger that old conflicts might be revived, they expressed confidence that this would not happen in the foreseeable future. But, when I asked how close relations with the Soviet Union could become, they acknowledged that they thought there would be severe limitations. In passing, they mentioned that "the three big mountain passes" to the Soviet Union had still not been opened (in 1988) to normal traffic and stressed that "political factors" still limited Sino-Soviet contacts. But they insisted that the border was "calm." I inquired specifically about the dispute between China and the Soviet Union over the Pamir mountains—a long-standing dispute involving about 20,000 square kilometers (approximately 7,700 square miles) of territory—and asked what the prospects for a total solution were. They had no answer, but they claimed that it was not a serious problem, even though the issue was unresolved. The area was quiescent, they insisted, and they expected that the status quo would continue to be maintained. (I got no clues as to what the prospect was for an eventual formal resolution of their conflicting territorial claims.)

The Chinese-Mongolian dispute over the Beidashan area—which was very active when I had visited Xinjiang in 1948—had been essentially settled, I was told. One member of the Academy's Institute of History said to me that the resolution was a result of a Sino-Mongolian agreement, the main basis for which was said to be compromise by the Chinese side. My informant claimed that, whereas China "kept control of the mountain ridge," in return it "gave up its claims to the north slope and the Burgan [Bulgan] river area," which had been ceded to Mongolia. The explanation that this scholar gave for the compromise was interesting. The Chinese had long considered the area involved to be Chinese territory, he stated, even though both the Soviets and the Mongols considered it to be part of Mongolia. "However," he said, "in the late 1940s a Chinese Communist publication in Yan'an had published the Soviet position on this area, without challenging its validity, and this gave Moscow a strong basis for arguing that China had accepted its position." Whether this was in fact the most important explanation for the compromise, apparently the Chinese had given up some of the territory that they had claimed and, my informant asserted, had subsequently made further small border adjustments. As a result, this border was no longer considered to be an area of contention.

Deputy Chairman Mao asserted, flatly, that there were "no current tensions over the region's borders" because both sides (meaning all sides) were willing to maintain the status quo under existing circumstances. The hope in Xinjiang, clearly, was that there would be continued calm and further improvement of overall relations among all nations within the region—and that this would lead to a significant increase of trade, particularly with the Soviet Union but also through the Soviet Union with Europe. Whether or not these hopes for the future will prove to be justified, the relatively calm international environment during the 1980s had clearly been beneficial to Xinjiang's modernization.[4]

All in all, Xinjiang's leaders were obviously concerned when I met them in 1988 that their region still lagged seriously behind China's coastal provinces, and they feared that this gap could widen in the period ahead. They nevertheless seemed to have considerable optimism about the region's prospects for future growth. Their urge to catch up, and to compete with other Chinese provinces, was very strong. So, too, was their desire to expand external economic relations as much as possible, to speed the process of modernization. They felt under considerable pressure to proceed with structural economic reforms, but, because of numerous special obstacles to the reforms in the region, they were cautious about introducing many of them. It was apparent that systemic changes in Xinjiang would be slower than in many other parts of China. One reason was the continuing domination of the People's Liberation Army (PLA) and the Production and Construction Corps. Another was the continuing complexity of ethnic problems and relations within the region.

The more that I learned about the role of the PLA and the Xinjiang Production and Construction Corps (hereafter, the Corps) in Xinjiang, the more I suspected that Xinjiang would be a difficult place to implement many of the reforms that Beijing was trying to promote throughout the country at that time. Nevertheless, as I did everywhere that I visited, I attempted to learn as much as I could about the extent to which the new reform policies had begun to change the local economy and society. My conclusion was that, although there had been efforts to implement many of the reforms and they had brought some changes, Xinjiang—even more than most other areas in west China—lagged far behind coastal China in moving in the direction of structural reform.

What had changed in Xinjiang during the reform period, it seemed to me, was the general political, economic, and social atmosphere. As elsewhere in China, I found that the old political and social controls characteristic of the Maoist era had been greatly loosened in the 1980s; ideology had eroded and become much less prominent; people seemed to speak with remarkable freedom and frankness, even with a foreigner; and, as the average standard of living had improved, expectations and hopes had risen. Important in all of this had been the rapid development of modern communications, which had helped to increase knowledge as well as raise expectations and had created new links with the rest of China and the outside world. Although Xinjiang was not as "open" as many eastern parts of China, by 1988 nine of its cities had been declared open to foreign travel, and the number of people moving in and out of the province had grown a great deal. The provincial leadership was trying hard to expand the region's external trade, but they were finding that this was not easy to do.

Top local officials readily acknowledged, as did local academics, that, even though they were making serious efforts to try to implement major economic reforms, many of these reforms were extremely difficult to implement and were taking root very slowly. Almost everyone agreed that the area had not gone very far in changing the basic structure of the economy—to say nothing of the polity.

Apparently the reform policies arousing the greatest hopes in Xinjiang were those associated with China's new open policy. The leaders and officials I met in Urumqi, like those in other inland areas, were ambivalent—to say the least—about Beijing's coastal policy, and they feared the possible consequences of giving special economic privileges to east China. One scholar said—speaking diplomatically and cautiously but nevertheless frankly—that "Xinjiang of course supports this policy, but in the academic world, as well as in the government, there are very different views. If the coastal areas sell more abroad, this may open up the domestic market more for the interior areas; . . . however, it is possible [and clearly he meant likely] that Xinjiang will fall further and further behind. It is really a challenge to us."

Some economic officials said to me that, because Xinjiang borders on the Soviet Union, Beijing had recently given the region some special trading privileges. Officials referred to a document that they called the "Nine Points," which they said permitted the regional government to engage directly, once again, in direct trade across the border, to hold trade talks with foreigners (meaning, in 1988, mainly the Russians), and to send trade exhibitions abroad. (Nobody explained precisely what the nine points were.) Clearly, these officials hoped to expand external economic relations as much as possible, as soon as possible. They also hoped to broaden Xinjiang's trade within China. Yet they felt that they were still far too limited by existing restrictions imposed by Beijing.

Xinjiang's overall economic targets for the rest of the century, as described to me, were very ambitious. The target set for the region's gross economic output in the year 2000, I was told, was six times that of 1980 (a target even more ambitious than the national aim of quadrupling output in the same period). Their hope was to raise per capita incomes accordingly. To try to achieve such aims, they said, they would continue to develop agriculture and animal husbandry; raise output of alloy metals and petroleum; intensify surveying of the region's underground resources; strengthen transportation, communications, and other infrastructure; and try their best to increase their earnings of foreign exchange. They expected the central government to continue providing large amounts of capital to Xinjiang, but their plans also called for an increase in the region's own investments, and they strongly hoped to obtain additional new capital from more affluent Chinese provinces—as well as some foreign investments (perhaps substantial foreign investment, if oil development could be opened up to foreigners).

DRU C. GLADNEY

Ethnoreligious Resurgence in a Northwestern Sufi Community

In this chapter, excerpted from Dru Gladney's significant book on the Muslim Chinese known as Hui, we learn about a community in the Ningxia Hui autonomous region in which the predominant religious orientation is the Sufi sect of Islam. Ningxia is a tiny province-level area of 66,400 square kilometers where the most populous minority group is the Hui, one of China's ten Muslim nationalities (see map 6.1). After decades of repression of religion, since the economic reforms of the late 1970s, there has been a resurgence of religious practice. Still, the state regulates and restricts religion, in part arguing that ethnic identity is separate from religious beliefs and practices. Gladney rejects this view, arguing that in fact religion is inseparable from other aspects of identity, at least for the members of the conservative Na Homestead in Ningxia. He writes of the tension between the state's view of religion as an "opiate" and practitioners' views of it, exemplified in the number of Party members—officially required to be atheists—who are practicing, observant Hui.

One of the impressions that one gets from Gladney's chapter is of enduring Hui struggles to construct and renegotiate an identity, even in the face of Han/state opposition. Yet, despite continuities in some areas, there are significant transformations under way in this area of Chinese life, including, notably, an increase in "ethnoreligious" identification. Gladney also points out the irony of the economic liberalization policies leading to an increase in religious conservatism, increasing ties with Muslims outside China as well as with other Hui within China itself—a "rerooting" of ethnic identity, in his words. As the government of China orchestrates a national symphony of multiethnic fraternity, the Hui have grown more skeptical of politics, distancing themselves from such administered solidarity by deepening their commitment to the practices of *qing zhen* (purity). So, rather than drawing ethnic minorities like the Hui toward the center of the predominantly Han nation, China's economic and political reforms have encouraged a centrifugal intensification of local and regional identity.—Eds.

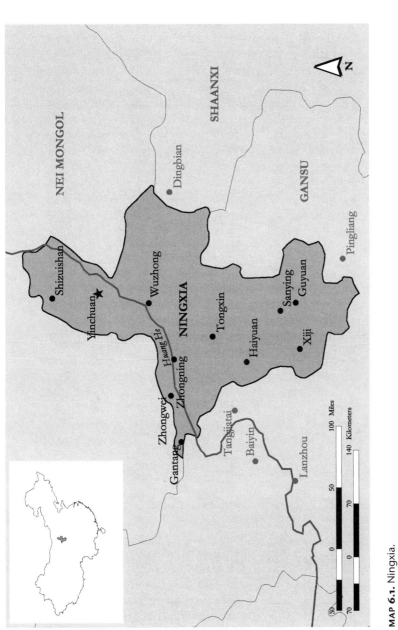

MAP 6.1. Ningxia.

In the Ningxia Hui autonomous region, where over 1.2 million of China's Hui minority reside, local cadres and government researchers are alarmed about the possibility of an Islamic "revival" among Hui youth. They are also questioning whether the private-responsibility system has engendered too much personal and religious freedom in rural areas. Cadres are surprised to find that some Hui peasants hold the mistaken idea that the Party, not only allows religious belief, but encourages it. In order to quell these rising concerns, studies by local academies of social sciences in Muslim areas are used to show that, while ethnic customs are maintained, religious belief is not necessarily strong. Reflecting traditional Chinese policy toward nationality religions, this approach clearly distinguishes between the minority itself and its religion. The policy often encourages the expression of traditional nationality customs and culture while depicting religion as extraneous to ethnicity (Ma 1989).

In this chapter, I argue that Hui ethnic identity in the northwest is inseparably identified with an Islamic tradition handed down to them by their Muslim ancestors. It is more than an ethnic identity; it is ethnoreligious, in that Islam is intimately tied to the northwest Hui's self-understanding. Recent reemergence of the meaning of Islam and stress on the requirements of a decidedly Islamic *qing zhen* (pure) lifestyle represent a return to northwestern Hui ethnoreligious roots. In this regard, an examination of Na Homestead discloses some of the expressions of this northwestern Hui ethnoreligious identity as well as its recent transformation in the midst of rapid socioeconomic change. A close analysis of salient Hui institutions, rituals, and texts reveals that a policy that seeks to make a clear distinction between religion and ethnicity is based on an inadequate understanding of Hui identity. The resurgence of Islamic practice and conservatism in Na Homestead, under recent liberalized policies, illustrates the importance of Islam in this context. The interaction of Na ethnic identity with recently liberalized government policies has also led to important changes in the expression of that identity and in the reformulation of local nationality policies.

A FUNDAMENTALIST REVIVAL IN NA HOMESTEAD?

Na Homestead is part of Yongning county, Yang He township, fifteen kilometers south of Yinchuan city in central Ningxia.[1] Traveling south on the main north-south highway linking Yinchuan with Wuzhong city and southern Ningxia, one finds a dirt road leading off to Na Homestead at the main intersection of the Yongning county seat. Separated from the intersection by three kilometers of fields, Na Homestead is a somewhat isolated, formerly walled community of mud houses clustered around a central mosque *(qing zhen si)*. The sloping eaves of the mosque rising up above the flat-roofed houses are visible from the road, providing a striking visual contrast with other surrounding communities.

This compact collection of households comprises nine teams that are almost 100 percent Hui, a rarity in central and northern Ningxia, where Hui are thinly distributed among the majority Han population. Yongning county is only 12.9 percent Hui, a relatively small minority in contrast to neighboring Lingwu county in the southeast, which is 47 percent Hui, and southern Jingyuan county, which is 97 percent Hui (the highest concentration of Hui in one county in China).

Just north of the all-Hui community in Na Homestead, separated by about two kilometers of fields, is another collection of households belonging to the village administratively and containing two teams (Teams 1 and 11) of mixed Han and Hui. All 22 households (264 people) of the Han families belonging to Na Homestead are located in this smaller community, separate from the nine all-Hui teams. Based on 1984 statistics, Na Homestead comprises 767 households, with a total population of 3,871. Hui households number 745, amounting to more than 95 percent of the population. Over 60 percent of the Hui in the village are surnamed Na.

Religious Revitalization in Na Homestead

I first became aware of changing Hui-Han social dynamics in the village from a discussion with one of the Han villagers in Team 1. She explained: "Since 1979, we have had less and less social contact with the Hui in the other teams. There are no problems between us, but the Hui are more devout [*qian-cheng*] now and less willing to come to our homes and visit or borrow tools. We raise pigs in our yards and eat pork, so they are afraid it will influence their religion [*yingxiang tamende jiaomen*]." Like many conservative northwest Hui, most Na villagers have become more conscientious about Islamic purity (*qing*) through attention to dietary restrictions. In order to preserve one's *qing zhen* lifestyle, conservative Hui who do visit Han homes accept, at the most, sunflower seeds or fruit when offered by their host. When Han come to their homes, Hui offer them tea from a separate set of cups that the family itself does not use, lest the family *qing zhen* utensils become contaminated. Hui are also free to offer Han prepared dishes of lamb and beef, but the Han cannot reciprocate. Gradually this imbalance of obligation leads to less and less contact. Increased scrupulous attention to the culturally defined notions of Islamic purity—especially in a culture that traditionally places high priority on extending social courtesies—has increasingly limited Hui-Han social interaction. This is not surprising. Careful Hui attention to this tradition maintains the purity/impurity power reversal in which Han, who can never fully reciprocate Hui hospitality by offering them social prestations and offerings of food in return, are placed in an inferior power relation to the Hui. As Marcel Mauss has so eloquently described, "The thing given is not inert" ([1925] 1967, 10), and Hui refusal to receive Han gifts places them in a position of moral superiority, though they may occupy a socially inferior and marginal position in the socioeconomic and ethnic context of northwest China.

This rise in religious activity and conservatism in Na Homestead stands in stark contrast to the closed mosques and restricted religious behavior common elsewhere in China since the 1958 Religious System Reform Campaigns (Zongjiao Zhidu Gaige). Frequent Na-villager participation in mosque ritual is also noticeably different from the lack of popular participation in urban mosques in northern and southern China. In those areas—with the exception of holidays, where large turnouts of the Hui community are becoming common—mosques are generally frequented only by a few bearded old men sitting on benches and sunning themselves while awaiting the next call to prayer. Not so in Na Homestead.

The Hui of Na Homestead are associated with the Khufiyya brotherhood, a very popular Sufi order in Ningxia that developed from a branch of the Naqshbandiyya introduced through Central Asia in the seventeenth century. Yet Na villagers, like many Khufiyya in Ningxia, do not subscribe to the *menhuan* (schools, orders, or sects) that venerate the descendants of Sufi saints. Hence, they resemble an isolated mosque-centered Gedimu community that maintains Sufi forms of ritual. Although they regard themselves as Khufiyya, Na villagers are not connected to the other Sufi Khufiyya networks extending throughout northwest China. This is not unusual in northern Ningxia and other areas where the Khufiyya have become more decentralized. While they are thus not closely connected to other Khufiyya orders, their Sufi background continues to influence daily life and ritual.

On any weekday morning, at least 150 people kneel at prayer on the hard floor of the mosque an hour before dawn. One wintry morning, I arose from my warm *kang* (heated brick platform bed) to the call for prayer (heard throughout the village) at 6:00 A.M. and walked over to the mosque. In this season, the ground is frozen, and the temperature hovers around thirteen to fourteen degrees below zero Centigrade. I was surprised to find the large prayer hall full of men when I arrived, illustrating that, though China was on one time zone, these villagers lived life according to a different clock. Many villagers prayed five times a day and followed the Islamic calendar, suggesting that the rhythm of their lives was much different than for the rest of China. As the service began, two or three stragglers came running up, hastily donning fleece-lined coats over their bare backs and removing their boots as they entered the prayer hall. They prayed in unison on the bare concrete floor for the duration of the thirty- to forty-five-minute service, some of them kneeling on lamb pelts or on small carpets purchased from a Zhejiang factory that makes the colorful rayon Islamic-style prayer mats sold throughout the northwest. Because of the sermon, the main prayer on Fridays (*zhuma ri*) generally lasts over an hour. This differed markedly from mosques in other parts of China, where latecomers straggled in at the last minute, knowing they could always "make up prayers" (*bu li*) later.

One official count of attendance on a Thursday morning in January 1985 recorded 141 worshipers, including 31 between fourteen and fifty years of age. On Fridays, an attendance of up to 500 worshipers is not unusual (13 percent of the village), with an average of 100–200 praying at least once in the mosque during the week. On holidays, the whole village, including women and children, turns out. While some say that participation has not yet reached 1950 levels, this is perceived as a new peak *(gaofeng)* since 1949 of religious activity among the Hui.[2] During the month of Ramadan in 1984, the mosque reported that one-third of all households had at least one member who took part in the fast. I have also visited concentrated Hui areas such as Linxia Hui autonomous prefecture, Gansu province, and southern Ningxia where 100 percent of the villagers above the age of twelve (boys) or nine (girls) fast. The level of participation in the fast among Na villagers is still considered rather high in a predominantly Han area.

Mosque income *(sifei)* derived from offerings *(nietie)* has also risen dramatically. According to the mosque's own careful accounting records, in the last two years it averaged over 20,000 yuan (U.S.$6,700) annual income from offerings. Based on an outside study, over a four-month period during 1984 and 1985, offerings of grain produce, goods, or money totaled 8,997.23 yuan (about U.S.$3,000). An economic survey of expenditures of 113 Hui households in Na Homestead revealed that average giving to the mosque was 47 yuan per household, or 8.40 yuan per person in 1984. If this average is applied to the entire Hui community of the village, then the mosque's total income last year was well over 32,500 yuan (U.S.$10,833). The money supports the staff of seven *ahong* (imam or "teacher"), including one "teaching" or head *ahong* (*kaixue ahong* or *jiaozhang*) and four student *ahong* (*halifat*, from *khalifa*, "successor," or *manla*, from *mullah*), and the daily upkeep of the mosque.[3] Offerings are given during the three main religious holidays and to individual *ahong* when they read the Qur'an at weddings, funerals, and naming ceremonies. Giving at funerals by the family to guests and to the mosque ranges from 100 to 1,000 yuan. As much as 2,500 yuan has been reported when the status of the deceased was extremely high.

On one holiday celebrated in Na Homestead, the "Prophet's Day" or "Muhammad's Birthday" (Shengji) on 7 December 1984, I witnessed offerings brought by children and adults—bags of flour or rice and fistfuls of money. A group of mosque officials dutifully registered each offering according to amount, name, and team number. Gifts totaled three thousand kilograms of wheat, twenty-five hundred kilograms of rice, and 300 yuan (U.S.$100), equal to approximately 3,313 yuan (U.S.$1,100). None of the donated money is required for the restoration of the mosque building *(qianliang)*. The mosque has received over 90,000 yuan (U.S.$30,000) from the State Nationalities Affairs Commission since it was identified as a national monument in 1981. Dating from the Ming dynasty's Jiajing period (1522–1567), it is the oldest remaining mosque in Ningxia.[4]

Donations to the mosque come from a village considered fairly poor by neighboring village standards, with an average annual income of 300 yuan (U.S.$100) per household.[5] Average per capita annual income in Yongning county for 1982 was substantially higher, 539 yuan according to the Population Census Office. Poor households (*pinkun hu*) occupy 2 percent of the village. Mosque income, however, does not necessarily reflect total giving per household. The mosque also received income from outside the village, such as from the state or from other Muslim communities. A study of seventeen households from three different villages belonging to different Islamic orders found that, out of an annual average income of 96.67 yuan, 8.96 yuan (9.26 percent) was given to religious concerns in 1980.[6]

The Ascendance of Quranic Education

A decrease in public school enrollment, and an increase in children studying the Qur'an in private *madrassah* (religious schools) attached to local mosques, is another phenomenon that concerns local cadres. This growing interest in pursuing religious education has not yet reached large proportions among the Hui in Na Homestead since only ten school-age children were not attending public school in 1985. Instead, they are studying the Qur'an at home privately. There are four officially permitted *manla* (students preparing to become *ahong*) in the village. In more heavily populated Hui areas, however, this is becoming a more noticeable practice. In Guyuan county, Jiefangxiang (Liberation township), only 12 out of 104 school-age children in the village are attending school, and 27 of those not in school are studying the Qur'an in the mosque.

In a *China Daily* front-page article entitled "Keep Rural Girls in School" (1987), Liu Su, vice governor of Gansu province, reported that, out of 157,300 school-aged children not in school in Gansu, 85 percent were girls. Children leave school for a variety of reasons, including the farm's need for income-producing labor under the newly introduced responsibility system. Yet many Hui point to traditional Islamic views that have made them reluctant to send their children, especially daughters, to public schools.

When asked about such reluctance, Na Homestead parents expressed doubts about "the value of learning Chinese and mathematics." "It would be much more useful," I was told by one mother, "for our children to learn the Qur'an, Arabic, and Persian." If a child excelled, he or she might become a *manla* and eventually perhaps an *ahong*. Their status in the village would be much higher than the average middle school or even high school graduate, as would their income (estimated at 100 to 500 yuan a month for a well-known teaching *ahong*). Children who are in poor health are often kept at home to study the Qur'an. In large families with more than one son, generally one child is encouraged to study to become an *ahong*. Although the government officially allows each mosque to support from two to four full-time *manla*—who should be at least eighteen years old and junior middle school graduates—many younger children study at home without official approval.

Ningxia, as the only autonomous region for China's Hui Muslims, tends to monitor *ahong* training and religious practice more closely than other areas where Hui are concentrated. In Yunnan's Weishan Yi and Hui autonomous county, several mosques had over 20 resident *manla* studying under well-known *ahong*. In Gansu's Linxia Hui autonomous prefecture, at the South Great Mosque there were over 130 full-time students. In Linxia city's Bafang district, where most of the Hui are concentrated, there were at least 60 full-time *manla* in each mosque. Mirroring the spiritual importance of Mecca and the centrality of theological learning of the Iranian city of Qum for China's Hui Muslims, Linxia's famous mosques and scholars attract students from all over China.[7]

Renowned mosques in Yunnan's Shadian and Weishan counties tend to attract students from throughout the southwest, including Hainan island. At an ordination (*chuanyi*) service I attended at the Xiao Weigeng Mosque in Weishan county in February 1985, the ten graduates included one Hainan island student and six students from outside the county who had studied there for five years. The Hainan student had a brother studying the Qur'an in Beijing. The next class admitted thirty students, ten from the local village, ten from other villages, ten from outside the county, including one from outside Yunnan. The fact that these *manla* travel long distances to study under celebrated *ahong* demonstrates that national ties continue to link disparate Hui communities. It also reveals the growing importance of religious education in the countryside.

THE RISE IN ISLAMIC CONSERVATISM

The increasing conservatism of the Hui in Na Homestead, noted by the Han villager above, is apparent to any visitor. Smoking and drinking are now prohibited in the village for the simple reason that "the elders are against it" (*laoren fandui*). When pressed for their reasons, the elders invariably refer to the dictates of maintaining a pure (*qing zhen*) lifestyle according to Islamic prescriptions. According to the local store clerk, very few people buy cigarettes anymore. Smoking and drinking were commonplace in the village during the Cultural Revolution. The clerk now keeps only a few bottles of low-alcohol-content "champagne" (*xiangbin jiu*) under a back shelf for rare occasions when outside cadres need to be entertained. When young men want to drink or smoke, they go outside the village to the Yongning county seat or to Yinchuan city. It came as quite a shock to the elders of this village when visited by foreign Muslim "friendship delegations" who openly drank or smoked.

While only the older women wear the head covering (*gaitou*) associated with the Muslim custom of purdah,[8] younger Hui admit that male-female interaction is much more restricted than in neighboring Han villages. Men and women rarely work together in the fields, and the majority of marriages are arranged through introductions. In a survey of fifty newly married young couples, only eight (16 percent) met their partners on their own, without an intermediary. The average courtship period was less than five months for 76 percent of the couples surveyed. While some younger Hui complain about this conservatism, change in the near future appears unlikely. In fact, "modern" marriage practice has continued to decline since the high point of male-female "free love" (*lian'ai ziyou*) encouraged during the Cultural Revolution. The only "love match" I knew of took place between a local Na villager who had met his bride while studying for two years at a vocational training college. One of a handful to receive higher education above the middle school level, the case of this young intellectual was anything but typical.

When I asked several Hui villagers if there was anyone in their team who did not believe in Islam (*buxinjiao de huizu*), I was always told that they did not know of anyone. By contrast, in urban areas such as Yinchuan, the capital of Ningxia region, Hui youth often openly discuss their belief in Marxism or secularism and the lack of relevance of Islam for their lives. Several have told me that they believe in neither Marxism nor Islam, but in "individualism," or only in "making money." This attitude is even more prevalent in cities like Beijing and Shanghai where urbanized Hui youth are becoming attracted to Western ideas. One Shanghai Hui youth married to a Han woman told me: "Buddhism is for peasants, Islam is for old Huihui, and Christianity is for those interested in the West."

In Na Homestead, however, even the local cadres who say they do not believe in Islam and belong to the Communist Party always invite the *ahong* to read the Qur'an at their family weddings, funerals, and parents' deathdays. The chairman of one team in Na Homestead, a prominent Party member, openly invited the *ahong* and participated in the reciting of the Qur'an at his son's wedding.

Perhaps of greatest concern to local Party officials in Ningxia is the lack of participation in the local Party apparatus and the "problem of Party members who believe in religion" (*dangyuan xinjiaode wenti*). There are sixty-three Party members in Na Homestead, representing only 1.7 percent of the total population. Of those sixty-three, twenty-two publicly worship at the mosque and say they believe in Islam. Three of these believers go to mosque five times daily, and one has officially quit his Party membership in order to become an *ahong*.[9] Many of these Muslim Party members have at one time been team-level chairmen, and four have been brigade (*da dui*) Party vice secretaries in the past. The United Front Department estimated that 70–80 percent of Party members in Hui villages take part in religious activities and about 10 percent openly admit they are believers in Islam (MacInnis 1989, 259). When I asked one Hui state cadre who openly prayed at the mosque in another city about this contradiction, he rationalized, "I believe in Marxism in my head, but I believe in Islam in my heart." Mason (1929) remarkably reported a similar explanation offered by Confucian Hui officials in the Qing dynasty: "It may be added that military officials in the Manchu times were not altogether exempt from certain ceremonies of worship at temples; but Moslems seem to have made a compromise with conscience and went with the rest; one said to me long ago in Szechwan [Sichuan] that though his bodily presence was there, and he shared in the prostrations, his heart was not there, so it didn't matter!"[10]

Local cadres give many reasons for religious behavior among Hui Party officials. In Na Homestead, it is explained that 80 percent entered the Party in the 1950s and are too old and uninvolved with Party affairs. As they grow older, these veteran Party members are becoming more interested in religion. Yet it should be noted that no one has been admitted to the Party in Na Homestead since October 1976.

Involvement of Party members in religious activities, state support of mosque reconstruction, and recent visits by foreign Muslims and guests to the historic mosque have been interpreted by some Hui as the Party's encouragement of religion. Na villagers have been quoted as saying: "Whoever does not believe in religion does not do good works [*xingshan*] and does not carry out the policy of the Communist Party." Acceptance of the Party's position on atheism has been declining in religious minority nationality areas, to the extent that some youths accept Islamic doctrines such as the creation of the world in place of scientific materialism. These trends have led many local cadres to argue that there has indeed been a revival of Islam among the Hui to the point of fundamentalist "fanaticism" (*kuanre* or *zongjiao re*, "religious heat").

Islamic Conservatism and Government Policy

What is the official response to these accelerating trends in religious conservatism? Based on several interviews with local and state officials, I find three approaches. (1) More conservative cadres say these religious activities and excesses should be stopped (*shoule*) immediately. (2) Others propose that political thought-reform campaigns should be taught again in the countryside to correct these misunderstandings of Party policy. (3) More moderate cadres would suggest reforms in the local Party itself rather than changes in policy; they point to recent research by Chinese sociologists that suggests Islam's influence is only superficial and is not important to youths and others in the village who are pressured to conform by mosque leaders and claim that Islamic activities merely represent maintenance of minority customs, not real religious belief.

To support this last position, a Ningxia Academy of Social Sciences (NASS) survey on religious belief was conducted among sixty Hui secondary school graduates under thirty years old; fourteen said they did not believe in Islam, while forty-six professed either complete or partial belief. Of those who did not believe, five expressed belief in Marxism, four in "individualism" (*geren zhuyi*), and five in both Marxism and Islam. Of those forty-six who said they believed in Islam, twenty-six expressed complete adherence, while the others professed only partial belief and unbelief. When the twenty-six believers were asked if this meant that they believed in an afterlife, heaven or hell, only one said he did. At one point, the young believers were asked:

"When you say you believe in Islam, can it be that what you believe is that you shouldn't smoke, shouldn't drink, shouldn't eat pork, and should go to mosque on holidays and give offerings?" The natural response was "That's exactly what we mean."

The NASS researchers cite this response to support their claim that few young people have "objective" reasons for believing in religion. Objective reasons, they maintain, would include beliefs in an afterlife, in the involvement of God in personal prosperity, and in Islam as the right religion. The researchers argue that most believe in Islam for "subjective" reasons, in which they include social pressure and ethnic background. The most common "subjective" answer given was: "We believe in Islam because we are Hui." This response, and the fact that over 70 percent of those who attend daily prayer service are over fifty years old, demonstrates that religion is unpopular among the young, according to the researchers. When the Hui villagers say they believe in religion, according to these observers, they have confused the influence of ethnic customs with Islamic belief.

Moderate cadres point out that many social benefits have derived from the relaxed religious policy. One of the most important advantages is the opportunity to use the mosque for disseminating Party and government policy. Imams have begun to preach both government policy and religious practice at the Friday prayer in a new style of preaching called *chuan jiang* (combined talks). Since 1979, the crime rate and social-disturbance problems that I was told were "fairly messy" (*bijiao luan*) in Na Homestead have declined dramatically. Wang Xiren of the Ningxia Academy of Social Sciences reported that only 0.06 percent of the whole Hui population had been charged with committing crimes, while the Han crime rate was 0.1 percent (Zhang and Zhang 1986). The government's family-planning policy and other reforms have been carried out quite effectively compared with other areas, a fact attributed to the willingness of the *ahong* to permit use of the mosque for promoting public policies. On 17 November 1984, the government invited sixty-three *ahong* from throughout the region to gather at the Yinchuan Hotel, where they were praised and encouraged in their efforts to raise the educational level of Hui in their areas, a ceremony reported in the national press ("Meeting Praising the Services of Islam" 1984). Most important, the religious policy has instilled in the villagers a new openness to dialogue with the Communist Party—a trust strongly shaken during the Cultural Revolution's "ten years of internal confusion" (*shinian neiluan*).

Moderate cadres argue that the solution to the misinterpretation of the Party's free-religion policy does not lie in restricting religious activity or returning to the reform campaigns of the Gang of Four period. Rather, they advocate resolving the problems and contradictions in the local Party apparatus whose inactivity and "paralysis" (*tanhuan*) is responsible for these false conceptions of Party policy. Errant Party members who openly believe should be educated or asked to resign. While the Party policy is one of "freedom of religion," it should be clearly explained that the Party itself does not promote religion and still regards it as an "opiate" that deters the masses from better production.[11] As one cadre in Yinchuan explained to me: "The Hui are allowed to maintain their ethnic customs that are influenced by Islamic traditions, but religion and ethnicity are two separate matters and should not be confused."

THE REROOTING OF IDENTITY IN NA HOMESTEAD

The policy of clearly distinguishing between religion and ethnicity is becoming the most important formula applied to the minority-religion question. This distinction is useful to cadres working in urban or Han-majority areas among minorities who no longer practice their traditional religion but who maintain certain ethnic customs. Many Beijing and Shanghai Hui who do not practice Islam continue to maintain Islamic dietary restrictions and celebrate traditional Islamic holidays. The distinction between ethnicity and religion is particularly evident among Hui along the southeastern coast; these recently recognized Hui eat pork and practice Chinese folk religion. What might be applicable to ethnic policy in these areas, however, does not make sense for the majority of Hui in the northwest. Nevertheless, this policy is promoted in these areas, as the cadre's comment above demonstrates.

The distinction between Hui ethnicity and Islam was an important corrective to the traditional Chinese idea that Islam was the "Hui religion" (*Hui jiao*), rather than a world religion in which most Hui believe. Controversy has arisen recently, however, over the idea that the Hui can be entirely separated from the Islamic religious tradition. This debate came to a head during the 1983 Northwest Five Province Islamic Studies discussion meetings held in Yinchuan. Conferees concluded that, while the Hui nationality must be distinguished from Islam analytically, nevertheless Hui cultural heritage has been intimately influenced by Islam. Without Islam, there would be no Hui minority.

The policy of distinguishing between religion and ethnicity arises from a Chinese Marxist approach to ethnicity that tends to view ethnic consciousness, customs, and religion as circumstantial, epiphenomenal traits. These cultural traits are often class based and assume importance only in the competition for scarce resources. Like Fredrik Barth's "situational" approach (Barth 1969), ethnic identity will lose its relevance when socioeconomic conditions change and eventually should disappear with erosion of class- or interest-based differences. Yet, for Na villagers, the religiosity is not instrumental (see Fabian 1982); it is part of their very sense of self and identity.

Islam is integral to their self-perception as Hui—it is part of how they see and construct their world.[12] What some might regard as a revival of Islamic fundamentalism in Hui communities is, I argue, but one aspect of a general return to and reinterpretation of their ethnoreligious roots. The resurgence in the countryside has come about in the midst of rapid socioeconomic change in the last decade since the liberalization of religious and economic policies. Current developments in Na Homestead illustrate that accepted cultural meanings of Hui identity are becoming more relevant in the social context under liberalized government policies that allow freer expression of Hui identity.

ETHNORELIGIOUS ROOTS

When I made my first visit to Na Homestead during a short 1983 trip through central Ningxia, I was immediately presented with the story that the Na villagers like to tell about their ancestry. This origin myth was often repeated to me throughout 1984 and 1985:

> We are all Muslims in this village. Most of us are surnamed Na. The Chinese character for Na is not in the classical book of Chinese surnames, and this proves that we are descended not from Han Chinese but from a foreign Muslim from the west. Our ancestor was none other than Nasredin, the son of Sai Dianchi (Sayyid 'Ajall), the Muslim governor of Yunnan under the Yuan dynasty. Nasredin had four sons, and those sons changed their names to Chinese under the Ming government's ethnic-oppression policy. The four sons adopted the surnames "Na, Su, La, Ding" corresponding to the four Chinese characters that made up his name. This is why so many northwest Huihui in the Ming dynasty had these surnames. The son surnamed Na moved to this place and had five sons, of which we still have five Na leading lineages [*men*] in the village. There is also a Na village in Yunnan province, Tonghua county, where some of our relatives live.[13]

Based partly on historical records and partly on oral traditions that may or may not be accurate, this story is nevertheless critical for illuminating Na self-understanding. The ability to trace ancestral origins to the five leading Na lineages is an important aspect of personal status in Na Homestead. Those surnamed Na are buried together in one part of the large cemetery connected to the mosque and village. The cultural reckoning of their descent from an ancestor not only foreign but Muslim is critical for Na self-identity.

The Cultural Organization of Na Identity

The cultural organization of space in Hui villages and homes distinguishes them from their Han neighbors. Hui homes are often decorated with brightly painted mirrors depicting Mecca or Medina as well as ornate quranic calligraphic drawings and paintings in Chinese and Arabic. These mirrors and texts are generally placed where Han traditionally would have their ancestral altars. Hui homes, like those of the Han, usually open to the south, but for the Hui there is generally no communication or doorways linking the side homes of the sons with the central hall of the parents. Hui claim that this reflects a more conservative perspective because the women are more secluded from their in-laws. The gates of Hui homes are less ornate than Han and not fixed according to *fengshui* (geomantic) principles. Hui also say their houses are cleaner than Han houses. Unlike most Han, the Hui usually do not allow domestic animals like dogs or chickens into the home. Hui often set aside places for ritual washing, and some even build separate small prayer rooms for the women to use. Hui pay scrupulous attention to order and cleanliness in their homes. I turn to Mildred Cable and Francesca French for a pithy description of northwestern Hui homes where they spent much time, which they contrasted with Han and Central Asian Muslim homes:

> In the home of the Tungan [Hui] there is neither shrine nor ancestral tablet but its pattern is as defined as the ancestor-controlled home of the Confucian, only here the scheme of life is ordered by the rules and regulations of the Islamic faith. Five times a day, beginning with the hour of sunrise, the man must prostrate himself with face toward Mecca and recite the liturgy of the hour. He never dares to neglect the endless ceremonial purifications which his religion demands, and for one full month of each year he observes the exacting and rigid fast of the Ramazan. . . . A visit to a Turki home is quite unlike a stay in a Tungan house. In the latter all is order, thrift and propriety, for existence has progressed on definite and established lines until it has mastered the technique of orderly conduct. Among the Turkis all is noise and turmoil. Gay clothing, swinging draperies and light muslin veiling combine with the rapid talk of girls and the gutturals of men's voices to fill the air with noise and movement. (Cable and French [1942] 1987, 166, 168)

The central location of the mosque in virtually every Hui village marks its importance as the focal point of the village in ritual and social organization. A Han temple, by contrast, is traditionally located wherever the *fengshui* determines best, which may place it either within or well outside the village. Those who maintain Han temples are not necessarily regarded by the locals as leaders or integral to the affairs of the village. The *ahong* in a Hui village, however, are regarded as the primary actors. They must approve every marriage and are intimately acquainted with the villagers' lives. Most *ahong* are regularly invited to Hui homes for meals on a revolving basis (*chuanfan*). The *ahong* also often assist in resolving local conflicts. For example, I witnessed the intervention by a Na village *ahong* in one dispute over the construction of a water pipe that one villager thought was being installed too close to his yard. If the pipe broke, the spillage would ruin his grain storage. As the argument escalated to the point of violence, several villagers ran to get the *ahong* to help settle the matter. When he arrived, the dispute calmed down considerably.

Unlike their Han neighbors, Hui often build their graveyards either adjacent to or within the confines of their village. This land is held in common by the community and often frequented by the villagers for regular prayer and meditation. Ekvall also noticed this unique aspect of the Hui social landscape: "The Moslems take great pains to make their graveyards like parks or semi-public groves, which become places for informal religious meditation and acquire a peculiar odor of sanctity. Among the Chinese the graveyards are open, and there is no prejudice against allowing sheep or cattle to graze over them—in fact, they are in a way community pastures" (Ekvall 1939, 23). Lattimore described two Hui graveyards outside Huhehot, Inner Mongolia, where "good Moslems" are buried in grave sites separate from the "backsliders" (Lattimore 1929, 17). In Na Homestead, an average of four to eight individuals went to the graveyard (shangfen) every day to pray, with thirty or more visitors on Fridays. Someone from the extended household made at least one trip a week to the graveyard. Hui do not believe in ghosts and gods like their Han neighbors and are not afraid of the graveyards at night. A popular Hui folk saying is: "When on the road the safest place for Hui to sleep is the Han graveyard; the ghosts won't bother us because we don't believe in them, and local Han bandits won't bother us because they are too afraid of the ghosts."

The role of the graveyard among the Hui and the influence of the ancestors buried there resembles the place of traditional temples dotting the Taiwan countryside. Women often take their daughters to these temples, seeking otherworldly help for them to have sons, or resolving financial problems. Miracles also are known to occur in the vicinity of these folk Chinese shrines, and they influence the natural powers of the earth, bringing good weather and fruitful harvests. Local communities may adopt nonlineage ghosts and historic heroes as patron deities over time. Similarly, among the Hui, especially well-known deceased religious leaders or hajji are often honored with local tombs (tu gongbei) that are patronized like these traditional Han temples. Deceased Sufi saints are built more elaborate tombs and shrines. The value attached to these local symbols has often been viewed as a threat to the state. While criticizing the Jahriyya shaykh (sheikh) Ma Zhenwu in 1958, prosecutors representing the state recorded the following ways in which he supposedly extorted money from his followers: "Before the Liberation, Ma Chen-wu even sold his hair, beard, the dirt from the 'kung-pei,' his household firewood ashes, dry bread, small pieces of his ragged clothes, and even his own manure to the Hui masses as 'miracle drugs' to cure their diseases. By so doing, he not only has swindled big sums of money but also has caused many deaths" (MacInnis 1989, 172).

While Hui do not have any known institutionalized practice of geomancy (fengshui) with professionals skilled in selecting sites for buildings and graves, it is interesting that many of these graves are placed in similar locations. Many Hui graveyards and tombs are on the sides of hills with a stream or plain below. The most notable example is the graveyard and gongbei complex at North mountain, in Linxia, Gansu. Following their own Islamic customs, Hui arrange their graves on a north-south axis, with the entrance to tombs almost always to the south. The body lies with the head to the north, the feet to the south, and the face turned west, toward Mecca.

Near the famous Bell Tomb of a Muslim saint buried outside Canton, there is a tombstone for the "Pure and True Religious Leader Ma *Ahong* by the Name of Yunting" (*qing zhen jiaozhang Ma lao ahheng zi Yunting*) dated 1939. It is engraved with the following epitaph: "Another Home for Purity and Truth (Islam)" (*qing zhen bieshe*). This marks the graveyard, and the ancestors buried there, as a powerful focal place in the *qing zhen* Hui village.

Marriage Exchange and Ethnoreligious Identity

Marital practices are an important indicator of changing social relations and ethnic solidarity. Growing prosperity in Na Homestead has led to an increase in the bride wealth given at marriage and a decrease in intermarriage with the Han. In Na Homestead, there were many Hui-Han intermarriages during the Cultural Revolution, when young Hui were strongly encouraged to marry Han as an indication that they rejected "local ethnic chauvinism" (*difang minzu zhuyi*). With the increasing conservatism in Na Homestead in recent years, however, intermarriages have been rare. The most recent intermarriage occurred in 1984; a Han woman living outside the village on the market street in the Yongning county seat married into a Hui family. This is typical of Hui-Han intermarriage in the northwest. Hui families take in Han women but rarely permit Hui women to marry out. The village chairman could remember only one marriage between a Han man and Hui woman, which took place ten years earlier. A Han villager told me of a thirty-seven-year-old Han man who married a thirty-five-year-old Hui woman in 1972. The man converted at marriage and is now regarded as a Hui. He maintains little contact with his Han relatives.

Marriage among the Hui within Na Homestead or with other rural Hui in the vicinity is the norm. Surname endogamous marriage between Na villagers still takes place—almost unheard of among the Han. Government regulations strictly prohibit endogamous marriage with someone who has a common ancestor within five generations. As more accurate government records restrict close intermarriage, the *lunzi paibie* system of marking generations by the first character of one's personal name has begun to break down only in the last two generations among the Na. The characters Wan, Yu, Zhang, Dian, and Hong mark the last five generations in Na Homestead. Surname endogamy is justified by some Hui to Han who reject this practice as unfilial because, the Hui reason, their surnames are translations of foreign surnames (e.g., Ma for Muhammad) and not indicative of familial relations. It is a different matter for Na villagers, however, who trace descent to a single ancestor.

Cross-cousin marriage, as well as marriage between matrilateral parallel cousins (*yibiao xiongmei*), is frequently practiced. The custom of "swapping relatives" (*huandui qin*), where a daughter is exchanged for a brother's son, is common in Na Homestead, as was the case in the venerable Wang Zixiao's family. He gave his daughter in marriage to his brother's son. A survey of fifty young people already married in Na Homestead showed that 4 percent were cross-cousin or matrilateral parallel cousin (*gubiao, yibiao*) marriages, with 8 percent in some kind of familial relationship with their spouses. Since dowry value was increasing throughout the rural areas in China, due to a general increase in rural income, I cannot tell if it correlated with rising surname endogamy. In general, however, Hui dowries tended to be 20–30 percent higher than Han.

Some Hui leaders believe that the preference for endogamous marriages among the Hui has led to mental illness among their offspring (*jinqin hunbing*). The Na Homestead chairman said that, in 1982, there were four cases of mentally handicapped children attributed to too close intermarriage. In one case, two malformed children were born to a household where a maternal uncle's (*jiujiu*) daughter was married to a paternal aunt's (*gumu*) son. In another household all three children were malformed, with one son dying at birth. I often encountered these mentally handicapped children (simply called *shazi,* "idiots") in Hui villages throughout the northwest.

Hui say mental retardation is a particularly serious problem in areas where certain conservative Islamic orders restrict intermarriage with Hui in other Islamic orders. Membership in various Islamic orders often significantly influences social interaction. While intermarriage between different orders of Hui is common elsewhere in China, in stronger Islamic areas of northwest China Hui prefer to marry within their own order. This is particularly true of the Jahriyya order, and, in Ningxia, Shagou, and Banqiao, *menhuan* branch members rarely intermarry.

In Chengdu, Sichuan, I met three Hui travelers from the northwest, who were easily marked by their strong Gansu accents, long beards, and distinctive dress. They were on their way to Kunming, where they planned to purchase tea; as Rossabi documented, this was an important trade niche of the Hui in this area over four hundred years ago (Rossabi 1970). Bringing the tea back to the northwest, they could sell it at a profit of 1 yuan per half kilo, averaging 300 yuan profit each trip, with three trips scheduled per year. Chengdu is a frequent stopping place for travelers from the northwest on their way to the southwest since it is the most central rail and transportation hub. This accounts for the high proportion of Hui restaurants and the large mosque in the city, despite a relatively small indigenous Hui population. The three businessmen complained that the religious fervor (*jiaomen*) at the local mosque was inadequate; they were the only ones at prayer that day. They then discussed their Islamic differences. One was a Gedimu, another a Yihewani, and the last a member of a Jahriyya Sufi order. When I asked if they would allow their children to intermarry, they themselves were somewhat surprised to learn that the Gedimu was willing to marry his child to the Yihewani but not to the Jahriyya. Neither the Yihewani nor the Jahriyya was willing to let his children marry someone from another order.

Birth Planning

The Hui minority in Ningxia follow a one-two-three policy: allowing one child in the city, two children in the countryside, and three children in mountainous or desert areas. In 1985, a law was promoted that minorities above 1 million population in urban areas would have to follow the birth-planning policies of one child only. In general, however, the Hui are often allowed to have at least one child more than their Han neighbors. This leads to not a little resentment among Han, who often feel the Hui are just the same as they and should not be given any advantages.

In rural areas where population is sparse, Hui have been known to have even more than their allotted children. One man from a village outside Guyuan told me his wife was pregnant with her ninth child. However, with the support of the *ahong* and use of the mosque for disseminating policy, birth planning has been judged relatively successful among most Hui. Infractions by the Hui tend to be judged more lightly than among the Han. I knew of one Hui village chairman with three sons and another child on the way in early 1985. A Hui villager north of Yinchuan had three daughters and was officially allowed to have one more child in order to see if he might have a son. He began spending every morning in the mosque praying for a son.

Perhaps because of this flexibility among the Hui, I heard of no female infanticide in Na Homestead or elsewhere in Ningxia. Hui villagers claimed that their Han neighbors practiced it and said they occasionally found Han female infants in the fields. Hui youth are permitted to get married two years earlier than Han, Hui girls at age eighteen and boys at twenty. I encountered several Hui weddings, however, where the bride was from fourteen to sixteen years old.

INTERNATIONAL ISLAMIC EXCHANGE

The Ningxia government is interested in promoting closer ties with foreign Muslim countries to foster economic development. In a 14 November 1984 *China Daily* interview Hei Boli, the Hui chairman of the Ningxia people's government, stated: "The delegations of the World Islamic Association that came to our region are quite impressed by the sincerity of the Party's policy of guaranteeing freedom of religious belief. Our Muslims are true believers and pay meticulous attention to Muslim customs" ("Middle East Trade Links Sought" 1984). In another article, Ye Zhikun, director of the region's economic commission, stated: "Ningxia, the home of Chinese Muslims, expects loans from Arab countries to help develop foodstuffs and light industrial goods for the Muslim world" ("Overseas Investors Sought" 1984). The government has sponsored several economic and "Muslim Friendship" delegations to the Middle East to correspond with the hajj, with the delegations including important religious leaders and well-known *ahong* fluent in Arabic.

Delegations of foreign Muslim government and religious leaders have been hosted by Ningxia and escorted to visit historic mosques in Yinchuan, Na Homestead, and Tongxin. Hui "Muslim Construction Teams" formed by collectives and encouraged by the government have been sent to Third World Muslim nations on state development projects ("Chinese Oil Workers in Iraq" 1986; "An Islamic Investment Corporation" 1986). While many of the workers are Han, several leaders are Hui, and some translators are Hui trained in the Islamic schools. The son of the current leader of the Jahriyya Shagou branch, trained in Arabic at Beijing's Foreign Language Institute, spent two years (1984–1986) in Yemen as the translator for a Chinese development project. He sought the roots of China's Naqshbandiyya Sufism in Yemen, where it is thought Ma Mingxin studied in the seventeenth century.

This exchange with the outside Muslim world and visits by foreign Muslims to Hui villages are having a profound impact on Hui ethnoreligious self-understanding. Na villagers told me that they were deeply impressed by the religious power and prestige of Islam after the first visit of foreign Muslims to their village in May 1984. Previously, they had no idea that foreign Muslims enjoyed such high levels of prestige and education. The excitement with which these foreign Muslims are greeted was evident to the Protestant missionary George Andrew (perhaps because they did not welcome him in the same way): "Itinerant mullahs from Persia, Arabia, India, Turkey, and Egypt are found, from time to time, visiting the Hwei-hwei [Hui]. . . . These visiting mullahs are greeted with great respect by the Hwei-hwei, who purchase from them copies of the Koran, prayer-caps and turbans. They not only provide them with the necessaries of life, but also bring them free-will offerings of money. They are escorted from one Hwei-hwei community to the next with great pomp and ceremony" (Andrew 1921, 45–46).

Religious knowledge of the Islamic world outside China is very limited among Na villagers and Hui throughout the northwest. I often asked if they knew of the religious differences in the Iraq-Iran conflict or the identity of Khomeini. Few people outside the city knew. Two young *halifat* in a mosque near Na Homestead who had studied in the *madrassah* for four years could not tell me why they faced west to pray. Few knew the country where Muhammad's birthplace is located. Mecca was generally known only to be in Arabia, the *Ahlabo* (the Mandarin pronunciation of *Arabic*) country west of China.

Now that Hui are becoming increasingly exposed to the Islamic world through visiting delegations and returned work teams or *hajji,* their awareness of the Islamic world is changing significantly. The Tongxin mosque *halifat* wear colorful silk turbans sent them by friends and relatives working in the Middle East or given to them by visiting Muslim delegations. While the government hopes for development assistance and increased trade through improved relations with the Middle East, many delegations are interested only in supporting religious development, mosque, and *madrassah* reconstruction. In the spring of 1986, an Arab visitor to the Central Mosque in

Yinchuan wrote out a check for U.S.$10,000 to assist its restoration and expansion.

ETHNORELIGIOUS TOURISM

The government is conscious of these unexpected results of its program, but, for the sake of improved international relations and the earning of foreign-exchange currency, it continues to promote travel to Islamic holy sites in China. Prestige associated with historic Islamic sites has led to a growing interest on the part of local cadres in developing "Muslim tourist attractions" in places like Na Homestead. While the mosque leaders are still not support-ive of the idea, economic interests are beginning to prevail. Construction was begun in 1986 on an "Islamic Hotel" (*Yisilanjiao binguan*), featuring Arab and Islamic architectural motifs. Na villagers do not want their mosque to become a tourist site like the South District Mosque in Yinchuan, which sells tickets at the gate to visitors interested in seeing the new Arab-style complex built in 1982 with government funds. The government's encouragement of tourism to foster better relations with Middle Eastern Muslim nations is an important factor influencing the ethnic identity of Na villagers, who are beginning to conceive of themselves in more international religious terms. This promotion on the part of the state is clearly evident in the introductory paragraph of the glossy pictorial *The Religious Life of Chinese Muslims,* pub-lished in English, Chinese, and Arabic, by the state-sponsored Chinese Islamic Association: "It is our wish that this pictorial will contribute to strengthening the unity among the Muslim community of China and encouraging leading Islamic personages and the rest of the Muslim commu-nity to do their bit in the socialist modernization of their motherland. At the same time, we hope this pictorial will help promote understanding and friendship between Chinese Muslims and their friends elsewhere in the world" (Chinese Islamic Association 1981, 7).

TRUTH WITHIN PURITY:
EXPRESSIONS OF NA IDENTITY

The influence of recent shifts in government policy and socioeconomic con-ditions illustrates the importance of Islam in the ethnoreligious identity of the Hui in Na Homestead. To be separated from Islam would be to cut them off from their ancestry. When I asked young Hui why they believed in Islam, the vast majority responded, "Because we are Hui," or, "Because we respect our parents and grandparents." To state-sponsored researchers, this indi-cated a confusion between customs and religion and a "subjective" belief in Islam. I would argue, however, that it demonstrates the inextricable place of Islam in Na villagers' identity as Hui.

Islam is an integral part of the identity of Na villagers—not easily distinguished from their ethnic identity. While Stalinist policy may seek assimilation through economic development and modernization, attempting to strip away Shelley's "loathsome mask" to get to the "pure" individual underneath, among the Hui just the opposite has been found to be true. As Hui continue to prosper and develop, they have become even more interested in their ethnoreligious roots. This does not represent an idealized nativism. Rising Hui interest in their Islamic and Central Asian heritage has led, dialectically, to a new revitalized identity. Instrumentalist approaches, such as Leo Despres's (1984) definition of ethnicity as a "mask of confrontation," are helpful for understanding opposition and symbolic representation, but in this case the masks are not easily removed or affixed. Interestingly enough, while seeking to employ a Stalinist policy of ethnicity that in theory should lead to the assimilation of minorities, the state, by registering the Hui as a nationality whose basic religion is Islam, has to some degree institutionalized and objectified this ethnoreligious identity. This local village now sees itself as part of a national imagined community that the state has helped to define. Policies that make a radical distinction between ethnicity and religion will serve only to alienate northwestern Hui from participation in the broader society.

While the renewed meaningfulness of Islam to the Hui might represent for some a fundamentalist revival of fanatical proportions, I argue that the unique ethnoreligious identity of these Hui communities reflects a return to ethnic roots—a rerooting, rather than a fanatic revival of Islam. The moral authority and purity (*qing*) of their identity as Hui is intimately tied to the truth (*zhen*) and authenticity of their religious heritage. Hui are motivated to take advantage of liberalized government economic and nationality policies in order to further express their understanding of *qing zhen* and its implication for their lives.

SOUTHWEST AND THE DIASPORA

The southwest includes the provinces of Yunnan, Guizhou, Sichuan, and Hunan, covering an area of approximately 1.1 million square kilometers. The first two provinces are known for their ethnic diversity as well as their historic poverty and marginality. Sichuan is a unique province, a central humid basin (the Red basin) with a population of 100 million (larger than that of Mexico!). Historically, it housed the Shu and Ba cultures but has often been isolated from the rest of China by its mountains. Hunan was historically part of the south, the site of ancient Chu culture (as mentioned by Friedman in chap. 3). Yunnan is especially remote and was only loosely joined to China for many centuries. It was traditionally considered a place of "malarial vapors" and primitive barbarians, and the Han people sent there were reluctant exiles, prisoners, soldiers, or desperate civilians.

Today, Yunnan is home to twenty-six ethnic minorities, constituting about 30 percent of its population. Ethnogeographically quite closely linked to Southeast Asia, many of the peoples of southwest China are virtually identical to people across the border in Burma, Laos, and Vietnam. Rivers known for their importance in Southeast Asia—the Mekong, Salween, and Red rivers— begin in Yunnan as the Lancang, Nu, and Hong rivers. (The Chang Jiang [Yangzi river] and the Huang He [Yellow river] also begin in Yunnan's western mountains as the Jinsha and the Dadu (one of the contributing streams). Economic ties across national borders are increasingly important now, and the region is developing rapidly. Tobacco and tea are major crops in Yunnan; Sichuan is very fertile and produces a wide range of grains, fruits, and vegetables. Along with Hunan, Sichuan is known for its peppers and—according to popular stereotypes—fiery revolutionaries.

Diaspora is a term commonly used for the forced migration of the Jews from a central homeland out into the world, but, with time, it has acquired a broader significance as a term for any substantial movement of a people away from their natal home. The *Chinese diaspora* refers to the great and steady migration of Chinese beyond the national borders of their homeland from the nineteenth century to the present. The causes for this migration are complex, but a significant political consequence is the global character of contemporary Chinese identity. And so it is that the definition of *Chineseness* has broadened considerably, as has the network of sentiment that draws substantial investment by wealthy overseas Chinese to the Mainland, while this same investment pulls Chinese consciousness out beyond the limits of an authoritarian state.—Eds.

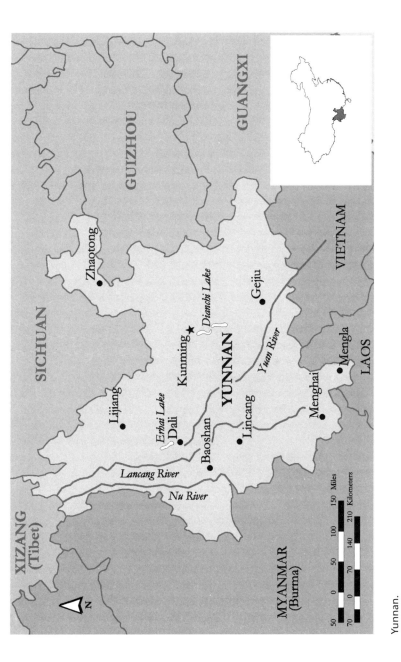

Yunnan.

7

Town and Village Naxi Identities
in the Lijiang Basin

This chapter, like the one that follows, was written specifically for this volume, as a contribution to readers' understanding of the relation between national and local cultures. Pulling out information about the setting of her research on plural medical systems, the anthropologist Sydney White describes the seat of the Lijiang Naxi autonomous county, called Dayanzhen (in a Mandarin approximation of the local Naxi pronunciation). This remote area, historically serving as a market for people traveling between Tibet and Kunming, is more prosperous than its marginal position might imply. The Naxi are known for their political astuteness and for being a relatively "advanced" and educated ethnic group. White's ethnography discloses the many ways in which identities are constructed in Lijiang and calls attention to the subtle movements of class in their determination. Some of these ways will seem very familiar to readers who know about other areas of China; some will seem quite unique, the consequence of the particular mix of environment, history, and ethnicity that obtains in this area.

White's essay also raises very important questions about the relation between ethnic minorities and the Chinese Communist Party while casting light on the political and ideological mechanisms through which the Party center affects the ethnic margins. It is because of the curious politics of long-standing Naxi loyalty to the Party that White's account may be read quite profitably alongside Mary Erbaugh's study (chap. 10) of the Hakka contribution to the Chinese Revolution.—Eds.

One of the most pervasive issues in contemporary China studies is the nature of the relation between the state and local society. China scholars are very much aware that, in understanding the contours of local histories, it is important not to underestimate the role of the state, whether in its imperial (206 B.C.E.–1911 C.E.), Republican (1912–1949), or Communist (1949–) manifestations. Nonetheless, it is also clear that analyses of local identities—both ethnographically grounded and historically situated—are critical to understanding the very real diversity of experiences among citizens of the People's Republic of China (PRC). This chapter specifically addresses the experiences of one particular segment of contemporary China, the Naxi residents of the town of Dayanzhen and of the village of Tiger Springs in southwest China's Lijiang basin, at one particular moment in the last decade of the twentieth century.

The chapter begins with an overview that both problematizes and historicizes the distinctive relation between Naxi and the Chinese state. The remainder of the chapter traces the basic contours of basin Naxi identities through an examination of the key statuses through which this identity is constituted, contrasting the lived experiences of Dayanzhen townspeople with those of Tiger Springs villagers. While the town/village distinction is clearly the most salient one affecting the lives of basin Naxi (and the experiences of most PRC residents in general), a variety of other statuses—including gender, generation, economic/occupation status, education, (former) class/family background, and Party membership—are also critical in understanding the contours of Naxi identities in the basin.

These are, in essence, the same statuses that inform Han identity on a national scale. Ethnicity, in contrast, which invokes the trope of the Naxi as a "minority nationality," is a status that informs Naxi identities in ways that are significantly different from Han distinctions of regional identities.

CONTEXTUALIZING THE NAXI: HISTORY AND POLITICS

While Naxi are officially classified as a minority, they are unquestionably in the majority within the Lijiang area, constituting approximately 250,000 of the 300,000 total population of Lijiang county. Most Naxi live within the bounds of what is now Lijiang Naxi autonomous county, in the northwestern corner of Yunnan province. The county seat is Dayanzhen, usually referred to by outsiders as Lijiang, and it has a population of approximately sixty thousand. Dayanzhen occupies the center of the seventy-four-hundred-foot Lijiang basin, above which towers the more than eighteen-thousand-foot Jade Dragon Snow mountain (Yulong Xueshan). Lijiang county extends mostly to the north and to the west of Dayanzhen, its borders determined by the sideways-S-shaped curve of the Golden Sands river (Jinsha Jiang) on its route to join the Yangzi river from Tibet. Owing to the uplift of the Himalayas, the topography of northwestern Yunnan in general is characterized by numerous snowcapped mountains and deep river gorges, with elevations ranging from approximately four to eighteen thousand feet.

The Lijiang basin represents the historical and political heartland of Naxi culture as well as a part of Naxi society that has been considerably exposed to and influenced by Chinese culture over the past millennium.[1]

Even after centuries of Chinese influence, Naxihua (Naxi language), a Tibeto-Burman language, still serves as the lingua franca among Naxi and the several other nationalities who live in Naxi-predominant areas; it also serves as a primary marker of "insider" versus "outsider" identity.[2] Historically, most Han who have come to reside in the Lijiang area have quickly learned that it was to their advantage to learn to speak Naxihua and to learn Naxi "folk customs" (*fengsu xiguan*) as well.

Naxi, like Tibetans, are believed to have been originally a "Qiang" people from the Qinghai plateau. Contemporary Han and Naxi historians estimate that the ancestors of contemporary Naxi migrated to the Lijiang area approximately fourteen hundred years ago, during the Tang dynasty (618–907 C.E.). Geographically, Naxi were sandwiched between the powerful non- Chinese Nanzhao state in the Dali basin to the south, the periodically powerful Tibetans in the mountains to the northwest, and the raid-prone Yi (as they are now referred to) peoples in the mountains to the northeast. While renowned as fearless fighters, Naxi were nevertheless quite conscious (at least as depicted in contemporary ethnohistoric accounts) of their relatively small population and consequent vulnerability.

Beginning in the Yuan dynasty (1206–1368 C.E.), the Naxi "kingdom" began a tribute relationship with the imperial state, under the terms of its *tusi* system, which entailed the formation of a two-tiered structure of elites and commoners in the kingdom. Exposure to Chinese culture was later facilitated by the in-migration of imperial armies during both the Ming (1368–1644 C.E.) and the Qing (1644–1911 C.E.) dynasties. These soldiers were stationed in the Lijiang area and frequently married Naxi women. Naxi were formally incorporated into the Chinese empire in 1723, during the Qing dynasty, under the system of "regular government" (*gaituguiliu*).[3] It has been suggested by some scholars that this historical shift had tremendous ramifications in reshaping Naxi social organization, particularly Naxi gender practices, along then-prevailing imperial Chinese norms, according to which women were the center of domesticity and bound to the inner quarters of the home. In addition to these normative Chinese practices, basin Naxi culture has historically been influenced by Buddhism in both Chinese and Tibetan forms, by Daoism, by Tibetan Bon practices, and by Chinese popular cultural practices.

Contemporary Naxi society in the basin manifests the unmistakable legacy of former imperial practices, despite widespread stereotypes in both Chinese popular culture and among visiting foreigners that Lijiang Naxi are "matriarchal."[4] Patrilineal descent, ancestor veneration, and clan exogamy, along with patrilocal residence, are the kinship and marriage norms that continue to shape Lijiang basin Naxi social structure. Arranged marriages were common before 1949, as were nonpatrilineally related cousin marriages (both of which were also common among Han in Kunming). Because many normative rites and rituals of the imperial era persist in the contemporary Lijiang basin today, it is difficult to determine what distinguishes many aspects of Naxi social structure from, for example, the social structure of Han Chinese cultures in surrounding Yunnan or neighboring Sichuan (at least in terms of rural Han practices).[5] With respect to gender, Naxi women consequently have borne the same official structural marginality as Han women given traditional norms. Although their status has been elevated by the changes of the last fifty years, Naxi women still consider their lot to be a hard one. However, this has to do with the interface between Han Chinese cultural practices and what appear to be distinctively Naxi cultural practices.

Economically, as is still the case throughout most of China, the rural/urban distinction is significant in the context of the Lijiang basin. In Dayanzhen, there is a long-standing practice of family-based small-scale entrepreneurialism among both men and women since Dayanzhen has for centuries been an important stop on the trade route between Tibet and Kunming. Private entrepreneurial activity has reemerged since the 1980s. Until very recently, a great number of town residents were still employees in either state or collective work units. In the villages of the basin, the post-Mao era (1976-1985) decollectivization of the communes and implementation of the household responsibility system has ensured a return to the patrilineal extended or stem family as the basic economic and social unit (Potter and Potter 1990).

Politically, Naxi of the Lijiang basin have tended to appropriate the politics of the socialist Chinese state in playing out power struggles within their own society. Perhaps their long-standing historical experience of being geographically sandwiched between powerful empires has contributed to this ethos. From the perspective of the central government, Naxi are seen as a "relatively advanced" (*bijiao fada*) and "obedient" (*tinghua*) minority. From the perspective of both Naxi and non-Naxi residents of the Lijiang basin, they are renowned for their zealousness in demonstrating adherence to the Communist Party status quo. There is a tongue-in-cheek expression in Dayanzhen that emphasizes this quality of Naxi political expediency: "Even before Beijing has made a move [in implementing a new political campaign], Lijiang has already started" (*Beijing hai mei dong, Lijiang yijing kaishi le*). Indeed, a large percentage of Naxi (some local estimates run as high as 90 percent) became participants in the underground Communist Party in the period just before Liberation in 1949, an implicitly acknowledged strategic move to jump on the Communist bandwagon. The Lijiang basin is, to my knowledge, one of the few areas of the PRC where land reform and class labeling were carried out, not once, but twice—the reason stated by basin Naxi being that these early 1950s political movements had not been carried out with sufficient vigilance (*bu gou lihai*) the first time around. Han from Kunming who were "sent down to the countryside" (*xia xiang*) to Lijiang during the Cultural Revolution testify to the political excesses (even by Cultural Revolution standards) of the basin area. While both the Chinese state and Chinese popular culture have played powerful roles in shaping the everyday categories of cultural distinction in basin society, it is important to understand how basin Naxi have negotiated these categories in historically and culturally specific ways.

DAYANZHEN

Dayanzhen lies more or less at the center of the Lijiang basin and was the site of the administrative offices of the imperial government for the Lijiang area from at least 1253 C.E. As mentioned above, it has consequently also been the area of Lijiang Naxi society most subject to Han influence through Chinese imperial and popular culture over the centuries. As was the case in other parts of Yunnan, most Han immigrants were soldiers who arrived during the Ming dynasty from the Nanjing/Jiangsu area and were promised land by the Chinese central government in return for their services. Many Dayanzhen residents trace their ancestry to these Han soldiers who migrated to Yunnan during the Ming and Qing dynasties, subsequently marrying Naxi women. In Dayanzhen today there are many families with surnames other than He or Mu (said to be the original surnames of Naxi people). On the one hand, these families will say that they are for most intents and purposes Naxi; on the other hand, they will say that their "old home" (*laojia*) is in fact Nanjing and that they are actually Han.

Dayanzhen currently serves as the administrative center for both the county and the prefectural governments. It is a town/city characterized by two significantly different sections: the "old town" and the "new town" (see fig. 7.1). The old town (*gucheng*, lit. "ancient city") represents the "historic" Dayanzhen just described. It is typified by narrow cobblestone footpaths that lead from the central town square ("square street," or *si fang jie*) to the five different neighborhoods (formerly referred to as *villages*) that made up the original old town. Stone bridges lead over the numerous spring-water-fed streams

FIGURE 7.1
Overview of Dayanzhen and the southern part of the Lijiang basin. (*Photograph by Sydney White.*)

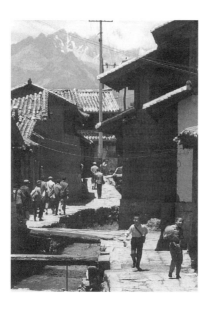

FIGURE 7.2
Street scene, Dayanzhen (old town). *(Photograph by Sydney White.)*

that flow throughout this section of the city, and Qing dynasty–style carved wooden gates open into the *siheyuan* (patiolike courtyards) of individual homes (see fig. 7.2). While plaques bearing the post-1949 formulated Chinese names of the streets are nailed above each entryway, most residents still use the pre-1949 Naxi names to refer to the streets.

In stark contrast to the tremendous aesthetic appeal of the old town is the new town (*xincheng,* or "new city"), which was built entirely after 1949. The new town is bisected by the People's Great Street (Renmin Da Jie) and is characterized by dusty wide cement streets and the Stalinesque concrete slab buildings that reflect the socialist modern architecture common throughout contemporary China. In many ways, this is the domain of the modern Chinese socialist state: all the major government and Party offices, the state-run department stores, the banks, the post office, the New China Bookstore, the (two) main hotels, and the former, Cultural Revolution–era Great Square of the People (now divided up to include various other architectural structures, including the very pink, multistoried "Children's Palace") are located in this section of Dayanzhen. Even Chairman Mao still has a central place in the (now much smaller) square in the form of one of the few larger-than-life-size statues that remain standing in the country. This is also the area of Dayanzhen where most of the Han who have migrated to the Lijiang area (primarily to work in state work units) tend to reside.

The population of Dayanzhen is approximately sixty thousand, including the "vegetable peasants" (*cai nong*[*min*], or *cainong*) who live in the villages immediately adjacent to Dayanzhen.[6] According to a number of Naxi Dayanzhen informants, who complain about the large numbers of Han

FIGURE 7.3
Naxi woman in
Dayanzhen market.
(Photograph by Sydney White.)

immigrants over the last two decades, Dayanzhen's population has approximately doubled during this period.[7]

Certain areas of the Lijiang basin, and Dayanzhen in particular, have been the centers of many centuries of entrepreneurial activities on the part of residents. These activities were very much divided along gender lines, with many Naxi men taking part in long-distance trade as far as Tibet and India, and with most Naxi women running local Dayanzhen businesses that catered to both Naxi residents and the many Tibetan and other clients who ventured to Dayanzhen for trade.

Just prior to 1949, most of the older generation of Dayanzhen informants (now in their sixties, seventies, and eighties) earned their livelihoods running small businesses, and, according to informants, most Dayanzhen residents were neither particularly poor nor particularly well-off. The overwhelming majority of Dayanzhen residents at that time were Naxi. Women ran businesses selling food products such as "bean flour gelatin" (*liangfen*), "bean curd" (*dofu*), Naxi "fried bread" (*baba*), pickled vegetables, preserved fruits, and a variety of other nonfood products (see fig. 7.3). Those of their husbands, brothers, and fathers who did not engage in long-distance trade either ran small shops, in which they performed the skills of their trade, or became white-collar employees for the Nationalist government (serving as teachers, officials, etc.). A fair number of men apparently did nothing in particular except rely on their wives (Goullart 1955, 79).

The 1980s and 1990s have seen the revitalization of small-business entrepreneurship in Dayanzhen. Yet, as previously pointed out, the majority of Dayanzhen residents continue to work in either state (*guojia*) or collective (*jiti*) work units.[8] There is a distinctly gendered pattern to the distribution of labor between these two types of work units, with men predominantly working for state work units (which have higher pay and much better health, retirement, and other benefits) and women predominantly working for collective work units (which have lower pay, irregular work, and few benefits). In general, however, contemporary residents of Dayanzhen enjoy a fairly comfortable standard of living and (unlike peasants in the surrounding basin), until very recently, the security of an "iron rice bowl" existence.

Dayanzhen women continue to be renowned (as they were prior to 1949) for their all-around capability—as managers of their households, as managers of their businesses, and as generally ceaseless workers. The *huo cuo* (loosely translatable as "credit association") is a Dayanzhen practice that reflects the central role of Naxi women as money managers and businesswomen and at the same time highlights the significance of friendship bonds within gender-specific age cohorts for Dayanzhen women. Most older women in Dayanzhen participated in *huo cuo* as young girls, and many of them have resumed participation in these organizations over the last fifteen years with the spread of national economic reform and liberalization.

While men's *huo cuo* exist now, they do not appear to have existed prior to 1949, and they do not seem to foster the same "through thick and thin"–type bonds that are found in the women's *huo cuo*. Nevertheless, age-cohort bonds appear to be significant for Naxi men as well as women, and "potluck picnics" (called *tutuzee* and *ddoddola* in Naxihua) were a popular practice for both genders prior to 1949. Older men and women alike (although men in particular since they seem to have much more leisure time) participate enthusiastically in the pan-PRC state-sponsored "associations for the elderly" (*laonian xiehui*) according to their Dayanzhen neighborhoods.

Older Naxi women describe their lives prior to 1949 as "exceedingly bitter" (*tai xinku*), attributing much of that bitterness to the imperial Chinese norms that informed their gender status. Despite the elevation of their status with the Revolution in 1949 and the Marriage Law of 1950, Naxi women still consider their lot to be a bitter one. Older and middle-aged Naxi women in Dayanzhen appear to derive a certain martyrlike satisfaction from their continuing ethic of ceaseless work; younger Naxi women in Dayanzhen have a decided preference for marrying Han men.

Education, following the classical model of Chinese scholarship through its respective Qing, Republican, and Communist period metamorphoses, has been highly valued for Naxi males for at least the past several centuries. Under the Nationalist government (1927–1949), Dayanzhen, along with Kunming and Dali, was the proud sponsor of one of the three key middle schools in the province. In the contemporary Lijiang basin, both the Number One Prefectural Middle School and the Number One County Middle School produce students with test scores (almost, although apparently not quite) equivalent to those of the top schools in Kunming. These scores are good enough to get Dayanzhen students into the Yunnan Provincial Minority Nationalities Institute as well as Yunnan University, Beijing University, and other key institutions of higher learning. Naxi are one of the few minorities who are denied having "affirmative action" bonus points added to their scores in competing with Han students for university and professional school admissions. According to local Lijiang sources (although I have not located statistics to confirm this), Naxi are second only to Koreans with respect to higher education levels among minorities in the PRC.

This high value placed on education (in the basin, at least) undoubtedly has gone hand in hand with the way in which the "literati" model of the gentleman scholar has been embraced by older Naxi men: physical or menial labor of any form is particularly avoided by Dayanzhen Naxi men, who prefer to leave such tasks to the women and while away their free time cultivating flowers, drinking grain alcohol (*bai jiu*) with their cronies, and playing cards or, in keeping with the recent rage, mah-jongg.

In contrast, prior to 1949, most Dayanzhen Naxi women received virtually no education, although during the 1940s a few young girls studied for one or two years. The daughters of wealthy Dayanzhen merchants, like other privileged daughters in China, were the only exception to this rule; these young women were subsequently ostracized in Dayanzhen. One of the direct consequences of the lack of schooling among Naxi girls prior to 1949 is that very few older Naxi women speak more than the barest amount of Hanhua necessary to communicate with customers. This pattern has been reversed among Naxi women who came of age after 1949, although excelling in school is still not seen as particularly appropriate for young Dayanzhen women.

Scholastic achievement is a marker of status for both young men and young women in the Dayanzhen context, although considered more critical for the former than for the latter. Whether one is only able to graduate from junior high school (*chuzhong*) as opposed to senior high school (*gaozhong*), or whether one is only able to test into a vocational training school (*zhongzhuan*) as opposed to a university (*daxue*), affects one's future job assignment and the prestige on which classmate and agemate relationships will continue to be based. Classmates who test into university-level schools tend to look down on (*kanbuqi*) those who do not.

Communist Party membership is another key variable in evaluating one's relative power and prestige in contemporary Dayanzhen. This is particularly true for the oldest generation of men in Dayanzhen, many of whom are now retired cadres (*ganbu*) who have *lixiu* status—a "retirement" status that bestows both monetary and prestige benefits on the bearer (as opposed to just plain "retired," or *tuixiu*, status) and that requires the bearer to have participated in the CCP prior to or during the 1949 Revolution. Closely related to political status in Dayanzhen is class background, which even in the current context of Dayanzhen continues to color social relations and influence education opportunities and job assignments. Education, Party membership, and (former) class background are all factors in addition to one's occupation that must be taken into consideration in formulating any notion of class in Dayanzhen.

A final important status distinction, made by Dayanzhen Naxi with respect to Naxi of the villages in the basin, was noted earlier in this chapter. It is the distinction between urban and rural residents found throughout Chinese society. In general, Dayanzhen residents consider the standard of living in the villages to be relatively "backward" and "unhygienic"; they also consider peasants to be relatively "uncultured"/"uneducated" and "conservative." By the same token, in describing Lijiang basin Naxi peasants, Dayanzhen Naxi use the same terms that Han employ in characterizing both minorities and peasants—"honest" (*laoshi*) and "hospitable" (*haoke*).[9]

TIGER SPRINGS

Tiger Springs (a pseudonym) is located in the northwestern part of the basin, nestled against the base of the Jade Dragon Snow mountain. In keeping with its name, Tiger Springs is known for its crystal clear spring waters that flow southward through the village across the basin to the town of Dayanzhen (see fig. 7.4). In current administrative terminology, Tiger Springs is designated an "administrative village" (*xingzheng cun*); during collectivization (1958–1983), it represented the brigade (*dadui*) level of administrative organization. Tiger Springs is made up of seven "natural villages" (*ziran cun*), which were divided into "production teams" (*xiao dui*) during collectivization.[10] As of June 1990, the population of Tiger Springs administrative village consisted of approximately two thousand individuals and five hundred households. One of these natural villages, Stone Bridge (also a pseudonym), was the principal site of my fieldwork.

Residents of Stone Bridge natural village, like residents of other parts of the basin, have their own geographic/climatological "map" of their position in relation to that of other villages. They see their water as the biggest asset of the village, their soil as not great but not terrible, and their climate as somewhat cool given their proximity to the mountain. Villages to the north of the basin are known for their poor soil and cold winds (as they are even more

FIGURE 7.4
Overview of Tiger Springs and northern part of Lijiang basin. *(Photograph by Sydney White.)*

directly exposed to these blasts from the mountain), and villages in the southern and southeastern parts of the basin are known for their fertile soil and warmer weather. These factors unquestionably play a role in marriage considerations for peasants (on the parts of both out-marrying young women and of young men who are bringing in new wives) because they directly affect the quality of life of the concerned parties. Stone Bridge villagers tend to marry people from villages with similar standards of living, either from the other natural villages in Tiger Springs, from the adjacent administrative village (see below), or from other villages in the basin.

Tiger Springs is essentially contiguous with an administrative village I refer to as *Culture Village*. Culture Village stretches to the east of Tiger Springs and has approximately the same size population. At the next highest administrative level, Tiger Springs and Culture Village are both part of Bai Sha (White Sands) township (*xiang*), of which Bai Sha administrative village serves as the township headquarters. Prior to 1949, and extending back to the Ming dynasty, Tiger Springs and Culture Village together with other nearby villages constituted the bustling agricultural and trade center of Shu He (Ten Rivers). Shu He was one of the key centers in the basin that catered to the trade between Tibet and other parts of China, along with Dayanzhen to the south and Bai Sha to the north.

Given Tiger Springs' location against the relatively rocky base of Jade Dragon Snow mountain, villagers before the Revolution did not have the same access to the more fertile land at the center of the basin enjoyed by Culture Village villagers. For this reason, Tiger Springs residents primarily earned a living from leather crafting (*pijiang*), although they supplemented this work with a few other trades. They specialized in shoes and Tibetan boots in particular, men doing most of the leatherwork and women either assisting them or rolling hemp into twine (*cong maxian*), which was then used to stitch the leather together. Women did virtually all the agricultural labor as well and ran small businesses selling *dofu* (bean curd) and *liangfen* (bean flour gelatin), much like the women of Dayanzhen. In another parallel with Dayanzhen, men (although sometimes accompanied by their wives and families) often left their home villages in Tiger Springs for years at a time to ply their trade in other more remote parts of Yunnan like Yongning (a Mosuo area), Ninglang (a Yi area), Zhongdian (a Tibetan area), and Shigu and Judian (Naxi and Han areas) and sometimes even as far away as Lhasa. Stone Bridge villagers and Tiger Springs villagers in general thus displayed an entrepreneurial ethos more in keeping with Dayanzhen residents than with the residents of other villagers in the basin who were primarily agricultural.

The primary concern of all young Lijiang basin men of the period just prior to 1949 (men who are now in their seventies and eighties) was conscription by the Nationalist army (first to fight against the Japanese, then against the Communists). Although Stone Bridge villagers were apparently better off than peasants in other villages of the northern part of the basin, they were not as prosperous as Dayanzhen residents; consequently, they were less able to come up with the requisite substitute mule that could buy their sons out of the Nationalist draft. Whereas Dayanzhen residents could sell their houses to come up with the amount of money necessary to purchase a mule, Tiger Springs house values could not compare with those of Dayanzhen. Thus, many young men from Stone Bridge would slip away from Nationalist conscriptors en route to Kunming or would run away to the Tibetan wilds of Xikang to escape the draft.

The pattern of young men disappearing into remote Tibet for years at a time was not unique to the Anti-Japanese War era (1936–1945) or the ensuing civil war (1945–1949), for it was an established practice prior to the 1930s and 1940s. In the meantime, the women who were their (usually young) wives held down the farm (so to speak), single-handedly raised the children, and often took care of their parents-in-law as well. There is an expression still current in the Lijiang basin that conveys this circumstance: "Whether your father is an official is not important; it is your mother's capabilities that determine whether you will fare well." This pattern certainly applies to the women of Stone Bridge who are now in their seventies and eighties and in fact has continuities among succeeding generations of women in the village. I suspect that opium addiction, which was widespread among Naxi men of the late Qing and into the Republican era (particularly since Yunnan in general, including the Lijiang area, was actively engaged in growing opium), contributed to this.

Most boys received at least a third-grade education or higher, depending on their aptitude and expendability from family-support needs. This was a reflection of the relatively good quality of Shu He schools prior to Liberation in contrast to other villages in the basin (albeit not as good as Dayanzhen schools). Girls, however, were entirely excluded from this possibility because education was considered completely superfluous to a Naxi woman's life of labor. In general, older women of Stone Bridge tend to look back on the pre-1949 era with contempt and resentment regarding the harshness of their lives and in particular the low social status that they held. Older men, in stark contrast, tend to be nostalgic about their past adventures.

The contrast between prerevolutionary Tiger Springs and contemporary Tiger Springs is much more dramatic (on the surface at least) than the contrast between the same two periods in Dayanzhen. Essentially, the 1949 Revolution entailed a process of "peasantification" and relative "decosmopolitanization" for Tiger Springs residents that has endured over the subsequent decades. After initial village moves toward cooperativizing the shoemaking/leatherworking trade in the 1950s, the task of making leather shoes and boots (for which Lijiang is still famous) was delegated to state factories based in Dayanzhen and other parts of the basin. With collectivization in the late 1950s, land that was formerly farmed by Culture Village peasants was redistributed to the jurisdiction of what became the Tiger Springs brigade (otherwise Tiger Springs villagers would not have had enough arable land to support themselves).

This political-economic transformation would have had dramatic impli-cations for the division of labor along gender lines in Tiger Springs, were it not for the fact that a number of large-scale state projects in the Lijiang area as well as in other parts of Yunnan created a demand for (primarily male, although some female) labor. These projects were, not only those of the Great Leap Forward (1958–1961), but also ongoing jobs through the 1960s, many of which were in the huge steel plants of Anning (near Kunming) and Panzhihua (now Dukou, on the Sichuan border). There were also a number of other heavy industry development and construction projects. Additionally, Lijiang basin Naxi had the education, the Party zeal, and the willingness to fill a number of low- and middle-level cadre positions in the more remote parts of northwest Yunnan that were then part of Lijiang's administrative area (such as Lanping, Bijiang, Deqin, Zhongdian, Ninglang, and Yongning), positions that most Han would have regarded as nothing less than exile. Young and middle-aged Naxi men, including the majority of men of those ages from Stone Bridge, enthusiastically harkened to the country's call.

Consequently, Stone Bridge women were once again in the position of holding down the farm, but without the additional sources of cash that their own entrepreneurial projects had formerly provided. Very few of their hus-bands who worked in far away work units sent back cash (part of a long-standing practice in Lijiang basin Naxi culture whereby men's money is their [play] money and women's money is household money). By their accounts, Stone Bridge women and their children actually experienced a drop in their standard of living during collectivization, which they see themselves as busily reversing in the last two decades through supplementing their cash income with entrepreneurial enterprises. Today, Stone Bridge women con-tinue to bear the responsibility for the vast majority of the everyday work in the fields, in the household, in collecting firewood and wild vegetation to feed the pigs, and in raising their children.

In contrast to the experience of Stone Bridge women, however, that of younger village men has, as a result of the economic and social changes of recent years, been one of downward mobility (at least in terms of cash flow). While a few village men are able to take over their fathers' respective jobs in either distant work units or in the basin vicinity (under the PRC system of *dingti,* or "reserving replacement"), most do not have the same sorts of guar-anteed, "iron rice bowl" (i.e., work unit) options that their fathers did, as the national economy has become increasingly privatized under the aegis of "socialism with Chinese characteristics." Village men often take jobs as sea-sonal laborers for which they are paid daily in cash. Otherwise, they periodi-cally carry out what they term *heavy* work, such as plowing, sending the cows, horses, or donkeys out to pasture, driving the motorized "hand trac-tors" that are the primary form of village transportation of goods, helping the women during the two busy annual harvest times, and assisting with periodic housebuilding efforts that involve stonework and the raising of structural timbers.

"Family class labels" (*jiating chengfen*), which were applied throughout Chinese society from the advent of the Cultural Revolution in 1966 until the early 1980s and which were unquestionably the single most important factor influencing an individual's experience, still color the memories and interpersonal relationships (both within and between village families) of villagers who came of age during the 1960s and 1970s.[11] While in absolute terms there were not significant socioeconomic differences between pre-1949 families (by the accounts of Stone Bridge villagers, the vast majority of them were "able to make a living" [*keyi guo shenghuo le*]), the labels were extremely successful in perpetuating the (frequently violent) class struggle that they were intended to foment. Economic realities in this instance were shaped by politics and ideology.

However, with the economic liberalization of the 1980s and 1990s, economics has overcome politics, and an interesting reversal of sorts has occurred with respect to class labels. In household management, education achievement, job opportunities, and the success of entrepreneurial projects, the families formerly labeled as *landlord* (*dizhu*) or *rich peasant* (*fu nong*) families have emerged as among the more successful in the village. These families attribute their success to the strength of will that they had to develop in order to survive the sociopolitical and economic discrimination that they encountered during the Maoist years (e.g., in terms of being social pariahs and scapegoats of every movement that came along, in terms of being assigned the hardest jobs for the fewest work points, and in terms of being denied education and other avenues to achievement such as Party membership).[12]

The most powerful families in contemporary Stone Bridge, nonetheless, are those that include members who have been longtime Party members and/or leaders and who have been able to capitalize on their "relationships/ connections" (*guanxi*). So, from a long-range perspective, politics has often been more influential than economics in determining status. One of the wealthiest and most powerful Naxi men in the basin lives in Stone Bridge and is the son of an early Naxi underground CCP leader. He runs a construction contracting business in a network that extends far beyond the basin to other parts of Yunnan. While most Stone Bridge families are faring reasonably well under the post-Mao reforms, there are a few families, most of them formerly labeled as *poor peasants* (*pinnong*), who no longer receive any political benefits from their "good" family backgrounds and are growing increasingly poorer.

In general, as in Dayanzhen, Party membership is still viewed as an asset, although more so for older generations than for younger generations. Although there have been some exceptions, it has for the most part been a primarily male domain for attaining power and leadership. While the current head of Stone Bridge in general laments the gradual undermining of his personal authority (and power) in the post-Mao era as well as that of the Party's, there are still several domains where state policies play a very potent role in Stone Bridge. These include agricultural policies (especially grain taxes), immunization policies, and (particularly) birth-planning policies.

Education remains one of the few avenues to a potential job in a bona fide state work unit, considered to be the ultimate in livelihood security in the villages of the basin. Tiger Springs' elementary school (*xiaoxue*) and junior high school (*chuzhong*) continue to have a relatively strong reputation in the basin, although still not as strong as that of Dayanzhen schools. Students who test into senior high school (*gaozhong*) either go as boarders to the "Number Seven" upper middle school in the basin or finagle a way into one of the top two upper middle schools in Dayanzhen. Most Stone Bridge boys attend school at least through the end of lower middle school and most girls at least through the sixth grade. The general attitude that education is superfluous for girls remains, however.

While age cohort bonds are clearly important in Tiger Springs, women's *huo cuo* organizations apparently are a uniquely Dayanzhen phenomenon and never existed in the villages. Prior to 1949, there were short-term credit associations (called *shi huo cuo,* or "ten [parts] money pooling") in both Tiger Springs and Dayanzhen. These were set up between ten different parties

FIGURES 7.5a and 7.5b
A Dayanzhen family (top); a Tiger Springs family (bottom). *(Photograph by Sydney White.)*

(households in Tiger Springs) along the lines of Chinese credit associations; interest was factored in, and they were devoid of the food, play, and close camaraderie aspects that the Dayanzhen Naxi women's *huo cuo* encompassed. Tiger Springs also organizes an annual "Elders Association" (*laonian xiehui*) feast and get-together for older Tiger Springs residents; this is apparently a state-sanctioned and state-created event, but it is nonetheless quite popular. Along the same lines, Tiger Springs also organizes an annual "Women's Association" (*fulianhui*) feast and day of activities on International Women's Day (8 March); also a state-sanctioned and state-created event, this is nevertheless also quite popular. There are also popular annual get-togethers for "middle-aged men" and "young people," although the role of the state is less clear in these events.

In sum, it is useful to return to the role of the urban/rural distinction as a status marker from the perspective of Stone Bridge villagers. While on the one hand Stone Bridge villagers agree with the stereotypes of the village as "unhygienic" and "backward" in comparison with Dayanzhen, they also view Tiger Springs and its historical connection to Shu He as endowing them with a relatively "civilized" and "cultured" legacy (see figs. 7.5a and 7.5b). Additionally, they maintain a certain smugness about the self-sufficiency of their lifestyle. Nonetheless, most Stone Bridge parents strongly encourage their children to do well in school in the hopes of eventually obtaining a job in a work unit.

CONCLUSION

Naxi of the Lijiang basin have for centuries been influenced by the various incarnations of the Chinese state, and the post-1949 Communist government has exerted a particularly powerful influence on its basin Naxi citizens. This chapter has addressed how many of the statuses that shape the everyday lives of contemporary Naxi are the same as those that shape the everyday lives of other citizens of the PRC. The difference between the experiences of town residents and those of village residents is a very salient one, although, as elsewhere in China, this is gradually beginning to change.

Nonetheless, contemporary Naxi residents of the Lijiang basin continue to be influenced by the legacies of a distinctive local history and of a distinctive set of cultural practices. Certainly, the socialist Chinese state's designation of the Naxi as a "minority nationality" (*shaoshu minzu*) has also shaped how basin Naxi construct their identities. And this has long been true for basin residents as well as for those who reside in other regions of the PRC. To be sure, PRC minority policies have influenced the making of basin Naxi identities vis-à-vis other Naxi, Han, and other "minority nationalities."[13] In addition, the commoditization of Naxi identity has been an integral part of the recent but profound economic transformation of the Lijiang basin into a national and international tourist destination. However, basin Naxi still constitute the dominant cultural group in the Lijiang basin, and official minority nationality status (in terms of how the Chinese state categorizes it) does not actually factor overly much into how these people forge an identity as members of a local society. My endeavor in this all-too-brief overview of town and village Naxi identities in the Lijiang basin has been to provide a contextualized and textured understanding of the lives of citizens in one part of contemporary China.

8

Ethnic and Linguistic Diversity in Kunming

In this chapter, Susan Blum, a cultural and linguistic anthropologist, describes some of the many types of people who live in and around Kunming, the capital of Yunnan province. Her urban ethnography fills out the linguistic and cultural complexity adumbrated by Sydney White's (chap. 7) portrait of rural southwest China. She points out that ethnic diversity is widely mentioned in accounts of this province and is usually associated with groups that are rural, "primitive," and colorful. The state catalogs fifty-five ethnic minorities in China; Yunnan has twenty-four, in addition to the Han majority. Yet popular consciousness of this diversity does not reach beyond Communist Party blandishments where emphasis is placed on the stewarding role of more advanced Han in shepherding their lesser minority brethren to modernization.

China's diversity is especially noteworthy in terms of linguistic practices. Other than the North China plain, most areas of China are characterized by a multiplicity of forms of speaking. Not all of them are codified, written, named, or studied. Most are referred to simply as the speech of "such-and-such a place" (*mou-mou qiang*). Although standard Mandarin is increasingly comprehended by people in China, especially among the younger ones, for at least 30 percent of the population it is not the mother tongue. Even in a predominantly Han city like Kunming, linguistic pluralism is the rule. Most people there speak a local version of Southwestern Mandarin (cf. Ramsey, chap. 4 in this volume). This multiplicity may be found in many other areas as well. When reading accounts of Chinese places in the future, remember to ask who is speaking what linguistic variety!—Eds.

Readers of this book are aware by now of China's complexity and of its multiplicity of standards, goals, ideals, and practices. Even within China's more familiar centers, questions of unity, homogeneity, and authority (including moral authority) are inconclusive. When one conducts investigations in areas remote from those centers, such fragmentation is even more striking. I have been conducting anthropological fieldwork in Kunming, the capital of

Yunnan province, over the course of most of the past decade (1991, 1994, 1996–1997). In this chapter, I describe some of the ethnic and linguistic diversity of Kunming. In some ways, Kunming's situation is very similar to other southwest cities in former border areas, such as Sichuan's Chengdu, yet, in other ways, it is unique.

KUNMING: COSMOPOLITAN LOCALE
ON THE BURMA ROAD

Yunnan province in China's southwest is bordered by Burma (Myanmar), Laos, and Vietnam on its south, the Tibet autonomous region, Sichuan, and Guizhou provinces, and the Guangxi Zhuang autonomous region on its west, north, and east. Ethnically and linguistically, Yunnan is extremely complex and claims to have the greatest proportion of ethnic minorities of any province in China: 31 percent of its population is non-Han. Its capital, Kunming, lies on the Yunnan-Guizhou plateau at an elevation of approximately nineteen hundred meters (fifty-seven-hundred feet). Its non-Han population is just slightly higher than that of China as a whole, at about 10 percent.

Despite its remote location from the perspective of "China proper," Kunming is an oddly cosmopolitan city as a result of its location on the old southern Silk Road and the modern Burma Road and of successive migrations over several centuries and continuing until the present; it is increasingly the locus of inland Southeast Asian trade from Burma and Thailand—including drug trade. Goods flow from Southeast Asia and out through Kunming to Hong Kong.

The name *Kunming* is that of an old ethnic group, known in Chinese sources for nearly two millennia, at least since China's first great "historian," Sima Qian (145–89 B.C.E.), mentioned it in his *Shiji* (Historical records), "Treatise on Southwest Barbarians"; it became the name of the city in 1276. The city, even as late as the beginning of the nineteenth century, has also been called *Yunnanfu*. Marco Polo claimed to have traveled through the major cities of Yunnan (contemporary Kunming, Dali, Baoshan; he called them *Yachi, Kara-jang,* and *Vochan*) on his way out of China through Burma.[1] The last province to fall under the direct control of China proper, Yunnan has been under continuous Chinese control only since the Yuan dynasty in the thirteenth century, when soldiers of the Mongol court came to extend political control of the Mongol empire in the west. Many Mongols stayed, marrying local women; there are a number of Mongol enclaves remaining in Yunnan, where people claim descent from the soldiers who arrived in the Yuan.

The greatest wave of Han immigration came in the Ming dynasty (1368–1644), encouraged by the Ming founder Zhu Yuanzhang (1328–1398), and continued immigration during the Qing (1644–1911) followed. A further influx of outsiders—mostly from the east, with a large number from the

FIGURE 8.1
Transportation in
Kunming. *(Photograph
by Susan D. Blum.)*

Nationalist capital, Nanjing—came fleeing the ravages of the Anti-Japanese
and civil wars between 1937 and 1945, driven south and west by bombings,
starvation, and a desperate quest for safety. Making a virtue of necessity, during the war an ad hoc constellation of professors "exiled" in Kunming from
Beijing, Qinghua, and Nankai universities formed the Southwest Associated
University (Xinan Lianxi Daxue, abbreviated Lianda). They included the
anthropologists Fei Xiaotong and Francis L. K. Hsu and the poet/revolution-
ary Wen Yiduo, among others. Lianda became the kernel of Yunnan Shifan
Daxue (Yunnan Teachers' University), one of Kunming's many institutes of
higher education.

Since 1949, a further wave of internal migration has brought people from
every part of China to Kunming, especially from contiguous and populous
Sichuan province. Yunnan is one of the least densely populated provinces of
China: Yunnan had 83 people per square kilometer in 1982, compared with,
for example, 175 in Sichuan, 265 in Hunan, 289 in Guangdong, 485 in Shandong, and 590 in Jiangsu (Banister 1987, 298–299). Although Yunnan is often
viewed as "backward," especially by the more privileged people from China's
major cities, it is also seen as providing possibilities for earning a livelihood
precisely because it has not yet been "developed."

All these influxes of people have left their mark on Kunming, as have the
sinicized minorities drawn to the provincial capital. The metropolitan population is around 4 million, yet, until the early 1990s, Kunming had the character of a sleepy, backward town (see fig. 8.1).[2] Horse and mule carts have,
until very recently, provided a great deal of the transportation in town,
although they are now restricted to the smaller streets or to the ring road that
circles the city. Building is proceeding with furor, as elsewhere in China, and
charming (although reportedly unsanitary and clearly land consumptive)
old neighborhoods of wooden houses built around courtyards are being
destroyed as soon as the cities can afford to do so to make way for ostensibly
more efficient and certainly more capacious new concrete and brick apart-
ment complexes, usually of six to eight stories. After its chalk outline is drawn

FIGURE 8.2
Mural of a stylized Stone Forest and Sani girl on a neighborhood wall, Kunming. *(Photograph by Susan D. Blum.)*

in the dirt, a new building can be completed in a matter of months—sometimes in just weeks!

The neighborhoods that remain have uneven pavement winding along narrow alleys, often with lovely traditional-style murals painted on specially provided plaster squares (see fig. 8.2), interspersed with the inevitable blackboards reporting on the latest political, social, or public-health campaign. When I was there, many campaigns were announced; these were campaigns in 1991 against drugs, to catch mice and rats, to increase adherence to the one-child policy, to respect the land-management laws, to follow the example of the selfless revolutionary hero Lei Feng, and to encourage celebration of the seventieth anniversary of the founding of the Party and in 1994 to take better care of oneself (by, e.g., relaxing and eating better food) and to get a lawyer (China was trying to persuade people that lawyers were useful rather than immoral, as they had been portrayed in earlier decades). The state reaches out into every alleyway, but its reception cannot be determined by the officials who prepare the slogans from their central place or by the mere presence of such written slogans. People seemed completely uninterested in these expressions of political correctness, weary after decades of changing political winds. There were new concerns blowing through China, mostly about economics and building. While in 1991 people grumbled about the state, by 1994 it was largely irrelevant, and by 1997 it was often seen by successful people as having provided the conditions for their success. *Progress, modernization, development, making, building, planning, starting*—these are the common terms I heard. Even Kunming was seen as eligible for transformation. But it is one of China's slower capital cities to join the modernization train. Most of the old houses have no indoor plumbing, so there is much use of public toilets, with their familiar odor. Kunming's ubiquitous banks of open, blue garbage cans are emptied regularly but filled just as frequently. On the hottest summer days, the stench can be overpowering. Any available land is used productively; a temporarily vacated field can grow a season's vegetables (see fig. 8.3).

FIGURE 8.3
Intensive crop
cultivation, southeast
Kunming. *(Photograph
by Susan D. Blum.)*

A few traditional-style teahouses endure, where mostly old men but sometimes old women congregate to smoke, drink an often-refilled cup of tea, read the paper, play chess, and tell stories. Near Cuihu (Green Lake) park in the northwest quadrant of the city, retired people play croquet on a sandy sidewalk; inside, old men play traditional instruments and sing opera during the day. This is also the location of regular gatherings involving "ethnic" singing and dancing, especially Yi. On Sundays the parks fill up with parents and children and with students taking breaks. Many people wear fine clothes in celebration of what had been their sole day of rest, posing for photographs at particularly presentable spots. (Since 1996 the weekend officially includes two days of rest, Saturday and Sunday, so even students go to school only five days a week now.)

Kunming's weather has earned it the nickname "Chuncheng" (Spring City); it has also helped the city acquire an exotic reputation and ensured its national status as a favorable site for vacations. The phrase most often offered to describe Kunming is *siji ru chun* (four seasons [i.e., year-round] like spring), just as New York might be reflexively called *the Big Apple* or Denver *the Mile-High City*. Street life is consequently evident all year, with open-air markets, repairpersons, snack suppliers, newspaper vendors, and, near the glitzy hotels appropriate for foreigners, minority people—mostly Sani women— selling handicrafts or offering to change money for a rate higher than the official one (the so-called black market), although, by 1997, they were con- fined to essentially one spot. Peasants come in from the nearby periurban areas to sell vegetables and fruits; most people agree that the fruit sellers are much more unscrupulous than the vegetable sellers, as the former buy fruit at wholesale prices and sell at a huge profit, while the latter merely sell pro- duce that they or their fellow villagers have grown.

The city markets are a miracle of abundance and color, and with each visit to China I find more variety available. Whereas in 1982 the only fresh produce that I could find in Nanjing in the winter were a few spotty apples, by 1994 in Kunming there were four kinds of apples, along with oranges, bananas, plums, peaches, litchis, *longyan* (longan), melons, pineapples, and more—and fruit is peripheral to the Chinese diet, with vegetables and other foods regarded as the main focus of the markets!3 By 1997 the markets offered the same wonderful varieties but were becoming permanent; structures were built with stalls for daily use.

Kunming's physical environment is quite pleasant, with many carefully tended flower collections, including perennial poppies, hollyhocks, and geranium bushes, maintained by both individuals and institutions. There are palm trees and evergreens and even eucalyptus. It has many parks, some quite lavish and popular, such as Cuihu (Green Lake) and Daguan (Broad Vista) parks, and a zoo that is one of the more humane and lovely in China.

Several of the large Buddhist temples, notably Yuantong temple, have been recently, and garishly, refurbished, as have several of the mosques, with vivid primary colors contrasting with the older, faded temples. Indeed, Islam and Christianity, both Protestantism and Catholicism, have many adherents, including people of minority nationalities, and Kunming's Hui (Chinese-speaking Muslims) constitute an important segment of the population, large enough to support several mosques. One of the mosques most active in 1991 was among the oldest in China, having existed on its central Kunming site since the early fifteenth century. However, just before my visit in 1994, most of the mosque's surrounding quarters had burned. The official caretaker, herself a Hui, told me that it would soon be rebuilt, more beautiful and "authentic"— that is, like in the Middle East—than ever. A poor, angry Hui woman who lived nearby confided in me, in the shadows of the destruction, that the fire had been set with the acquiescence of officials because the department store immediately adjacent to the mosque wanted to expand onto the property. She claimed that the fire department purposely responded too slowly. Accusing the caretaker of lying, she said bitterly that the mosque would never be rebuilt. But in late 1996 it was indeed being constructed—or so I was told. It was still closed to outsiders.

Indigenous religious activities flourish as well; on the street one can buy abundant spirit money and various spirit "goods" such as paper clothing and cars to burn for ancestors. One can stumble across neighborhood shrines tucked away in corners; some of them were renovated during one of my stays—only to fall to development by my next visit.

Kunming is home to many colleges and technical institutes, bringing students from throughout the province and even from outside Yunnan. Yunnan University and Yunnan Teachers' University are the most well-known, but there is also the Yunnan Minorities Institute, just a few blocks down the ring road from the other schools. The Yunnan Academy of Social Science does not conduct classes but is a further source of intellectual activity, with a branch concerned solely with minority affairs. Kunming also has the Kunming Teachers' College, the Kunming Metallurgical College, Kunming University, and the Yunnan Institute of Technology. Other institutes of higher education pop up occasionally, willing to take in students who can pass the entrance examination—and pay tuition.

ETHNIC AND LINGUISTIC VARIETY IN
THE CONTEXT OF CHINESE NATION BUILDING

Occasionally on the streets one can see people who by their dress and demeanor are obviously from elsewhere: overseas Chinese from Hong Kong or Taiwan in clothes that strike a Westerner as stylish, Mainlanders from coastal areas in Kunming for business, foreigners on tours, foreigners studying, teaching, or surreptitiously evangelizing in Kunming, peasants in town for the first time, and ethnic minorities still in their native clothing. In most cases the latter means women in traditional costumes; the exception is Tibetan men, mostly sellers of (illegal) medical supplies like tiger paws and deer horn, wearing striped cloth draped across one shoulder.

The human diversity of Yunnan, and of Kunming, is promoted in tourist guides prepared for foreigners and natives; even a website promoting Yunnan speaks mostly of its minorities. Yet the street life is much less evidently plural than such guides suggest. Inquiry into ethnicity in Kunming always provokes the suggestion that one would best investigate (*diaocha*) a minority area. Ethnic minorities are assumed to be more like peasants than anyone else. Minorities who move to Kunming often mask their ethnic identity in order to avoid ridicule, so the visible markers of ethnicity, such as clothing, are an inadequate source of information about the actual ethnic makeup of the city.

China is often considered a quite homogeneous nation-state, with the Han majority constituting 92 percent at the last census (taken in 1990). There has been a sudden increase in the proportion of those claiming minority status, from 6 to 8 percent in only ten years, indicating that, even by official ethnic criteria, the Chinese nation-state may be less ethnically "pure" than had previously been believed. Add those desiring but not granted minority status, add those who choose to follow the ethnicity of their Han parent, add the distinctions between vast regions of China, and it seems that we must reflect much more critically on the issue of China's homogeneity.[4] Western analysts, such as Edward Friedman (see chap. 3 in this volume), have begun to question the very possibility of China remaining unified in the face of such great ethnic and regional diversity and identification. The way in which one regards the possibility of Chinese unity depends on one's model of a nation. It is evident that the idea of a timeless, homogeneous, well-bounded polity underlies some such conceptions, but the only sorts of states that approximate such a model (such as Japan) do so only through the sometimes violent suppression of memory and difference or through the inculcation of a racial mythology of cultural sameness (through the national education system).

We may consider China a new nation-state in the sense that, with the founding of the Republic of China in 1911 and of the People's Republic of China (PRC) in 1949, a new, nonimperial identity for China had to be forged. With the improvement of transportation and communication (*jiao-tong*, a term covering both "transportation" and "communication") and the increased complexity of participation in the nation-state, people's identification with their fellow Chinese had to be encouraged, even with those from other regions, ethnic groups, and classes. One powerful way in which this was fostered was by renaming some of the entities in the Chinese universe, including linguistic varieties. What had been merely *guanhua* (administrative vernacular, hence "Mandarin") was renamed twice: the years after 1911 saw the coining of the term *Guoyu* (National Language), a term that persists in Taiwan and many overseas Chinese communities, and the years after 1949 saw Guoyu become *Putonghua* (Common Language), to emphasize that this is a shared lingua franca but to downplay its connection to any particular group, or *Hanyu* (Han language), to emphasize the fact that there were other languages spoken as well in the new Chinese nation-state, an attempt to bring ethnic groups into the "family" of Chinese citizens.

Ethnic groups were renamed as well, pejorative terms were changed, and all groups were encouraged to assimilate to the new socialist ideal. Despite repeatedly changing goals and methods for achieving them, the problem of integrating ethnic minorities has been salient to China's leadership since 1949 and, indeed, is one that troubled even the Qing rulers before Republican and "new" China.[5]

ETHNIC GROUPS IN YUNNAN

Yunnan is officially said to "have" twenty-four ethnic minorities. The official counts of each in the 1990 census were as follows:

Yi	3,352,000	Tibetans	96,000
Bai	1,120,000	Jingpo	93,000
Hani	1,060,000	Bulang	58,000
Zhuang	894,000	Pumi	24,000
Dai	836,000	Nu	23,000
Miao	752,000	Achang	20,000
Lisu	467,000	De'ang (Benglong)	12,000
Hui	438,000	Jinuo	12,000
Lahu	300,000	Mongolian	6,200
Wa	298,000	Buyi	4,900
Naxi	236,000	Dulong	4,500
Yao	147,000	Shui	4,000

These groups live either in "compact communities" (*juju*) or scattered throughout the population (*zaju*). Many live in economically marginal,

FIGURE 8.4
"Ethnic" dancers (Lahu),
Minority Villages (ethnic
theme park), Kunming.
(Photograph by Susan D.
Blum.)

mountainous areas, forced by Han migration into their territory to subsist on inferior crops. Many are considered "primitive" and "backward," a judgment based on the PRC assumption that cultures "evolve" in a single manner (technically, this is called the idea of *unilinear cultural evolution*) and that all groups can be placed somewhere along this continuum. Western anthropologists no longer believe in this nineteenth-century idea but rather take the position that different societies should be understood on their own terms. Still, the notion of cultural evolution is taken as commonsense fact about ethnic minorities, as is the sense that the state has the right to classify and identify such groups.

The ethnic minorities are often represented in particularly intriguing ways. One of the most colorful is in song-and-dance performances on television, in theaters, and in restaurants and nightclubs. These are occasions on which a troupe of dancers, not all necessarily from the same ethnic group, dresses in stylized traditional costumes and performs to allegedly traditional music. Sometimes these performances are extremely long, with all ethnic groups being represented, and sometimes shorter, with only a few groups being represented. The performers are not necessarily performing their own people's dances; indeed, it is common for Han Chinese to don the garb and assume the role of any number of ethnic minorities, something equivalent to the performance of African American spirituals by white minstrels (see fig. 8.4).

Border provinces also capitalize on their ethnic minorities for publicity and public-relations purposes. Yunnan especially advertises itself as the home of many different groups. Representations of minorities are used on the paper money of China, especially the smaller-denomination bills.

In Yunnan, one can also visit minority museums/theme parks. The "Minority Village" (Minzu Cun), for example, outside Kunming, includes replicas of houses typical of minority groups, attended by young people representing their people through dances and costumes. Visitors can also put on costumes and pose for photographs (see fig. 8.5).

FIGURE 8.5
"Commoditized"
ethnicity: Dai village,
Minority Villages (ethnic
theme park), Kunming.
(Photograph by Susan D.
Blum.)

As I have discussed elsewhere (Blum 1992, 1994, 2001), Chinese minority groups are most well-known for their many festivals. Tourists can attend these festivals, the most popular of which are the Water-Splashing Festival of the Dai and the Torch Festival of the Yi. Such festivals are often quite well attended by outsiders, including foreigners. Many of their original "messy" aspects, such as their movement according to the lunar calendar, have been tidied up, to make them more convenient for tourists.

The PRC established "autonomous" areas, places where minority populations constituted a third or so of the population. Some of the administrative officials were to come from these minority groups. There are three levels at which autonomous areas are found: (1) *zizhiqu*, or autonomous regions, which are province-size units, of which there are five, with Tibet (the Tibet autonomous region) the most famous; (2) *zizhizhou*, or autonomous prefectures; and (3) *zizhixian*, or autonomous counties. Yunnan has eight autonomous prefectures, of a total of fifteen.

In Kunming, where the Han are the clear majority group, ethnic-minority languages are occasionally heard. But much more common is, not the standard national language (Putonghua), but rather a breathtaking assortment of local varieties.

ATTITUDES TOWARD LANGUAGE

Language demonstrates some of the challenges for a central state that wishes to forge national integration. In addition to the so-called dialects of Chinese, which were considered similar enough to be written with the same characters as Mandarin, prior to the 1950s many of the minority languages had never been written. Alphabets had to be devised with which to represent their sounds.[6]

Throughout the world there is a wide range of attitudes toward linguistic standards, something very well established in the professional literature of linguistics and linguistic anthropology. These attitudes have everything to do with the political and cultural situations in which the languages are found; people often think that they hold a given attitude toward a language or variant, but invariably it is toward its speakers or the location in which it is native that they have their strongest feelings. Would Americans so readily say that German is "guttural" if we had not fought Germany twice in World Wars and if stereotypes of harsh, cruel military commandants were not prevalent? North Americans often dislike the sound of Cantonese, but Chinese speakers of various dialects overwhelmingly find Cantonese to be pleasing—a consequence at least in part of the contrasting social standing of the Cantonese in the two societies. (The fact that Cantonese has a large number of tones also figures into the dislike that English speakers feel.) Chinese often feel that Japanese sounds like inconsequential chatter and is not pleasant to hear at all—not surprising given the fact that Chinese in general abhor the Japanese.

Attitudes toward languages, and the speakers of languages, are often held subconsciously, especially where there is not a good deal of ideological concern or explicit discourse about such matters. Such attitudes, if discernible, are fruitful sources of information about relations between groups—between the speakers of languages and their hearers.

The linguistic situation in China is quite complex, with nine major language groups (Altaic, Tibeto-Burman, Mon-Khmer, Tai, Sinitic, Austronesian, Hmong-Mien [Miao-Yao in Chinese], Indo-European, and Austroasiatic) and countless local dialects, many of which are mutually unintelligible. The languages spoken by ethnic minorities belong to all the above-mentioned language families. While Mandarin (Putonghua) is defined as the official, standard language of China, there are many situations in which it is not spoken or is spoken in a "nonstandard" way. Official treatment of linguistic diversity in China has fluctuated, but the predominant concern is that everyone learn Putonghua. It is assumed that, in time, the other varieties will fade away through disuse. In my fieldwork, I found the local varieties to be flourishing.[7]

In this chapter and elsewhere (see esp. Blum 2001), I am also very interested in what people in China say about such languages and dialects, although I am little concerned with the actual linguistic description. For the most part, I use reports about attitudes toward languages to reveal attitudes toward their *speakers*. Ultimately, such attitudes reveal how identity and difference are conceptualized and talked about in China. People say that every town in Yunnan has its own dialect, some variant of Southwest Mandarin, and many ethnic groups have their own languages, languages that are representatives of several different language families. As the provincial capital, Kunming attracts people from throughout China in addition to those from throughout Yunnan. The most common language in Kunming is Kunminghua (Kunming language), a dialect of Mandarin that is phonologically quite distinctive, with tone reflexes different from those of standard Mandarin and with both grammatical constructions and lexical items that set it apart from other Mandarin dialects. A speaker of only standard Mandarin might take a week or two to comprehend even simple Kunminghua with ease.

In Kunming, one hears almost no standard Mandarin spoken in the course of everyday life. Kunming residents speak Kunminghua at the market, in hospitals, school corridors, post offices, and restaurants, and on the public bus (everybody but the driver, who announces the stops in Putonghua). On private buses, the so-called *mianbaoche* (bread loaf vehicles), named after their shape, even the stops are announced in Kunminghua. People from the countryside speak their own variants of Yunnanhua, and, while understood, they are immediately recognized as being from somewhere else, *shanqu* (mountain area) or at best *xiancheng* (county seat). The differences between Yunnanhua and Kunminghua lie principally in vocabulary and phonology, including tones, and do not constitute an insurmountable barrier to communication. Still, they are markers of identity; within the context of Yunnan, Kunming is the big, shiny, fast-paced city that sets the standard for a variety of matters. Kunminghua is the dominant language in Kunming, at least as measured by frequency of use.

Putonghua is spoken in Kunming only by outsiders—mainly those outsiders whose positions permit them to evade the social pressure to learn Kunminghua (teachers, officials, foreigners). People like small-time entrepreneurs must make the effort to learn the local variants; if they do not, they are seen as having unjustifiable attitudes of superiority. Only people from Sichuan can get away with retaining their own dialect; Sichuanhua and Yunnanhua together are considered variants of "Southwestern Mandarin," and Sichuan people—*Sichuan haozi,* "Sichuan rats," who scurry everywhere away from their crowded province in search of opportunity—are familiar, comprehensible neighbors, if not especially well liked. The Yunnanese may dislike the Sichuanese automatically: witness the thirteen-year-old neighborhood ice-cream and yogurt seller who, having had his eye blackened by a Sichuanese bicycle repairman working the same alley, commented, "What do you expect from a Sichuanese?" Such dislike seems to be that between people nearly alike, competing for what are perceived as limited goods—in this case an economic niche in an increasingly competitive service sector.

Some people in Kunming speak what is referred to derogatorily as *Mapu* or *Majie/Magai Putonghua* (street Putonghua). This arrogant term suggests that Mapu speakers are aiming to speak Putonghua but are falling short because of lack of education.

Kunminghua, Yunnanhua, and Putonghua (even Mapu) would seem clearly to be different varieties of Chinese. Indeed, people never hesitated to identify the variants that they heard around them. Although Kunminghua and Yunnanhua are mutually intelligible, so much so that both will be used in a single conversation, Putonghua is rather more different. Putonghua is the only language officially taught in schools (with exceptions in some autonomous areas). Nearly all educated people, especially young people, can understand Putonghua, but they cannot necessarily speak it without effort, practice, and extensive exposure. The same is true for Putonghua speakers who would speak Kunminghua or Yunnanhua, except that they may not be able to understand detailed conversation without practice, and unlike the case for Putonghua there is no official channel for learning Kunminghua or Yunnanhua. Putonghua and the Yunnan dialects, of which Kunminghua is one type, are not merely different varieties of the same language, as, for example, Black English and Standard English, but different branches of Mandarin. For example, pronouns are pronounced differently in the two, as are the tone categories, and there are regular phonological variants.

The sum of these small differences is a considerable barrier to effortless communication. The following two sentences are indicative of the differences between the two varieties (the numbers indicate tones, with 5 being high in the speaker's vocal range and 1 low; 0 is neutral, following the contours of the syllable just preceding):

Kunminghua: T'e22 ji44 suei22 la44?
Putonghua: Ta55 ji21(3) sui 51 leo?
"How old is s/he?"

Kunminghua: xiao44 hom31
Putonghua: xiao21(3) hong35
"(My friend) Hong"

People who are willing to learn Kunminghua have to learn correspondences between sound categories, a fairly manageable task and one familiar to Chinese speakers of Chinese dialects. Minority languages, in contrast, are considered to be unintelligible by Han; with no genetic relation believed to exist between Chinese and most minority languages, these latter are seen as truly other (if not foreign).

Clothing and appearance are also signs of difference, marking ethnicity as well as sophistication or *class* (a term used advisedly in the context of this self-proclaimed classless society). Precise origin, however, is best indexed by speech. (And Hans are distinguished primarily by speech.) Just as in the United States accent betrays regional origin (the Texan without the twang is inconceivable), so it is assumed in China that "accents" (*kouyin, kouqiang, difang qiang*—different phonological patterns employed within a given linguistic variety) and "dialects" (*fangyan*—different linguistic varieties) reveal the origins of the speaker;[8] persons wishing to disguise their identities must choose carefully the variety of speech used and make an effort to speak without the telltale accent, as when speakers from the stigmatized area of Shanghai known as Subei avoid Subei dialect when away from home to escape the disdain that would automatically be directed toward them (Honig 1992, 117).

For many Chinese especially in the south, Putonghua is a second language. Even southerners who learn Putonghua well often retain their "southern accent," usually in the form of loss of distinction of certain consonant pairs: *c* and *ch* (International Phonetic Alphabet [IPA] /ts'/ and /tʃ/), *s* and *sh*

(IPA /s/ and /ʃ/), *z* and *zh* (IPA /dz/ and /dʒ/), *l* and *n*, final *n* and *ng*, and sometimes the vowels *i* and *ü*. Despite what Westerners may feel on the basis of analogies with the prestige of standard languages and what they learn as students of Chinese from their northern teachers, the southern accent in Chinese is not stigmatized to the extent that southern accents may be in the United States. The ditty *Tian bu pa, di bu pa, jiu pa Guangdongren shuo guanhua* (Heaven and earth I am not afraid of; I only fear/dislike a Cantonese speaking Mandarin) does not reflect all attitudes toward southerners. An extremely sophisticated Cantonese friend told me in 1988 of a student she had known at college in Beijing, originally from Shanghai, who feigned a Canton accent for the cachet conferred. The Cantonese accent is quite controversial. Many people with whom I spoke in Kunming wrinkled their noses at the mere mention of Canton or Cantonese, while others seemed genuinely drawn to them. We see here what is common throughout the world: nonstandard linguistic varieties can have prestige if the corresponding loci of populations confer economic and political advantages, as is increasingly the case for Guangdong.

Minority languages are legally permitted to be used at least in certain contexts, such as on signs on government buildings in autonomous areas. Uneducated minority nationalities in Kunming are likely to speak their minority language in small, private groups of conationals, but, outside such settings, they speak either the local Hanhua of their region (the Han language in contrast to a minority language, whatever version of Yunnanhua is the local lingua franca) or Kunminghua. Putonghua would be used only if an interlocutor initiated a conversation in that language; otherwise, using it would be seen as putting on airs.

One might expect the minorities institutes to be full of talk in minority languages, but such is not the case: many of the students at the Minorities Institute were officially classified as being members of an ethnic minority but in fact had one Han parent. And many of them could not speak their "own" language. Some could understand it since their grandparents spoke it, but a number of the students were from urban areas and minority in name only. (This applied as well to minority students at Yunda and the other colleges and universities in Kunming.) When I told a Chinese friend that I had done some research on China's minorities and that I had a particular interest in the Miao, he brought a Miao student to see me. We talked for a while; I asked him about his parents, his hometown, his language. It turned out that he had been raised in Kunming, that he did not speak Miao, and that he had been to his ancestral village in Wuding county (in Yunnan's northeast) only once or twice, finding it very dirty. His parents, he said, could speak Miao, but not as well as his grandparents.

Of course, in order to do well on the college entrance examination, this student had to have been fairly well educated, even taking into consideration the extra points given to most minorities and the fact that he was paying for his education himself. The best educated minority students are in general those living in urban settings, usually in areas dominated by Han, and often the regional county seat; many speak the Han language even at home.

In the linguistic marketplace of Kunming, languages have far different amounts of power. Nationally, Putonghua is powerful and desirable and is known to be the sine qua non for economic and occupational advancement in the state political system. Minority languages are permitted in all-minority regions, but monolingual speakers tend to be confined to the obscurity of border areas.

As demonstrated by Susan Greenhalgh's (1993, 1994) recent studies of de facto and de jure family planning and of the relative strengths of state and society in determining policy, language use instantiates a disjuncture between state and society. Policies regarding the education of minorities appear quite benevolent, but, as carried out, they are less effective than they appear. While one may cite the numbers of minorities in higher education, we must recall that a good number of them are thoroughly sinicized; that is, they are virtually indistinguishable from the Han, having accepted the Han culture and learned to speak the Han language. Often they are the children of "mixed marriages," which in China means an ethnic minority and another minority or, more usually, a Han. ("Mixed-blood" marriages with foreigners is another issue, one that elicits great interest on the rare occasions on which it occurs.) This form of gentle assimilation promises to eradicate differences between minority and Han to a far greater extent than did the more violent attempts that occurred during periods of political radicalism.[9]

EDUCATION AND LANGUAGE SOCIALIZATION

Education has been depicted by some anthropologists as one of the primary means of social reproduction; language is directly involved in such a process. How closely reality matches the ideal, however, is a matter of some interest here as well.

Putonghua is the official medium of instruction in the classroom at all levels of education. For speakers of other forms of Chinese, this is sometimes challenging. Written Chinese does not merely transcribe speech. It has many formal aspects that transcend the actual spoken language and thus can be pronounced according to the reader's own version of Chinese. Yet Chinese people in general, like most people with a long, admired written tradition, find it much easier in practice to pay attention to the written form. Many academic linguists in China focus on the written language—grammar, lexical items, etymologies—and awareness of spoken language in use is, as in most societies, minimal. Education in China revolves around written texts, much as it has for millennia, even though a recent policy is in place stating that Putonghua is the spoken medium of education. In part to witness the extent to which Putonghua has penetrated the lower levels, I observed classes at an elementary school and a junior high school.

The elementary school was an ordinary one, with no particular claim to excellence. The two classes were selected so as to show the foreign researcher the best that the school had to offer. One of the elementary school classes was a first-grade Chinese (language) class. The teacher's Putonghua was fairly standard, although my research assistant later commented that it was not especially standard (Was this to demonstrate *his* mastery of the rules defining the standard?). During class, the teacher made virtually no effort to correct students' pronunciation; when the new word *bangyang* (model) was being taught, she pronounced it "properly"; the class repeated it as [*bongyong*], and she said nothing. One correction, however, was made when a student offered a compound of *chuanxie* (put on shoes): he pronounced *xie* as *xi* and was corrected.

The teacher of the second class at the elementary school had extremely nonstandard Putonghua. Her focus was on preparing the sixth-grade students for their upcoming examinations, in which knowledge of characters and compounds, grammatical structures, and other formal aspects of Chinese was certain to be tested. Already, the deference shown in the education system to the written language was evident.

I also observed two classes at the junior high school: seventh-grade literature and eighth-grade geography. The junior high was an exemplary "key" school associated with Yunnan University. The geography class was indeed conducted in Putonghua. Most of the children—many the children of university faculty with origins outside Yunnan—spoke it fairly well. In the first class, the teacher had a slight Yunnan accent when speaking Putonghua quickly, although, when being very formal and careful, he could approximate a strict standard. He never corrected the pronunciation of the students, who for the most part had fairly standard Putonghua. They tended to reveal their origins by the loss of contrasts in the retroflex fricative and affricate series (merger of /s/ and /sh/, /z/ and /zh/, and so on). The class monitor, however, had impeccable Chinese (Putonghua). She welcomed me to the class with great fluency and aplomb. (People given public, speaking roles are selected in part because of their standard pronunciation.)

When I spoke with the teacher during the break, I asked about correcting pronunciation. "Oh, yes, we must correct it." "Do students speak Kunminghua in class?" "No, it's required that they speak Putonghua in class, and teachers should even speak it out of class." Earlier in the conversation, he had said that many fewer students than usual had raised their hands to answer that day because they were afraid that I would not understand Kunminghua. The contradiction apparent in his two remarks about language variety should serve to caution any reader inclined to believe that language functions to signal identity. Reports about language use are to be taken as both metalinguistic and linguistic acts; that is, they both say something ("We never speak Kunminghua in class") and do something ("I am giving a sophisticated impression of the correctness of the behavior of the well-educated teachers at our school").

There is great disagreement about what linguistic varieties are in actual use in schools. People responsible for setting standards and acting as models may emphasize the successes of the promulgation of the standard. (A linguistics professor who was also an assistant dean at a university told me that 70 percent of the classes were conducted in Kunminghua.) Officials, as one might expect, tend to present optimistic pictures of the work for which they are responsible.

I was able to get another view of language diversity through a group of university students studying Western-style linguistics with a foreign teacher. During the unit on code switching and multilingualism, I asked the foreign teacher to pose the question of what varieties of language were actually used by the students' teachers when they were in school. (In this case, the reports might have been shaped in the direction of increasing the reported diversity to please the foreign teacher.) Although the responses were not entirely reliable because they depended on memory, they were nevertheless quite revealing. Only four of twelve students in the class responded that all their primary school teachers used Putonghua. Of those four, two mentioned that there was a regulation about language use, and one qualified her response by saying that there was code switching even though the primary variety was Putonghua. Three of the twelve mentioned that their Chinese (language) teachers used Putonghua and that all their other teachers used the local dialect.

As for their middle school experience, three of the twelve reported that all their teachers used Putonghua. Two mentioned that most of their teachers had used Putonghua. One student mentioned that no teachers at her school spoke Putonghua outside class; all spoke Kunminghua. As for their experience at the university level, two reported that all their professors used Putonghua. Two said "most," and one specified "almost all use Putonghua (in class)," indicating that, again, outside class, no matter what the ostensible regulations about living an exemplary life, teachers speak the varieties with which they feel comfortable—and that is often something other than Putonghua.

A more detailed survey of the linguistic division of labor came from a questionnaire that I administered to eighty-five people in Kunming about their language use in diverse contexts (see Blum 2001, 32–36). Even assuming self-reports to be biased in favor of more prestigious varieties, the responses that I obtained reveal enormous variation. Of eighty-three usable responses (thirty-eight were men, thirty-eight were women, and seven did not specify gender), only seven people, or 8.4 percent, claimed to use only a single variety. The overall impression received is of a cacophony of dialects spoken in various settings, such as the dormitory where each person claims to speak his or her preferred variety.

Dividing up the responses according to the institutional affiliation (Yunnan University, the Kunming Metallurgical Institute [now the Kunming Metallurgical College], and the Kunming Metal Factory), then according to hometown (Kunming, elsewhere in Yunnan, another province), we find some revealing patterns.

First, the language of instruction varies even at the most prestigious institution in the province. In fact, there is more variation at Yunnan University than at the Kunming Metallurgical Institute (Putonghua was used 62 percent of the time at the former and 77 percent of the time at the latter), a difference that may be attributed to the equivalent of what the sociolinguist William Labov ([1966] 1972, 132) termed the *linguistic insecurity* of the lower middle class: the students at the latter institution are trying hard to succeed, despite the fact that they were not admitted to the best school. For them, using Putonghua in class may be perceived as the best route to success. Or, alternatively, they may be *reporting* such usage because they are aware of the greater prestige of Putonghua. Random observations turned up *no* instances of classes conducted in Putonghua at the Metallurgical Institute.

Further, people generally spoke a local dialect at home, whether the Kunming dialect or the dialect of a smaller town. Only eight people claimed to speak Putonghua at home. Only "in class" or "traveling" did a majority claim to use Putonghua, and there is reason to suspect overreporting. Policies with regard to language and education are often quite remote from actual practice.

For example, the Minorities Institute students told me that those from the more numerous nationalities, such as Yi, could speak their own languages there since they had fellows with whom to converse. Those from the smaller groups or from groups little represented in higher education, such as Hani, did not often speak their own languages. Some did not speak "their" language at all, especially those with one Han parent or those from urban areas.

A sign on the stairway of one of the buildings of the Minorities Institute advocates the sole use of Putonghua. When I asked one of the institute's professors about it, he said that, while such a policy was in existence at all universities and was enforced at the institute, it was not enforced at, for example, Yunda (where a majority of classes were conducted in Kunminghua) because it was so much harder for the minorities to learn Putonghua effectively that they had to be forced to use it. At other universities, students were assumed already to have mastered Putonghua and, like their teachers, to prefer their local dialect unless the standard was necessary.

CONCLUSION

From the above sketch of Kunming, one can observe several things. Although there is a great deal of centralization in terms of economy and policy, ordinary people's lives are shaped equally by local factors, which in this case include ethnic and linguistic pluralism. No matter what the official policy, linguistic diversity has been tolerated, and the result is that most of the population is at least bilingual (speaking their native dialect and at least passively understanding the national standard language). Nods toward the official policy of standardization reassure bureaucrats at the center that their goals are accepted. Ethnic differences have been tolerated in recent decades, within limits. As long as the ethnic groups do not demonstrate separatist tendencies, as long as the ideal of harmony and unity is espoused, differences of clothing, language, and subsistence have been tolerated.

Still, the ultimate aim for China is that a unified national language and culture be born, led by the Mandarin-speaking northern Han from the cities. Whether this will happen any time soon is an unanswered question. What *is* clear is that, for the foreseeable future, such a goal remains elusive, and, beginning at the edges, and going inward, challenges to the central ideal are vibrant and multifaceted. As long as people act and speak in their own terms, national unity is a phantasm, perhaps desired, perhaps dreaded, but always beckoning like mist around the corner.

9

The Construction of Chinese and Non-Chinese Identities

If we wish to discuss the contemporary Chinese experience in its broadest sense, we must take into account the "overseas Chinese" (*huaqiao*). Not only do they account for a substantial amount of the world's wealth—in 1992, the *Economist* estimated their liquid assets to be roughly $3 trillion, equivalent to "all of the bank deposits in Japan" ("The Overseas Chinese" 1992)—but they live in a wide variety of nation-states, retaining their Chinese identity in varying ways. The following chapter addresses one of the principal areas of contention among scholars of the Chinese diaspora—what the author terms *the construction of Chinese and non-Chinese identities in frontier China*. It offers a footing in the empirical aspects of the ethnic genesis of the Bai people and also serves to increase our understanding of the complexity of Chinese identity and its representation. Here is another perspective on the ethnic pluralism of China and what such pluralism means for a new, global "imagined community" of Chineseness.

Wu's chapter does much to broaden the criteria of Chinese identity beyond the limitations of cultural chauvinism. His study of *huaqiao* in Papua New Guinea vividly depicts the different ways in which Chinese imagine and represent themselves abroad and also shows how far was the reach of Guomindang nationalistic indoctrination in earlier decades of the twentieth century. His analysis of southwest China's Bai people, whose ethnicity he distrusts, believing them to be Han, is arresting in its demonstration of the plasticity of ethnic identity in China. But, above all, it is Wu's well-illustrated disbelief of a uniform Chinese culture that offers the greatest single critique of the commonplace view of a uniessentialist China, as he contends that a uniform, Han-exclusive Chineseness is a fiction.

If the Bai are "Chinese," in the sense of being culturally Chinese, then the definition of *Chineseness* must be further expanded or qualified and, moreover, must not be delimited by the considerations of race usually implicit in the notion of *Zhongguo*, "the central country." At the geopolitical margins, Chinese identity is fluid, its claimants inventive and resourceful. This is no less true in China proper, near the center, but, the "processes of identity construction," writes Wu, "have been seldom documented by Chinese scholars in China." All too often, in official accounts of Chinese life and in the narratives of sinologists, representation falls short of reality.—Eds.

Concepts of Chinese and non-Chinese as the Chinese perceive them are complicated. The single English word *Chinese* not only misses certain meanings but may cause confusion. In Chinese, in both the spoken and the written language, many terms are used to reflect racial, cultural, ethnic, and national attributes (*Zhongguoren, Zhonghua minzu, huaren, huaqiao, tangren, hanren,* and so on). These terms have evolved through time; some are recently invented; some originated before the Christian era but are still popular among Chinese. Such singular terms alone, however, cannot describe the complex situations of Chinese identity. The modern cultural concept of *Chinese*, for example, must be understood in the context of China's recent political history. In order to create a modern identity to cope with conditions created by China's confrontation with the Western world, the Chinese were obliged to deal with foreign concepts, including those of nation, state, sovereignty, citizenship, and race, and, more recently, with cultural and ethnic identity. Chinese officials and intellectuals since the end of the nineteenth century have had difficulty accepting these Western concepts, especially as they apply to Chinese living abroad, who are often regarded as foreign nationals under international law.

The Chinese have also had to deal with the powerful national and racial groups who are not themselves Chinese but who at one time or other conquered parts or the whole of China and continue to live today in China's vast frontier territories. Both these peripheral situations not only raise interesting intellectual questions about the nature of being Chinese and the formation of Chinese identity, but also reveal cultural and political constructs of identity that have had local, national, and international interpretations, leading to negotiations about identity and manipulations of policy by the governments of China and other nations.

To ordinary Chinese, the traditional view of being at the center of existence has always been an important aspect of being Chinese. This anthropocentric view is based on a deep-rooted sense of belonging to a unified civilization that can boast several thousand years of uninterrupted history. Such a sense of unity and continuity was, until recently, common among all Chinese, even among those who had moved abroad permanently to settle among non-Chinese people. What is the reality of such sentiment today?

Let us first recall the movement of Chinese within the territory of present-day China. Throughout history, the Chinese have moved southward, from the center to what is today the southwest, traditionally perceived to be the location of the kingdoms of the southern "barbarians." Then, of course, there has been the migration and settlement of the Chinese abroad. In the last two centuries, hundreds of thousands of Chinese have left their homes in southeast coastal China to work and eventually settle in, primarily, Southeast Asia, Oceania, and North and South America. The physical separation of many Chinese from their homeland—the center of their culture—has not precluded the continuity of a Chinese identity. Although it seems natural for Chinese emigrants to maintain their cultural heritage, to emphasize their home-oriented identity this sentiment has in the last sixty years been reinforced from the "center" through deliberate efforts by the Communist government in China to promote a state version of Chinese identity. As a result, many Chinese in the periphery share common sentiments, although they are physically far removed from China.

Two sentiments identify all who see themselves as Chinese. On the one hand, as *Zhongguoren,* which carries the connotation of modern patriotism or nationalism, they feel a connectedness with the fate of China as a nation. Associated with this is a sense of fulfillment, of being the bearers of a cultural heritage handed down from their ancestors, of being essentially separate from non-Chinese. Such primordial sentiments were very common among Chinese in the peripheral areas, especially among those living in the frontier lands but also among the overseas Chinese, who were forced to intermingle with non-Chinese.

The Chinese also see themselves as being members of *Zhonghua minzu;* a close but inadequate English translation would be "the Chinese race" or "the Chinese people." Since ancient times, the Chinese have viewed themselves as being at the center, surrounded by culturally inferior barbarians on the peripheries—the Yi in the east, the Di in the west, the Rong in the north, and the Man in the south. *Zhonghua minzu* is a rather modern concept that emerged only at the turn of the twentieth century (Han and Li 1984; Wu 1989b). The term *minzu* (*min* for people and *zu* for tribe or clan) was adopted from the writings of the Japanese Meiji period, although the two characters used separately were borrowed by the Japanese from classical Chinese writings. By 1895, *minzu* began to reappear in Chinese revolutionary journals, but it was not until 1909 that it became popular among intellectuals.

The term *Zhonghua minzu* was first used by intellectuals during the time of the early Republic of China, where it was often associated with nationalistic writings warning the Chinese people of the danger of annihilation under Western invasion. In his article entitled "The Explanation of the Republic of China" (*Zhonghua minguo*), the leading intellectual of the time, Zhang Taiyan, proposed an authoritative definition of the Chinese people—*Zhongguoren* (people of the central country) (Zhang cited in Hu [1964]). He writes that the ancestors of *Zhongguoren* (the ancestors of the Han) have, since ancient times, been centered (*zhong*) in North China (yet no mention of territorial boundaries) and have called themselves Hua Xia. His article, later cited by leading ethnohistorians, concluded that *Hua, Xia,* or *Han* could be used interchangeably to mean China the nation-state, Chinese the race (or tribe), and China the geographic location. According to his word and logic and that of many Chinese intellectuals who supported him, any of the terms

Hua, Xia, or Han designated a unity—an undifferentiated race originating in north China that emerged during the legendary Xia dynasty and was in the process of becoming a modern republic. Zhang Taiyan's vague and inclusive definition marks the beginning of a modern concept of Chinese national identity. Later efforts were made both in and out of China, through intellectual discourses and government promotions, to construct a Chinese identity based on his nationalistic view.

Both *Zhongguoren* and *Zhonghua minzu* represent an identity based on concepts of cultural and historical fulfillment rather than the more conventional modern notions of nationality or citizenship. Since most Chinese have believed that the Han people were *the* race of China, one that had absorbed people of all languages, customs, and racial and ethnic origins, the meanings of being Chinese in the sense of ethnicity, culture, citizenship, or residence were almost never addressed. According to the intellectual discourse in the early Republic, *Zhongguoren* was thought to be the same as *Zhonghua minzu*— meaning the five major stocks of the Hua people of the middle land—an idea that is still deeply rooted among many educated Chinese today. By the early twentieth century, this concept of a "Chinese people" included four major non-Chinese races, descendants of what were formerly referred to as barbarians: the Man (Manchus), the Meng (Mongolians), the Hui (ethnic groups of Islamic faith in northwestern China), and the Zang (Tibetans). It was also believed that these minority groups, like hundreds of others in the past, had been assimilated into the Chinese culture because of the irresistibly superior Han civilization that had carried on unchanged for thousands of years. For several decades, the perception that racial and cultural composition delineated Chineseness dominated the minds of Chinese under Nationalist education and party propaganda.

Recent studies, however, have shown that the existence of a superior Chinese culture is, at best, a myth. The Chinese people and Chinese culture have been constantly amalgamating, restructuring, reinventing, and reinterpreting themselves; the seemingly static Chinese culture has been in a continuous process of assigning important new meanings about being Chinese. However, the Chinese people have not been conscious of using such a cultural construction, and it has significantly affected Chinese individuals in peripheral areas because they are socially and politically situated on the border between the non-Chinese and the category of people considered Chinese. Chinese, be they *hanren, tangren,* or by the 1980s *huaren* (the Han people, the Tang people, or the Hua people), in the peripheral areas have embraced an unspoken but powerful mission: to keep themselves within the acceptable definition of *Chineseness* and to engage other members of the Chinese community in the preservation of Chinese civilization despite their non-Chinese environment. Although these processes of identity construction have occurred both in and out of China, they have been seldom documented by Chinese scholars within China.

CONSTRUCTION OF
CHINESE IDENTITY OVERSEAS

In the Chinese mind, the overseas Chinese, or *huaqiao* (the Hua sojourners), are natural members of Zhonghua minzu as well as Zhongguoren. Following the traditional thinking of the Chinese people and state, overseas Chinese (regardless of racial mixture) remain Chinese in the fullest sense as long as they are able to claim a Chinese male ancestor, a home place in China from which this ancestor supposedly emigrated, and observe some manner of cultural practices.

For ordinary people in China, the term *huaqiao* invokes the image of a certain type of Chinese—one who is Chinese but partly alien, wealthy, often associated with the United States and the Cantonese—but, in some instances, with Nanyang, the South Seas, and the Hokkienese. Overseas Chinese refer to themselves using a variety of terms in Chinese as well as in other languages, with and without political connotations; these include *huaren* (Hua or Chinese persons), *huayi* (descendants of Chinese), and *huaqiao* (Chinese nationals living overseas).

Rising nationalism since the early Republic, the threat of Japanese invasion, and discrimination against the overseas Chinese in most host countries all created the necessary environment for a strong China-oriented identity outside China. After the Nationalist government was established in Nanjing in 1928 following the northern expedition, China entered a period of "political tutelage" under the authoritarian rule of the Guomindang (GMD). The entire school system of China became a major arena for nationalist indoctrination—especially allegiance to the GMD and its leaders (Li 1990). Nationwide inculcation of GMD ideology in school classes included the teaching of Sun Yat-sen's Three People's Principles and speeches of GMD leaders along with lessons on citizenship and patriotism. Outside the schools, the GMD introduced the daily flag salute and national anthem and sponsored weekly gatherings in the name of Dr. Sun Yat-sen for lectures on GMD teachings and military training. This kind of nationalist indoctrination was also brought to overseas Chinese schools via branch organizations of the GMD and other overseas Chinese organizations, including the Overseas Chinese Commission of the Nationalist government. Even today, the commission regularly sponsors cultural and educational activities in North America and Europe, under the guise of promoting Chinese cultural tradition, in order to induce loyalty to the Nationalist government in Taiwan.

The case of the Chinese living on the remote islands of Papua New Guinea illustrates how Chinese in the center, primarily government officials and intellectuals, were able to forge a Chinese nationalist identity overseas. I conducted research there from 1970 to 1973 on people recognized by themselves and others as Chinese (Wu 1982). During our first encounters, they often complained that they had suffered for years from discrimination by the

European colonists or, in Cantonese, the *loufan* (barbarians). They maintained that they were a people without a country to look after them (*guojia*), although the majority had become Australian citizens during the 1960s.

When I first arrived in Rabaul on the island of New Britain, I was astonished to find the New Guinea GMD headquarters, which was also the center of local politics as the majority of the local Chinese elites were GMD members. Only after a year of study did I realize that the New Guinea Chinese had been recruited and initiated by the GMD during the 1930s, when about one-fifth of the total Chinese population of New Guinea joined the party. In addition to the GMD headquarters in Rabaul, three branch offices were set up in Kokopo (on New Britain Island), Kavieng (on New Ireland Island), and Madang (on the New Guinea mainland). GMD leaders, primarily wealthy Chinese merchants, functioned as political representatives of the Chinese population vis-à-vis the Australian colonial administration and represented the central power of China in presentations of Chinese culture and education. Until the late 1950s, all Chinese in New Guinea were educated in Chinese schools under the wing of the GMD, who recruited teachers from China to infuse New Guinean Chinese youths with a proper understanding of Chinese language, culture, and national identity. These Chinese schools appear to have had a profound influence on the New Guinea Chinese in their formation of a nationalist Chinese identity. A photograph taken in Rabaul in 1953—which I obtained from a family album—depicts a community gathering on a playing field, with New Guinea Chinese Boy Scouts parading through a Double Tenth celebration arch.[1] The inscription on the poles of the arch reads: "Donate generously to fill up the national treasury: To counterattack the [Chinese] Mainland is the duty of overseas Chinese."

During my stay in New Guinea, I was introduced to GMD members or managers through GMD networks. The organization appeared still to be intact and GMD branches in Port Moresby, Lae, Madang, Kavieng, and Rabaul were in close contact with the GMD headquarters in Taiwan. Not only did New Guinea Chinese send representatives to the annual Double Tenth celebration in Taipei, but, according to one regional GMD head, they were also sometimes invited to sit in on the National Assembly of the Republic of China to show global support for the government of Taiwan. At the time, neither I, then a student of anthropology, nor the Chinese in New Guinea had begun to understand the concept of *huaren* (used—with no political connotations—to mean ethnic Chinese). The New Guinean Chinese considered themselves either *huaqiao* or *Zhongguoren,* using expressions like *ngo de wuakiu; ngode jonggokyan* (we are overseas Chinese; we are Chinese nationals). They accepted Chinese patriotism as a matter of duty to one's fellow man, although they were predominantly naturalized Australians. After the Second World War (and until the Republic of China's withdrawal from the United Nations in 1971), the Rabaul Chinese celebrated the Double Tenth holiday each year by performing a lion dance or, as they called it, a dragon dance. Each year they organized a party at the GMD hall that was sponsored by the

New Guinea GMD and was attended by the Chinese community on the island of New Britain.[2]

During this period, the Chinese in New Guinea publicly expressed their association with the GMD and the Nationalist government in Taiwan, but they also quietly gossiped about the rise of the People's Republic of China as a world power. By the late 1960s, Chinese merchants gradually increased their imports from China—first through Hong Kong and later through direct trade. Because of the conservative, anti-Communist sentiment of the Australian people—especially the colonial administration in New Guinea—the Chinese never openly expressed their pride about being Chinese and their continuing association with the Mainland, although their "ancestral land" had successfully tested the atom bomb, had sent a satellite into orbit, and had reportedly cured the blind and the deaf with traditional Chinese medicine.

The influence of Chinese schools in teaching a China-oriented identity has been even more profound in the larger countries in Southeast Asia that have a substantial ethnic Chinese population. Indonesia is a good example. Before 1957, there were two thousand Chinese schools in Indonesia. These schools were divided between those that were pro-Taipei and those that were pro-Beijing: "In 1958 there was an anti-Guomindang campaign in Indonesia because of Taipei's involvement in the regional rebellion. The Chinese schools associated with the Guomindang were closed down. In 1965 there was an abortive coup in which the Communists were involved. Beijing was implicated in this coup, which resulted in the closing of pro-Beijing schools, marking the end of Chinese education in Indonesia" (Suryadinata 1988). The 5 million ethnic Chinese in Indonesia considered themselves divided into two ethnic subgroups: the *peranakans,* predominantly locally born and residing on the outer islands; and the *totok,* or in the Chinese Fujian dialect *sinke* (new arrivals), which included a large proportion of non-Indonesian-born Chinese people concentrated in Java. However, in 1965, the government suppressed the use of Chinese languages, theatrical performances, and religious practices in public. By the 1970s, with the closing down of Chinese schools, the majority of the Chinese children in Indonesia, including the less acculturated *totok,* had lost their ability to speak Chinese.

CONSTRUCTION OF CHINESE AND NON-CHINESE IDENTITIES IN FRONTIER CHINA

It was not until the 1960s, under a Marxist ideology and a Russian model of policy, that the People's Republic established a new concept of being Chinese, one that clearly demarcated the Han (ethnically and racially Chinese) and the non-Han (a number of exclusive groups of people representing different cultures, languages, races, and territorial boundaries).

In the 1980s, I conducted research on the minorities in China that raised serious questions about the meaning of being Chinese and non-Chinese inside China. The term *Chinese—Zhongguoren*—officially consists of fifty-six *minzu*, or nationalities. The majority of Chinese, who once called themselves *Zhongguoren*, now consciously refer to themselves as *hanren* (of the Han nationality), although the Han Chinese are only one of the fifty-six nationalities in China. The Han constitute almost 94 percent of the entire population of China, but the remaining fifty-five minority nationalities—including the Man, the Meng, and the Hui, well-known since the early Republic—reside in over 60 percent of China's territory.

Does being Chinese (or non-Chinese) mean the same thing for the Han, the minority nationalities, and the Chinese overseas? In a recent discussion of ethnic group conflict in China, Stevan Harrell (1990b) provides an interesting observation. He proposes that the distinctions between the Han and the minorities in China and those between two groups of Han from different regions of China are *ethnic* differences (in the contemporary social scientist's understanding of the term). But he makes the important point that being Han (ethnic Chinese) does not include a self-perception of being "different" from the mainstream of Chinese culture. The regionally defined groups of Han—Cantonese, Shanghaiese, and Taiwanese, including those living overseas—have obvious ethnic differences in speech, dress, customs, religious beliefs, and so on. Any expert on ethnic studies today will notice that the difference between two Han groups can, in some cases, be more pronounced than that between a Han and a so-called minority nationality group. From their ethnocentric view, however, the Han do not believe that the culture and territorial claims of minority groups are equal to those of the superior Han civilization.

In view of these confusing senses of ethnic and cultural identity among the "Chinese" and "non-Chinese" in China, what is the meaning of the resurgence of minority cultures? Government authorities in China, as in other modern nations, have played an active role in changing and promoting ethnic or national identities. To classify a group as *non-Chinese* in China today is to reinterpret the meaning of minority culture rather than to preserve parts of a past tradition. The present cultural system has been undergoing constant change and is the reinterpretation or creation of an already changed system, similar to the case of the modern Hawaiian or other "native" American cultures. The new classification of nationalities in China officially emphasizes that each of the minorities has its own language, culture, and history. China's State Nationalities Affairs Commission has even published an official ethnography, linguistic study, and ethnohistory for each nationality. Furthermore, one can observe officially sponsored festivals, officially sanctioned religious celebrations, and officially approved songs, dances, and costumes in minority regions to represent the distinctiveness of the newly named non-Han groups.

Such concerted efforts by the government have been necessary given the fact that, under the new ethnic classification, many previously anomalous groups, whether by tribal name or by cultural characteristics, have now been subsumed under single ethnic labels. As a result, the revival of minority culture in China has required the creation of new unified, centralized, and pannational sets of cultural symbols and activities. Thus, official efforts to promote Chinese minority groups have also included giving assistance to minorities to create a written language, compile a minority history (glorifying legendary heroes), and restore minority medical practices as well as to compose music, opera, and literature. Field data gathered in the summer of 1985 on one minority group, the Bai in Yunnan province, illustrate the above processes of cultural construction and interaction between the Han Chinese and the non-Han minorities.

The Bai are the second largest minority of Yunnan, with a population of 1.2 million (the largest minority group, the Yi people, numbers 3 million). The core of the Bai population resides in northwestern Yunnan, surrounding Erhai lake, in the Bai autonomous prefecture. The capital city includes the ancient town of Dali, which has long been a trade center in the region and has recently become a popular tourist attraction for foreign visitors. The rest of the Bai people are scattered in east Yunnan, including Kunming—the capital city of the province (see Blum, chap. 8 in this volume).

Bai as an ethnic label was unknown to both the Bai themselves and others until 1958, when an official list of nationalities was compiled. Before 1958, the Bai had been known by a number of names, depending on where they resided and whether they were referring to themselves or being referred to by neighboring groups. The most commonly used name was *Minjia*, literally meaning "the civilians," a term developed during the Ming dynasty when the Han military settlers were distinguished from the local residents. In the 1940s, one Chinese sociologist observed that the Bai were "not quite a minority, but not quite Chinese either" (Tao 1943). According to ethnographic reports, the Bai who lived in towns and cities were so assimilated to Chinese culture that they were indistinguishable from any other so-called Chinese (or Han, in today's terminology). They maintained their own language only in the countryside (yet more than half their vocabulary was Chinese) and practiced only a few customs that could be considered non-Chinese by anthropologists (Wu 1990a).

The Bai assimilation to Chinese culture had been going on for centuries, perhaps millennia, even before their ancestors in the eighth century C.E. established a powerful kingdom—Nanzhao (Nan Chao)—which dominated the Indochinese peninsula and influenced what is today Burma, Thailand, Laos, Cambodia, and Vietnam (Wu 1990b). During the 1940s, when sociologists and ethnologists entered the Bai territory to conduct field research, the Bai people denied their non-Chinese origin and would feel offended if regarded as not being Chinese. Therefore, the Bai, until very recently, considered themselves to be ethnic Chinese and enjoyed treatment as such. One of the best-known works on Chinese culture, written by the anthropologist Francis L. K. Hsu (1963), was based on fieldwork among the Bai people during the 1930s. Hsu's field site, in the heart of today's Bai autonomous prefecture, consisted of a township and several surrounding villages. It appeared to be a typical local Chinese center of commerce and agriculture. During World War II, local trading firms expanded their business to international ports as far away as Calcutta. The "Chinese" in the Minjia territory (as it was known then) were so typically Chinese that their family and kinship systems as well as their rituals for ancestors, as described in Hsu's book, were thought to be the ideal representation of Chinese society and culture from the late 1940s through the early 1970s.

In 1985, I conducted field research in a Bai autonomous district, a cluster of five villages situated in a hilly valley with a total population of two thousand. The majority of the villagers were farmers who grew rice, vegetables, and some fruit, but a small percentage were employed at factories in the neighboring districts. Local legend had it that the original Bai families migrated here from Dali—the heart of the Bai territory—about 250 years ago. Most villages had once been dominated by one or two surnames, but, since the Communist Revolution, the local patrilineal clans had officially been dissolved, although local politics continued to revolve around prominent figures still carrying those surnames.

My initial concern was to collect general ethnographic data. As is the convention in my discipline, I expected to find and document a minority culture that was quite distinct from that of the "Chinese"; I did not expect to make a connection between this "minority nationality" and Hsu's Chinese (the Minjia). I soon noticed that the Bai villagers did not appear to be different in physical features, appearance, behavior, or custom from other ethnic Chinese villagers in the region. I therefore inquired how a Bai, or the Bai people as a whole, could be distinguished from the Han—the ethnic Chinese. No one was able to answer the question save for mentioning language differences. The Bai claim to be bilingual—speaking the Bai language and Chinese Mandarin (Yunnan dialect, or Yunnanhua) with a distinct Bai accent. Linguists have long argued about the likeness of the Bai language to other minority languages in the region, but all have agreed that it is basically a Tibeto-Burman language with a high percentage (60 percent) of its vocabulary adopted from the Chinese. The Bai language has always been easily accepted by other people living in and around the area as a local, rural dialect since it is common in other parts of China for people to speak mutually unintelligible dialects or languages in places of close geographic proximity (Fitzgerald 1972). In terms of both language and culture, the Bai themselves believe that they are different from others, especially the ethnic Chinese, yet they could not give a convincing explanation for these differences.

Further observations also failed to reveal cultural characteristics that could differentiate the Bai from the ethnic Chinese. Bai family and kinship structure and their social and political organization at the village level are all similar to those of the ethnic Chinese villages in the region. Although they used to be Buddhists and practiced rituals for Chinese deities on special occasions, these religious activities had stopped in the 1950s. Since the early

1980s, however, some villagers, usually women, have resumed the worship of gods at home and in restored temples. Rituals in memory of ancestors and marriage and funeral ceremonies—all traditional Chinese practices—have become popular for every family. Furthermore, since ancient times, the Bai have celebrated folk holidays and festivals celebrated by Chinese elsewhere. Even the Bai architecture shows an adoption of traditional Chinese construction styles. A few wealthier families have even torn down their old houses (of mud bricks) and built modern cement houses, thus making their village houses less distinctly Bai.

All these observations leave an outside observer with the impression that the Bai people have little cultural uniqueness. What is clear, however, are the many cultural elements that, although distinctly "Chinese," have been associated with the claim of Bai ethnicity in the writings of Chinese ethnologists.

There are great similarities between Hsu's interpretations of the 1930s and my own findings in 1985. Most of the change in self-perception among the Bai has occurred because of their officially named identity; where they previously claimed to be ethnic Chinese, they now claim to be a minority—"non-Chinese." The case of the Bai reveals how the official policy of advancing a minority group's social status and the minority's acknowledgment of its new status have had a profound effect on ethnic identity in China.

My research in China demonstrates how policy can influence the passing on of ethnic identity from Han (Chinese) to non-Han (non-Chinese) for an entire ethnic group. Such a move by a group, or, rather, the changing of official labels under an authoritative policy, does not require members of the group to change their culture; but it does require a change in their perception and interpretation of their culture so that they can justify a new identity. This is the essence of being Chinese or non-Chinese in China today. Such a scenario has applied to many other minority nationalities in China, such as the Miao-Yao groups in southwest China, the Zhuang in Guizhou and Guangxi provinces (the largest minority, with over 13 million), the Tujia (2.8 million in Hunan and Sichuan), some of the urban Mongols, the She (in Zhejiang and Fujian), almost all the Man (Manchu) in the northeast and elsewhere in China, and the Hui (the assimilated Muslims residing in urban centers) (Wu 1989).

BECOMING CHINESE OR NON-CHINESE: PERANAKANIZATION

Throughout the long history of Chinese civilization, Chinese cultural chauvinism notwithstanding, many non-Chinese have been absorbed both culturally and racially into the Han Chinese group since traditional values have held that being Chinese is culturally and socially superior to being non-Chinese (barbarian). Therefore, we rarely find statements in Chinese literature of

Chinese becoming acculturated with non-Chinese. Many in the overseas Chinese communities, however, have long observed that some of their members have "gone native" and have developed special terms to distinguish them. Many examples can be cited from Southeast Asia, where the migrant Chinese are numerous and have had a long history of settlement.

Peranakan is a Malay word popular among ethnic Chinese in Indonesia to refer to the native-born Chinese who have gradually lost their mother tongue and cultural characteristics. *Peranakans* may speak the indigenous language of the host country (or a creolized version of it), may observe some very old Chinese customs and ceremonies as well as acquiring indigenous ones, and are regarded by both the unassimilated Chinese migrants (the *totok*) and the indigenous people as belonging to neither group. While the "pure" Chinese may question the legitimacy of the *peranakans'* claim to being authentic Chinese, the *peranakans* themselves are quite confident about the authenticity of their Chineseness. They are often heard referring to themselves as *we Chinese.* Conspicuous examples of *peranakan* communities are also found in Malaysia and Singapore, where they are known as the "Straits-born," or *baba* (Tan 1982, 1988).

Until recently, it was inconceivable for the Chinese in China to admit that it would be possible for a Chinese within China gradually to give up superior Han Chinese cultural practices, adopt the native way of life, and eventually become a *peranakan* or "native." However, owing to the change in minority policy to favor minority groups in China and the apparent advantage of having a new minority status, as promoted by the authorities, the acculturated Chinese settlers in some minority regions have even sought official recognition as a distinct ethnic minority. "Peranakanization" (migration out of China, acculturation to an indigenous culture, and subsequent loss of one's Chinese identity) has occurred repeatedly throughout history. The following is one example of how a Han family became acculturated to the indigenous culture in Yunnan, as described in a prewar ethnographic report (Tao 1943).

A Chinese man arrives in a minority region and becomes an itinerant trader. After toiling on the road among local villages and market towns, he saves enough money to settle down. He either purchases a piece of land or opens a shop in a market town and marries a native woman. As he prospers and his family grows, he decides to send one of his mixed-blood sons or grandsons to a school in the regional capital or even in the capital city of Yunnan, to acquire a proper Chinese education and eventually to become an official. The idea is that this son, if successful, will carry on the honorable Chineseness of his family, although the other sons who stay at home may eventually become natives.

To be established in a native-dominated region, a Chinese merchant or landlord must become acculturated to the indigenous culture and use his sociocultural abilities to build friendships with the natives—such a settler is usually a bilingual and bicultural man. The Chinese ethnologist Tao, who conducted fieldwork in Yunnan in the 1940s, was not ashamed to admit that a Han settler as such, as opposed to a truly native person, was usually the best informant for visiting ethnologists (Tao 1943, 23). It is not unreasonable to assume that some of the Han Chinese settlers whom Tao observed might have, in a generation or two, changed their ethnic identity to become members of the minority group they lived with, as many Chinese colonists in Yunnan did during the fifteenth and sixteenth centuries (the Ming and Qing dynasties).

It is highly possible that some of the Bai people described earlier were descendants of early Han migrants who acculturated with the indigenous people when the Chinese were not as numerous or as powerful as they later became. These "indigenized Chinese," or Bai, may have later become reacculturated to the Han when further waves of Chinese migration and domination reached the old Bai territory. Turning to the Chinese communities in Southeast Asia, we begin to understand that a comparable process of peranakanization has repeatedly occurred among Chinese migrants overseas.

There was a Hokkien (south Fujian dialect) saying among the early Chinese settlers in Malaya: *sa dai sheng ba* (in three generations a Chinese will become a *baba*) (Tan 1988). If a Chinese man married a Malay woman and their son also married a Malay, it is unlikely that the grandson would maintain his Chinese language skills and practice Chinese customs. What Chinese ethnologists observed in Yunnan appears to be typical of early Chinese migration and settlement in Malaya. Ethnographic reports in recent years still document the process of Chinese (considered pure) incorporation of Malay customs, language, and other cultural practices. One interesting example is the way in which the Malayan Chinese have included Malayan gods, spirits, and non-Chinese figures in the traditional Chinese cosmology and religion. In other words, although the Malayan Chinese continued to live as Chinese on foreign soil, many foreign elements became part of their existence. The anthropologist William Newell reports that the Chinese "hierarchy of gods was parallel to the government hierarchy in the world. The gods were sometimes regarded as subordinate to officials in this world." In the 1950s, for example, a tree spirit was making trouble for workers during road construction work in a Chinese village in Malaya:

> In desperation, the Chinese community and the workmen petitioned the [British] District Officer to come and order the tree to be cut down. The District Officer took the axe and gave the tree one stroke. After this, the tree was easily destroyed. In another village the [British] District Officer had to perform a similar task. Underneath the present new village, there used to be a cemetery. Each time the cemetery was cleared, mysterious rumblings and groans were heard so that the workmen became frightened. Finally the District Officer had to sign a notice [in English!] ordering the spirits or ghosts to remain quiet. From then on no trouble was experienced. (Newell 1962)

Chinese flexibility in cultural and religious identity can be seen in the inclusion of native gods in their worship. In north Malaya, Chinese peasants worshiped local tutelary gods. Newell writes: "One family has built four shrines to [the local gods] in each corner of their property. In other cases, the earlier Malay inhabitants of the land have worshipped a tree or other object believed to have mystical power, and the Chinese inhabitants have continued to worship the same object" (Newell 1962, 99).

I observed similar patterns of Chinese becoming non-Chinese in Papua New Guinea, cases that parallel that of the Yunnan Xian described by Tao as well as that of the Malayan Hokkien mentioned above. The Chinese settled in New Guinea at the turn of the century. By the 1970s, at the eve of the country's independence from colonial rule, the Chinese community of some three thousand included a minority group of mixed-blood descendants (numbering about seven hundred) whose identity depended on the other's labeling and interpretation.

The example of a particular family further illustrates the peranakanization process. At the turn of the century, a Chinese migrant worker from Taishan, in Guangdong province, arrived on New Ireland. He became a coconut plantation manager for a wealthy uncle, married a native woman, and had three sons. His eldest son (who was least noticeably of mixed blood) was sent back to China for education at the age of eight and was raised there. By the time he reached his forties, life in China had become less acceptable to him. He returned to New Guinea with a Chinese wife and their children, where they were received as "Hong Kong Chinese" by the locally born Chinese and the native people of New Guinea. His two younger brothers had stayed on the island, and both had married mixed-blood women. One of the brothers became a local politician and was successful enough to serve a term as prime minister of this newly independent nation. His dark skin and physical features made it difficult for people to distinguish him from the rest of the Melanesians on the islands. Yet, during his recent visit to China with a government delegation representing Papua New Guinea, he spoke Cantonese—a common language of the island Chinese community, which he had learned as a child. He was treated, in one sense, as an overseas Chinese returning home. The youngest brother of the three, whose physical appearance was obvious enough to be recognized as a *bun tong* (a Chinese translation of the colonial English term *half-caste*), became the proprietor of the family business established by his father. In three generations, a Chinese migrant's offspring had become Chinese, New Guinean, and mixed-blood New Guinean–Chinese; each could claim any one of these multiple identities.

In the early 1970s, almost one-third of the locally born Chinese in Papua New Guinea (second and third generation) were of mixed blood. In earlier work, I observed that, "judged by its ethnic as well as its cultural characteristics, the Chinese population in Papua New Guinea is not a homogeneous group. Among the Chinese included in my survey only 77 percent are *chin tong* (the Cantonese word for pure Tang people), the rest are *bun tong*" (Wu 1974a). The Chinese on these remote islands were able to construct a Chinese identity using very flexible criteria. Irrespective of the extent of ethnic mixture in a person's progenitors, if he was descended from a Chinese man, maintained a Chinese surname, and spoke a little Chinese, he was accepted by the Chinese community as a Chinese—*tongjan* (in Cantonese, Tang person). In Kavieng, all the Chinese, regardless of ethnic makeup, lived in the Chinese quarter of town. I often heard the Sino-Niuginians, who closely resembled indigenous people in appearance (in one instance a man's complexion could be described as charcoal black), refer to themselves as *we Chinese*. For many communities, being Chinese depended on one's wealth and social status, not one's skin color or degree of knowledge about Chinese culture. A mixed-blood Chinese, if poor, was regarded as a member of the *bun tong* community; however, if he owned a prosperous commercial business, he was accepted as Chinese (Wu 1974, 95). No matter how well the New Guinea Chinese could demonstrate their Chinese language skills or their knowledge of Chinese culture (by, e.g., reciting stories from the *Romance of the Three Kingdoms* as some did to show off to me, a person of the center), they all ate with a plate, a spoon, and a fork, as opposed to the "universal" bowls and chopsticks.

The Indonesian Chinese are another example of Chinese who may have lost all possible ethnic and cultural traits, including language, but are still able to improvise a Chinese identity. Media reports, for example, have revealed that recent government relaxation has allowed the revival of public displays of Chinese identity in the form of temple renovations and celebrations of Chinese folk festivities. A recent article in the *Far Eastern Economic Review* reports that, although there has been a revival of Chinese culture by the *totok* in the performance of *po-te-hi* (hand puppet theater, which originated in Fujian, the homeland of the Indonesian Chinese), these Chinese puppet theaters now perform in the Javanese language: "In the early 1960s one could still watch *po-te-hi* performed entirely in Hokkien, but now only the chanted parts are in the dialect, and even then only if the puppeteer masters it. Otherwise, he merely chants nonsense syllables" (*Far Eastern Economic Review*, 15 October 1987, 52–53).

CONCLUSION

For centuries the meaning of being Chinese seemed simple and definite: a sense of belonging to a great civilization and performing properly according to the intellectual elite's norm of conduct. This is what Wang Gungwu (1988) referred to as the Chinese *historical identity*. The Chinese as a group traditionally believed that, when a larger Chinese population arrived in a frontier land, sinicization was the only possible course. It was inconceivable that any Chinese could be acculturated by the inferior non-Chinese "barbarians"; however, such acculturation has been a common course of development for Chinese in the frontier lands and overseas, although people still insist that an unadulterated Chinese culture is maintained by the Chinese migrants.

In an article in which he reviews social scientists' concepts of identity and ethnicity and applies them to the Chinese experience in Southeast Asia, Wang (1988) points out how complex the Chinese identities are from multiple perspectives of ethnic, national, local, cultural, and class considerations. My discussion has focused on how Chinese conceptualize their own Chineseness in the peripheral situation, demonstrating the complex process whereby they are able to incorporate indigenous language and culture without losing their sense of having a Chinese identity—not even their sense of having an authentic Chinese identity. A comparison of the situation of overseas Chinese with that of those living on the frontier of China allows us to understand how similar processes of acculturation can have very different political interpretations. Within China, official policies alone can label acculturated Chinese *non-Chinese*. In the situation overseas, owing to the politics and conventional thinking about race and culture, many Chinese who have acculturated to the indigenous population are still labeled *Chinese* and subject to suspicion, discrimination, or exclusion from sociopolitical participation. In part, this suspicion is not unreasonable given that identity for the overseas Chinese has been inseparable from a China-oriented nationalist sentiment for most of the twentieth century.

Since the formation of the early Republic of China, nationalism has preoccupied Chinese intellectual thought both in and out of China. The organizational efforts of the GMD and the Nationalist government, through the activities of the Overseas Chinese Commission, continue to exert their influence in many parts of the world where large numbers of ethnic Chinese reside. This nationalism has been defined in Western terms and is manifested in modern organizational activities such as the GMD and its affiliated associations, such as the Boy Scouts and summer camps for Chinese cultural learning, national anthems, and other rituals and ceremonies for public demonstration of the ties between the Chinese overseas and their ancestral land of China.

The China-oriented identity of the overseas Chinese will continue as long as the Chinese government—whether Nationalist or Communist—as well as Chinese intellectuals and community elites overseas continue to recognize its significance. Despite continual cultural change among the peripheral Chinese, the official interpretation of their Chineseness will sustain their meaning of being Chinese.

SOUTH AND SOUTHEAST

The south and southeast of China are usually considered its wealthiest, most advanced, most modern areas. This portion includes the cities of Shanghai and Nanjing, Canton (Guangzhou), and Xiamen (in Fujian); it is the area settled by Chinese first during the Song period as the north was invaded by powerful, organized "barbarians" and industrialized first in the twentieth century. Most of the foreign investments made—usually by overseas Chinese—are found in this area; with the exception, perhaps, of Beijing, per capita income is highest here, as are rates of computer usage and car ownership and adherence to contemporary fashion trends. Yet poverty abounds as well. The greatest wave of migration has come from south and southeast China, and most Chinatowns in the world are filled with people whose ancestors left south and southeast China, often in profound desperation. Thus, it is the artifacts of the life ways of these peoples that are instinctively recognized by Westerners as "Chinese," so it is that we are far more familiar with the cultures of these regions.

The foods that most Americans associate with China come from southern China: chop suey, fried noodles, sweet and sour dishes, dim sum. Indeed, until most recently, only south and southeast China had rice as their staple food. In northern China, wheat products—noodles, steamed bread—are daily fare, while, in western China, wheat, buckwheat, corn, and potatoes constitute the foundation of the cuisine. The stereotype is that north China is dry, serious, and poor and south China wet, artistic, and wealthy. The south is certainly favored by its climate, suited for growing a dazzling assortment of crops. Transportation out of China is also favored by its southern ports and rivers. It is the area of China most open to the outside world; many films and much music have their source here; it is often possible to trace influences that have coursed into China from outside and then been transformed.

At the same time, although the south and southeast have been exporters of Chinese culture, the "Chinese" aspect of that culture is far from monolithic. Indeed, the linguistic and cultural diversity of this section of China is staggering, perhaps resulting from the isolation caused by its numerous mountains and rivers. Villagers living scarcely a few kilometers apart may speak mutually incomprehensible dialects; gods familiar in one village may be unknown in the next.

Although southerners call themselves *Tangren*, "people of the Tang dynasty," in contrast to northerners, who call themselves *Hanren*, "people of the Han," both believe themselves to be typically Chinese. As Edward Friedman (chap. 3 in this volume) points out, a rivalry is growing that pits the south against the north in terms of claims of greater historical influence, authenticity, and time depth. Archaeological research is a weapon in this war for the real "origin" of Chineseness.

History is often a symbol that is used in struggles over pride and centrality. Facts, in some random way, may exist on their own, but they are always employed in a narrative context that has consequences. Students are unknowing participants in battles in which their elders engage for resources—cultural as well as economic—that produce images of "China" as its ancient culture moved from one center to another. Many would argue that China's most vibrant centers are currently, as they have been for a millennium, southern, despite the government's location in the north. In contemporary China, as the reader will learn, this evident contradiction is worked out in interesting ways in the rewriting of history, nation, and identity.—Eds

10

The Secret History of the Hakkas

The Chinese Revolution as a Hakka Enterprise

The Hakka, "guest people" (*kejia*), are considered a "subethnic" branch of the Han, speaking a Han dialect and with little officially recognized history of their own. In this detective-story-like chapter, the linguist Mary Erbaugh shows how significant Hakka participation is and has been in Chinese political life—within China and in the Chinese diaspora as well. She pieces together bits of evidence from a variety of sources, coming to the conclusion that the Hakka have played a central role in recent political history. Nevertheless, in late imperial China, they were considered an ethnic minority in the southwest and southeast regions where they settled following migration from north central China in the twelfth century. In fact, in the middle of the nineteenth century, ethnic feuds (*xiedou*) between the Hakka and native residents (*bendi*) of Guangxi led to the formation of the Society of God Worshipers, later known as the Taipings, a militant millenarian Christian sect that led a popular revolt against the Chinese state. The Taiping Rebellion raged across southern and central China between 1850 and 1864 and represented the single greatest domestic threat to the Manchu rule of the Qing dynasty. Later ideological engineers and official historians of the Communist Revolution identified this moment as prefigurative of the twentieth-century revolution of peasants and workers that created the People's Republic of China (PRC) in 1949. Thus, Hakka, correspondingly, are revolutionaries and Han.

Today, Hakka constitute 60 percent of the population of the provinces of Fujian, Guangxi, and Jiangxi; there are 80 million Hakka worldwide, 40 million of whom live in the People's Republic. Since in the official taxonomy the Hakka are not recognized as an ethnic minority—in fact, some Hakka were offended at the suggestion that they were not really "Chinese"—to emphasize leaders' Hakka identity would be seen as promoting disunity among the Han. For this reason, and as a nod to the famous *Secret History of the Mongols,* an oral transmission in verse of the origins of the Mongols transcribed into Chinese, Erbaugh titles her chapter "The Secret History of the Hakkas," emphasizing in this way the curious conveying of their authoritative identity through official inscription in Chinese. She shows an uncanny overlap between areas heavily populated by Hakkas and both areas that were the pre-1949 Soviet bases (where the fledgling Chinese Communist Party [CCP] practiced its techniques and tactics) and areas traversed during the 1934–1935 Long March; it appears as if the Communists went from one Hakka area to another as they fled the pursuing Nationalists (Guomindang, or GMD).

Hakka language is the tie that binds Hakkas across vast regions of China. It is spoken by 3 percent of the PRC population (and 3 percent are considered Hakka, or 36 million—a proportion larger than the largest ethnic minority, the Zhuang, with 15.5 million) and by 10 percent of the population in Taiwan. Although Hakkas have been poor, they have emphasized education, literacy, and gender equality. (Hakka women never bound their feet.) Their participation in national life exceeds what one would expect of their numbers. At one time three of the six members of the Standing Committee of the Politburo (the highest decision-making group in post-1949 China) were Hakka.

Erbaugh traces similar disproportionate representation to late-imperial (1850–1911), Republican (1912–1949), and Communist (1925–) moments, focusing especially on the early days of the CCP, the CCP-GMD civil war, and the first decades of the PRC. Although most of the early participants in the Chinese Revolution are no longer alive, Erbaugh points out some of the ways in which subethnic identities can be employed or denied. Also, her "secret history" casts into relief the politicization of ethnicity in China, revealing, much as White (chap. 7 in this volume) did in her study of the Naxi of Lijiang, that it is politics, not religion or culture, that is efficacious in contemporary life and that the meaningfulness of identity is always constrained by politics. Moreover, the essay's ironic tone accentuates the tensions between the rigidity of official taxonomy and the fluidity of real experience and history, a phenomenon that we have observed in several earlier chapters. In this regard, it is illustrative to compare the function of migratory identity in the Communist Revolution (where it is accorded a positive valence) with the significance of that identity for China's contemporary political economy (where it is heavily stigmatized). The contrast effectively conveys the astonishing breadth of change that the nation has undergone in this century of political, economic, and ethnic revolution.

Note. In this essay, readers will encounter quite a number of political personalities and significant events of the Chinese Revolution. Do not be daunted by the references; read for the argument. To assist in the reading, we have provided a selected glossary of terms and names at the end of the chapter.—Eds.

Few China scholars or Chinese citizens know one of the most basic facts about Deng Xiaoping, Hu Yaobang, Zhu De, Chen Yi, Guo Moruo, or many other modern leaders: they are all Hakka. Most popular and official histories, in China and abroad, ignore this basic ethnic bond. The title of this chapter is used ironically, in deliberate parody of the genuine *Secret History of the Mon-*

gols. The subtitle points toward an ironic but serious effort to illuminate a major facet of revolutionary history that remains almost entirely unexplored.

THE PARADOX OF HAKKA OBSCURITY AND HIGH POLITICAL POSITION

The Hakka are an impoverished and stigmatized subgroup of Han Chinese whose settlements are scattered from Jiangxi to Sichuan. Socialist revolution meshed well with the Hakka tradition of militant dissent, with the result that their 3 percent of the Mainland population has been three times more likely than other Han to hold high position. Six of the nine Soviet guerrilla bases were in Hakka territory, while the route of the Long March moved from Hakka village to Hakka village (cf. maps 10.1, 10.2, 10.3, and 10.4). In 1984, half the Standing Committee of the Politburo were Hakka, and the People's Republic and Singapore both had Hakka leaders, Deng Xiaoping and Lee

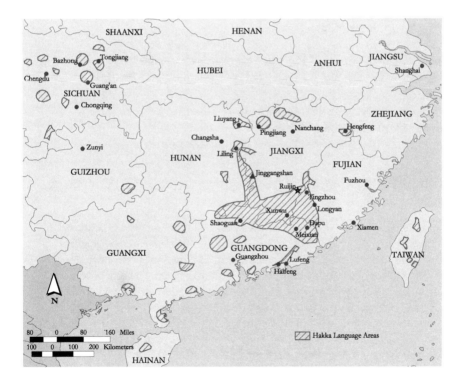

MAP 10.1 Hakka language areas.

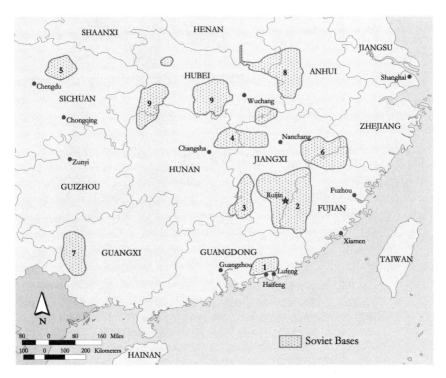

MAP 10.2 Soviet bases. 1 = Hai-Lu-Feng Soviet (1927-1928); 2 = Central Soviet (southern Jiangxi, western Fujian; Min-Yue-Gan); 3 = Southwest Jiangxi Soviet (Gan-Xi-Nan); 4 = Hunan-Jiangxi Soviet; 5 = East Sichuan Soviet (Chuan-Shaan, 1932-1935); 6 = Northeast Jiangxi-Fujian Soviet (Gan-Min-Wan); 7 = West Guangxi Soviet (Zuo-You Jiang); 8 = Hubei-Henan-Anhui Soviet (E-Yu-Wan); 9 = West Hunan-Hubei Soviet (Xiang-E-Xi).

Kwan Yew. The group of influential Hakkas was augmented when Lee Teng-hui became president of Taiwan in 1988.

Hakka political history remains almost entirely undiscussed, and Chinese sources virtually never use the word *Hakka,* but a vital subset of political alliances appears as soon as Hakka networks are decoded. Hakka solidarity also illuminates how a small subethnic group can gain significance when it meets a historic opportunity. In the early twentieth century, Hakka poverty made land reform worth fighting for at precisely the moment when socialist organizers desperately needed the traditional Hakka strengths: mobility, military prowess, strong women, and a strategically useful common language. After 1949, Hakka history from the Long March era was reified as an icon of dissent that Deng Xiaoping's faction promoted as an alternative to Maoist invocations of Yan'an. Since the Beijing massacre of 1989, Deng's allies have reprocessed these Hakka-based images yet again to praise the military and solicit overseas investment.

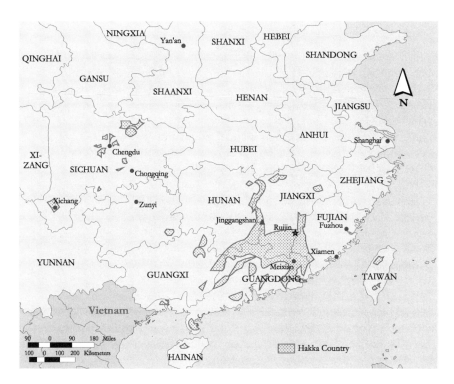

MAP 10.3 Hakka country.

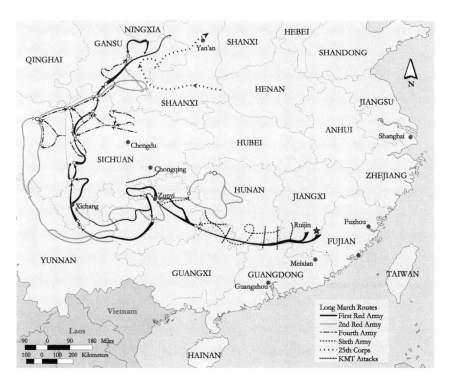

MAP 10.4 Long March routes.

The Importance of Hakka Connections

Chinese traditionally avoid public discussion of subethnic ties. The all-important backgrounds and personal connections of the leadership remain largely hidden, even though nominal political position often understates actual clout, given the underdeveloped legal and legislative systems. Analysts spend decades tracing the alliances forged by shared province, hometown, alma mater, intermarriage, military service, and political patronage. "Connections charts" made popular posters during the Cultural Revolution and the 1989 democracy movement. But even these analyses do not mention ethnicity.

Hakka ethnicity, in fact, predicts high office more reliably than native province, Long March veteran status, or military factions based on field army loyalties. One list of eleven "national heroes" is 27 percent Hakka, nine times the chance rate. Included on the list are Zhu De, Chen Yi, and Song Qingling (Madame Sun Yat-sen), daughter of a Hainan Hakka (Seagrave 1985, 17, 53).[1] The Central Committee has often been disproportionately Hakka (Leong 1985, 314). And Hakkas appeared at triple the chance rate among the 105 leading politicians at the level of minister (*buzhang*) or above profiled in 1989. Many would expect a Deng Xiaoping–Sichuan connection to inflate the number from Sichuan, but these appear at one-third the chance rate. And two, of the three, Sichuanese are probably Hakka.

The Obscurity of Hakka Roots

Most Mainland Chinese have no idea that leaders such as Deng are Hakka. "What's a Hakka?" asked a Beijing intellectual when I mentioned Deng. Others protest, "Deng can't be a Hakka! He's from Sichuan!" These responses are understandable. The only Hakka frequently identified as such in the Chinese media is Ye Jianying, a native of the Hakka "capital" at Meixian in eastern Guangdong, and he is invoked as a token, much as the Panchen Lama served as a token Tibetan. Confining the official image of Hakkas to Ye Jianying as an individual and to Meixian as a location obscures the importance of the 33 million Mainland Hakkas whose settlements stretch all the way to Sichuan. Efforts to combat Han chauvinism account for some of this silence, which contrasts dramatically with the routine highlighting of national minorities, such as Long Marcher Wei Guoqing, who is proudly labeled as a Zhuang. Ye Jianying is the only leader identified as Hakka in a dictionary of revolutionary figures and in a forty-one-volume set of biographies of Party heroes. Autobiographies and memoirs are equally silent. The 1979 edition of the officially sanctioned *Ci hai* (Sea of words) dictionary devotes only nine lines to the Hakka people and eight to their language. In contrast, West lake in Hangzhou receives eighteen lines, while the Zhuang, Miao, and Yi minorities receive seventeen to nineteen lines each, with an additional twelve to fourteen lines on their languages. Chinese ethnographic dictionaries include many entries under *Han* but none under *Hakka, Min,* or other Han subgroups.

However, Chinese leaders may bring up their Hakka roots with foreign reporters who have little idea what they mean. Yang Shangkun, who knew Deng Xiaoping for more than seventy-five years, described Deng's Hakka roots to the American journalist Harrison Salisbury (Salisbury 1985, 136).[2] Deng, born in Xiexing village, Guang'an county, in central Sichuan, is descended from Meixian Hakkas (Alley 1980, 8; Hsin 1978, 4; Franz 1988, 11). Zhu De told Agnes Smedley about his poor Hakka family in northern Sichuan's Yilong county (Smedley 1956, 14). In his celebrated intellectual biography of Guo Moruo, David T. Roy, the Chinese literature scholar, discusses Guo's Hakka family from the village of Leshan in western Sichuan (Roy 1971, 19). And Zhang Guotao (Chang Kuo-t'ao), who was born in Jishui, Jiangxi, and raised in Pingxiang county, quotes his mother as saying that she did not know why their Hakka ancestors had moved to the mountains on the Hunan-Jiangxi border during the Ming-Qing transition (Chang 1971, 1:23).

SOME CAVEATS

Taboo topics tempt researchers toward conspiracy theories and reductionism. Consideration of Hakka ties helps clarify the view of modern China, but these ties alone explain little. The high tide of Hakka leadership appears to rest on revolutionary status as much as ethnicity. The Hakka are only one of hundreds of subgroups that won the Revolution, and ethnic bonds compete with dozens of other demands, even for Hakka politicians. Additional caveats include the difficulty of tracing ethnicity by birthplace, degrees of assimilation to the dominant Han culture, and individual variations in worldview.

Difficulty of Tracing Ethnicity by Birthplace

Explicit proof of Hakka roots is elusive, a problem that the sinologist Vincent Shih faced in writing a history of the Taiping movement (Shih 1967, 305). Chinese biographies virtually never mention Han subethnic ties, but they do scrupulously list birthplace, so Hakka insiders can decode a network of Hakka genealogies. Birthplace in one of the thirty-three counties that were pure Hakka in 1933 very strongly implies Hakka background. For the purposes of this chapter, I count as Hakka people born in a pure or partial Hakka county who have supplemental Hakka documentation. Chen Yi, for example, chronicled his genealogy to his oldest son. Their ancestors left southern Hunan (Xinning county on the Guangxi border) in search of good land during the Qing transition, eventually settling in Sichuan, at Ma'an village near Lezhi city in Yilong county, just a few kilometers from Zhu De's native village. Most Sichuan Hakkas migrated along precisely this route at the same time. Hakka historians claim Chen Yi as Hakka and print his probable family tree in a Hong Kong compilation of Hakka genealogies (Han 1965, 22–23).

I define "probable Hakkas" as natives of pure Hakka counties or of the additional 150 strongly Hakka counties for whom I find no additional documentation (Hashimoto 1973, 6–13; *Yuyan wenzi* 1988, 237–239). Eighty years ago, most Hakkas grew up in ethnically isolated villages. (Central Guangdong Hakkas were more likely to live in mixed Cantonese and/or southern Min districts [Norman 1988, 188].) Impoverished background, early revolutionary activity in Hakka districts, ability to speak Hakka, and lifelong alliance with Hakka leaders reinforce the likelihood of Hakka roots. Explicit confirmation would require raising direct, often taboo, questions with relatives or contemporaries.

Deeper investigation can document some probable Hakkas as definitely Hakka. Hu Yaobang, for example, was a poor peasant from Hunan's majority Hakka Liuyang county. At the age of fourteen, Hu walked six hundred kilometers south to the overwhelmingly Hakka Jiangxi Soviet to do youth and propaganda work, tasks for which the Hakka dialect would have been almost indispensable (Yang 1988, 160–165). Wang Zhen, another Liuyang county native, left home at thirteen, fought as a guerrilla in Hunan's strongly Hakka Pingjiang county, then rose in communications and propaganda work in the Central Soviet before joining the Long March. Liu Binyan (personal communication, Portland, Oreg., 22 June 1991), the former *People's Daily* reporter and a native of Manchuria, confirms that Deng Xiaoping, Chen Yi, Hu Yaobang, and Wang Zhen were all Hakka.

Variable Degrees of Assimilation

Hakka identity varies. Ethnicity is classically defined by common race, religion, customs, and language. But Hakkas are genetically the same as other Han and share very similar religions and customs (Blake 1981, 63–66). Comparing Hakka identity with Jewish identity can be illuminating. In the United States, Jews are scattered by diaspora and tiny in numbers (less than 2 percent of the population). Individual Jews vary in assimilation and politics, from Christian convert Felix Mendelssohn to Zionist Chaim Weitzmann to feminist Gloria Steinem. Yiddish, which transcended political boundaries, once provided the very name for European Jewish solidarity, *Yiddish keit*. And language is the most important Hakka unifier, even though many Hakka have long been multilingual. Ye Jianying himself attended a Cantonese primary school, then spoke Mandarin at the Yunnan Military Academy (Klein and Clark 1971, 1009). Zhu De used Mandarin to study for the imperial exams (which he passed as a *xiucai* [see the glossary]), when he studied physical education at normal college, and in military work in Yunnan. Deng Xiaoping learned Mandarin and French at his Catholic middle school (Franz 1988, 14). Currently, most Hakkas under sixty years of age in the People's Republic and Taiwan speak some Mandarin; virtually all Hong Kong Hakkas also speak Cantonese (Blake 1981, 111–113).

Other Hakkas are more assimilated still. Charlie Soong—a southern Chinese Christian merchant, supporter of the Revolution, and father of some of the most influential figures of the nation's modern political and economic transformation—from Hainan's Wenchang county, changed his name and married a rich Shanghai Christian. Their children, Song Qingling, Meiling, Ailing, and T. V., were most unlikely to have spoken Hakka, for they grew up as highly assimilated cosmopolitans. Hakkas may even be unaware of their ancestry. Lee Teng-hui, the former president of Taiwan, who speaks Mandarin and southern Min, did not know about his Hakka ancestry until a Mainland reporter traced his genealogy.

Individual Variations in Worldview

Hakka roots do not guarantee a particular worldview. Educational, professional, and political alliances are likely to outweigh ethnic ties among revolutionaries. Nor do ethnic ties ensure cooperation. Hakkas fought the civil war among themselves as well as other Han. Many warlords and Nationalist military leaders and politicians were Hakka. The Nationalists made Hakka Shaoguan city its Guangdong capital from 1937 to 1945; nearby Lian county became a model Nationalist county (Vogel 1989, 229–230). The role of Hakkas among the Nationalists must remain beyond the scope of this study, but it will probably prove even more hidden in their official histories than in socialist accounts. Certainly, Chiang Kai-shek's inner circle of fellow Zhejiang natives formed a major barrier to Hakka political aspirations.

THE ROOTS OF HAKKA OBSCURITY

First studies of taboo topics can only sketch lines for future inquiry, as early feminist, gay, and black histories were forced to do. The secrecy surrounding Hakka history means that many findings must be given tentatively, in terms of "probable" Hakkas and "contributing factors." No other Han subgroup approaches the Hakka combination of diaspora, stigma, pride, and silent solidarity against outsiders. The Worldwide Hakka Federation has many members outside the Mainland, but its anti-Communist and Christian constituencies are reluctant to discuss Party history. Non-Chinese sources often openly discuss ethnicity but are all too often uninformed or vague.

Why are Hakkas so obscure? Revealing the concentration of Hakka leaders would certainly fuel charges of nepotism. But other, more neutral trends mask Hakka importance: Han unity, a bad fit with official historical categories, and the stigma of rootlessness. This stigmatized subculture of migration and self-reliance produced many precedents for reforms that the Communists later promoted nationwide as modern and revolutionary.

The Ideal of Han Unity

Seamless cultural unity is a Han ideal that the Hakka share. Chinese traditionally abhor public discussion of subethnic divisions as encouraging the all-too-frequent blood feuds and civil wars. Ordinary people share this reticence, as when an elderly Hakka villager in Hong Kong's New Territories told an anthropologist, "I really don't like to talk about the Hakkas and other Chinese. This issue has disturbed the unification of the Chinese race" (Nicole Constable, personal communication, 27 November 1990).[3] Hakkas who achieve national success glory in their achievements as Chinese; ethnic labeling seems factional and graceless. Rulers from the Qinshi emperor to Mao Zedong are hailed for unifying the empire, whatever the cost (Cohen 1991, 113–134; Wu, chap. 9 in this volume).

Sun Yat-sen, who despairingly called China a "plate of loose sand," provides the ultimate example of a national leader whose Hakka roots, if any, cannot be documented securely. Non-Hakka southerners would be horrified if they were, for Sun is always discussed as a national hero, "the father of the country" (*guo fu*). "Sun the silent," as his biographer called him, did not refer to himself as Hakka, but Hakka historians claim him as their own. Details from Sun's life are provocative. His family were recent migrants to the multisurname village of Chong Hung (Mandarin: Cuiheng), in a mixed Hakka-Yue Cantonese area of the Pearl river delta. Local Hakkas were quite assimilated, but marauders frequently attacked the fortress-like village houses. Sun attended a village school that admitted girls. The schoolmaster, a Taiping veteran, inspired Sun with tales of Hong Xiuquan, the addled visionary leader of the Taiping Rebellion. Most Chong Hung men worked overseas, and, at thirteen, Sun joined his older brother in Hawai'i, was said to have spoken Hakka there, and was nicknamed "Hong Xiuquan." Sun described how, when on trips back to his home village, "the first matter for my care was to see my rifle was in order and to make sure plenty of ammunition was still left. I had to prepare for action for the night."[4]

The chief evidence against Sun's being Hakka is a reconstruction of his genealogy as definitely non-Hakka. The other is Sun's mother's refusal to unbind his sister's feet. Sun quoted her exclaiming in horror, "Would you have your sister as a Hakka woman or a Chinese woman? Would you have her as a stranger or as one of us?" Paul Linebarger, Sun's biographer, interviewed Sun at length. He devotes an entire chapter to the foot binding and makes much of a family photograph in which Sun's mother and two sisters-in-law have bound feet (Linebarger 1925, 25–31). Yet Linebarger does not discuss two other women relatives in the same portrait whose feet are unbound. The controversy over Sun's ethnicity probably cannot be resolved. He may have come from a mixed background or possibly been Yue Cantonese.

The Rigidity of Official Categories

Official history is centralized in China, commissioned from northern capitals. The basic historical categories, *dynasty* and *province,* can render migratory people borderline or marginal. Local history is often literally provincial. A study of Fujian revolutionaries, for example, may omit all mention of

Jiangxi or Guangdong, completely ignoring important movements that cross provincial boundaries. The claim that Deng cannot be Hakka because he is Sichuanese testifies to the strength of traditional categorization. But the Hakka diaspora scattered successive waves of migrants athwart half a dozen provincial boundaries. William Skinner analyzes Chinese economic organization in terms of eight regional subsystems organized around lowland market and transit hubs (Skinner 1977a, 212; Skinner 1977b, 216). Hakkas straddle the mountain boundaries of at least five of these subsystems (see maps 10.1 and 10.3 above).5 And even explicit histories of the Hakka obscure the record under archaic, incorrect, or confusing terminology, such as referring to them as *the Cantonese*.6

Migration and the Stigma of Rootlessness

Dominant Han tradition worshiped the native place, and the Min and Yue Cantonese disdain the Hakka as rootless. Four mass migrations shaped Hakka identity. In the first, the Hakkas left Henan and Shandong during the chaos of the Jurchen attacks between the Tang and the Song dynasties (907–959 C.E.) and settled around Changting (Tingzhou) in the underpopulated highlands of the Fujian-Jiangxi border. In the second, they moved into northeastern Guangdong during the period of the Song-Yuan dynastic transition (1127–1279), settling around Meixian and the North river highlands. In the third, many Hakkas claimed untended land on the southeast Guangdong coast during the early Qing dynasty (1644–1800). Others, like Chen Yi's kin, moved up to the Hunan-Jiangxi border. By 1800, Hakkas had also settled permanently in Guangxi, Hainan, Taiwan, and famine-depopulated Sichuan. The fourth migration came in the mid-nineteenth century, after nearly a million died in the Hakka-Bendi land wars, and in the aftermath of the Taiping Rebellion (1850–1864). Hakkas dispersed further away from Guangdong, into Sichuan, Hong Kong, and overseas.

The word *Hakka* is as blatant a brand of impoverished wandering as *Gypsy* or *Okie*. It was originally a hostile outside coinage, the Cantonese pronunciation of the characters for *guest family, settlers* (the Mandarin pronunciation is *kejia*). *Guest* is often pejorative in Chinese. *Jia* is used in derisive names for minorities but not for other Han except the even more benighted Danjia (Tanga, Tanka) boat people. Old population registers called migrants from outside a province *keji*, "guest population." Many *keji* are Hakka; Zhu De used this term to identify himself as Hakka (Zhu 1981, 115). (*Keji* can also refer to the impoverished "shed people" [*peng min*] migrants [Averill 1983].) Long-settled Han call themselves *locals, natives, bendi* (*punti*), literally "rooted in the soil." In Guangdong, *bendi* implies *Cantonese*. But long-settled Fujian and Jiangxi Hakkas also call themselves *bendi*. Other Hakkas have no special name for themselves but, if pressed, describe themselves as *Tingzhou people*, for the small Fujian town through which 90 percent of Hakka forebears passed. Guangdong and Hong Kong Hakkas prefer a more courteous *guest person* (*keren*) form (Blake 1981, 50–51, 60–62). Non-Chinese sometimes wonder whether the Hakkas are a national minority (*shaoshu minzu*), but this, implying that they fall outside the glories of Han civilization, outrages them. Guangdong Hakkas protested against a 1930s government publication that described them as "barbarous" and "speaking a bird-like chatter" (Leong 1985, 316). Hakkas also complained about a 1958 Beijing University publication that referred to them as "a national minority" (see Yin 1958, endpaper). Greater Han ethnicity as a "Han race/group" (*Han zu*) belongs to the "civilized and civilizing" Han 94 percent of the population, an identity that exists only in opposition to small numbers of "real" minorities such as the Yao or the Tibetans. Han subethnics typically refer to themselves simply as *people* (*ren*), specified as Hakka or Min or Wu.

STIGMATIZED CULTURAL TRAITS USEFUL IN REVOLUTION

Hakka identity centers, not on birthplace, but on ancestry and culture. Migrants repeatedly dug up their ancestors' bones and carried them in jars to new settlements. Hakkas, in fact, see themselves as more Chinese than other Han, as preservers of ancient northern Han culture. Thus, Hakka associations are called *associations for those who revere the true Chinese tradition* (*chongzheng hui* from *chongbai*, "revere," and *zheng tong*, "the true tradition"). The Yue and the Min deride the Hakkas as troublemakers, as poor, stingy, crude fighters who overwork their women and remain hopelessly clannish. Hakka historians herald many of the same traits as adaptations to mobility, conflict, and poverty that yield strong women, military prowess, a useful common language, and an openness to innovation, traits that they claim underlie both traditional Chinese culture and continued progress: "Carrying with them the culture of Central China the Hakkas have built a great mobile army, rich in the pioneer spirit. They have built roads where no roads went before. They founded homes in the wilderness. They have offered hope and promise. Thus, they do not have a narrow concept of territory and are not strongly tied to any one local region. Having a very cosmopolitan outlook, they feel at home anywhere in China" (Yang 1988, 163). The stigmatized traits merit further discussion, for, in the socialist revolution, many were eventually adopted nationwide while the Communist Party carefully avoided any mention of parallels of such traits in Hakka tradition.

History of Conflict

Chinese traditionally avoid discussing unresolved conflict. Northerners may not know what a Hakka is. But the Yue and Min do: their great-grandfathers fought them. Cantonese gazetteers often referred to Hakkas as *Hakka bandits* (*ke fei*) and Hakka gentry as *rebel chieftains* (*ke shen*) or *bandit chieftains* (*zei shou*) (Cohen 1968, 275). Hakkas, as late migrants, often ended up with hilly, marginal land or squatted on land deserted after war, famine, or plague had passed through. Conflict was inevitable when the original owners returned. The central government, however, sometimes backed Hakkas when it feared sedition. When the Ming dynasty emperor Taizu (Zhu Yuanzhang, 1328–1398) feared rebellion in the border area between Hunan and Jiangxi, he drove the original population off with high taxes, and Hakkas later moved onto the vacated land. The early Qing suppressed rebellion by evacuating the coast in 1660. Fujian and Guangdong were worst affected; as many as 90 percent of the coastal Cantonese died. Few returned after resettlement was allowed in 1684, so the Hakkas moved in (Cohen 1968, 275). The Kangxi emperor (r. 1662–1722) paid southeastern Hakkas in silver to repopulate Sichuan after famine, peasant rebellion, and brutal Manchu reprisals decimated the population (Han 1965, 20–23).

Poverty

Hakka migrants had, not only bad land, but also less time to develop the local connections so essential for accumulating wealth. In pure Hakka western Fujian in the 1920s, 85 percent of the population were tenant farmers who paid between 60 and 80 percent of their crop in rent. Peasants ate rice for only three months of the year. More than 90 percent of the men were illiterate, and more than 25 percent were jobless wanderers (*liumang wuchan*), compared to 5 percent nationwide. In the country as a whole, Hakkas were much less likely to be landlords than other Han and far more likely to work as miners or making paper, salt, or textiles (Averill 1983, 1987; Polachek 1983, 810).

Scholarship and Open-Mindedness

The Hakka scholarly tradition is not widely known, but an unusually high number of Hakkas passed the imperial exams. Eighty percent of Meixian men were literate a century ago, while many Hakkas studied in Europe or Japan. In 1934, even impoverished Xunwu county in the Jiangxi Soviet had four hundred living *xiucai* scholars who had passed the imperial exam. Mao estimated that 40 percent of Xunwu males were at least minimally literate, although he stressed that half of these knew only two hundred characters (Mao 1990, 191, 194). Nevertheless, Yan'an was only 1 percent literate in the same period. Hakkas could also be more receptive than other Han to new, even heterodox, ideas. They continue to cherish their meticulously kept family trees, but religion and ancestor worship are often less elaborate among Hakka than among other Han. Families honor a single ancestor tablet, not a whole altarful. Hakka shamans also abounded, and Hakkas converted disproportionately to Christianity (Cohen 1968, 164–165). In the late 1920s, Xunwu city, a market town of twenty-six hundred, had five churches (and twenty brothels); Shanghang, Fujian, had six churches, which occupied one-sixth of the city land (Mao 1990, 116, 211).

Strong Women

Hakka women adapted to their lifestyle with physical strength and self-reliance. Except for a few members of the upper class, they have never bound their feet. Women traditionally kept substantial cash reserves from their dowries, nursed their own children, and worked for cash outside the home. Even today, Hong Kong Hakka women often work in markets or on construction sites. Hakka tradition also strongly encouraged monogamy and discouraged daughter selling, concubinage, and prostitution. Poverty often forced Hakka men overseas, so the women ploughed the home fields and handled the money. Women's self-sufficiency also promoted a relative freedom of association between the sexes as well as a tradition of women's love songs and public protest as voiced in bridal and funeral laments (Han 1965, 27–28; Shih 1967, 317–318; Blake 1981, 43–44, 51–52; Johnson 1984; Johnson 1988, 135–164; Ono with Fogel 1989, 1–22).

Military Prowess

Military heroism is central to the Hakka tradition. Hakkas have often been under siege from their neighbors. Many still live in huge adobe or stone fortresses (*tulou*), elegantly designed multistory circular complexes, some built as recently as the Cultural Revolution. Large central courtyards contain wells, granaries, and animal pens, an arrangement that allows several hundred residents to stave off attack for months. Hakkas have long participated heavily in regional and national armies as well as in irregular troops. Land wars with the Bendi fueled the Taiping Rebellion. Hong Xiuquan, a Hakka native of Hua county, Guangdong, led the rebellion, along with his fellow Hakka warrior Shi Dakai. Taiping opposition to foot binding and opium smoking meshed with Hakka values, as did Hakka promotion of women workers and officials. The earliest recruits were Hakka tenant farmers and miners, followed by soldiers, blacksmiths, barbers, and masons, all disproportionately Hakka trades. Some three thousand joined after defeat in a battle with the Bendi. (In Guangdong, however, many Bendi joined the Taiping, then tried to expel the Hakkas.) After the Hakka-Bendi wars of 1864–1867 killed nearly a million, including tens of thousands in Taiwan, the government moved many Hakkas out of Guangdong and set Hakka quotas for military and civil service exams.

Hakka militancy and separatism remained a serious problem in the Republican era. The Hakka warlord Chen Jiongming (1878–1933), a native of Haifeng, fought for the secession of eastern Guangdong and western Fujian in the 1920s. Chen had served as governor of Guangdong and commanded the Guangdong army. His cousin, General Chen Jiongguang, backed the secession efforts before Sun Yat-sen deposed them (Boorman and Howard 1967, 173–180; Galbiati 1985, 37–38, 81–85). Paramilitary fraternal organizations were especially common among the poorer hilltop Hakkas. Many were Taiping admirers or descendants. Zhu De was a member of the anti-Manchu Older Brother Society (Ge Lao Hui), one of several brotherhoods that ran special "reception bureaus" in the Soviets (Smedley 1956, 87–88, 114–115, 135–136; Schram 1966). The Hakka settlement at Qionghai, Hainan, had produced Communist guerrillas since 1927. The revolutionary opera *The Red Detachment of Women,* set at Qionghai, probably features fighting Hakka women.

HAKKA LANGUAGE AS ETHNIC BOND
AND STRATEGIC ADVANTAGE

Language is the affiliation that produces the meaning of Hakka ethnicity. Urban occupations, schools, and military mobilizations often subdivide on linguistic lines (Cohen 1968, 217, 264; Bennett and Montaperto 1972, 5–6). Guangdong Hakka tradition stressed language over surname with the slogan "acknowledge your dialect, not your surname" (*ren sheng, bu ren xing*). Guangxi Hakkas considered the refusal to speak Hakka as a betrayal serious enough to bar violators from ancestral halls and ban their names from family gravestones (Yang 1985, 184).[7] Sichuan Hakkas still say, "You can sell your ancestral land, but never sell out your clan's language" (*neng mai zu tian, bu neng mai zong yan*) (Cui 1985, 12).

Forty million people speak Hakka, including at least 33 million in the People's Republic (3 percent of all citizens), 2 million in Taiwan (10 percent), and sizable enclaves in Singapore, Malaysia, Indonesia, Thailand, Vietnam, and the Philippines.[8] Some cite the Hakkas' Shandong and Henan ancestry to support the erroneous claim that Hakka is closely related to Mandarin; indeed, it has a similar vocabulary and fewer tones than Cantonese or Min. But a thousand years of residence south of the Yangzi triggered extensive language change. Linguists class Hakka as a southern dialect, close enough to the Gan dialect of Jiangxi that both Hakka and Gan used to be classed as a single language (Ramsey 1987, 110–115; Norman 1988, 210–213, 226–227).

Unlike Cantonese, Min, and Wu, dialects that vary so much that one village often cannot communicate with its close neighbors, Hakka is clearly intelligible across its entire territory. Recent migration, frequent travel, and solidarity allow it to serve as a lingua franca, as Yiddish once did among Jews of the diaspora. Sichuan Hakkas who visited Guangzhou in 1976 overheard some teenagers speaking a dialect identical to their own. They turned out to come from the Guangdong branch of the family that had migrated to Sichuan's Yilong county two centuries before. Zhu De's family had followed the same route. Foreign scholars attest that Meixian Hakka is understandable in Sichuan (Myron Cohen and William Skinner, personal communications, San Francisco, 20 April 1990).

Strategic Uses for Hakka Language

Hakkas have long used their language strategically. They developed an early written vernacular, an innovation especially valuable when classical style prevailed. The Taiping "kings"—the five leaders of the rebellion and rulers of the heavenly kingdom in Nanjing—objected to linguistic barriers between scholars and commoners. Hakka vernacular strongly influenced Taiping documents, reinforced group identity, and promoted literacy. The distinctive style also helped mislead the enemy, especially in coded military documents. Communist reliance on Hakka as a common language helps explain how organizers from all over China managed to communicate with illiterate peasants in the linguistically splintered south.

A Hakka-based underground railway supported an intelligence network in the Soviets. Hakka women, long a familiar sight walking along the ridgetops to market, did extensive reconnaissance. Messages went from Ruijin to Meixian to Shantou and then by boat to Shanghai. No radio sets reached the Soviets until the early 1930s, and, on the Long March, codebooks were often missing, so messages had to be sent uncoded. Transmission in Hakka, with circumlocution, provided a partial shield, much as Navajo was successfully adapted for top-secret American military dispatches during the Second World War. As the early Long March moved through the Hakka settlements, Hakkas were better able to question local people and beg favors. They also had more experience with minorities. Even today, many of the She people in the southeast mountains speak Hakka (Ramsey 1987, 285).

HAKKAS IN SOCIALIST REVOLUTION

Hakka militance made many receptive to Marxism. Orthodox Marxists targeted the proletariat, and some of the earliest worker organizations developed among Hakka workers in southern cities far away from family ties. Many Guangzhou ricksha pullers were Hakkas from Hai-Lu-Feng; Peng Pai (a Party peasant organizer and founder of the Hai-Lu-Feng Soviet in Guangdong) organized them successfully. Most members of the early anarchist-organized unions of barbers and teahouse clerks were also Hakka.[9] Many Hakkas were miners, and many of the most militant mined coal in pure Hakka Shanghang, Fujian, and at Anyuan, Jiangxi, just five kilometers south of the heavily Hakka Pingxiang city. Mao went down the shafts at both sites, but Li Lisan was the most important labor organizer. Li was a probable Hakka, born to an impoverished family in Liling county, Hunan, just over the border from Anyuan. He organized the thirteen thousand Anyuan miners and mechanics for the 1922 strike that was one of the most important worker actions. Anyuan workers survived brutal reprisals to support the 1927 Autumn Harvest Uprising (Shaffer 1982). Li eventually became the main proponent of proletarian revolution at central Party headquarters in Shanghai.

Peasant revolution struck orthodox Marxists as implausible, if not absurd. But peasants made up 80 percent of the population, workers less than three-tenths of 1 percent. Hakka peasants were particularly receptive. Mao investigated rural Hunan in 1927 and reported that about half the peasants were organized. Hakkas constituted only 1 percent of the Hunan population, but five of the thirteen counties that Mao judged "almost completely organized" were heavily Hakka. Mao could not speak Hakka, although he may have understood a good deal. His investigations relied on dozens of interpreters and consultants, including the activist Gu Bo, a native of Jiangxi's pure Hakka Xunwu county on the Guangdong border. Mao's *Report from Xunwu* includes glossaries of Hakka vocabulary and texts of Hakka songs (see Mao 1990).

In Guangdong, Peng Pai worked with Lin Boqu to organize peasant associations across the province. Lin, a probable Hakka from Hunan's Liling county, headed the Guomindang Peasant Department, then became a founding member of the Chinese Communist Party. The peasant associations attracted many disenchanted soldiers from Chen Jiongming's separatist army. The leader of the Meixian Peasant Association, Gu Dacun, was a poor, semieducated native of Anliu village in pure Hakka Wuhua county. Gu led a land reform that brought many landlords to trial, became military director of a short-lived Fast River Soviet, then survived its annihilation to lead five thousand guerrillas.

Soviet Bases in Hakka Country

Six of the nine major Soviet bases were in heavily Hakka areas (see map 10.2 above). The first successful base was the Hai-Lu-Feng Soviet (1927–1928, labeled 1 on the map). The Western Fujian Revolutionary Soviet controlled ten counties at its founding in 1929. Five were pure Hakka (Changting, Shanghang, Wuping, Yongding, and Ninghua); the remainder had substantial Hakka populations (Qingliu, Guihua, Liancheng, Longyan, and Jianning). In 1931, the Central Soviet moved near this area (labeled 2 on the map). The capital at Ruijin was in a pure Hakka county guarded by mountains one thousand meters high. The Central Soviet eventually controlled twenty counties. Four were pure Hakka (Ruijin, Huichang, Anyuan, and Xunwu); most of the remainder were heavily so (especially Yudu, Xingguo, Ningdu, Shicheng, and Guangchang). Only two fell outside Hakka territory (Nanfeng and Liquan). "Provincial" Soviet capitals tended to be Hakka as well.[10] The Southwest Jiangxi Soviet at the Jinggang mountains (labeled 3) was strongly Hakka (particularly Ninggang, Suiquan, Yongxin, and Chaling counties). The Hunan-Jiangxi Soviet (labeled 4) included the heavily Hakka Pingjiang and Xiushou counties. The East Sichuan Soviet (labeled 5), organized in Hakka country by Sichuan Hakka Zhang Guotao, centered around the miserably poor highland towns of Bazhong, whose residents were in rags, and Tongjiang, where one thousand families supported two hundred opium dens (B. Yang 1990, 134). The Northeast Jiangxi-Fujian Soviet (labeled 6) fell largely in Min and Gan territory, although its capital at Hengfeng has many Hakkas. Soviets outside Hakka territory include the West Guangxi Soviet (labeled 7) at some distance from the Hakka settlements in eastern Guangxi. However, many of its organizers, including Deng Xiaoping, moved to the Jiangxi Soviet, then made the Long March. The Hubei-Henan-Anhui Soviet (labeled 8) and the West Hunan-Hubei Soviet (Number 9) are far outside Hakka country. Hakkas are not native to Yan'an or Shaanxi.

Ethnic Conflict

Ethnic conflict caused chronic problems. Mao's report from the Jinggang mountains describes the Hakka-native conflict as "a peculiar feature" of the border counties, one that weakened the Revolution because it undercut class struggle. Mao apparently could not bring himself to use the word *Hakka* (*Kejia*), using *settler* (*keji*) instead. (He may have been trying to avoid inflammatory language, or Beijing editors may have changed his wording.) The "settlers," Mao explained, lived on bad, hilly land, were oppressed by the "natives" (*bendi*), and had "never had any political rights. They welcomed the revolution, thinking that 'their day had come.' " Conflicts were worst in Ninggang, Suiquan, Ling, and Chaling counties—each strongly Hakka. Landlords would claim that settlers were about to massacre the natives and call in troops. When the Red Army left, the settlers would retake native land. The Party had extreme difficulty making settlers return seized property: "In theory, this rift between the native inhabitants and the settlers ought not to extend into the exploited classes or workers or peasants, much less into the Communist Party. But it does, and it persists by force of long tradition. . . . Inside the Party, education must be intensified" (Mao 1969b, 93–94). In late 1927, the only real Red Army was the local, heavily Hakka Hai-Lu-Feng army. Its commander, Zhu De, joined forces with his old Berlin classmate, Ye Ting, a Hakka from Huiyang, Guangdong, who, like Zhu, had supported Chen Jiongming. After the defeat of the Nanchang Uprising, Zhu and Ye retreated with two thousand troops, still under the Nationalist flag, to the pure Hakka Sanheba district between Meixian and Dapu, then south to the safety of the Hai-Lu-Feng Soviet. By 1929, Zhu De, backed by Chen Yi, wanted to "enlarge Communist operations" (Harrison 1972, 142) into the Hakka heartland of eastern Guangdong and southwest Fujian. Mao opposed this as bad strategy. Zhu carried out his raids alone. But he was defeated in central Fujian, and Mao reasserted his power with his essay "On Correcting Mistaken Ideas in the Party" (1969a). By 1930, the Central Committee opposed setting up Soviets on the Guangdong-Fujian-Jiangxi border as a "conservative error."

Western Fujian guerrillas defied orders with an attempt to liberate the Hakka heartland all the way to Meixian. They linked up with Fang Fang and the East river guerrillas but were defeated by May 1931. Yet, in June, Li Lisan called for the liberation of all Jiangxi, then a march to Wuhan, and, by July, the Western Fujian Soviet vowed to liberate the whole nation, starting with Hakka country. The rebels of the Western Fujian Soviet proceeded to attack on their own just over the Guangdong border at Dapu but were defeated again, and, by September, their numbers had dropped from three thousand to four hundred.

Yet Fujian rebels grew increasingly radical, particularly in Longyan, on the border between Hakka and Min country. Youth gangs forced women to bob their hair, banned incense and ritual candles, and forbade people to worship gods, sweep tombs, or tell fortunes. A ban on extravagant weddings forbade dowries, banquets, and gifts down to the bride's parents' gift of a chicken. Such moves, coming largely from Hakkas, disproportionately affected the more prosperous and ritually active Min. Vigorous negative reaction led to a harsh purge. Even so, at the Ningdu Revolt in December 1931, an entire Nationalist army of twenty thousand mostly Hakka men defected to the Communists. Other rebels established a people's revolutionary government in Fuzhou (a northern Min area), which the Politburo suppressed.

Long March Separatism and Survival

Preparations for the Long March were minimal. Xiao Ke later recalled that his troops made the entire trek with just one map, a page torn from a high school history text. Zhou Enlai did as much of such planning as was done, along with the Comintern adviser Otto Braun (Li De), Zhu De, and the guerrilla Su Yu. Zhou negotiated a relatively smooth evacuation with the Hakka warlord Chen Jitang. Ren Bishi (a Hunan Xiang, like Mao) and Xiao Ke (a probable Hakka) scouted the early route around Xiao's native Jiahe, Hunan, near the Guangdong border (see map 10.4 above). Xiao and Ren proposed establishing a new Soviet there, a plan that the Party Center vetoed immediately (Whitson with Huang 1973, 146).

The main flank of marchers left the Central Soviet on 18 October 1934. Zhu De led the First Army with eighty-six thousand troops and supporters; Ye Jianying was chief of staff. An extremely high percentage of the footsoldiers were Hakka, including some twenty thousand western Fujian locals. Mao, who had been exiled to pure Hakka Wudu county in Jiangxi, joined the march when it passed through. Peasants along the route were often angry and out of supplies, but casualties remained low until the marchers moved outside Hakka territory at the Xiang river. Nie Rongzhen, a probable Hakka from Sichuan who had attended middle school with Deng Xiaoping, later described the difficulty of leading fractious troops while the leadership itself was split. As many as twenty-five thousand marchers deserted before the first major battle; desertions were especially common among the heavily Hakka

Eighth and Ninth Corps. Some twenty thousand died in the fight to cross the Xiang river, leaving only thirty thousand. Morale improved briefly with a proposal to create a Guizhou-Yunnan-Sichuan Soviet, partly in Hakka country, but Nationalist attacks forced the march to continue (Chen 1958; Alley 1977, 16–30).

Mao's faction gained control at the Zunyi conference in Guizhou, which may have been held there partly because it was away from Hakka territory and supporters. The conference called for linking up with Zhang Guotao at the Sichuan Soviet. But Zhang and his heavily Hakka Fourth Front Army had long been out of contact. Radioed with orders to link up, Zhang declared the Long March a failure, then marched out of range, vowing to establish a new Soviet in northwest Sichuan Hakka country to "dominate the heights above the rich Chengdu plain" (B. Yang 1990, 125). Zhu De mediated, but conflicts with the Party center continued.

The army split in August 1935. A newly formed Eighth Route Army continued to march north with the Party center, Mao, Ye Jianying, and Deng Xiaoping. Mao, Ye, and Deng were uncertain whether a Shaanxi base even existed until Nie Rongzhen sent a clipping from a Nationalist newspaper about the location of a Shaanxi "red bandit extermination campaign." Convinced, Mao denounced Zhang Guotao and justified the northern route as an anti-Japanese action. The newly formed Left Route Army, under an all-Hakka high command, marched away with all the communications equipment, so communication with the Party Center ceased. Zhu De was general commander, Zhang Guotao the political commissar, and Liu Bocheng the chief of staff. Liu was a probable Hakka, born to a traveling musician in eastern Sichuan's Kai county. Zhang Guotao proclaimed a new Central Committee and Politburo, then an All-Sichuan Soviet. Zhu De and Liu Bocheng later rationalized their service on the rival Central Committee by claiming that Zhang had kidnapped them.

Some thirty thousand First Army troops stayed behind in the Hakka homeland near Ruijin. These were largely sickly, local men with just one gun for every three soldiers (Benton 1989, 70–71). The Central Committee may have found Hakka peasants more expendable, for it left orders that "those working personnel who were natives of the Soviet area should stay behind as much as possible to carry on the struggle" (Kuo 1970, 2:4). The First Army commander, Chen Yi, lacked the code to decipher the final message from the Party. In two months, the Nationalists took over sixteen thousand prisoners. Even so, Hakka counties fared better than others in the resistance. Seasoned Nationalist troops from Guangdong had particular difficulty fighting there because they did not speak Hakka. Hakka guerrillas, including Su Yu, Zhang Dingcheng, Deng Zihui, Gu Dacun, Tan Zhenlin, Tan Cheng, and Fang Fang, led raids in the mountains. Party leaders in Yan'an gave them up for dead, but, in 1938, remnants of this force emerged to form the New Fourth Army (Harrison 1972, 242–243; Benton 1989, 62).

Fewer than twenty thousand Long Marchers reached Yan'an. Once there, the use of Mandarin cooled southern ethnic rivalries by putting all dialect speakers at a disadvantage. Mao was probably ambivalent about Hakkas, grateful for their militance, but relieved to have their power diluted. As Mao consolidated his power, he tried to integrate urban revolutionaries with the rural base. The 1942 rectification campaign also attempted to unify these factions. New rural investigations forced both Long Marchers and Shanghai intellectuals to focus on issues relevant to Yan'an, an area that Hakka guerrillas must have found almost as unfamiliar as Jiang Qing did.

Rectification also targeted abuses often associated with Hakka guerrillas: "adventurism" and "mountaintopism" (*shantou zhuyi*), the tendency for border region commanders to ignore central authority and stress their own importance. Only the armies of the highly educated Liu Bocheng and Chen Yi consistently coordinated actions. Zhang Guotao joined the Nationalists after a final dispute. Professional soldiers and the guerrillas were also divided. Soldiers from the Central Soviet "considered themselves intellectually and socially superior to the ruffians from the wilds of western Hunan" (Whitson with Huang 1973, 466). Chen Yi urged the factions to learn from one another. Uneducated local volunteers tended to put local needs first but were seasoned fighters. Soldiers from the Central Soviet might be formally trained, but they knew little about the local language, people, or topography. Chen stressed that outsiders needed to study local customs and integrate themselves into the community.

Certain factional leaders remain as symbols of dissent even today. Deng Xiaoping supporters often invoke Ye Ting as a conveniently martyred hero. Ye Ting, an old friend of Zhu De's, became commander of the New Fourth Army despite a lack of guerrilla experience, partly because Chiang Kai-shek found him acceptable as a compromise United Front commander. But the New Fourth Army, composed of Jiangsu peasants supplemented by Fujian guerrillas, tended to be apolitical and unused to formal discipline. When Nationalist troops attacked and killed Red Army troops in the New Fourth Army Incident of 1941, Chen Yi court-martialed Ye Ting and imprisoned him until 1946. Ye Ting died in a plane crash soon afterward.

POST-1949 POLITICAL AND MILITARY POWER

Chen Yi himself led the New Fourth Army in liberating east China. Shanghai vanity was shaken when Hakka commanders marched in with troops from the backwaters of northern Jiangsu, Jiangxi, and Fujian. Under the new government, many Hakka heroes gained high positions. Chen Yi became mayor of Shanghai (where even he needed an interpreter) and then foreign minister; Li Lisan became minister of labor; Ye Jianying held nearly every high post in Guangdong; Guo Moruo headed the Academy of Sciences. Deng Xiaoping, a protégé of Liu Bocheng's, administered Sichuan and assigned his own loyal subordinate, Hu Yaobang, to administer the northeast, including Deng's home county—much as Mao assigned his successor, Hua Guofeng, to administer Mao's native county in Hunan.

Hakkas were especially prominent in the military, particularly among the four thousand Long Marchers who survived to 1950. In 1955, ten seasoned fighters became marshals, a rank above general. Three, Chen Yi, Ye Jianying, and Zhu De, were indisputably Hakka. Two more, Liu Bocheng and Nie Rongzhen, were probable Hakkas. By 1966–1968, some five hundred Long March veterans were in the military elite, 80 percent of them from central and south China. The highest-ranked Hakka below the marshals was probably Yang Chengwu (Changting, Fujian). Yang had served under Zhu De, helped lead the capture of Zunyi, then headed the heroic Dadu river crossing. After long service under Nie Rongzhen, he commanded the Beijing garrison, then became a colonel-general in the air force. Fang Fang, the former Meixian guerrilla, held many posts in the Southern military district under Ye Jianying before transferring to overseas Chinese liaison, where his ability to speak Mandarin, Cantonese, and Hakka was an important asset.

The Cultural Revolution

Hakka power waned during the Cultural Revolution. Mao, Kang Sheng (Shandong), and Lin Biao (Hubei) promoted a Yan'an-style ideology and may have felt some animus for their Hakka coworkers. The military had certainly been relatively outside central Party control, but strictures tightened as the Cultural Revolution proceeded. Resistance proved difficult. Chen Yi, for example, rallied former guerrillas, including Tan Zhenlin, to the "February Adverse Current" of 1967 that attempted to slow the tide and protect subordinates. But they were bitterly denounced as plotting to restore capitalism. Chen Yi talked back to a crowd of ten thousand Red Guards and kept his post, although he was forced into seclusion. Ye Jianying himself came under attack and spent much of the era under People's Liberation Army (PLA) protection in Guangzhou. Zhu De, whom the *Ci hai* later described as "ceaselessly struggling against Lin Biao and the Gang of Four," died in 1976. Many other military leaders were dismissed after 1973. Zeng Sheng, former commander of the East River Guerrillas and 1950s mayor of Guangzhou, was wounded and imprisoned.

Deng Xiaoping ranked second only to Liu Shaoqi as a target for abuse. Deng was exiled to an old Jiangxi base area in December 1966, an infantry school in Xinjian county, a Gan-Hakka area just northwest of Nanchang. There he oiled machinery every morning and played bridge every afternoon until he was rehabilitated in 1973. When he fell again in April 1976, Ye Jianying secretly flew him to safety in the Guangdong military region, hid him in Sichuan, and then continued to lobby the Central Committee on his behalf.

After his second rehabilitation in July 1977, Ye Jianying and Li Xiannian strongly backed Deng against Hua Guofeng. Hu Yaobang's career mirrored the ups and downs of his patron.

Many Hakkas, of course, weathered the upheavals. Yu Qiuli was probably the highest-ranked Hakka below Ye Jianying to survive the Cultural Revolution without severe damage to his career. Yu's story hints at how a skilled survivor might use a bit of ethnic solidarity to fortify an intricate combination of hard work, luck, and technical and political skill. Yu was born near the Jinggang mountains at Ji'an, Jiangxi, and made the Long March with Zhang Guotao. At Yan'an, Yu backed Mao but managed to remain allied with Zhou Enlai, Wang Zhen, and Deng Xiaoping. He followed Deng to Beijing and promoted the Daqing oil fields. During the Cultural Revolution, Zhou Enlai supported Yu even after Deng fell. After 1973, Yu realigned himself with Deng. By the 1980s, he headed the General Political Department of the PLA (Lampton with Yeung 1986, 151, 160, 184).

As the Cultural Revolution proceeded, Mao's faction invoked the Yan'an legacy with increasing fervor. Yan'an ideology had special resonance for the northern Party stalwarts who "went down" to work in the south (the *nanxia ganbu*). After Mao died, "localism" and other Long March–era issues closely associated with Hakkas became code words for attacks on Deng. Hua Guofeng used a eulogy for Zhu De as a crypto attack on Deng, denouncing Zhang Guotao, the Sichuan Hakka general who defected in 1938, for "splittism" and betrayal. No one directly criticized Yan'an iconography, but a parallel iconography developed around Long March imagery and praise for Hakka heroes. Yan'an and Long March imagery alternate: they do not coexist even in the patriotic tales selected for children's books. Immediately after Deng's rehabilitation, coded Long March imagery was used in a spate of biographies of Hakka heroes, including Zhu De, Chen Yi, and Ye Ting. Speeches by Ye Jianying and others on the fiftieth anniversary of the PLA also lauded them. And Ye Jianying himself delivered the much-edited official Party critique of Mao on 1 October 1979.

Deng cleverly highlighted his own role in early communism by using the Maoist legacy in 1981–1982. Deng had worked in pure Hakka Xunwu county, so he argued that both he and Mao had been there "seeking truth from facts." He also published many rural investigations from 1934–1943, including Mao's report from Xunwu that had been omitted from the definitive 1967 edition of Mao's *Selected Works*. Deng authorized a new edition to include the report, then published his own *Selected Works* in 1983. Officially sanctioned histories elevated Deng's role on the Long March, even claiming that "it never occurred to this old adherent of Mao's to follow Zhang Guotao." As Deng consolidated his power, a flood of Long March memoirs appeared. Ye Ting came to symbolize resistance to Maoist oppression. Popular posters showed him dressed in a long cape, writing poems on the wall of his prison cell; there was a flattering portrait and biography of him in the long-delayed 1979 *Ci hai*. Newspapers published poignant accounts of re-unions between Long March heroes and the children whom they had been forced to leave behind with Hakka peasants.

Fewer than one thousand Long Marchers survived into the 1980s, but they climbed back into power. Yang Chengwu, for example, a colonel-general in the air force who was purged in 1968, became commander of the Fuzhou military district by 1982. The only non–Long Marcher on the 1984 Standing Committee of the Politburo was Zhao Ziyang. (The other members were Ye Jianying, Deng Xiaoping, Hu Yaobang, Chen Yun, and Li Xiannian, the first three being Hakka.) Seventeen of the twenty-five Politburo members were Long Marchers, four of them Hakka, as were four of the nine members of the Military Affairs Commission—that is, five and fifteen times their respective chance rates. Other probable Hakkas above the minister (*buzhang*) level in 1989 included the former Beijing mayor Chen Xitong (Anyue county, Sichuan), an early Deng associate. Liu Fuzhi, Deng Xiaoping's longtime secretary and later a top security official, was a Meixian native, as was Yang Taifang, a Ye Jianying protégé who headed postal and telephone communications (Li 1988, 274–275, 230–231).[11] The Hakka heritage of capable women is not apparent at this level, although Nie Li, the daughter of Marshal Nie Rongzhen, is a colonel-general.

CONTINUED POVERTY IN HAKKA COUNTRY

Despite the successes of individual politicians, Hakka districts remain bitterly poor. Peasant life span has doubled since 1949, and income has risen, but none of the Yan'an, Hakka, or other inland peasants has prospered. Hakka leaders evidently avoided pumping gigantic sums into their home districts, and, in any case, the extreme poverty and population density of Hakka country overwhelmed whatever aid did arrive. Deng Xiaoping's home county, for example, has the only silk factory backed by foreign capital in the whole of China as well as half a million dollars in foreign aid. But, by official standards, it is still a poor county (WuDunn 1991). The only major investment that may have benefited Hakkas more than other peasants was the Third Front industrial development of 1964–1971. Even then, the motive was not rural development but national security. China felt threatened by the Soviet Union and the United States and so built heavy industry in the interior far from coastal attack. Whole railway lines and factories were moved inland, largely to areas over five hundred meters in altitude. The Sichuan highlands, including some of the remote western Long March route and the old Shaan-Chuan base, received much of the earliest investment (Naughton 1989). Most of Guangdong's "little Third Front" centered on Shaoguan prefecture, twelve especially rocky, mostly Hakka counties on the Hunan border. Third Front investment also built factories in old Fujian base areas, including Changting (Tingzhou) and Qingliu, counties so poor that land reformers had classed people as landlords if they had sweet potatoes to eat. Xiamen Red Guards made their way there in 1967 to recruit the peasants whom they had heard were "brave but ignorant, and therefore easier to command." But the city teenagers found that the language barrier presented "the greatest difficulty" and became ill on the local diet. One banker's son delivered his ultimate insult: western Fujian was like "Black Africa" (Ling 1972, 297–304).

By the 1980s, many Third Front enterprises had closed. Investment had never been adequate, and many enterprises were not viable economically. But their loss was a serious local blow, for little new investment appeared. A PLA munitions factory in Changting moved to the more prosperous Min-speaking coast, where it now makes motorcycle parts and brassieres. Every single Hakka worker and dependent eagerly relocated to Fuzhou.[12] Meixian prefecture also remained poor, for it includes three of the four poorest counties in Guangdong (Wuhua, Fengshun, and Dapu). In the late 1980s, the social scientist Ezra Vogel noted that many villages were still not connected by paved roads; even Meixian city was twelve hours from Guangzhou by car. (Air service began in 1987.) Meixian had no major hotel, and department stores did not stock towels because people dried themselves on rags. Meixian does have one of Guangdong's few key schools outside Guangzhou, thanks to Ye Jianying's patronage, but classes are very traditional. Meixian is also the single remaining inland area of Guangdong to export migrants. Overseas descendants outnumber current residents two to one, but the Hakka stress on professional rather than commercial success led sons and daughters to become soldiers, bureaucrats, or teachers, with little cash to invest back home. Xiamen and Guangzhou have thriving overseas outreach and scholarship programs, but Meixian publishes few books on Hakka history and had no research institute. However, most Meixian people still speak Hakka (Vogel 1989, 242–247). The language does have some economic clout; Fuzhou and Xiamen newspapers advertise Hakka lessons for entrepreneurs with expanding businesses in Southeast Asia.

CURRENT DECLINE OF HAKKAS IN HIGH OFFICE

Hakka power is now on the wane. Vogel claims that "more than 20 high Beijing officials of deputy rank or higher are of Hakka descent" (1989, 245), certainly an underestimate. But the Hakka gerontocracy seems not to have spawned a new Hakka elite. The only probable Hakka on the 1989 Politburo was Yang Rudai (Renshou, Sichuan), who retired in 1992. No Hakka sits on the Standing Committee. Ye Jianying's son, Ye Xuanping, was governor of Guangdong in the 1980s. Chen Yi's son, Chen Haosu, was deputy minister of radio, film, and television but was purged in June 1990, probably for anti–Li Peng activity (WuDunn 1990). This decline suggests a relative lack of corruption: in China, southern peasants led the unification of their nation, which, paradoxically, opened up more high posts for northerners.

Public discussion of Hakka history is increasingly possible, now that Hakkas are no longer a threat. The highest Hakka leaders are dying off, and the culture is being homogenized. The traditional Hakka militance and alternative common language are no longer in demand, even while the revolutionary ideals that once appealed disproportionately to land-hungry, iconoclastic peasants have steadily dimmed. Taiwan Hakka demands that the Nationalists "give us back our language" and share power undoubtedly shamed the Mainland into more openness. But, as traditional culture fades, the most reactionary central powers, Deng and the military, increasingly invoke Hakka iconography. Since the Beijing massacre of 1989, a burst of activities that benefit Hakkas has appeared. Many glorify the PLA and thus indirectly justify Deng's role. Song and dance troupes visited long-neglected Hakka base areas on the Fujian-Jiangxi border to perform local songs, local plays, and opera for retired Hakka veterans. A propaganda poster commemorating the founding of the Chinese Communist Party centers on a large portrait of Deng, surrounded by smaller images of Mao and other Long Marchers, including Zhu De, all ringed by Long March scenery and the wild geese that symbolize exile and reunion.

The word *Hakka* came "out of the closet" and into the headlines of the *People's Daily* for the first time in 1991 in a belated attempt to solicit overseas investment. Proposals included urban renewal for Meizhou, a research institute, a Hakka folk festival, and a Beijing museum of overseas Chinese history that would prominently feature Hakka history. Deng's Hakka ancestry was leaked to the Chinese public by a traditionally indirect and deniable route when a Communist-sanctioned Hong Kong newspaper with considerable Mainland circulation published the news as a "foreign expert's findings," summarizing an article of mine without my knowledge (see Sun 1991). But the iconography of Hakkas in patriotic dissent, now recycled to glorify geriatric central control, could backfire if it encourages a revival of stereotypes of Hakka crudeness. For now, it at least gets laughs. Even Party members parody Wang Zhen's rustic accent, while Deng Xiaoping, like the aged Mao, has his conversations rerendered in the accents of his youth by a daughter who shouts in his ear.

CONTINUING ISSUES FOR
HAKKA LANGUAGE AND IDENTITY

Hakka history clarifies the extremes of ethnic conflict, assimilation, and sacrifice for the national good. Of crucial importance was how the Hakka people used their language during a major transformation of broader Chinese society. Spoken Hakka is the primary unifier of what Benedict Anderson ([1989] 1991) calls "the imagined community." Seldom has a language so strongly defined ethnicity without other powerful ties of race or religion. Hakka dialect remains a powerful bond even in a nation united beyond all others by a national written script. And seldom has an ethnic group or its language been so strategically placed to serve a political movement of worldwide significance. Twentieth-century Hakkas worked their way to center stage in an era when national levels of literacy, partially modern communications, and a need for oral reconnaissance made Hakka literacy and vernacular writing, and its widely dispersed but partially shielded common language, exceptionally useful for guerrilla war. The low prestige of and lack of formal instruction in Hakka render this achievement all the more impressive.

How powerful can Hakka identity remain as monolingual speakers disappear? Only 3 percent of Chinese speak Hakka, but ethnic ties can endure even after a language dies, so long as a distinct identity remains useful, as the case of Irish Gaelic also shows. Many other issues remain unexplored. What is the role of ethnicity in Chinese socialism? How does Hakka ethnicity differ from other Han subethnic bonds? How does Hakka culture relate to modern movements for women, to social organization, to antilandlord movements, and to the military? How does it differ within China, in Taiwan, and overseas? What sort of Hakka factions survive in the army and the Central Committee? Did the First Front Army have more Hakka officers than other armies? Did Hakka factions play a role in later military district reorganizations? During the Cultural Revolution, did Hakkas disproportionately oppose Lin Biao and follow Ye Jianying? How do other personal ties interact with ethnic loyalty?

To what degree do Hakka connections still carry weight? Official China often sidesteps sensitive issues by publicizing a loyal individual. Ye Jianying was the token Hakka, but that position is too sensitive to be filled under the Deng regime. The government was not packed with Hakkas under Chen Yi, Deng Xiaoping, or Lee Teng-hui in Taiwan, but the struggle to balance ethnicity with equality continues.

GLOSSARY OF TERMS AND NAMES

Terms

Chinese Revolution: The revolution began with the overthrow of the Qing dynasty in 1911, but *the Chinese Revolution* refers to the Chinese Communist Party's 1949 liberation (*jiefang*) of the nation from the oppression of foreign imperialism following a five-year civil war against the Nationalist Party and its military. It was this revolution that established the current political regime.

Long March: The year-long retreat (October 1934–October 1935) of the Communists from their first Soviet in the Jinggang mountains of Jiangxi province to escape the Nationalist army that sought their extinction. It was a harrowing ordeal of human endurance that took peasants, Party members, and loyalists throughout marginal areas of southwestern and western China. Roughly ninety thousand people began the march; fewer than twenty thousand arrived. From the Party faithful who survived the ordeal has come a good number of the political leaders of this century, figures such as Mao Zedong, Zhou Enlai, Zhu De, Lin Biao, Bo Gu, and Deng Xiaoping.

Nationalists (Chinese: Guomindang [GMD], "National People's Party"): The ruling party of China from approximately 1912 to 1949. Following the Chinese Revolution, the party's principal leadership and followers fled to Taiwan and established the Republic of China. Until very recently, the Guomindang dominated the politics of this island. Taiwan is now a multiparty democracy.

Soviet: The base camps in which the pre-PRC Communists set up their system of collective ownership and equality, a rehearsal for later years when they came to power. The most important of these was established at Yan'an in the Shaanxi, Ningxia, Shanxi border region of north central China.

Xiucai (cultivated talent): First level of scholarly attainment in traditional China for those seeking bureaucratic appointment and roughly equivalent to an undergraduate degree. Increasingly irrelevant following the abolition of the imperial examination system.

Yan'an: The Communist base in northwestern China during the war with the Nationalists (1935–1949) where the peasant mobilization strategies of self-sufficiency, mutual aid, land reform, and guerrilla warfare—hallmarks of the CCP—were successfully implemented.

Names

Chen Yi (1901–1972): Hakka. Former commander of the First Army. Vice chairman of the Central Military Commission and foreign minister.

Deng Xiaoping (1904–1997): Hakka. Vice premier and former chairman of the Central Military Commission who was responsible for the economic and political reforms that opened China to the West.

Guo Moruo (1892–1978): Hakka. Romantic poet of the 1920s, founder of the Creation Society, Marxist literary critic. Vice premier of the PRC and president of the Chinese Academy of Social Sciences.

Hong Xiuquan (1813–1864): Hakka. Founder of the Society of God Worshipers and leader of the Taiping Rebellion. He was the "Heavenly King" of the Five Kings and emperor of the Taiping Heavenly Kingdom.

Hu Yaobang (1915–1989): Hakka. Last chairman of the CCP (the office was abolished), general secretary of the Party Secretariat, an advocate of liberal political reforms whose sudden death in April 1989 fomented the student discontent that led to the democracy protests in Tiananmen Square.

Hua Guofeng (1921–): Premier and later chairman of the CCP. Mao's appointed successor.

Li Lisan (1899–1967): Hakka. Effective labor organizer who insisted that national revolution could be provoked through targeted urban uprisings of workers in alliance with the Communist Party. Led the CCP from 1928 to 1930.

Li Xiannian (1909–1992): Minister of finance and president of the PRC (1983–1988).

Liu Bocheng (1892–1986): Hakka. Communist military commander. Marshal of the PRC and Politburo member.

Peng Pai (1896–1929): Hakka. Early CCP peasant organizer who founded the Hai-Lu-Feng Soviet in Guangdong in the late 1920s.

Shi Dakai (1831–1863): Hakka. One of the most brilliant generals of the nineteenth century, military commander of the Taiping forces and one of the "Five Kings" of the Taiping Heavenly Kingdom.

Song Qingling (1893–1981): Hakka. Madame Sun Yat-sen. Vice chairman of the Standing Committee of the National People's Congress, honorary president of China (1981).

Sun Yat-sen (1883–1925): Hakka. The national father of both China and Taiwan, he was a southern revolutionary leader who led the 1911 revolution that brought down the Chinese imperial government, helped found the Guomindang, and served very briefly as president of the Chinese Republic.

Wang Zhen (1908–1993): Hakka. Long March veteran and proagandist. Member of the Politburo and the Central Military Commission, vice premier of China.

Wei Guoqing (1913–1989): Zhuang. Long March veteran and former director of the General Political Department of the People's Liberation Army.

Yang Shangkun (1907–1998): Hakka. Vice chairman of the Central Military Commission and former president of the PRC.

Ye Jianying (1897–1986): Hakka. Former marshal of the People's Liberation Army, Party secretary, and governor of Guangdong.

Zhang Guotao (1897–1979): Hakka. One of the founding members of the Chinese Communist Party, and an effective union organizer and military leader. Favored the development of a multiparty system in the wake of the Revolution, and was accused of "splittism" for deviating from Mao's authoritarian insistence that the Communist Party alone would be supreme in politics.

Zhao Ziyang (1919–): Former Party general secretary and premier in the late 1980s. Demoted in 1989 for his opposition to the Party repression of the Tiananmen protests; he remains under house arrest today.

Zhou Enlai (1898–1976): Hakka. Former premier and foreign minister of China. A political and economic "moderate," he was the originator of the Four Modernizations.

Zhu De (1886–1976): Hakka. Founder of the Red Army, forerunner of the contemporary People's Liberation Army, and long-standing member of the Politburo of the Communist Party.

PART III
Social and Cultural Margins

To name something *marginal* is to claim that a center exists, which is contradictory to the aims of this book. Yet the *belief* that a center exists is something else again. There is a psychological center in views of China's society and culture; for Westerners, it may involve the exotic East, and, for Chinese, it may involve state-sponsored extravaganzas. It is such centers that dominate Western and Chinese representation of contemporary life and permit a facile understanding of China. The realities, however, are much more complex. It is not the case that we can generalize about *Chinese*, nor can we say anything definitive about *Chinese culture*. What we have done in this part of the book is to portray what we believe are little-known aspects of Chinese society and culture. Students have tended to be surprised when they learn that such things exist in contemporary China.

This part has chapters on sexuality, gender and work, migrants, rock and roll, and spiritual life. Sexuality in China, like sexuality in other societies, takes many forms. Yet each variation may be evaluated too; acceptance of a range of practices is familiar in the United States but not often found in China. Sexuality is front and center today, explicitly displayed in billboards, in magazines, on film and television, and in forms of dress, but, because it is not spoken of, sex stands on the edge of Chinese social life. Gender and work open up the difficult topic of what are believed to be the proper roles for men and women as well as the realities of who does what work. The centers of economic vitality may appear familiar to residents of U.S. cities, but the margins—which are now growing—may not. Because of China's recent economic and political history, people who had formerly been employed by state-sponsored factories or provided for in rural enterprises are now left to their own devices, creating one of China's largest social problems as they wander by the millions from countryside to city and from city to city. Popular music in China has many forms. One form favored by younger people is rock and roll, although it may not be entirely the same thing as what we find on our charts. Contemporary musical styles—including rap, hip-hop, grunge, and heavy metal—popular in the United States are manifest in China, and their local appropriation by young musicians has produced a new discourse that competes with, but does not overcome, politics. Finally, although religious and spiritual life is not well represented in the Western press, it is extremely varied in contemporary China, as the reader will learn from the small slice of religious life that we present below.

The sections in this third part may not fit together into a coherent picture of what a "typical" person in China is like, but they will ambiguate common assumptions sufficiently to provoke further reflection on the manifold splendor of this vast nation's real life and perhaps open space for comparison of the readers' culture with that of those they seek to understand.—Eds.

SEXUALITY

In this portion of the book readers are offered an opportunity to explore more easily the complexities of contemporary life through insight into the degree of change in sexual attitudes and practices among the Chinese. Although sex is a very private matter in the West, just as it is in China, we are very conscious of our less repressive but nonerotic sexual culture, but not inclined to regard it as a foundation for cross-cultural comparison. It is customary to credit China's celebrated economic and political reforms that began in the early 1980s and have continued unabated to the present with the increasingly liberal sexual consciousness of the national population. As a generalization this is accurate, but, as with many of the accurate generalizations about China that have been presented and questioned in this book, it has but contextual validity. Certainly, when the artifacts of contemporary sexual consciousness and practice are placed against the historical backdrop of the decades-long, post-Revolution, puritanical repression of desire mandated by the Party, where clothing styles for men and women were monochromatic, uniform, unrevealing, and unisexual, it is obvious that the changes of the last twenty years constitute a revolution.

In certain locales, such as the hyperurbanized enclaves of the south and southeast coast (Shanghai, Guangzhou, Hong Kong), Shenzhen and other special economic zones, and the northern capital, Beijing, sex sells and is inescapable. There is much evidence of this radical shift: public displays of affection between young couples, risqué clothing styles, brazenly shown tattoos, national anti-HIV/AIDS campaigns, prostitution, sex slavery, pinup calendars, women's fashion magazines, pornographic books and magazines, explicit condom promotion, and breast enhancement advocacy, along with a proliferation of visual images of the body, clad and scantily clad, strewn throughout the commercial blandishments of the new urban landscape.

In the countryside, the sexual atmosphere is less thick yet perhaps more real in that, there, sex is more immediately about life choices and is not so easily commoditized as a consumer product. Sex outside marriage is unusual in this setting, and a great number of marriages are still arranged according to the time-honored pattern of the parents of the couple and a go-between negotiating the alliance. The ideal of romantic love and its presumption of sexual parity are communicated to rural China via film, television, and the frequent movement of village family members to regional capitals for work. The chief consequence of this infusion of sexual knowledge is a refunctioning of traditional marriage practices so that the union of the rural couple may be predicated on love but accomplished through a deliberative process involving family members and friends.

As long as we accept that the commercial representation of desire reflects popular will and individual practice, then we may conclude that, with respect to sex, China is a lot like the West. Of course, this is not the case. According to Harriet Evans (2000, 239), even though "extramarital sexual relations are on the increase," choosing not to marry or to have a male lover is widely considered a sign of some "abnormality." Evans also observes that it is common for patrons of popular Beijing singles' bars to register if they are actively seeking a marriage partner. Simply because Chinese attitudes toward sexuality are more liberated does not mean, however, that the independence that Westerners associate with untrammeled exploration of sexual possibility with multiple partners has taken hold. Social boundaries governing the discussion and the practice of sex are firm and easily recognized in both urban and rural China, and there are areas such as homosexuality where little has changed in the way of public and legal opposition to individual habit.—Eds.

DALIN LIU, MAN LUN NG, LI PING ZHOU,
AND **ERWIN J. HAEBERLE**

TRANSLATED BY **MAN LUN NG**
AND **ERWIN J. HAEBERLE**

II
Sexual Behavior in Modern China

Roughly five years following the inauguration of China's economic reform and
"opening to the West," scholarly treatments of sexuality in China began to
appear. The 1980s saw the conducting of public seminars and conferences on
sexuality and contemporary sexual problems as well as publication of a number of academic journals. By 1990, there were a number of centers for sex
research in Shanghai, Shaoguan, Shenzhen, Beijing, and Heilongjiang. This
scientific pursuit of sexual knowledge and sexual practice paralleled the liberalization of Chinese social life and the marked increase in sexual expression.
This chapter is but an excerpt of a much larger English translation of a national
survey that represents the first attempt to study the most private, personal,
and individual aspect of people's lives in contemporary China: their sexual
behavior. Often compared to the Kinsey reports of U.S. sexual behavior in the
1940s and 1950s, China's "Sex Civilization Survey," as it is known, has been revolutionary and pioneering in the Chinese context.

Designed and administered by a team of sociologists, physicians, sexolo-
gists, and other practitioners of health-related and political fields in Shanghai,
the survey (conducted from February 1989 to April 1990) sought to establish
some general knowledge of the prevalence of premarital and extramarital sexual relations, homosexual relations, sources of information about sexuality,
satisfaction with sexual practices, and so forth. Twenty-one thousand five hundred questionnaires were distributed by 538 fieldworkers in twenty-eight
regions located in fifteen of China's thirty-one provinces. Ultimately, 19,559 of
the surveys were returned (94.4 percent): 6,092 from high school students,
3,360 from college students, 7,971 from married couples, and 2,136 from sex
offenders. Although the number of respondents was large, the survey was
drawn from a nonrandom sample, and, as sampling errors could not be eliminated, the findings reflected the habits of willing, cooperative respondents
and were, thus, not generalizable to the entire population. Although the findings did not yield many surprises, they present researchers with a baseline
from which to proceed. This information is essential for carrying out birth
planning and for preventing the further spread of HIV/AIDS, a considerable
national threat now that the government has acknowledged that there are

600,000 cases nationwide. (Chinese medical experts in the field confess that the number is closer to 2 million.)

The authors of the survey also provide a fascinating glimpse into a society that has had a reputation for prudishness and repression for most of the second half of this century. With an eye on comparison, they find that, in many areas, sexual behavior in China is similar to that in many other societies—yet with expected culturally shaped differences as well. They also examine differences within Chinese society, especially in terms of city and country, male and female, more and less educated. They provide their findings as a baseline from which future work on this heretofore controversial topic may proceed.

It is important to note that the survey or poll is an uncommon information-gathering mechanism in China and that complete candor when responding is unlikely to be obtained. Moreover, considering the rapid pace of social change in China, especially in the areas of premarital sex, prostitution, and masturbation, the figures from this survey, now ten years old, must be regarded as a mere glimpse of changing practice. Nevertheless, the trends are manifest here as well as in the admissions of public-health officials and Party members concerning the exponential increase in prostitution (the World Health Organization, among other organizations, estimates the number of prostitutes in Beijing alone to surpass 300,000) and the increasing incidence of AIDS and sexually transmitted diseases.

It is not prurience that drives us—or, for that matter, the researchers in China—to disclose these practices. Instead, it is our belief that the documented changes in this most private of activities convey a great deal about the changing experience of Chinese men and women. There is an urgent need for sex education in China; this survey aims at improving society's understanding of sexuality as a healthy expression of personhood. At the same time as it discloses a startling array of sexual interests and practices, the survey gently but persuasively gestures toward the moralistic interdiction of sexual license common to Party pronouncements. In addition to information about college students and married couples, this project includes a section on "sex offenders," that is, criminals incarcerated for sexual pathology. There is clearly a normative dimension to such an inquiry. It is important to point out that college students by law must be unmarried, so direct questioning about their sexual behavior constitutes something of a bold move, daring to point out something that is best covered up.

Finally, the authors point out that China has a severe lack of readily available information about sexuality, and they believe that a healthy society must include couples whose sexual and married lives are satisfying—which can be possible only if information about this is clearly transmitted to those on the brink of participating in sexual behavior. Indeed, in a compelling statement of this public-health concern about popular Chinese ignorance and repression of sex, one of the survey's authors, Liu Dalin, opened a sex museum in Shanghai in November 2000. The mild controversy that greeted this event suggests that, in China as well as in the United States, sex provokes intense reaction from those seeking to inculcate a healthy public attitude and from those wishing to stifle embarrassment and discomfort. The survey makes clear that, even with minimal data, sexual liberation has not occurred in China on the scale that it has in the West, but what we do learn about Chinese intimacy lessens the distance between our cultural worlds.

Caveat lector. What follows is an edited version of the introduction that accompanied a largely tabular presentation of the survey data. It was too cumbersome to reproduce the many tables from the original book's chapters (data for each of the survey's many questions were presented according to category: high school students, college students, married couples, sex offenders). For the intriguing questions about views on dating, numbers of sex partners, premarital sex, and age at first intercourse, we have reproduced the narrative account of the statistics, reordered from general to specific topics. Finally, we reprint the study's conclusions. This may seem an inelegant mechanism for presenting such fascinating data; however, the massive documentation of the survey in text and tables was not easily accommodated within the anthology as a whole, and we strongly urge interested readers to peruse the entire contents of *Sexual Behavior in Modern China* at their leisure.—Eds.

This is a report on the nationwide survey of sexual behavior conducted in China in the period ranging from February 1989 to April 1990.

In our survey, we included data on adolescent sexual physiological development, the extent and source of sexual knowledge, sexual attitudes and their changes, marital relationships, family planning, and sexual offenses. We considered all of this to be part of our sexual and social culture. The findings touch on the most personal experiences of the individual and have important implications for family life and society as a whole.

In the China of the late 1980s, people looked, above all, for social stability and therefore paid a great deal of attention to their marital and familial systems. However, in doing so, they overlooked some important things, as Alfred Kinsey wrote:

> Sociologists and anthropologists generally consider that the family is the basis of human society, and at least some students believe that the sexual attraction between the anthropoid male and female has been fundamental in the development of the human and infra-human family. . . . But whatever the phylogenetic history of the human family, the evidence is clear that the sexual factor contributes materially to its maintenance today. . . . Success or failure of a marriage usually depends upon a multiplicity of factors, of which the sexual are only a part. Nevertheless . . . where the sexual adjustments are poor, marriages are maintained with difficulty. (Kinsey, Pomeroy, and Martin 1948, 563)

Of course, the purpose of studying sexual matters is not only the strengthening of marriage or family. It will also benefit adolescent education, and ultimately it will contribute to the stabilization and solidarity of society.

This report can give only an introductory analysis of the data obtained in the survey. It is introductory because the wealth of the data is too great for an in-depth analysis within a short time. More detailed studies on the results may take another eight to ten years. In this report and introductory analysis, we hope to make a modest contribution in several areas:

1. **Information.** This is basic to any survey. We are aware of the limitations of any single survey. However, we make certain comparisons with other, smaller Chinese sex surveys of the last ten years and also with surveys in neighboring countries such as Japan.

2. **Theory.** By analyzing the large amount of data obtained, we aim to define and clarify a number of issues concerning the sexuality of the modern Chinese:

   a) **The relation between sexual attitude and behavior on the one hand and sociocultural factors on the other.** As social and cultural factors keep changing, parallel changes are expected in sexual attitudes and behavior. It is the task of this survey to identify these changes and their relations to find out the direction of the work needed in sex education and sex policies.

   b) **The commonalities and differences in Chinese sexuality.** The Chinese are an ethnically heterogeneous people. Their sexual attitudes and habits are also heterogeneous. The current process of modernization forces the Chinese to accept many great changes, including those in their sexual attitudes and behavior. It will be helpful to see how modernization influences sexuality in general and what the Chinese could or should do on their road to further development.

   c) **The quality of marriage in China.** Poverty and backwardness often go hand in hand with unhappy marriages. It would be good to know how much and what kind of marital counseling is needed and to whom and how much adult sex education should be provided.

   d) **Adolescent sexual problems.** Adolescents are our future leaders. Their need for sexual knowledge and sexual ethics has to be recognized, characterized, and measured for the planning of adolescent sex education.

   e) **Women's problems.** Sexual oppression especially victimizes women. Any sexual liberation should therefore begin with women. This survey aims to study the sexuality of Chinese women, how oppressed they are in their sex lives and how repressed in their sexual attitudes. On the other hand, are the rates of female sex offenses indicative of degrees of sexual liberation?

   f) **Sexual control.** In all societies, sexuality is regulated in many ways. This survey aims to discover how these control mechanisms work in modern China. Are they effective? Are they humane? Can or should they be changed? Should they be stricter or more lenient?

3. **Instruction.** Information leads to theoretical formulation. We hope to be able to arrive at some guidelines for teachers, health professionals, and policymakers in China.

However, in our present society, where multiple ethical rules coexist, it is very difficult for any suggestions to be absolutely neutral. Biases may be due to problems in information collection, for example, in the selection of study areas, the way questions are framed, and the method of conducting the study. All we can do is to try hard, looking at the facts from a distance, then make a preliminary analysis. Most important, we should not draw any rash conclusions.

In our simple survey there are many inadequacies of which we are well aware. It is practically impossible to estimate the number of subjects required for a representative sample for the whole population of 1.16 billion Chinese, not only because the population is vast, but because of the multiple racial and social characteristics in the many different regions of China. A large proportion of Chinese are farmers. Our sample on the other hand had only 20 percent who were farmers. This was much lower than we originally planned because of the difficulty in doing field studies in some of the rural areas and because many of the villagers were illiterate.

Another problem is that, because of the national attitudes toward sex, we either could not ask certain questions or could not find out significant details. For example, in the case of married couples, we could ask only about changes in sexual positions, not about the frequency of each type of position. Considering the general degree of sexual knowledge, we also asked only about the feeling of sexual pleasure and not about orgasm. These modifications made our studies less precise. Also, we surveyed only those groups of subjects that were of special concern to us, that is, high school and college students, married couples, and sex offenders. We did not survey the physically disabled, minority groups, the army, old people, or self-defined homosexuals. All of these are, without question, very important for a truly comprehensive survey. Such groups need to be surveyed in the future.

However, we did make some effort to ensure a certain degree of representativeness of our information. In our survey design, we aimed at surveying two large groups of subjects: a large group presumed to consist of social conformists and a smaller group of nonconformists, in this case sex offenders. In the conformist group, subdivisions were made into married and unmarried (students). The unmarried were further divided into those who were below or above age eighteen (high school and college students). By this way of linking and grouping, we try to trace the information following the paths of physiological, psychological, and social development. Thus, we tried to make sure that the information can be cross-validated. We hope that, by tracing the main line of development, we can obtain some reliable information about the sexual behavior of "mainstream" modern China.

All scientific research has its subjectivity and its limitations, and our survey is no exception. We see this survey as a first step on a long road to truly meaningful sexological research. It was a difficult yet rewarding step. We dedicate this survey to all those interested in sexological studies. It has to be emphasized that this survey represents the work of forty researchers and five hundred additional fieldworkers. The present report was written by the few of us who synthesized, analyzed, and reported the results.

HOW THE SURVEY WAS CONDUCTED

This survey was organized by the Shanghai Sex Sociology Research Center. We wanted to obtain data on the physiological development of both sexes, sexual knowledge, sources of sexual knowledge, the sexual attitudes of young people, the marital and sexual relationships of married couples, and their family-planning practices. We also wanted some information about sex offenders. Thus, the subjects of our survey were high school students, college students, married couples in cities and rural areas, and sex offenders. Of the usable questionnaires, 31.1 percent were from high school students, 17.2 percent were from college students, 40.8 percent were from married couples, and 10.9 percent were from sex offenders.

The regions covered in this survey are Heilongjiang, Liaoning, Beijing, Tianjin, Shandong, Shanxi, Jiangsu, Shanghai, Zhejiang, Fujian, Guangdong, Henan, Sichuan, Xinjiang, and Ningxia. All in all, there were twenty-eight regions located in fifteen provinces of China. Five hundred and thirty fieldworkers participated in the research. The fieldwork began in February 1989 and ended in April 1990.

Social Background

The fact that this survey could be conducted at all was mainly due to the changing social and political climate in the China of the late 1980s.

Beginning in the early 1980s, China took rather bold steps to implement a new "open policy." With an increasing exchange between the Chinese and Western societies, a market economy developed and greatly elevated the average Chinese living standard. As a result, new and varied social contacts became possible, with an increase in basic needs. More and more people escaped from the prison of traditional thinking and came face to face with reality. Seeking love, affection, and marital happiness, they felt entitled to a healthy and harmonious life. These aspirations gradually led the Chinese of all ages to investigate the hitherto secret world of sex for themselves and talk more openly about it.

Another reason for this new preoccupation with sex was an increase in sexual problems manifesting themselves in the wake of the open policy. Generally speaking, the speed of reform greatly exceeded the psychological ability to follow. Most people were unable to anticipate and study, much less modify, the negative influences of Western civilization and of the new market economy suddenly growing in China. Sexual problems became more prevalent, and sex education was unable to keep up. Problems became visible in the following major areas:

1. **An increasing rate of early love relationships between young people.** According to the yearly Shanghai 1985–1988 survey, of the senior high school students, about 60 percent had love affairs. There also was significant percentage among junior high school students.

2. **A great increase in premarital sex.** According to the statistics of a few major hospitals, in 1986 there was a 16 percent overall increase of premarital pregnancies and requests for induced abortions.

3. **A great increase in extramarital sex.** According to a few surveys from 1988, the number of divorces due to adultery increased to the point of accounting for 25–40 percent of all divorces.

4. **An increase in the reported cases of sexual disharmony in married couples.** In 1984, in Shanghai, 23 percent of divorces were due to sexual disharmony. Two years later, in 1986, nearly twice as many couples, namely, 45 percent, reported sexual disharmony.

5. **An increase in sex offenses.** According to Shanghai statistics, from 1979 to 1983, the number of rapes increased more than $3^{1}/_{2}$ times, and the age of rapists became lower. There were more group rapes, and not only were these more violent, but they also turned out to have been premeditated.

6. **An increase in prostitution.** In the last ten years, prostitution has spread from coastal cities to medium-sized cities in the country's interior and from there even to the villages. In 1987 the number of prostitutes arrested in China was 240 times that in 1979.

7. **Spread of sexually transmitted diseases.** In recent years, the rate of sexually transmitted diseases has been increasing by 300 percent a year in China. AIDS has reached China as well.

8. **An increase in pornographic publications.** The government reported an increasing number of campaigns to eradicate pornography, indicating a spread of these materials in China.

9. **Confusion in sexual attitudes.** In China, feudalistic sexual attitudes still retain some influence. Add to these Western capitalism, which seeped into China over the last one hundred years, mixed with Communist teachings in the new China, modified again by the latest American and European fads and fashions, and the predictable result is a great deal of confusion among Chinese young people. China is still searching for a new, healthy, and rational attitude toward sexuality.

10. **Family planning is facing great difficulties.** China aims to control population, trying to keep it under 1.2 billion, but, in view of the difficulties in teaching and implementing family planning in distant regions, there is a high probability that the goal cannot be reached. This is another reason why the government and the people both realize the importance of sex education.

All of the above are real problems, but most of them are difficult to admit—especially prostitution and sexually transmitted diseases. Some people think that to admit these problems is to shame the country and the Communist doctrine. Yet, with the progress of modernization and the open door policy, facts cannot be hidden for long, and it is therefore a historical necessity to face and solve these problems.

The Tortuous Path

A few years ago, although worried about its feasibility, we had thought of doing a large-scale national sex survey. Obviously, we would need enormous resources as well as government and public support.

By the autumn of 1988, however, there were some hopeful signs. A letter from Jiang of Xiamen University invited us to help organize a sex survey. We explored the possibilities, and, to our surprise, there were more people throughout the country willing to help than we had expected. Not a single request we mailed out received a negative reply.

Hence, the initiation of this survey was the result, not of some capricious impulse on the part of a few workers, but the answer to a true social need. There were, of course, warnings that we should be cautious. A colleague in Beijing wrote to us that such a survey should be planned very carefully, that it should take national sentiments into account, and that 80–90 percent of the attempts at this type of survey were known to fail anyway. In response to such warnings, we decided to undertake some pilot studies in what were possibly the most difficult regions.

Thus, we decided on a pilot survey in the villages. Farmers constitute 80 percent of the population of the whole country. Yet they are the least educated and usually the most conservative group. If the villagers would receive our project well, there would be even fewer problems in the cities.

The village pilot survey was made possible with the help of Huang, vice principal of Shanghai Women Officials Training College, who was also a member of the Shanghai Sex Sociology Research Center. Through the Women's Unions of four *xians* (towns), Jinshan, Jiading, Qinpu, and Songjiang, four hundred men and women in the villages were surveyed. We learned from the experience and modified the questionnaire in order to make it more acceptable. We also reinforced the efforts to prepare the respondents by giving detailed instructions and explanations and by assuring them of the strictest confidentiality.

The last step before starting this large survey was to secure adequate financial resources. China had very limited funds for any kind of scientific research. The Shanghai Sex Sociology Research Center, being just a public academic body, in order to run a survey of this caliber, had to look beyond its own resources. At the beginning, some businesses within and outside of China promised support, and therefore we started the survey. The well-known events in June 1989, however, caused some unexpected difficulty; foreign financial restrictions imposed on China and the recession that followed caused many of the original resources we had relied on to disappear. But, since we had started, we decided not to give up.

Soon after the beginning of the actual survey, however, we were unfortunate enough to confront a number of social campaigns that caused us serious difficulties. There was a campaign against permitting capitalism, followed closely by a national campaign against obscenity. To our way of thinking, however, the best way of eradicating obscenity was the dissemination of scientific information about sex and the promotion of healthy and rational ideas. But it seemed that the general public was not yet ready for our approach. Anything relating to sex was considered obscene and was therefore faced with the threat of eradication. Some people asked our fieldworkers: "Is this really the right time to ask people about sex?"

Hence, many of our fieldworkers could not successfully interview the selected subjects as planned. One of the regional team leaders, Yao of Shanghai, started with an agreement from ten universities to participate in the survey with their students, but, when she approached the universities after the social campaigns mentioned above, all ten universities refused to honor that agreement. So did the high schools that earlier had made the same promises to Liu of Beijing. At the universities in Xinjiang, after half of the students were surveyed, cooperation was suspended by higher officials, and other universities had to be found as substitutes in order to complete the survey. One fieldworker was criticized and disciplined by her superiors for having participated in the survey.

These were not the only difficulties. Many villagers were illiterate, so the fieldworker had to read the questions to them one by one and then fill in the answers. Interviewing prison inmates, the fieldworkers had to endure poor and hot environments and deal with the resentment of people to whom the survey made no sense at all. A great deal of effort was required to help inmates understand the questions in order to obtain their cooperation.

There were some advantages, as well. A closely linked structure is a characteristic of Chinese society. Our survey made full use of this and thus was channeled through all regional bureaus concerned, such as Planned Parenthood committees, the Women's Federation, the Workers' Union, schools, police departments, correctional facilities, social science institutes, publication networks, and others. The implementation moved all the way down from provincial bodies to cities, to towns and villages, step by step. Hence the process of work distribution and duty allocation was quite simple.

Because our survey was implemented through official organizations, our surveys on students and sex offenders were conducted in groups. Group questionnaire completion is a better method in this kind of situation because: (1) When questionnaires are administered by a trusted official and in a group situation, the subjects are more likely to cooperate as they find it easier to believe in the worth and seriousness of the survey. (2) When so many others are filling in the questionnaires at the same time, some of the individual fears of "sticking out" or being identified diminish. (3) Individual interviews, especially on sexual matters, tend to provoke anxiety in the individual.

Sampling and Statistics

The ideal sampling procedure for this type of survey is random sampling, but under the current conditions in China, on a topic that most people were yet unable to fully understand, it is a sampling method that could not be used. Since the survey was neither funded nor officially supported by the government, we did not have access to the central government population statistics and their breakdowns according to age, occupation, marital status, level of education, and other demographic characteristics. This made the process of random sampling or stratified random sampling in the cities and villages impossible. The lack of uniform cooperation in a district area also made the selection of representative samples using random or semirandom procedures impossible.

Thus, although we realized the value of using random sampling as much as possible, we could use only nonrandom procedures. Our procedures can be divided into two stages. In the first stage, we selected survey points. Based on our knowledge of the size of the cities and their locations, we chose about the same number of cities and villages in the interior, coastal, northern, and southern regions of the country. However, admittedly, our choice was also influenced by "convenience" in the sense that we picked places where cooperation was likely to be obtained.

In the second stage, we specified the sample characteristics and calculated the sample size needed for getting representative data at the survey spot. The team leader for that region then was free to decide how he would go about obtaining the sample—by random or intentional sampling—as long as the subjects met the required characteristics and number. Hence, in this second stage, various types of sampling procedures, such as intentional, random, convenience, or others, were used by different regions.

By these standards, the survey should be seen as a nonrandom sampling survey. Since it is impossible to eliminate sampling errors under these conditions, the data obtained from the sample cannot be generalized to the whole population. We believe, however, that, because of our interest in and our acquaintance with the population in question, the subjects chosen represent those that are of interest to us, as well as to sex educators and policymakers in China, and that they have a certain degree of representativeness for all Chinese.

In interpreting the results, some other defects of this survey must be acknowledged and taken into account. The questionnaire design left much to be desired in terms of the method of measurement, sequencing, and categorization. Occasionally, the vocabulary and usage of terms might not have been clear enough to prevent misinterpretation. Some answers were missing for various reasons, and the sample distribution could still be biased despite a deliberate attempt to survey representative regions and groups.

We believe, however, that our experience with this survey—including shortcomings and mistakes—could serve as a basis for better studies of a similar nature in the future. During our survey period, for example, Keng successfully finished a sexuality survey on 2,050 city couples and 2,080 university students using more representative samples. We are glad to know that her findings closely match ours in many of the sexual behaviors surveyed, for example, on physiological sexual development, masturbation frequency, the ways couples get married, the rate of premarital sex, sexual satisfaction, and so on.

FIRST SEXUAL INTERCOURSE

Age at First Sexual Intercourse

The mean age was 25.45 for the city couples and 22.88 for the village couples. The mode was between 21 and 30. Intercourse before age twenty-one (i.e., below the nation's legal age of marriage) was reported by 5.7 percent of city couples and 17.6 percent of village couples. Obviously, then, to a certain extent, early (illegal) marriage or premarital sex is being practiced, more so in the villages.

Partner for First Sexual Intercourse

Of all the subjects, 81.9 percent of the city subjects and 92.5 percent of the village subjects had their first sexual intercourse with the individual who would later be their spouse; 3.1 percent of city subjects and 3.2 percent of the village subjects had their first sexual intercourse with nonspouses. (The remainder reported "unknown.")

More females had their first sexual intercourse with their eventual spouses, indicating that probably the females were more cautious with their first sex partners and took the whole encounter more seriously. Of all the cities, Guangzhou (Guangdong province) and Xiamen (Fujian province) had the greatest number of subjects who had sex with nonspouses, probably indicating the degree of sexual permissiveness in these cities.

Among the city subjects, the younger the subjects, the more they had their first sexual intercourse with nonspouses. It could be that the city subjects, especially the younger ones, were more liberal in their sexual attitudes. They were also less likely to get married due to financial constraints, high mobility, and a time-consuming education.

For the village subjects, however, there was no significant relation with age. For the village wives, those who had first sex with nonspouse were subjects of ages forty-six to fifty-five or below age twenty-six. The village husbands showed even a reverse relation; that is, the older the subjects were, the more they had had their first sexual encounter with nonspouses.

Among the city subjects, education level had little to do with the type of partner for first sexual intercourse, but more of the less educated had their first sexual encounter with nonspouses. Among the villagers, there was a significant relation with education.

Occupation had very little to do with the type of partner one had first sexual intercourse with.

Premarital Sex

Of those surveyed, 62.4 percent of the city husbands, 70.8 percent of the city wives, 69.3 percent of the village husbands, and 62.3 percent of the village wives had their first sexual intercourse on their wedding day.

The younger the couples were, the more they had had premarital sex. Education level had little to do with premarital sex, except among village wives. In general, the trend indicates that the more highly educated had premarital sex. Occupation also had little to do with premarital sex.

Our findings were different from those of Kinsey, who found that the better educated had less premarital sex. In Kinsey's view, it was because the well educated had more self-control.

In the past, the Chinese believed premarital sex to be a corruptive influence from the West. But, in the 1980s, premarital sex gradually spread in China, almost becoming a common practice. The figures of premarital pregnancies can give an idea of the increase. In 1982 in Shanghai, the figure of premarital abortions was 39,000. In 1983, it had grown to 50,000. In 1984, it was 65,000. In Wuxi in 1986, the figure was 5,112, and 16 percent of the subjects were above age twenty. In Jinhua Xian of Zhejiang in 1988, there were 1,704 cases of induced abortion for first pregnancies, and 90 percent of these were premarital. Some of the subjects had induced abortions up to ten times.

MARRIAGE AND LOVE

The Paths to Marriage

How the spouses become acquainted and how they get married, to a certain extent, influence the mutual perception of the marriage. It can be an important factor in the subsequent development of their feelings for each other. For the Chinese, there are many different ways of finding a spouse. These ways could be divided into two groups: free and arranged marriages. The free marriages result from chance acquaintances or from informal introductions by various intermediaries. The arranged marriages are usually set up by parents, sometimes for economic reasons, and there are also cases of forced marriage.

Two percent of city couples and 4.3 percent of village couples were married through arranged marriages. For free marriages, the percentages were 97.0 and 95.2, respectively. More city couples than villagers got acquainted by themselves.

Our data show that most couples had met as a result of some introduction by others. In a 1984 survey in Shanghai, Beijing, and Guangzhou, 65.1

percent, 68.3 percent, and 60.8 percent of couples were married as a result of introduction. A survey in Heilongjiang in 1986 showed also that, in the period from 1982 to 1986, 67.23 percent of newly married couples reported that they had met as a result of introduction. This dominant form of getting acquainted was found, not only in the less educated, but also in the well educated. In a survey in Tianjin in 1983, 71 percent of the college graduates had found their spouses through introduction. This shows that the social circle of many Chinese is probably rather small.

The overall finding relating to the type of marriage is that the proportion of arranged marriages in modern China is low—at around 2.4 percent of all marriages. Yet, if the large Chinese population in China is considered, this percentage represents a total of about 5 million couples in arranged marriages. This is about the total number of couples in a medium-sized country. Furthermore, arranged marriages are still found in some subjects under the age of thirty-five. This shows that freedom of marital choice has not yet been achieved everywhere in China.

Arranged marriages in China are not due only to low education levels; economic need is also a cause. Under the pressure of poverty, women are still considered family property to be "given in marriage" for profit. There are many ways in which one can dispose of this property. A direct way is to actually sell women in the market, as still practiced in northeastern villages. In the 1950s and 1960s, the price was 200 yuan for single-eyelid women, 400 yuan for double eyelids. The price is known to have increased considerably in the 1980s. More commonly, however, parents gave a girl away in return for a "wedding gift" (often a certain sum of cash) from the bridegroom. According to the study of the National Marriage and Family Research Society, in the 1980s, about 0.5 percent of villages asked for wedding gifts at a price of over 3,000 yuan. In 1986 the percentage rose to 10.5 percent, and, in certain provinces, the percentage was up to 47 percent. This over tenfold increase is disproportional to the average income of the inhabitants, which barely doubled during the same period.

There is another way to sell a bride directly. For example, in Heilongjiang, a father had twice forced his daughter to get married in order to pay debts, first for 1,000 yuan and later for 3,000 yuan. In Shaanxi province, a villager sold his three daughters to three mental patients for 13,300 yuan. Many female suicides were found to be related to this kind of forced marriage.

Nothing but Love?

A commonly held view is that love is more important than anything else: "Everything can be given up for the sake of love!" For young people, this view translates into the following conviction: "As long as a pair of lovers are in love, they can have sex, even if they are not married to each other." With this view, 34.3 percent of the males and 16.0 percent of the females agreed. This agreement did not vary with the education level of the subjects.

The agreement, however, had a significant relation with the subjects' sexual histories. Most of these subjects had not had their first sexual experience with their spouse or future marital partner. This shows how much sexual attitudes influence sexual behavior.

Most scholars do not agree that love should be put above all other concerns. After all, love must be considered within the context of other good things in life that it enhances and that, in turn, color its character. If the importance of love is exaggerated to such a degree that it renders everything else insignificant, it loses its original meaning and purpose. As a Chinese scholar, Fu Lei, said, "In my whole life, I have never taken love as being above everything."

SEXUALITY ON COLLEGE CAMPUSES

Sex Partners

By *sex partner,* we mean a partner with whom one engages in coitus. Of the 640 subjects who answered this question, 312 (48.8 percent) reported none; 213 (33.3 percent) reported having one such partner; 101 (15.8 percent) reported having had two to five; 6 (0.9 percent) reported having had six to ten; and 8 (1.3 percent) reported having ten or more partners. Hence, a total of 328 (51.25 percent) of the college students had had sex partners.

Of the male students, 12.5 percent had sex partners; of the females, 6.3 percent had such partners. A greater proportion of the males had multiple sex partners. Based on the desired professions of the students, those with partners were: arts, 11.0 percent; science, 9.3 percent; engineering, 10.3 percent; agriculture, 9.8 percent; and medicine, 7.5 percent.

The older the subjects were, the higher the percentage became of those who had sex partners.

Of those who had sex partners, 328 used contraception. Of these, fifty-eight (17.7 percent) took pills, twenty-five (7.6 percent) used spermicide, sixty (18.3 percent) used condoms, fifteen (4.6 percent) used a diaphragm, forty-two (12.8 percent) practiced coitus interruptus, ninety-nine (30.2 percent) used the rhythm method, twenty-seven (8.2 percent) used miscellaneous methods, and two (0.6 percent) did not specify any method. This shows that, among college students, there was sufficient knowledge of contraception, but the fact that 30.2 percent of them used the rhythm method indicates that they either could not afford the cost of other, more effective contraceptive methods or were ignorant of the rhythm method's poor effectiveness.

Sexual Attitudes

The core content of sexual attitudes is one's ethical evaluation of sexual issues. There are three levels of sexual ethics: the level of penal law, the level of social mores, and the level of personal convictions and choices. Of all segments of the population, college students represent most those that are young, knowledgeable, and sexually open-minded. Their sexual attitudes are likely to influence individuals of the immediate future in China.

Views on Dating in College Students

Of all the students surveyed, 0.9 percent replied that dating among college students should be forbidden, 1.8 percent thought that it should be controlled, 66.4 percent thought that it should be put under guidance, and 28.8 percent thought that it should be freely allowed (2.1 percent did not answer clearly).

Significantly more females than males replied that it should be put under guidance. Significantly more males than females thought that it should be freely allowed. The higher the grade level, the more students think that dating should be freely allowed. The reverse is true for those who thought it should be guided. This shows that the senior students were more confident of their ability to take care of their own affairs and did not wish to have their dating behavior interfered with by others.

Of the various professions, the highest percentage of arts students thought that their dating behavior should be allowed to develop freely.

Before 1985, dating among college students was considered misconduct. The students involved were criticized, reeducated, and even punished. But this policy proved to be impractical. It only drove the students to secret or underground dating and to outright lying. It also put them under tremendous pressure. After 1985, friendships among male and female college students were allowed to be more open. The school authorities in general did not interfere with dating, although they hardly encouraged it. But this policy still did not face reality. The result was that dating affairs could not receive any proper guidance, something very much needed, as shown by the responses of the students in this survey. We believe that college students should be allowed to get married or should be allowed to love and date freely, but, in China today, this still cannot be done.

CONCLUSIONS

1. Contemporary Chinese society is undergoing rapid change. Many obsolete ideas have been rejected, but not all. Our survey shows many of these contradictions:
   a) Many women and men want to marry for love, but often have only the vaguest concept of love; that is, they do not know what exactly love is and is not.
   b) Many claim satisfaction with their marital sex life generally but are not satisfied with many of its details.

c) Many are interested in knowing more about sex, and are open-minded about it, but take no initiative to look for information.

d) The status of women has improved, but few are concerned with the quality of their sex lives, including the women themselves.

e) Many have some sexual knowledge, but it is often fragmentary and not comprehensive enough.

f) Many try various ways of enhancing sexual pleasure (e.g., different sexual techniques and positions), but they do so only secretly, and there is no open agreement that it is all right.

g) Many understand the importance of family planning for the nation, but many still practice contraception reluctantly or deliberately avoid it.

h) There is a general open-mindedness about divorce and extramarital sex, but not necessarily when it comes down to one's personal life.

i) There is an increase in premarital and extramarital sex, but there is a great deal of controversy concerning its meaning.

j) The problem of sex in the aged has been identified but not yet given its due attention.

These and many similar matters have to be dealt with in the future sexual culture of China. In order to find solutions, one will have to improve the people's quality of life, and this is inseparable from an improvement in economic circumstances.

2. The usual idea about Chinese families is that they are very stable, and this is believed to be an asset in Chinese society. Our survey, however, raises the point that it is not always enough to be satisfied with outward stability. We must look at the basic reason for the stability. It is obvious that marriage and family as examined and described by us are of high stability but low quality. For example, outward satisfaction often hides underlying frustration. Therefore, one may ask whether outward stability is, in fact, hiding inward instability? It is important to identify these problems and to solve them.

3. To improve the quality of marital sex, it is important to help people to have a proper attitude toward sex. Previously, sex was considered "dirty" by many people, but now we encounter many different attitudes. It may be appropriate today to emphasize the pleasure function of sex and to put it in a social perspective.

4. To enhance the quality of sex for married couples, it may be necessary to emphasize the role of affection and love in marriage. Our survey shows that there are still many married couples who consider sex as nothing more than a duty or a means of producing offspring. This is likely to make sex monotonous, lowering the quality of the marriage.

5. There are still moral controversies about some sexual issues, such as masturbation, premarital and extramarital sex, divorce, and chastity. It is quite impossible to find one universal morality governing such matters.

Sex education should probably teach the moral principle that any behavior is permissible as long as it is harmless to others and takes place by mutual consent.

6. There is a need for adult sex education. It should emphasize the importance of and difference between affection and moral duties, rights, and responsibilities. To maintain a happy and enduring marital relationship, it is not effective to depend only on the force of morality and the law because they can, at best, maintain only a superficial stability. Teachings about mutual respect and love, on the other hand, will strengthen the foundations of a stable and happy marriage.

7. A greater emphasis should be placed on the sexual needs of women and the aged. Our survey shows that women remain largely under the influence of traditional concepts and are therefore more removed from factual sexual knowledge and flexible sexual attitudes. The sex life of the elderly is also largely neglected by most people.

8. Our survey shows that sexual behavior is determined very much by sexual knowledge and sexual attitudes. If we want to minimize conflict in this area, we must popularize sex education and see it as part of our society's civilizing process. In view of the social changes now occurring, we must work for a more open and tolerant atmosphere. Only this way can we hope to adapt well to the rapidly modernizing world.

12

The Cut Sleeve Revisited

A Contemporary Account of Male Homosexuality

The national sex survey presented in chapter 11 provided an incomplete cata-
log of sexual practices, and Vincent Gil's essay takes up one of the most glaring
deficiencies in its respondent pool: male homosexuals. The article's title is a
reference to the book by Brett Hinsch, *Passions of the Cut Sleeve* (1990), and to
the use of a "cut sleeve" as an indication of sexual preference from the Han
dynasty (208 B.C.E.–220 C.E.) onward.[1] Here, Gil, a medical anthropologist
and sexologist, discusses what he learned from an ethnographic interview
with an acknowledged homosexual, comparing what he learned to the official
denial and repression of homosexual behavior. Through a mutual acquaintance, the author meets "G.I. Joe," a singer at dance clubs in a city in southwest China, and discusses the complexities of being a self-acknowledged gay
man in contemporary China. Clearly, homosexuality is not officially tolerated,
but Joe knows how to negotiate the external constraints imposed by Chinese
society and lives a life of artistry, with a series of short-lived encounters. Gil
puts all this in context and in turn suggests something of the way nonmain-
stream behavior coexists with official proscriptions against it.

Although homosexuality is stigmatized in many (but not all) human societies, the particular forms that it takes in China disclose some of the struggles
and contradictions peculiar to selves in that society. In China, unlike the
United States, individual free choice of "lifestyle" exerts no dominance over
social expectations. For a more quantitative contextualization of homosexuality in China, we refer interested readers to Pan, Wu, and Gil (1995). This pioneering research, based on interviews or brief meetings with nearly eight
hundred acknowledged gay men in cities throughout China, reveals an enormous range of sexual behavior and attitudes. Most gay men marry; there is no
organized movement of homosexual identification, although informal identification appears to be increasing compared to earlier periods in the People's
Republic when austerity and puritanism dominated Chinese sexuality. Still, it
is very difficult to find private places to meet, and, thus, many trysts occur in
anonymous, public places. Beijing has a "gay park"; gay men also meet at cer-

FIGURE 12.1
A very clean public
latrine in contemporary
China. (Photograph by
Dr. Louis C. Liley Jr.)

tain clubs, hotels, restaurants, and "corners" in addition to other portions of parks, public toilets, and public baths (Pan, Wu, and Gil 1995, 6, 9) (see fig. 12.1). The closeted and ominous nature of homosexuality in China has the consequence that long-term relationships among homosexual men are difficult to pursue, despite much explicit value placed on such relationships by the men interviewed and surveyed. From Gil's courageous ethnography, the reader learns much about the difficulties of love and intimacy while obtaining a better sense of the grave public-health consequences of contemporary Chinese sexual behavior.—Eds.

This report is based on material collected during a brief ethnographic interview with a self-disclosed male homosexual in China. I was part of a medical delegation to the People's Republic of China assessing the status of HIV/AIDS and providing collaborative exchanges on the management of the infection throughout the country. The visit was undertaken in November 1990. As the sole medical anthropologist and sexologist on the delegation, I was privy to departures from the schedule for ethnographic observations. During one such departure, at a dance club (not "gay" club) in a provincial city of southwest China, I was introduced to "G.I. Joe."[2] Joe, who is a self-admitted homosexual, agreed to a brief interview—in his flat with a mutual Chinese friend/interpreter present. This interview was tape-recorded and later transcribed and translated.

Joe's story, while certainly not to be taken as wholly typical, does provide rare insights into the life of a homosexual in Mainland China. As such, this ethnographic narrative contextualizes biographical material within the political realities of the culture in which Joe functions. It is hoped that this brief ethnographic interview also articulates those intricate details and hidden experiences of living as a homosexual in contemporary China.[3]

Before the Revolution of 1949, China had a long history of dynastic homosexuality (Pan [1947] 1970; Van Gulick 1961; Ruan and Tsai 1987; Lau and Ng 1989; Hinsch 1990), courtly love among rulers and subjects of the same sex being elevated to a noble virtue (Hinsch 1990). This tolerance for male sexual diversity throughout much of Chinese history was accumulated in a well-developed literature, which allowed the male homosexual a modicum of introspection and self-reflection about his orientation, particularly if the person was literate. The surviving literature of the Spring-Autumn period (770–475 B.C.E.), of the Warring States period (475–221 B.C.E.), and of the Qin and Han dynasties (221 B.C.E.–220 C.E.) indicates that homosexuality was accepted by the royal courts[4] and its custom widespread among the nobility. Even Puyi, the last Qing emperor (r. 1908–1911 C.E.), was steeped in an awareness, if not the practice, of the ancient icons of male custom (cf. Ch'en 1965). The dynastic record is one, then, of general tolerance for the male homosexual and an amoral, if not moral, construction of the lifestyle itself.

The evolution and transformation of homosexuality into a moral negative in Chinese society has been well elaborated by Hinsch (1990). Suffice it here to say that it was only in the final epoch of dynastic history that intolerance began to build, the product, as Hinsch (1990) proposes, of an admixture of neo-Confucian familism, Manchu concepts of sexuality, and a reaction against Ming sexual permissiveness. Increased intolerance of homosexuality also infiltrated China along with Western contacts (Ruan and Tsai 1987). The growing antipathy accelerated in the twentieth century under Mao Zedong (cf. Ruan and Tsai 1988).

Fueled by the remnants of Confucian morality, the Revolution of 1949 ensured that homosexuality would be swept away, at least to the underground (Butterfield 1982; cf. Ruan and Tsai 1988), as a bourgeois and decadent practice. A puritanical, if not heavy-handed, sexual "primness" became firmly established (Stafford 1967). This included a denial of romantic love and the affirmation of the absolute role of the collective over the individual as a basic tenet toward which one should direct any affections. The Great Leap Forward demanded, in Communist parlance, the "renunciation of the heart." Party policy deliberately constructed an altruism that sought (for every man and woman) hard work through the day, without being "deflected or confused" by love, sexual desire, or any strivings for private happiness. However, by the end of the 1950s and the early 1960s, life had become hard and all but hopeless in Mainland China, so that there were few escapes except in the pleasures and delights men and women could give each other bodily (Stafford 1967).

During this period, the breaking up of millions of marriages formerly arranged by Party cadres, the separation of millions more of young lovers by massive transfers of population, had one general effect: Many of those who had suffered at the hands of the state turned cynical and hedonistic. Others, young people separated by gender in dormitories, escaped into homosexual liaisons, although the very existence of these activities has been historically and strenuously denied (Ruan and Tsai 1988).

Even now, in this post-Maoist period, it is argued that no "homosexual tradition" as such exists today or is known, even among the educated (Hinsch 1990). In Mainland China there is an adherence to seeing the sexual world according to moral ideals rather than empirical realities (Gil 1991). This leads contemporary authorities to underplay any homosexuality in the population and to underscore emphatically that Chinese people innately experience a far lower rate of homosexual attraction than Westerners (Hinsch 1990; Ruan and Tsai 1988).

This does not, however, erase the reality that homosexuality has again surfaced and enjoys an invigorated openness among the younger generation, that is, those "children of the [Cultural] Revolution" now in their mid- to late twenties. For example, I was assured by several university professors in Beijing, and elsewhere, that there is a strong male homosexual contingent in university campuses across the nation. Recently, Pan (1990), a Mainland sociologist, also estimated 7.4 percent of respondents from his survey samples—all individuals from urban areas—to have had same-sex sexual relations. When homosexuality is discovered, authorities continue to denounce it openly.[5]

While China lacks explicit laws against homosexuality, several laws that attest to "hooliganism" (*liumang*), "lewd conduct," and "perverse or immoral acts" are sufficient to try homosexuals and send many to prison (cf. Gil 1991; Ruan and Tsai 1988). Given such contemporary contexts, openly acknowledging one's homosexuality pits one against a politically hostile system. It is in this context of tensions that homosexuality is negotiated by individual Chinese.

MEETING "G.I. JOE"

Dance "clubs," the rage in the late 1980s and now an established fixture among younger urban Chinese (Schell 1988), function as meeting places for both heterosexual and homosexual men and women. Amid tight security, no alcohol, and seemingly rigid standards,[6] these clubs serve as an "underground" of sorts where a broad clientele can exhibit a range of behaviors—from covert seduction to outright propositions—that are not possible outside of these confines. Joe, incidentally, is a prominent singer at several of these clubs in his provincial capital city.

Since women can dance with women and men with men, signaling they are "available" to the opposite sex, this openly nonhomophobic custom can mask two male homosexuals meeting and then dancing together. As long as the externals presuppose heterosexuality (and this can be accomplished by dancers respecting the prescribed physical distance while gyrating), no one finds the practice of same-sex dancing eye raising. Hong Kong and Taiwanese businessmen, aptly dressed with expensive suits, are often seen dancing with local young(er) men.

At twenty-eight, G.I. Joe has been singing for about eight years and is considered the best male vocalist in the city. (His tonal range and English interpretations of pop songs are extraordinarily well developed.) He is thus sought after by clubs and can command 300 yuan (paid in FEC)[7] per week per club for a full six-day schedule. The schedule is two to four songs (fifteen to forty-five minutes) in each club, and he does two clubs a night unless he is ill. Since club singing is an "entrepreneurial activity" and always done in the evenings, Joe devotes his daytime to the pursuit of his "real" (government-appointed) job in the local college of performing arts.

We were introduced by a mutual Chinese friend (another singer) during my visit to one prominent club at a hotel. Joe wasted no time asking our friend if I knew about him. It was explained to Joe who I was and why I had asked to meet him. While our singer friend performed, Joe sat beside me, shoulder to shoulder, and conveyed through gestures that he wanted me to know he was "homosexual" (*tongxinglianzhe*). While he knows no English and I a very faltering Mandarin, Joe proceeded to sign explicitly his message. While first pointing to himself, his palms then united horizontally and were inverted repeatedly. The message of his self-proclamation as an "invert," while repugnant by Western gay standards, was communicated clearly. He smiled and asked via another set of hand signals whether I understood. I replied that I did (in Mandarin) and repeated the hand gestures, pointing to my brain.

In a culture where most homosexuality is hidden, Joe is an admitted homosexual. In the artistic communities to which he gravitates (and in which he works), he is humorously tolerated and often appreciated for his piquant statements. Also, those males who surround him often humorously chide him about his overtly feminine manner. (Joe would be considered "swishy" by Western standards. I was told he is also effeminate by west China standards of masculinity as well.) Joe seems to relish the attention, and he has a well-developed ambience about his sexual orientation.

Such began a comfortable exchange. After our singer friend had concluded his number, Joe suggested that we all retire to his flat—"more comfortable and private there" was the translation.

THE INTERVIEW

As an ethnographer, my inclusion into the world of another, much less the world of one with an alternate lifestyle, was achieved only through formal introductions and having been seen as an "authority" or as a "foreign sex expert." However, to create a mutual sense of rapport, I shared American perspectives on sexuality with my interviewee. I also allowed the other individual, our mutual friend, verbal leeway in the course of the interview so as to reduce the risk of making the entire process seem like an interrogation.

Because he is the best male singer in his city, Joe is accorded special privileges. For example, one of the dance hall managers also manages a small building of rental flats. Usually artists are rented flats in these buildings at very low rates but must coexist in crowded conditions. By Western standards, these would be nearly intolerable: four and oftentimes more individuals living in small dormitory-type rooms, communal water closets and shower in the halls, and no privacy whatsoever. However, Joe has a flat all to himself, which affords him both the privacy necessary for sexual liaisons and the luxury of personal space. (Our mutual friend also indicated that Joe lives by himself because other male artists will not live with him owing to his homosexuality. Joe is unsure of this reasoning, or so it was explained to me.)

Joe's flat was clean, sparsely furnished, and modest. His few clothes were hung on a rack against the bed wall. A small hotplate, ice chest, and rudimentary food pantry were well in view. So was an Akai stereo tape system. Next to the stereo was a desk-vanity with three lipstick containers and one makeup compact. These were the only visible items of decidedly feminine identification, and Joe quickly pointed out that these were for his "shows" (songs). On the two armchairs opposite the bed lay a knitting project: Joe knits well and also sews many of his show clothes himself:

> When I like a man, and he is a regular [at the dance club], I will knit him something. Most of the time it will be a vest, something warm for winter. I'll be bold enough to present it to him myself if I feel the timing is right. Otherwise, I'll send it to him with a messenger. By then they will know about me. . . .

Pictures of Joe on the wall, all formally posed and poster sized, encouraged my questioning about them:

> These are what I use when I am being billed in one of the nightspots. Do you like them? Do you think they really look like me? Some say I don't . . . but you are a Meiguoren [an American man], and I will trust your judgment!

Proceeding from those parameters, I asked about his career, his life, and his orientation. Excerpts follow verbatim translations:

> I do not remember when I decided that I liked men. . . . [I]t seems like forever. When I was first introduced to singing, about nine years ago, I had my first "male encounter" [nan-xing-chu-nian]. I was about nineteen years old. Since then I have met many men through my singing career. On occasions, I am approached after I am done singing. Sometimes I approach others, even singers, but I have less success there. [Laughs.] I used to meet some men in the toilets, but since I am now so visible . . . famous . . . and I have many possibilities through the clubs, there is no need to go there [any more].

Toilets?

Oh yes, in this city there are public toilets in such-and-such a park. When it is nighttime, especially late, they are not patrolled very well. It is common knowledge that some who "split peaches"[8] and men who like men frequent these places. It is an easy way to be in contacts [*sic*]. Now, I am careful who [*sic*] I approach. Like I said, I like to be attracted [to a man first], and that usually means having seen a regular and "liked" them from the stage. If that regular seems mutually attracted, I may knit him something. Sometimes, though, I don't knit the person something until we have had our first love [*chu-nian*].

How do you know if a "regular" is attracted to you?

I know. Believe me I know! It is sometimes the smile or sometimes the way they look at you and you at them. It is very much . . . I can't explain . . . a feeling that this is a possibility. I have to like what I see, though.

How do you "love" another man?

Well I don't know how Americans do it, but in China there are essentially two ways: You receive or you give. For me, I have never done both . . . (I am embarrassed) . . . I receive . . . but I like to feel close and love a lot under the covers. I'm a touchy person, you see. [*Hugs our mutual friend and laughs.*]

You know, in China this [homosexuality] was a tradition of the higher classes, not something like it is stated now. I have studied it! Sometimes people say homosexuals are the remnants of the imperial China or Western corruption; but I disagree! I know for me, it was just something that I came on. I liked this man who was my song teacher [*sic*]. I felt he liked me. We talked about it, a lot, after classes. One day I went to his flat, and it was love. I was young, but I know it was love.

That did not last long, though. I told a friend, who already suspected, and he threatened to tell if I didn't stop [with this teacher].

And now, do you keep steady relationships?

I have had some that have lasted, but most often I am not satisfied to be with one person only. I meet too many good men [*sic*] in my profession! [*Laughingly jokes about this.*] Besides, if they saw me with one partner for too long, they would be more suspicious of me than they already are!

Who are "they"?

Well, for one, people who know me from distances [afar] but who don't really know me. Let me explain to you something. Life in China is very different. Everybody minds everybody else's business because that is supposed to be good for everyone. So it is never really private here [life]. Usually one has to be careful outside of the singing friendships; but lately I haven't had to worry. I have no long-term relationships! Anyways, everybody around here seems to know I am attractive [attracted] to men, and they just look the other way. The reason is, I am the best singer in ———!! Perhaps, too, it is because I sometimes date the sister of a friend, who is very beautiful. She sometimes accompanies me to clubs when I first start singing there. She's a good friend and knows about me. She knows I sometimes need to make believe [as heterosexual].

Then there are the *danwei*. These committees are supposed to report any illegal activity at work by the people. I am illegal! But I do not get reported. Imagine that! [Our friend] can tell you, it is because I am a good singer that they do not care. They think everyone now who is doing cultural activities is something wrong [*sic*] [are somehow different]! They do not understand and I think do not care! In this city you can get by with things like that . . . but not so in other parts of China.

Do you ever have [sexual] relations with your friends at work?
I try all the time . . . [*laughs*] but they don't let me [*laughs again*]. No, I really have to be attracted to someone, like I already told you. I can choose now, so why not?

G.I. Joe also explained that he wasn't feeling too well lately; he had increasingly experienced bouts of "swelling" inside and therefore was to see a traditional Chinese medicine doctor in the morning.[9] This opened up another avenue of exchanges:

What kind of "swelling" are you experiencing?
My "insides" often swell up, I think, because I do not take good care of myself.

Exactly where is the swelling?
Down there [*points to the groin*], probably because of my activities [sexual activity].

G.I. Joe lifted his pant legs to reveal a generalized edema of the lower extremities. Joe relies on traditional medicinal herbs for treatments. He mentioned that, within a few days, the swelling would leave and the groin pains disappear. Not to worry, he said, he would be all right in a few days. (Our mutual friend later volunteered that Joe has been hospitalized several times with bladder, kidney, and liver infections. He suspected syphilis at one point and hepatitis at another.)

Do you ever use condoms (biyuntao)?
Well, not really, not me. Some of the men I have been with have used condoms, but only very few. Why do you ask me about condoms?

My response emphasized that condoms can prevent sexually transmitted diseases, especially for the "receptor" during anal intercourse. G.I. Joe was not ignorant of these facts but did not consider them relevant at the time of sexual activity.

When this brief interview ended, I invited G.I. Joe to join us (myself and the mutual friend) for dinner the next evening. Although he willingly accepted, he was too ill the next evening to attend.

DISCUSSION

Excerpts from this brief interview reveal something about the cultural parameters that impinge on the male homosexual in Mainland China and about the strategies developed to negotiate these. To G.I. Joe, the strictures of the system (legal risks, cultural stigmatization) are but inconveniences to be negotiated outright. He has elected to facilitate his choices by pursuing music (and an artistic environment), which provides both cover and contacts.

Like many others in China, Joe initially sought casual involvements with great risks, such as in the "tearoom trade" in his provincial city. Increasingly, and gradually, the environments in which he established himself professionally allowed greater and (politically) safer sexual choices. In this respect, Joe transcends the more normative lifestyle and sexual options of other Chinese homosexuals (cf. Hinsch 1990; Ruan and Tsai 1988). He has utilized his professional prestige and economic independence to situate himself optimally in his relations with men. Joe can "afford" his privacy and, as such, is in a position to control key variables required by his orientation.

Consequently, I sensed no great trauma or anxiety and suffering, as has been reported elsewhere in the case of Mainland China homosexuals (Lau and Ng 1989; Ruan and Tsai 1988). G.I. Joe thus presents an example of adaptive strategizing within a cultural context that denounces homosexual sex.

The etiology of Joe's homosexuality obviously cannot be deduced from this interview material. He presented no information to suggest there were developmental or physiological factors that would distinguish a rationale for his orientation. The strands of his life as told to me, however, do present factual and conceptual similarities with the lives of other homosexuals across cultures (cf. Weinberg and Bell 1972; Bell and Weinberg 1978; Silverstein 1981): Joe's sexual involvements tended toward multiple partners; he operates within a romantic ideal; he engages in casual as well as longer-term sexual encounters; he can be distinguishably effeminate; he sometimes feigns heterosexuality; he uses wit and determination to master opposition and derision; and he exemplifies an "uncloseted" lifestyle, as much as anyone can in Mainland China.

Finally, Joe's expression of his orientation also conforms to traditional role ideals found in Chinese male homosexual pairs. His explanation of roles is clearly circumscribed to an "either/or" dichotomization: the passive (receptor) or active (insertor) identifiers for the sexualizing pair. The passive partner, Joe's particular role, is often associated in the literature with the feminine (Hinsch 1990; Ruan and Tsai 1988) and is thus consistent with Joe's self-presentation as an effeminate male.

GENDER AND WORK

It is often believed that "traditional" societies have clear-cut, timeless divisions of labor along gender lines and that, with "modernity," such roles are called into question. We caution readers to distinguish ideology from practice, ideals from behavior. In some conflated "traditional" China—far from unitary or homogeneous throughout time, in actuality—there were said to be proper roles for men and women. Men were to be like emperors in the home; women were to follow their fathers when they were children, their husbands when they were wives, and their sons when they were widows. Women were called *neiren*, "the people inside." As Ida Pruitt shows so poignantly in *A Daughter of Han* (1945), only the most desperate of the poor permitted their wives or daughters to leave the home. Foot binding was the most visible symbol of this binding inside.

Yet, throughout the centuries, there were millions of desperate poor. The rule—often violated—that widows must not remarry meant that widows were often on the verge of starvation. In *The Death of Woman Wang* (1978), Jonathan Spence describes the kinds of work that a respectable but destitute widow could undertake in seventeenth-century China: sewing, washing, and so forth. Such women worked, but they were modest and invisible.

In traditional elite Chinese views, agriculture was the most venerated of domains and therefore off-limits to women. It was believed that a menstruating woman would pollute the fields and destroy the crops. Traditionally, agricultural work was shared among males related by blood and marriage. Families who could not manage their own land hired workers. People without their own land worked for others.

In the founding years of the People's Republic, gender equality was espoused. At the height of the Cultural Revolution, images of women driving tractors and working on high electrical wires were everywhere. One of the goals of the communes was to free women from the repetitive, reproductive domestic work of child care and cooking, in order to allow both men and women to work in productive labor. This backfired, as one might suspect; men did not want women to work with them, nor did they want women to earn as many work points as they did. Still, the taboo against decent women working "outside" was broken.

With the economic Reforms of the late 1970s and early 1980s, the types of work available to men and women have changed. To domestic and agricultural work has been added industrial work (often divided into "light" and "heavy"). In rural China, many men have left their farms to find more lucrative employment in factories in towns. This has left women doing most of the agricultural work. At the same time, young women have also sought employment in light industry, often textiles and manufacturing. The conditions for such workers have often been execrable—with no protection for their health or safety—since theirs is seen as a temporary situation that will end with marriage. The coastal cities, especially in the south, are a favorite destination for young women hoping to make huge amounts of money prior to marriage, but such women often find themselves exploited by greedy firms that forbid them to leave the dormitory or factory. A significant proportion find themselves working in the sex trades, essentially enslaved by an employer who promised them fortunes and lured them from their inland provinces.

Men have often aspired to do industrial work since the Reforms began, ideally in heavy industry. Those employed by state-owned enterprises in cities or towns have a full range of benefits, but such enterprises are now decreasing. More and more men are roaming China in search of employment, leaving behind their families and banding together with other men in "villages" that attempt to provide a modicum of social order.

At the highest levels of privilege, men and women are able to find employment in high-tech firms, in broadcasting, and so forth. Many firms prefer to hire men, and, in fact, many are subject to government limitations in that no more than one-tenth of their employees can be women. But one can see successful men and women in urban cafés, cell phones in hand, and the troubles of inland rural China seem—but are not—a thing of the past.—Eds.

JAMES TYSON AND
ANN TYSON

13
"The Moon Reflecting the Sunlight"

The Village Woman

Rural Chinese life has little resonance with the Western reading or television-viewing public, so this chapter offers a brief, but very valuable, glimpse at the gender and labor realities of the contemporary countryside. This chapter comes from James and Ann Tyson's innovative *Chinese Awakenings* (1995). In the early 1990s—a mere five years following the widespread institutionalization of China's "capitalist" economic reforms—these two journalists traveled throughout China, living with ordinary people and speaking with them about the details of their lives. This chapter recounts some of the history of Zhao Xinlan, in many ways a typical middle-aged resident of rural China. Zhao's own life is increasingly comfortable materially; among her household possessions is a television, and her home boasts electricity. Rural life since the economic reforms of the late 1980s has paid a price, however: many men have been enticed into cities, leaving behind wives who now have the double burden of household and agricultural labor to shoulder alone. In the humid and subtropical climate of Zhao's village of Xiaodian, Henan, 90 percent of the farm labor is performed by women.

Zhao tells of the bitterness of her own mother's life, as she was virtually sold to Zhao's father when still very young because of her family's poverty. Women were considered the property of their husbands' families. Since 1949, the selling of daughters has been outlawed, curtailing the practice somewhat, and women of Zhao's generation grew up with increased security. Yet boys were and still are valued over girls, and girls are still regarded as dependents being raised for their future husbands' families. The increasing responsibility of rural women has not resulted in equal valuation of boys and girls, however. You will read in this story about the enduring preference for boys and some of the increasing difficulties that poor women face in the China of recent years. Paradoxically, it is women who, according to the often-quoted Maoist dictum, "hold up half of the sky" but have suffered the greatest burden of the new inequities introduced by China's profit-driven reforms.

The Soviet ideologue Bukharin once spoke of the Bolsheviks "riding to socialism on the nag of the peasants," a bitter sarcasm that, with slight modi-

FIGURE 13.1
Field work. (Photograph
by Dr. Louis C. Liley, Jr.)

fication, suitably describes the path of China's economic reforms: riding to prosperity on the backs of women. Although Zhao Xinlan's recollections and observations give us pause, it is crucial to recognize that her experience is better than that of many others. The dramatic decline in family integrity and values, paired with the numerous difficult labors of the female head of the rural household (see fig.13.1), has transformed the countryside into a site of anomie and, increasingly, suicide. China has more than 300,000 suicides per year, and the highest rate of death is among rural women. In fact, 90 percent of these suicides occur in the countryside; so great is the number of women that their deaths account for more than 56 percent of suicides among women worldwide. Zhao's story is nowhere near as bleak, but it does provide telling documentation of contemporary upheaval, to wit, the transformation of the rural economy and the sexual division of labor that has taken women from liberation to indenture.—Eds.

Zhao Xinlan rises early, quaffs a ladleful of cool water, and leaves her farmhouse before the June day grows too hot. She walks a mile down a dirt path to the family plot, passing acre after acre of golden wheat that seems to touch the sky. As she walks, a migrating cuckoo pipes its whimsical song from a nearby poplar. For Zhao, the cuckoo's call is the surest sign that harvest time has come again to her village in China's heartland. "Cuckoo, cuckoo. Sprinkle vinegar on the noodles. First harvest the barley and then the wheat," Zhao hums as she walks, reciting the summer harvest rhyme she learned as a girl.

Zhao's song does little, however, to lighten the backbreaking task that lies ahead. She sets to work, stooping and cutting the bundles of ripened grain with a sickle. Her body is wiry; her hands are rough and tanned dark brown. As in many summers past, Zhao will bring in the harvest alone, laboring to feed her three boys without help from her husband, a coal miner in a distant city. "I do all the work, the man's half as well as the woman's," says Zhao, tucking a loose strand of hair behind her ear. "If I didn't do it, who would?"

For the first time, millions of peasant women like Zhao have been left in charge of what was men's work in China for centuries: the grueling, never-ending production of food. In many villages, such as Zhao's home of Xiaodian in China's central Henan province, women now shoulder 90 percent of the farming. Nationwide, women handle from 60 percent to 70 percent of farmwork in addition to their traditional household tasks, official figures show.

Zhao's life shows the kind of sweeping change that market-oriented reforms have brought to the lives of China's 430 million rural women since 1980. The reforms have spurred tens of millions of men to quit the land in less developed regions like Henan and migrate to more lucrative jobs in cities and towns. As a result, rural women like Zhao have assumed the vital economic role of farming.

The shift in roles illustrates how reform has brought new responsibility but also greater hardship to many women in the countryside, especially in poor regions. Zhao and others like her have gained pride and self-esteem as they run family farms. However, like Zhao, most peasant women are managing China's farms not by choice but by necessity. Left behind by their husbands, these women find that their opportunities to move beyond the toil are almost nil. Just as bound feet kept women close to the hearth in traditional China, rural women today are bound to land and home by the endless chores of farming, sewing, housekeeping, and caring for their children.

In other ways, China's peasant women have faced growing, sometimes vicious discrimination under reform. As Maoist social controls have eased, women in Xiaodian and thousands of other villages have seen a revival of customs such as wife buying, concubinage, the arranged marriage of child brides, and the sale or abandonment of baby girls. Widespread in China's patriarchal society before the 1949 Revolution, such practices are again rampant in many parts of rural China.

In addition to old oppression, women face new forms of exploitation in China under reform. As crude, unbridled capitalism spreads outside the state-run economy, many women are maltreated by unethical bosses who profit from a buyer's market for labor. Some rural women, although far fewer than men, migrate to towns and cities seeking jobs. Most of these are unmarried teenage girls, who work as maids or baby-sitters or in unskilled, low-paid factory jobs. In the cities, these girls often labor fourteen hours a day in dangerous sweatshops. They sleep crowded in locked dormitories of corrugated tin despite the threat of fires that have killed thousands of others like them. They are easy victims of wage exploitation and sexual abuse. A handful of these girls marry city residents and escape their poor villages for good. But most eventually return to the countryside to wed, bear children, and farm the land.

The plight of rural women shows how social justice and equality lag behind gains in prosperity in China under reform. Many of the harmful offshoots of reform most hurt women, both rural and urban. As a group, peasant women are especially vulnerable because they are among the least-educated Chinese. One out of three women in China's countryside is illiterate. In the cities, better-educated women also face new pressures from reform. As employers gain the freedom to hire and fire workers, qualified urban women are increasingly denied jobs because of the widespread bias that men are more competent. Women employees work longer hours for less pay than men and are twice as likely to be laid off by state firms. Women and others who have faced setbacks under reform—the poor, state workers, the elderly—are growing disaffected as the Communist Party gives them no outlet for defending their interests.

Many rural women are traditional in outlook and lack the confidence and resources to fight discrimination. Unlike the millions of Chinese who have grown more assertive under reform, women like Zhao and her neighbors in Xiaodian tend to accept their fate. Deeply influenced by the prejudices of China's ancient patriarchal culture, they still see themselves as naturally subordinate to men, even as they shoulder unprecedented responsibility on the farm. They are "the moon reflecting the sunlight," the shadowy, negative force of yin enlivened only by the masculine brightness of yang. Passively, they often allow their lives to be molded by the needs and demands of others rather than pursue their own aspirations.

One morning in the middle of June, Zhao returns home from the market with a basketful of spring onions. She has finished the difficult summer harvest. Her four thousand pounds of wheat have been threshed, sun dried, and stored in gunnysacks. Once again, the busy season has passed, and Zhao has begun the lighter work of hoeing and weeding her newly planted cotton crop. This morning, she can afford to stay home. As often happens, several neighborhood women drop in. They pull up wooden stools and chairs in the main room of Zhao's two-room farmhouse, chatting as they clean the fresh onions. Country women like to talk together as they work, Zhao says, because it makes the chores go more quickly. She joins her circle of friends to trade jokes as well as stories of the bitterness life has dished up.

"I am truly an ill-fated person," sighs Guo Yunfang, an elderly neighbor of Zhao's, as she carefully strips the thin outer leaves off the onions. "We women in this village are made to suffer, worked to the bone, oppressed, and given no freedom!" She tosses the dirty leaves on the brick farmhouse floor.

Guo's words are harsh, especially for a woman in her seventies. But they flow from years of abuse beginning when Guo was a girl in the 1920s. She was born in 1919, the daughter of a rich landlord in nearby Yanjin county. In the 1930s and 1940s, her father, a stern disciplinarian, served as an official of the Nationalist regime. Guo's simple but perfectly tailored clothing hints of her wealthy past. Her snow-white hair is neatly held back with combs. She wears gray trousers, black cotton shoes, and a white short-sleeved shirt that buttons at the shoulder. But the most telling sign of Guo's past status—and suffering—are her tiny pointed feet, which look grotesquely out of balance with her rotund figure.

"My feet were wrapped up when I was ten years old," Guo recalls. "First, all my toes were broken and forced under. It hurt terribly. Then, they were wrapped in long cloth strips eighteen inches long and five inches wide," she says, remembering every agonizing stitch of the cloth that bound her feet, day after day. After some time, the flesh of her feet atrophied, leaving only shrunken, misshapen appendages of skin and bone.

"Why did they do it? Well, when a girl married in those days, everyone looked at her feet, not her face," Guo says. "If she teetered along, 'ta-ta-ta,' on dainty feet, she was considered pretty. Big feet were ugly."

Foot binding was one of the cruelest, most flagrant forms of subjugation of women in China's old society. Euphemistically called *lilies* and meant to give erotic pleasure, bound feet crippled millions of Chinese women like Guo. The tiny deformed stumps made even simple movements painful and awkward for the women and forced them to stay close to home.

In any case, Guo, like other girls, was barred from leaving her family courtyard without permission. Girls were to stay at home, sewing, embroidering, cooking, and keeping house. According to Confucian tradition, Guo was essentially the property of her father until her marriage. Then she became the subject of her husband, whom she addressed as *zhangfu* (master). In Henan, a man still calls his wife "the person inside the room" after this ancient tradition. Even when her husband died, a woman was not free from the domestic tyranny. She was obligated to obey her son.

"My sister's marriage was arranged when she was only two years old. She couldn't even talk," says Guo. "Mine was settled when I was fourteen. Of course, I hadn't set eyes on my husband before our wedding day. That night, we were two strangers in one bed!" she says with a loud laugh, drawing chuckles from her neighbors.

Zhao's brother-in-law, a gray-haired man in his late fifties, peers in the open farmhouse door with a quizzical grin.

"Who invited you?" Zhao asks him. "Go on, now," she says. Reluctantly, he shambles away.

When the laughter subsides, another village woman with short steel-gray hair and a squarish face turns to Guo. "You suffered a lot, for sure. But what about me? I had twelve children!" says the woman, a peasant in her sixties named Wang Shenglan.

"My goodness! Twelve children. She just couldn't control herself. Those two together, all they did was make babies!" says Guo loudly. Laughter again bursts from the peasant women.

Wang, who is one of the village's two hundred Christians, blushes deeply. But she recovers and goes on with her story. "I had twelve children, but only seven of them survived, five boys and two girls. Those were considered lucky numbers. But it was not lucky for me. It was a lot of trouble and hardship. Every year I had to spin and weave to make shoes and clothes for them. I felt so irritated with all the children crying."

Like all Chinese women, Wang had an unshirkable duty to bear sons, the more the better. Beyond that, though, her life and the lives of other women often seemed to have little value. In Chinese kinship rites, women were treated as fleeting vessels made of flesh. Their bodies served to perpetuate the all-important male line before melting away, soon to be forgotten. Only men, whose essence was symbolized by the enduring bones, had the hope of attaining immortality if their descendants worshiped them long enough. When Wang was young, as today, a woman who failed to produce a boy was often harshly chastised by her husband and in-laws. Adding to the insult, her husband almost certainly took a concubine if he could afford one.

Although men yearned for sons, they usually left all the care of children to their wives. Wang's husband refused even to pick up their youngsters. "After giving birth, I could only rest three days before getting up to work again," Wang says. "I couldn't even eat eggs to get my strength back. Once, we had a few eggs. But my husband told my son to sell them at the market and buy him tobacco. My son argued that I should have the eggs. But my husband refused. I still remember that." Her face darkens.

"My husband is ill tempered, too," says Guo. "He is always beating me and cursing at me. He hardly allows me a mouthful to eat. I've had to accept a sack of grain from my [married] daughter." Guo winces at the humiliation.

Women like Guo and Wang had little recourse against such abuses once they moved into their husbands' households after marriage. Traditionally, a husband had the right of virtually complete control over his wife. Indeed, according to one interpretation, the Chinese character for woman, *nü,* is based on an ideogram of a woman kneeling. For centuries under ancient Chinese law, a man who murdered his wife faced no punishment; if she committed adultery, he was legally free to kill her. Yet a woman who injured or killed her husband, even in self-defense, was severely punished or beheaded. In the Qing dynasty (1644–1911), women belonged to a legal category of subjects called the *petty and low.* They were routinely held responsible for crimes committed by their husbands, who were categorized as the *elder and better.* As late as the 1940s, a man in financial straits could sell his wife. Or he could engage in *dianqi* (wife mortgaging), lending his wife to another man for a few years.

Worst off were the young girls from poor families, like Zhao's mother, who were often sold by their fathers as child brides, servants, concubines, or prostitutes. Their lives of slavery started in girlhood. "My mother's life was miserable," Zhao tells the neighbors gathered in her farmhouse. "When she was nine years old, her parents died. They were very poor, so her uncle sold her as a *tongyangxi* to a family with some money."

Tongyangxi (daughter-in-law-to-be) was one of the lowliest of social rankings. An ingenious invention of China's patriarchal system, it allowed a family to train its son's future wife to be submissive and obedient from childhood. For girls like Zhao's mother, this meant giving up the relative freedom of her parents' home for years of servitude. "The family bound her feet. She was just like a slave in their house. She was very unhappy," Zhao says.

Zhao's mother was not alone. She was born in 1920, the first year of a devastating famine caused by severe drought in Henan and neighboring provinces. At least 500,000 people died in the famine, and nearly 20 million more were left destitute. Deadly epidemics plagued survivors. Refugees filled the roads, trying to escape the disaster. Unable to feed themselves and their offspring, adults sold tens of thousands of children like Zhao's mother.

One day, however, Zhao's mother managed to escape her mother-in-law's watchful eye and flee. At first she ran to her uncle's house, but he was away. Inside, there was no food. In desperation, she ground up some old peanut shells she found on the floor. For several days, she hid in a ditch, eating the ground shells, weeds, and anything else she could scavenge. But soon the family found her and dragged her back to Le village, not far from Xiaodian.

Each day, Zhao's mother was put to work milling flour, cooking meals, spinning and weaving cloth, or stitching shoes. She hated the tedious work, especially the long hours sitting cross-legged and rocking to and fro as she spun cotton on a hand-rotated wooden spinning wheel. Her outstretched arms ached as she turned the wheel with one hand and drew the other back and forth spinning wad after wad of cotton into one long thread. But, as the years wore on, she accepted her fate, glad simply to have food and shelter.

In 1938, when Zhao's mother was eighteen, the family fled Le village during a massive flood of the silt-laden Yellow river, some thirty miles to the south. The flood was triggered by Nationalist leader Chiang Kai-shek, who had ordered his engineers to blow up the river dikes to slow the advance of Japanese troops. Full-scale war between China and Japan had erupted the year before. The huge flood wiped out more than four thousand Chinese villages and shifted the course of the Yellow river south nearly three hundred miles. But it merely stalled the Japanese for three months. Before long, the family found itself again on the run as Japan's army moved deeper into China's heartland. "My mother and her family were always running from here to there, but somehow they lived through the war," says Zhao.

The widespread atrocities of Japanese troops terrified Zhao's mother and her in-laws. During the 1937 massacre in Nanjing, Japanese invaders raped an estimated 20,000 women and murdered some 200,000 civilians. Zhao's mother told Zhao the tragic story of one young mother she knew who hid behind a door petrified as Japanese troops stormed into her house. To keep her baby from crying, she pressed it hard against her breast. Finally, the soldiers left without detecting the woman, but her baby had died of suffocation. Zhao's mother knew other women who had babies while fleeing in 1938 and were forced to abandon them.

Zhao's mother did not have a child until after the Anti-Japanese War ended in 1945. In about 1946 she gave birth to a son, the first of six children. At the height of China's civil war between the Nationalists and the Communists, she bore her second child, Zhao. Zhao was born on 12 April 1948, as Communist armies in Henan seized the nearby city of Luoyang. In a little more than a year, the Communist victory was complete, and Zhao's mother and father settled down to a life of farming back in Le village. During the land redistribution campaign in 1950, Zhao's parents were classified by the Communists as *middle peasants,* which meant they escaped the beatings meted out to landlords and rich peasants but also received none of the land and property reallocated to poor peasants. Still, they were allowed to keep what land they had.

Zhao grew up in a period of relative calm in China. But domestic battles raged inside her mud-walled home. Although Zhao's parents had been raised together, they had a stormy relationship. Zhao's father was a coarse man with a fierce temper. Although he never beat his children or derided them, he fought constantly with their mother. For her part, Zhao's mother had always resented being sold as a *tangyangxi.* As she grew older, her resentment over the thankless role grew. She went about her chores muttering to herself. "These lazy, good-for-nothing men! I'm tired to death!" she complained over and over.

Zhao remembers her mother busy from dawn until dusk as she single-handedly cared for six children, cooked the meals, spun, wove, hand stitched cotton clothes, and also did a little farmwork. "My father would come back from the fields with his pant legs rolled up and squat on his heels, smoking tobacco," Zhao recalls. "The household was chaotic, and my mother was frantic trying to get things done, but he just sat there."

"Now, it's the same." Zhao swats a chicken with the back of her hand and sends it flapping out the farmhouse door. "The men all want to squat on their heels, play cards, play mah-jongg. They are all alike. 'Every crow under heaven is as black as the other,'" she says, quoting a Chinese adage. "This is the reason for most of the conflicts in the countryside today: The men are lazy, and the women are tired."

As a girl in Maoist China, Zhao grew up in a world radically different from her mother's. Mao Zedong advocated women's equality under the slogan "women hold up half the sky." Shortly after taking power in 1949, the Communists announced a program that promised women equal rights and pledged to end their "bondage." In 1950, a new law banned compulsory arranged marriages and the sale of women and girls as brides. It promoted the freedom of Chinese to choose their spouses and allowed women to seek divorce. Also, the law gave unmarried, divorced, and widowed women the right to hold land in their own names. (Married women were still denied that right.)

Communist propagandists campaigned against foot binding, concubinage, prostitution, and other traditional practices that oppressed women. "Big feet are good. Big feet are steady. Big feet won't let you slip and leave you muddy!" went the propaganda ditty Zhao sang as she played in the village as a little girl.

Although the Communist Revolution promised Chinese women some new political and legal protections, it fell far short of liberating them. Old prejudices lived on for girls like Zhao, especially in rural villages, where the subordination of women had been ingrained for centuries. Many peasants like Zhao's father still viewed girls primarily as household labor and hesitated to educate them. Zhao went to primary school for only two years before dropping out because her father and grandfather withheld tuition. When she was only seven, Zhao was put to work spinning cotton. By the time she turned thirteen, Zhao could manage all the domestic chores and often did.

Moreover, it quickly became apparent that Maoist policies were dictated less by the aim of freeing women than by the necessity of tapping female labor for radical economic programs. Beginning in the 1950s, the government aggravated the burden of peasant women by forcing them to take part in often grueling collective farm labor. In 1958 China launched the Great Leap Forward. Under the slogan "release men and substitute women," millions of men were drawn off the fields to smelt steel and build irrigation works. Rural women, meanwhile, were enlisted for field labor on an unprecedented scale, with some 90 percent of able-bodied women taking part. Zhao was only ten years old, still too young for strenuous farmwork. But her mother and millions of other Chinese women were organized into rural production teams in Henan as the province led China's drive to abolish private plots and create people's communes. In order to free women from domestic chores, the communes set up mess halls, nurseries, shoemaking shops, laundries, and other services. But this pooling of household work quickly broke down as the Great Leap collectivization movement brought starvation.

"At first, we had the big rice pot," Zhao said. "We all took our bowls to the canteen, where workers ladled out gruel from a big basin. Then we carried the bowls home to eat. But later the gruel became thinner and thinner. All the peasants started to complain. 'The big pot of rice is too watery!' they said."

The Great Leap ended in a severe nationwide famine. Zhao and her family struggled to fight off starvation. The village grain supply was exhausted, some of it shipped out to fulfill state quotas and feed China's cities. The family subsisted mainly on carrots and other root vegetables. Meal after meal, they ate steamed buns made of carrot flour, broth of carrot tops, and sweet potatoes. Sometimes Zhao, driven by hunger, crept into the communal fields to dig up carrots and turnips. She stuffed them into her mouth, dirt and all. But, later, even these disappeared. Zhao and her family ate wild leaves and weeds.

The famine was hardest on women like Wang Shenglan, the mother who bore twelve children. Wang had her first baby when she was only eighteen. By the peak years of food shortages she was in her late twenties and already had several more children. Wang, like most peasant women at the time, was ignorant about methods of contraception and could not refuse her husband's advances. Even if she had known how to prevent conception, Communist Party policy during the Great Leap discouraged her from doing so. The party declared that due to the success of people's communes China faced a labor shortage. In 1958, Mao declared that China could manage not only 800 million people but 1 billion. As a result, countless undernourished women like Wang suffered the agony of becoming pregnant, giving birth, and lacking enough breast milk to keep the weak infant alive. "I had no milk, so the babies got sick and died," Wang said. Some peasants, realizing the bleak prospects that awaited their newborns, resorted to infanticide.

In 1962, when Zhao was fourteen, she was assigned to a women's production team. By then, the Party had reversed many of the disastrous Great Leap policies. Local officials had decentralized the commune's powers and redistributed small individual plots in Le village. Communal mess halls had shut down, and domestic labor was no longer pooled. But, as women once again shouldered the household chores, they were not free to quit working the communal fields. Maoist radicalism combined with traditional prejudices had locked peasant women like Zhao and her mother in a double bind: They were compelled at once to be revolutionaries on the farm and wifely at home. "If we didn't work, we didn't eat," Zhao said.

Shoulder to shoulder with other peasant women, Zhao labored to earn the work points that were converted into grain at the end of the year. At first Zhao found the farming awkward and difficult. Food remained scarce in the village, and she was still weak from malnourishment. She earned only seven or eight work points a day. Later, as she grew stronger and more skilled, she received the women's daily maximum of fifteen points, worth about 40 Chinese cents. "I pulled a plow and harrow, work an animal should do," she said.

But no matter how hard they worked, Zhao and her teammates on the women's production team could never earn the maximum of twenty points reserved for men. A man was always considered a more able farmhand than a woman. Rural communes claimed to liberate women, but discrimination was built into the work point system.

The outbreak of the radical Cultural Revolution in 1966 heightened pressure on rural women like Zhao to emulate Mao's "iron girl," the unadorned, sturdily built peasant woman with short-cropped hair and baggy clothes glorified by propagandists. Already in the early 1960s, millions of women like Zhao were organized into "red women's shock brigades." They underwent basic military training, marching into the fields with crude rifles as well as hoes on their shoulders. The iron-girl model forced women like Zhao to suppress any display of femininity, as if womanliness itself was at odds with the Revolution.

Women were also masculinized by their mandatory role in political violence during the Cultural Revolution. Many rural communities were spared severe turmoil in the decade-long movement, but Le village saw its share of "class struggle." Maoist extremists recruited Zhao and other women for mass struggle sessions against peasants accused as enemies of the people. As Red Guards dragged victims before a packed-dirt square in the center of the village, Zhao had to scream out charges with the crowd or risk being accused as a sympathizer. Often, the hapless peasants were twisted into the torturous "airplane position," their arms pinned behind them and heads jerked forward. If victims failed to confess their "crimes"—often something as minor as stealing vegetables from communal fields—they would be beaten.

But, even as Cultural Revolution fanatics smashed ancestral shrines, preached revolutionary puritanism, and painted life as an endless struggle between class enemies and the people, relations between peasant men and women remained essentially traditional in Le village and across rural China.

One summer day in 1968, as Zhao was pruning cotton, a teenage girl in a straw hat ran up to her through the rows of green shrubs. Breathlessly, the girl said that her mother's younger brother, Ran Wenli, had just returned to nearby Xiaodian village after four years in the People's Liberation Army. Zhao perked up but said nothing. She knew a hint of courtship when she heard one. The girl had been instructed by her mother to draw Zhao's attention to Ran. Not long afterward, the girl and Zhao had occasion to go together to the local market town. "Oh, there's my uncle now," the girl said, squeezing Zhao's arm as they walked past the local wheat station.

Zhao glanced over and saw a tall, handsome young man hoisting sacks of grain. She instantly turned away again, feigning a lack of interest. But, in spite of herself, she felt her heartbeat quicken. "He caught my fancy. He was good-looking. And, as a returned soldier, he had a good class status."

A matchmaker for Zhao's parents conducted a detailed inquiry on the family and character of their prospective son-in-law, just as Ran's family had checked on Zhao's background in advance. From Ran's friends and relatives, a picture emerged of an even-tempered young man of twenty-two. As a former soldier from a poor peasant's household, his revolutionary credentials could not have been "redder." Soon, in the traditional fashion, the go-between arranged for Zhao to be formally introduced to Ran.

On the day of the meeting, Zhao's stomach was taut. She and her parents met with Ran's parents, according to tradition, in the eastern room of his family's home. After some polite small talk by the elders, Ran and Zhao were left alone briefly. "Do you have any complaints?" he asked simply. It was the first time he had ever addressed her. "If not, then it's settled," he said.

Zhao felt the blood rushing to her face. Her heart leaped upward and blocked her throat. She shifted in her chair, stared down at her cotton shoes, and said nothing.

Finally, she looked up. "I don't have any complaints," she replied.

Smiling, Ran unfolded a pretty yellow scarf and tied it gently around Zhao's neck. In accordance with the local custom, Zhao also gave Ran a scarf as a token of her affection. They were engaged.

In 1969, the wedding was set for an auspicious day in the second lunar month. That morning Zhao dressed in her best shirt, a red, white, and green plaid. She wore matching plaid cotton shoes and also the yellow scarf from Ran. When all was ready, she stepped into the back of a wooden horse-drawn cart accompanied by two women relatives. Six men followed behind carrying her dowry of a cabinet, a table, and a dresser containing a wadded-cotton quilt and mattress. As the driver clucked to the horse, Zhao's parents firmly shut the door of their house and climbed into the cart. Tradition dictated that, from this day, Zhao would belong to her husband's household in Xiaodian.

Zhao sobbed all the way to her wedding. She cried out of shame because she thought her dowry was too small. She cried from a lingering fear of Ran and his four brothers. She cried as Chinese women had for centuries on their wedding days, because there was no going home.

The ceremony was an odd mixture of traditional ritual and worship of Mao. When they arrived at Ran's home, the two mothers met alone for a customary chat. Then, as friends and relatives gathered, the bride and groom paid their respects to cosmic and earthly authorities.

"First we prostrated before heaven. During the Cultural Revolution that meant we kowtowed in front of Mao's portrait," Zhao explained. Next, Ran and Zhao bowed to the northern wall of the simple courtyard home, where Ran's parents stayed, to show their obedience. They bowed to each other. Finally, amid the crackling of firecrackers bunched on long strands, they bowed to the guests.

At the wedding feast, the hosts toasted everyone with cups of rice wine. The guests sampled eight plates of cold dishes and eight bowls heaped with fragrant meat and vegetables and gave Zhao and Ran small packets of money as gifts. After nightfall brought the festivities to a close, the newlyweds withdrew to their room behind doors marked with the red-painted Chinese symbol for "double happiness."

For seven months, the couple lived with Ran's family. Zhao was happy, although her workload was heavier than that of men in the household. Every morning she rose early to prepare meals and wash clothes. Then she left for work in the fields to earn her grain ration. In the evening, Zhao often had to attend political meetings. She had been put in charge of her women's production team in 1969, and the meetings were mandatory for a low-level cadre. However, like many younger Chinese women who became cadres in the Maoist era, Zhao had little real power. Although far more women served as officials under Mao than ever before in China, their jobs tended to be menial, low ranking, and therefore unattractive. Many women quit after a brief time or once they bore children. Zhao resigned in 1970 after being criticized for arriving late at meetings.

Zhao's double burden in the home and fields was by now not only accepted but glorified as politically virtuous by the Party leadership. The Party badly needed women's labor as it launched a campaign to achieve agricultural self-sufficiency in the early 1970s. But it lacked the resources to set up collective nurseries and cafeterias to relieve women of their household chores. So Party propagandists created a new female paragon to encourage women like Zhao to work harder. Known as the mother with "four goods," this superwoman excelled at collective labor and opposing revisionism as well as bringing up children and keeping house.

After less than a year of marriage, Ran left Xiaodian to accept a job as a state worker in a leather shoe factory run by the county. As a returned soldier, he qualified for the coveted state job, which offered financial security even though it paid only 40 yuan a month. A few months later, he was offered another job in a coal mine on Henan's northwestern border. The couple knew the job would mean years of separation before Ran would be allowed to retire. But it also offered him an urban residence permit, along with state grain rations, medical care, and other lifelong benefits. "All the peasants wanted to get urban residence. Workers ate much better than peasants. Peasants exhausted themselves in the fields every day and still ate poorly," Zhao said. "We believed the urban residence was worth it."

One day not long after Chinese New Year, Zhao watched Ran hoist his bedroll and knapsack onto a crowded provincial bus and squeeze through the doors. As the bus rattled away, she waved good-bye with her yellow scarf, and tears ran down her cheeks. She did not imagine, though, how deeply she would regret his absence.

In the spring of 1971, after one of Ran's home leaves, Zhao began feeling queasy. It was a busy farming time, and she had to rise at dawn and join her production team in the fields before breakfast. Several times, she returned home at midmorning dizzy and with her stomach heaving. Exhausted and yet too nauseated to eat, she lay on the bed, her face pale and drawn. She "had happiness," as Chinese say.

Despite her pregnancy, Zhao had no respite from fieldwork. But, fortunately, she was healthy and suffered no complications. Harsh working conditions and a lack of even crude medical care meant that the maternal death rate was high in China. The loss of infants was also common. When it came time to give birth, Zhao was attended only by her mother, who came from Le village to help. The baby was a ruddy boy. Because he was born just before the lunar New Year in 1972, Zhao named him Fachun (Bringing Spring).

Zhao would give birth to two more sons, Fatai and Fayang, whose names together mean "Bringing Sun," in 1975 and 1979. By that time, she had moved out of Ran's parents' home and lived with her children in a simple thatched dwelling. Her mother helped with the second birth. But Zhao delivered her third baby alone. Her mother had died a few months earlier at the age of fifty-nine. "My mother died too young. She died of exhaustion."

The period after her mother's death was one of the hardest in Zhao's life. She felt an intense loneliness. More than anyone, Zhao's mother had supported her in Ran's absence. Now, she needed that support more than ever. With a baby and two small children to care for, Zhao found it hard to do much fieldwork. Her work points fell to seven or eight, and so her grain allotment dropped sharply. The family received some cash from Ran each month, but the food still fell short. With her children hungry, Zhao often had to hide her shame and ask for handouts of grain from relatives.

In 1980, China's market-oriented reforms began alleviating poverty in Xiaodian and thousands of other Chinese villages. Collective fields were broken up. The revival of family farms spurred huge gains in productivity. As farms nationwide reaped record harvests with fewer hands, millions of peasants began quitting the land for factory jobs.

Ironically, however, the reforms only compounded Zhao's difficulties. In 1980, she received her own small plot of land when she was least able to farm it. Still, she had to till the land in order to feed her family. "I had three children and no one to help me," Zhao said.

Zhao dreaded most the strenuous jobs of harvesting, hauling, and threshing the wheat. Each day before dawn in the summer of 1980, Zhao walked the mile to the field with her baby, Fayang, tied to her back and two other sons dawdling behind. Because of the constant bending and stooping, Zhao could not carry Fayang as she harvested the wheat. "I had to lay the baby in the dirt and let him cry."

Later, in desperation, Zhao sometimes locked her children in the house while she did the farming. Her overwork and lack of vigilance proved tragic. When Fayang was about twelve months old, he crawled over to the stove and toppled a pot of boiling corn gruel. He screamed as the hot gruel spilled on his face, badly burning it. Zhao rushed the howling child to the neighbors and borrowed some ointment. The cream did little good, however, and within days the burn was seriously infected. Fayang grew feverish. Zhao carried him to the nearest hospital, which was several miles away. With treatment, his infection slowly healed. But Fayang's left eye and most of the left side of his face were grotesquely disfigured for life.

In the early 1980s, Zhao was unusual as a woman single-handedly running a farm. Today, she is the norm. Every day in Xiaodian, peasant women like Zhao shepherd their children down dusty tree-lined paths to the fields. As the mothers farm, their youngsters play, throwing rocks, chewing on twigs, or digging up clumps of soil. At the end of the day, the women head home, often with a sleeping child on one shoulder and a hoe on the other.

Scenes in Xiaodian reveal how China's market-driven reforms have been a mixed blessing for rural women. A walk through the village at harvest time leaves no doubt that the reforms have ended hunger for Zhao and most other villagers. Golden wheat lies piled on the village's only paved road, to be threshed by tractors and other passing vehicles. In the village market, peasants buy swirly flat breads called *huo shao* as a vendor browns them on an iron skillet. A young married woman walks past with her arm hooked through a basket filled with fragrant fried dough twists, a customary harvest time gift for her mother back in the home village. Zhao's family is now self-sufficient in grain, and, by selling cotton, goats, and chickens, Zhao earns a cash income of about $550 a year.

Yet, as reform has brought greater productivity and prosperity to Xiaodian, it has been almost exclusively the men who have seized the opportunity to escape the drudgery of farming. As fewer of Xiaodian's one thousand villagers were needed to farm its eight hundred acres of land, men left in droves to seek higher-paying jobs in construction, manufacturing, carpentry, and mining outside the village. Peasant men also occupied most positions of power in China's newly emerging rural enterprises and commercial networks. In contrast, only a few young women have ventured out of Xiaodian. They work mainly as baby-sitters and maids or at menial factory jobs. Many rural enterprises pay women workers less than men, retaining the assumption of the collective work point system that any man will do more than a woman. Virtually all of these young women return to Xiaodian to marry, raise children, and till the land. Older and married peasant women like Zhao have stayed in the village. For them, any fleeting leisure enjoyed as a result of the reforms ended with the departure of their husbands. "When the man leaves home, he leaves all the farming to the woman," said Wu Cuilan, a stout middle-aged matron who runs Xiaodian's agronomy station.

Women like Zhao handle all the painstaking work of growing Xiaodian's annual 640-acre cotton crop. They fertilize the soil, apply pesticide, and carefully clip off the twigs of cotton plants that have not borne heads of cotton. In the fall, women pick the cotton and also harvest corn, peanuts, beans, and vegetables. During the summer wheat harvest, some men who work in nearby factories take leave for a few days to help. Otherwise, bringing in the grain is also left to women. "Now, the women's burden is relatively heavy. Every day they bury their heads in hard work," said Wu. "When they return from the fields, from the moment they enter the door they have to cook, wash clothes, and care for the children."

As Zhao knows well, a husband's absence adds nagging loneliness to the hours of toil. Although Zhao is convinced her husband has remained faithful to her, many migrant men are promiscuous, according to Chinese experts and the official media. "Peasant women today have a big problem," said Ren Qingyun, a Chinese professor of women's studies in Henan. "After the reforms began, a lot of their husbands went out and found work, earned money, and took lovers. These women are brokenhearted when they discover their husbands with other women. They face great hardship on the farm. Without some sort of moral support, they really can't handle it."

Although their lives on the farm are physically and emotionally taxing, Zhao and other rural women can at least take pride in their new farming skills. Zhao finds satisfaction in the easy, graceful way she swings a hoe, in her deftness at pruning cotton, and in the two kids born to her herd of white goats one summer morning. She tends a brood of thirty chicks. In addition to the staple crops of wheat, corn, and cotton, she grows cash crops of peanuts and vegetables. With the help of villagewide broadcasts by Wu, Zhao and many other Xiaodian women have learned about modern farming technologies, seeds, and pesticides. "How can I afford not to be skilled? I have farmed this land for so long just to feed a few mouths!" Zhao says as she squats in her field of sprouting cotton, inspecting the plants. "We depend on the land to survive."

Even if Ran returned today, Zhao said she would still manage the farm.

"He doesn't know how!" she exclaims. "My husband is good to me, but he can't handle anything here. Women these days have more ability than men," she says, standing up and brushing the dirt from her hands.

In the company of other women, Zhao describes her husband as an honest, gentle, and simpleminded man. With an earthy, irreverent affection typical of Chinese peasant women, she calls him a "big, dumb dick" *(da sha diao)*.

Zhao's confidence suggests that rural women are gaining self-esteem as they master the once male-dominated occupation of farming and prove their economic worth outside the home. In a few cases, peasant women have risen from threshing grounds to boardrooms, launching highly successful rural enterprises and leading whole villages to prosperity.

Ten miles from Xiaodian, a large, headstrong woman named Liu Zhihua has transformed the village of Jinghua into a rural corporation with yearly profits of over $500,000. Jinghua's 360 villagers now earn double the average per capita income of Chinese peasants. No one had believed Liu could succeed in 1971 when she and a few other women took over the village production committee. At that time, Jinghua's impoverished villagers were almost completely dependent on resold state grain.

"The first day we organized people for work, peasants came from all around to watch. It was as if we were a local opera troupe," she laughed. "The Party branch decided to let us try. Their attitude was, 'If the pot is cracked, why not smash it to pieces?' But I had confidence. I knew the men we were replacing were terribly incompetent."

Liu recalls one day asking a group of men to thresh some wheat. This was heavy work. It required pulling a half-foot-thick stone roller over the wheat to remove the husks from the grain. Defying Liu's authority, the men refused. They thought the women would be helpless without them. But Liu organized the women cadres in the village to do the work; they finished by late afternoon. "Those men were put to shame," Liu recalled with a smile of satisfaction. "After that, I asked all the village women to learn such methods of farmwork."

By 1973, thanks to Liu's promotion of fertilizers and other farming techniques, Jinghua was no longer short of grain. Over the next decade, Liu launched a variety of rural factories making products ranging from rope and dried tofu to asbestos shingles. By 1987, Liu's Jinghua Industry Corporation was recognized nationally as a leader in rural enterprise. Her latest goal is to raise the incomes of Jinghua's villagers to equal those of people in middle-income developed nations.

To a degree, Liu has succeeded in changing the status of women in Jinghua. Her corporation is something of a matriarchy, with more than 90 percent of the workers and managers women. So eager are men to move into the wealthy village that a full third of Jinghua husbands have "married in" to their wives' homes. In Xiaodian, in contrast, only the poorest bachelor will stoop to become a *nüxu,* or son-in-law in his wife's household. Still, Liu's female workers are beaten by their husbands, and Liu herself faces sexual discrimination and hostility.

"In more than twenty years as village production team leader, people have never stopped cursing me," Liu said. "The village Party branch didn't make me a member until 1983 because all the male cadres were afraid I would fire them! Other people claim that my husband is behind everything I do. They don't want to give me credit."

Despite some striking achievements, the vast majority of rural women—from talented entrepreneurs like Liu to common peasants like Zhao—are still restrained by lingering, ancient prejudices in China's patriarchal society. For many, this means a lack of opportunities to move beyond the dirt and toil of the farm. For some, it means a life of virtual imprisonment and cruel abuse. In Xiaodian today, discrimination against women is widespread, many faceted, and at times severe.

Chen Wensheng squats on his heels in the doorway of his run-down brick home in Xiaodian, slurping a bowl of noodles. As he eats, the shirtless young laborer idly watches people passing on the dusty dirt road out front. Above Chen in the doorway hangs a ribbon of red, the Chinese color symbolizing happiness, announcing the birth that morning of his first child.

In a dimly lit back room of the filthy, cluttered dwelling, Chen's wife lies on a bed wrapped in a quilt, perspiring in the summer heat. Her hours-old newborn lies swaddled beside her. She smiles weakly as she shows off the baby, greeting a visitor in the thick accent of her native Sichuan province.

"It's a boy," Chen says, flashing a proud smile.

In his delight over fulfilling his Confucian obligation to father a son, it makes no difference to Chen that he bought his wife as he would a mule or sow. Indeed, Chen is one of several Xiaodian men who have bought brides from Sichuan in recent years amid a resurgence of China's traditional trade in young rural women. The trade was widespread before 1949. It was revived after Beijing began to unleash market economic forces and loosen social controls in the 1980s. Now, China each year reports at least ten thousand cases of rural women being abducted and sold, mainly as brides but also as prostitutes. More than fifty thousand abductions of women and children were reported in 1991 and 1992, according to official figures. The actual number of sales is believed to be far higher, especially as cadres and police increasingly assist the tens of thousands of "people mongers" (ren fan).

Abductors often lure women from poor mountain villages in Sichuan, Guizhou, and other hinterland provinces with promises of jobs. Most are sold as wives for less than $1,000 to farmers in slightly better off areas like Henan who cannot afford the exorbitant cost of formal weddings. Thousands of women are sold to Henan men each year, according to Chinese experts in women's studies. The trade is so widespread and accepted in Henan that one Party secretary listed the number of women sold into his village to "solve marriage problems" for local men as one of his main achievements.

Villagers in Xiaodian, like many rural Chinese, take a pragmatic view of bride buying. "Here, the men from rich households who are handsome and have good class status all find local wives," explained Zhao. She lives a ten-minute walk from Chen's house. But "men from poorer families who are short, old, or have bad class backgrounds take Sichuan wives."

Chen is short. He is also the fifth son in a poor family. He admits that he lacked the more than $2,000 required to build a new house and host a respectable wedding in Xiaodian. So, in 1991, he paid only $200 to a matchmaker who delivered his twenty-one-year-old bride from Sichuan's Mianyang district. Chen was pleased with the trade. "She's pretty, she can till the land better than a northern man, she's a good housekeeper, and she saved me a lot of money," said Chen. He earns $1 a day doing odd jobs.

At first, Chen and his family kept a close watch on his new bride to make sure she did not run away. Some farmers beat wives who disobey or try to flee. Others threaten to resell them to older bachelors, according to official reports. Once the women bear children, as Chen's wife did, they are often ashamed to go home. Many of them resign themselves to their lot. In the end, Chen's wife stayed. "Not many run off," said Zhao. "The Sichuan women want to come here. They come here because the work is lighter. They are poor. In the mountains they eat corn. They want to come down to the plains where they can eat wheat and rice. It is a good thing," she said.

Zhao's attitude toward the Sichuan brides shows how greatly the mistreatment of women is tolerated by both sexes in China's countryside. Millions of rural women like Zhao are so molded by Confucian customs, and so inured to lives of hardship and humiliation, that they are blind to even the most glaring injustices. Although they complain about their difficulties, Zhao and her neighbors passively accept many traditional beliefs that lie at the heart of sexism in China. In Xiaodian, such old biases have reemerged widely along with the easing of social controls under reform.

Boys, for example, are preferred by couples in Xiaodian and throughout rural China because of the importance in Confucian culture of carrying on the male line. Women are largely held responsible for the sex of their offspring, as many peasants are unaware that sperm determines a baby's gender. According to Chinese superstition, even what a woman eats and does during pregnancy can decide the sex of the child in her womb. The pressure on women to produce sons has grown since China imposed its "one couple, one child" birth-control regime in the 1980s, as each additional child brings the risk of greater sanctions by the state.

"If people have boys, they are happier," said Zhao. "If they have no son, they think of all possible ways to have another child, even running off to join the 'guerrillas,'" she said, referring to Chinese couples who take to the road to dodge family-planning authorities.

As Zhao speaks, her year-old niece, the second child of her sister-in-law, plays on the floor. Across the room the child's mother, Wang Shijie, makes wheat noodles with a hand-rotated press. The toddler was born secretly and is a "black child," one of an estimated 1 million over-quota children who have not been registered with the government because their parents fear official retaliation.

Many women like Wang are caught in an emotional vise between the conflicting demands of family members and birth-control officials. If they resist trying repeatedly for a son, they will face the wrath of their husbands' families. But, if they become pregnant without approval, they are likely to be forced to undergo the physical and psychological trauma of sterilization or abortion, sometimes as late as the third trimester. "If I have another child, they will tie my tubes at the township hospital," says Wang. She speaks in a dull tone, without emotion. The procedure is common enough not to cause excitement in Xiaodian.

Women in Xiaodian suffer greatly from the family-planning regime and preference for boys, but young girls stand to lose even more. "Here, girl babies are not killed, but some people give them away or abandon them for others to find," Zhao said. Girls in rural villages like Xiaodian are several times more likely than boys to fail to enter school or drop out to work, according to Chinese statistics.

The pervasive custom of girls "marrying out" of their home villages into their husbands' households perpetuates discrimination against women of all ages in Xiaodian. Girls are less valued in their own homes since they will leave on marrying. Unlike sons, they are not expected to care for their elderly parents. They rarely inherit land or houses, and therefore only by marrying can they secure a livelihood and place to live. Yet, as outsiders in their husbands' homes, they are vulnerable to mistreatment, especially if they do not bear sons.

Zhao's own efforts to find a suitable match for her eldest son, Fachun, reveals how strong remains the practice of the *popo* (mother-in-law) dominating the *xifu* (daughter-in-law)—the custom that so oppressed Zhao's own mother. "Here it costs about 10,000 yuan [$2,000] to get a *xifu,* and it's not easy to find a good one," Zhao explained. "My son courted five or six girls. But many of them were too fierce and sharp tongued. I was afraid I couldn't manage them, so I refused to give my approval. In the countryside, parents still have a lot of power over their children's marriages."

Eventually, Fachun was introduced to a girl his mother liked. He married her one early spring day in 1992 at the age of twenty, as Zhao and her husband proudly looked on. "She says what she should and does what she should," said Zhao approvingly as she hurriedly swept out her house on the day before the wedding. "And she's quiet." Although Zhao is not as tyrannical as many Chinese *popo,* she clearly expects her son's wife to heed her.

Even in old age, some women cannot escape the miseries inflicted by the system of marrying out. Guo, the snowy-haired grandmother with bound feet, is often beaten and cursed at by her husband, a factory watchman. Her grown son, who lives at home with his wife, is equally cruel, refusing to give his mother grain to eat unless she cooks and cleans the house.

Often, Guo must eat cornmeal given to her by a sympathetic daughter, who is married and living in another village. Guo would like to move in with her daughter, but she is bound by deep-rooted Confucian mores to stay with her abusive husband and son.

"If I moved to my daughter's house, the other elderly people in the home would say, 'How unlucky!' And, if I died there, I would bring insults on my daughter," said Guo. According to custom, Guo's daughter must devote herself to caring for her parents-in-law, and Guo must rely on her own son in old age. "When I'm old and sick, I have no choice but to depend on my son to take care of me," Guo said, tears welling up in her eyes. "In the end, the leaf must fall at the base of the tree."

After hoeing all afternoon in her cotton field, Zhao returns home to make supper. She uses a hand pump in the courtyard to fill a large bucket with water and carries it to a brick hearth that stands in an open shed. She pours the water into a large iron pot sitting on the hearth. Fachun sits on a wooden stool, stoking the fire with wheat stalks and kindling.

Back in the house, Zhao beats a spongelike dough of wheat flour and water called *mian jin* (wheat cloth). Her two-room brick-and-tile dwelling is an eclectic jumble of new and old. Guardian spirits glare fiercely from the double doors at the courtyard gate. Chinese New Year couplets at the entryway celebrate the coming of peach blossoms and fragrant grass. In the larger room, old newspapers and Henan opera posters cover the wall. A small white bust of Mao sits on a wooden table. An electric ceiling fan whirs overhead, while a soap opera plays on a new television set, a wedding gift for Fachun and his bride.

When the dough is ready, Zhao walks outside and plunges it into a peppery stew of eggs, vinegar, fungus, and other ingredients now boiling on the hearth. "You take a bowl, I take a bowl, and we all squat on our heels and talk together. This is how we eat here," Zhao tells a visitor, a wide smile crinkling the corners of her large bright eyes.

For a woman who has shouldered as much as she has in life, Zhao seems fairly content. She often laughs and jokes, poking fun at herself and others. "We peasant women are comfortable. We sit here and do some cooking, watch the children. We are happy," Zhao says in a tranquil moment after dinner. Things are easier for Zhao now that her boys are in school and old enough to help a little on the farm. Her husband is kind compared with other men. But there are other reasons for her sense of satisfaction. Zhao contrasts her life, no matter how harsh at times, to that of her mother and other women of the older generation. "My mother suffered much more bitterness. I am better off than my mother," Zhao says.

Zhao's own life hints that the worst abuses against rural women will be alleviated only by slow, generational changes in attitude. For example, Zhao out of necessity raised her three sons to cook and sew as well as to till the fields. Unlike many men of his father's generation, Fachun helped mind his younger brothers and now delights in caring for his one-year-old cousin. Fachun, Fatai, Fayang, and many rural boys now being reared by their mothers alone are less likely to become aloof, traditional fathers.

As for Zhao herself, her low expectations, limited education, and traditional peasant values keep her from moving beyond the boundaries of home and farm. Instead, she is resigned to her demanding life as a full-time farmer and mother.

"Here on the farm, you work for a year's worth of grain. Sometimes it is busy. Sometimes there is not much work to do. You can manage to farm with children; you just put them on the ground. How could a woman with children work in a factory? If she put her child on the factory floor, it would be crushed! And how could she nurse her baby?"

"I believe a woman's most important task is to raise her children and take care of her husband," Zhao says. "Let the men go out and earn money."

As Zhao looks back on her life, she derives a sense of well-being from the knowledge that she has fulfilled her traditional womanly obligations. As for the future, she looks forward to Ran's retirement in a few years and return home from the mine. But most of all, she said with a smile, "I want to find brides for my sons and hug my grandchildren."

ECONOMIC MARGINS

Before the end of 2001, China was admitted into the World Trade Organization (WTO), a very long twenty months after it had been granted permanent
normal trade relations with the United States. China's admission into the WTO
signaled ceremoniously what most of the world already instinctively acknowledged: China was the world's fastest-growing economy and the globe's chief
manufacturer. In this context, it may seem willful paradox to have a section on
economic margins. There is nothing at all marginal about WTO accession. It is
a privilege extended to only the most exclusive economic winners, the
mighty, not the marginal. However, as the reader will have learned by this
point, the readings in this book assist a specific process of rearranging conventional perceptions, and this section is no exception.

To assert what is least evident in the commonplace triumphalism of glob-
alization—China is a developing country, and its present as well as future economic circumstances are perilous. The peril—human dislocation, the displacement consequent on rapidly developing economies throughout history—
emerges clearly in this next reading, hovering in the margins of the national
economy a decade ago and now salient in the Chinese urban landscape. There
are apparently 150 million "floating" people (*liudong renkou*) in China. This
population consists of those who are not tied to the residences where they are
officially registered by the government. Since the late 1980s, and more starkly
since the 1990s, the floating population has left the countryside, where economic reforms have brought about labor redundancy and class polarization,
to pursue the prospect of economic benefit inherent in the sale of their
unskilled or semiskilled labor. This economic and demographic development
resembles uncannily what Marx described in volume 1 of *Capital* as a "reserve
army of the unemployed." Today in China, as in late-nineteenth-century
Europe, this unemployed mass proved critical to the maintenance of low
wages for workers and the high profitability of industry. Of course, this is an
ironic but not sufficiently explored problem for Chinese, one that will soon be
intensified by the government's privatizating and closing of the great majority
of state-owned enterprises (SOEs) and township enterprises, which employ

40–45 percent of the population. The agreements that China has signed as a condition for its admission to the WTO call for the establishment of rational and efficient enterprises that are above all else profitable. SOEs have long been the least profitable sector of the Chinese economy.

The privatization and downsizing of unprofitable state enterprises began in 1998 and have already cost hundreds of thousands their jobs. The government has offered, albeit passively, programs for retraining displaced workers and, in some cases, severance packages that permit a few months or more of sustenance. But there is no larger safety net within which this first wave of China's urban unemployed could be caught. Labor unrest is not reported in the Western press very much, but it is increasingly common. In a recent analysis of labor unrest in China, Weston (2000, 260, 261) reports that, in March 1997, some of the "worst labor unrest since the 1949 Communist Revolution" occurred in Sichuan, adding that, throughout 1998 and 1999, similar labor disputes were reported in other interior provinces, including Shanxi, Henan, Hubei, and Gansu.

At the same time, the out-migration of peasant families from the countryside is likely to produce an explosion when these many millions contend with displaced SOE workers for increasingly scarce urban employment. The margins are swiftly becoming China's economic mainstream.—Eds.

14

The Floating Population in the Cities

Markets, Migration, and the Prospects for Citizenship

The *liudong renkou,* or "floating population," offers one of several key windows on the adverse unintended consequences of the dismantling of China's
collectivist social system and rural household registration, coupled with the
exaggerated economic advantage of urban versus rural life. China's "migrant
laborer" population has been officially estimated at about 100 million,
although estimates by scholars in the field suggest that the figure is 150 million—about two-thirds the U.S. population! Many of these people are uneducated male peasants who flock to urban centers seeking the livelihood that the
new economy of China promises, although increasingly entire families leave
their natal homes in the provinces to attempt life in the city. And, most
recently, a growing number of younger women and girls have abandoned the
poorly paying light industrial work of township enterprises in the country to
ply their bodies in the more profitable sex trade of most cities.

Dorothy Solinger, a political scientist whose work on China's migrant
population has merited national recognition, describes and analyzes the features of the migrants themselves and of the "receiving society" in which they
hope to make their place. She discusses the gender imbalance among the
migrants and what consequences this may have on their plans to remain in
the cities (most are unmarried). One of the most important aspects of the situation is the fact that employment in contemporary China often depends on
patronage. Migrants without some preestablished connection may be rele-
gated to the least desirable occupations. This troubling demographic aspect
of China's "modernizing" economy must be understood as one of its enduring
cultural features. Readers are asked to keep in mind that China is currently in
the process of forcing its "state-owned enterprises" in the cities to become
profitable and self-supporting, which will result in coming years in the unemployment of many millions of urban residents. The competition between
urban residents and rural migrants is intensified under conditions of rapid
economic development and has in recent years led to significant unrest.

The principal portion of this movement is from the countryside to the
city. Rural labor migrants are known, somewhat dismissively, as *mingong,* and,

FIGURE 14.1
Squatters' shacks.
(Photograph by Susan D.
Blum.)

FIGURE 14.2
Temporary housing.
(Photograph by Susan D.
Blum.)

as their number has escalated in the last decade (there are 3 million migrant residents of Beijing alone), they are officially referred to as *mingong chao*, or "rural laborer tide." The tide is moving across China and is especially pronounced in larger cities, where such wanderers take up residence on the floors of unfinished multistory buildings, hang around transit stations, or eke out a life on the street in makeshift housing fashioned from cardboard and scraps of wood and metal (see figs. 14.1 and 14.2). Given their primitive education and skills as well as a marginal awareness of public-health risk, the latest threat to the precarious existence of *mingong* is, not political repression, but the enhanced transmissibility of the HIV/AIDS virus.—Eds.

INTRODUCTION

The waves of internal migration pulsing through China over the past decade provide us with a window on a major transformation going on. The migration represents one crucial form of the human dimensions of the nation's change from plan to market. This movement of peoples can be both a symbol and a measure of the decline of the Communist regime's institutional structures and of its social system. It also suggests the possibility of the demolition of long-standing barriers erected by the post-1949 government between city and countryside, in contrast to the lack of labor mobility before the reform era. Those involved in the movement are members of a new urban grouping, the floating population, chiefly peasants no longer domiciled where they were initially registered to live and estimated in the range of 50 million to 70 million persons.[1]

Some observers seize on this flow as an emblem of an imminent demise of the Party's previous pattern of rule where class structure is concerned. They adopt a positive outlook, alleging that this human tide stands for freedom, for peasants unbound from the sometime shackles of the commune, released from the countryside. Farmers venturing into the cities and towns can hope for the enrichment of their daily lives and for the betterment of their social lot in life, such arguments hold.

But pitted against that view is the fact that the state, by refusing to grant these transients an urban *hukou*—the legal right to household residence in the city and the whole panoply of special privileges and access that that affords (discussed in detail below)—forces them to remain in the *temporary* category. This denial and its accompanying designation, while limiting their total numbers and so reducing somewhat the inevitable pressure on municipalities, exclude most of them from normal city life. Thus, the "retreat of the state" is far from complete.

Depending on personal circumstance and skill, the two-thirds or so of the floaters who enter the urban job market (the other third coming for social purposes or for reasons connected with what have been called *urban functions:* to visit or stay with family and friends, to attend meetings, to undergo training, for tourism, or to see a doctor) have widely varying ways of life in the city.

According to a major government study of seven of China's biggest municipalities, the largest group of them (about 30 percent) earn their living on construction projects, often bound to specific projects or else to annual contracts; another 22 percent peddle in produce markets, not uncommonly remaining for years on end; some 18.5 percent engage in "household service," many of whom are nursemaids for periods as little as three months; and about 6 percent work in the repair trades (including such activities as shoe, bicycle, pots and pans, and knife repairing).

A catchall category of *other types of hired labor,* amounting to 21.7 percent, includes those in state factories (of whom the majority work in textiles) on three- to five-year contracts, day laborers hauling freight, sanitation workers, coal deliverers, and garbage collectors. Other occupations that attract floaters include barbering and tailoring, street performing, fluffing cotton quilts, popping popcorn, bricklaying, restaurant work, and handicrafts and furniture manufacture. Despite real differences, in the eyes of the authorities, as defined by the Fourth National Census, held in 1990, anyone living away from his or her place of legal residence for less than a year is called *floating*. What will be the fate of these displaced persons as the Communist system in its social sense unravels with the progress of market reforms? How much is the state plan, with its coercively mandated residential system, giving way to the market, with its governance purely by economic forces and its purely economically driven status and class categories? How much can the floaters expect to become integrated into the dominant social order (or, put otherwise, to become a part of an incipient social order)? Taken a step further, can they venture to imagine not just assimilation for themselves but an actual upward climb for their children, a shot at transferring out of the "peasantry" to a higher social class? I am less concerned here with the formation of autonomy, more interested in processes and potential for incorporation.

In the remainder of this chapter, to address these questions I will draw on findings about migration from comparative, historical, and theoretical literature on this subject. I have culled from this material two sets of variables: first, traits that characterize migrant populations; and, second, factors present in receiving societies that determine the life chances of transient peoples. This framework shows that integration for the floating population is blocked, stymied, or distorted because of the stamp of the socialist state and its long-standing social and economic systems. My focus is on the world of the larger metropolises, whose magnetism is most apt to draw migrants from far and wide.

TRAITS OF THE MIGRANTS THEMSELVES

The traits of the migrants relevant to this inquiry are their resources (both material and "human capital"); the class characteristics of the migrant community; their family strategies; their "ethnicity" (defined in a special way in the Chinese context, as explained below); their intention to remain in the city; and their subculture. Each of these is conditioned by the residue of the Communist order in ways that affect the integration and mobility chances of the transients and their children. The discussion that follows distinguishes between two groups of migrants: Some of them, undoubtedly a tiny minority, come to town blessed with either the funds or the social connections to enable them to enjoy entrée to at least some of the benefits of the genuine urbanites; others are braving the odds without monetary means or ties to the influential.

Comparative researchers have identified both material and "human capital" resources that can either magnify or limit the chances of migrants in their adjustment to new environments (Morawska 1990, 198, 201). While material wealth is obvious, relevant forms of human capital for our purposes include special work-related skills, job training and experience, education, and parentage. As for material capital, those with either financial resources or a way of gaining some can hope to use these resources to enter urban society. This they may either do directly, by acquiring some of those goods that the Communist system offers free or at a low price to urbanites, or indirectly, by bribing the gatekeepers of those goods, thereby obtaining cheap grain, better housing, a good job, or schooling for their young. Often enough money and a "route" (*lu*) are both required, in the words of a Beijing cab driver.

It is not just that variously endowed migrants have different levels of success in their efforts to seek goods reserved by the state system just for urban insiders. Their very chances even to gain the essential material and human capital for seeking these goods in the first place were in the past shaped by that same system. For it is likely that the relevant skills among those who possess them were developed by virtue of their own Party membership or by working at jobs in the past in such commune enterprises and units as warehouses, supply and marketing cooperatives, and village industries. These are advantages of which only some of the floaters can boast.

As for parentage, all the rural in-migrants start from a more or less common base, cursed by a low-status *peasant* household label. And, while their level of schooling admittedly varies, for the most part they have as a group been educated in inferior institutions. Although a portion may have completed senior high school, the nationwide average education level of peasants is low. According to one sample survey, migrants with a junior high school education represented 20 percent of the sample, those who had only attended primary school were 40 percent, and illiterates and semiliterates accounted for 30 percent.[2]

The second trait, the class characteristics of the migrant community, relates in the comparative literature to whether a group of migrants in a given locale creates what is known as an *ethnic enclave* (Portes and Rumbaut 1990, 21), which tends to generate its own *enclave economy* (Smith, Tarallo, and Kagiwada 1990, 20). For this not just capital but some individuals with business expertise who are willing to hire compatriots are required. Some of the major theorists in the field of migration have recently pointed to the opportunities that such communities provide for job formation and eventually capital accumulation for coethnics—capital that ultimately can become useful in investing in the education and, hence, presumably the upward mobility of the next generation (Portes 1990, 160–184; Tilly 1990, 92–93).

In the Chinese case, we see again the bifurcation between two groups of in-migrants. Those who have or are in the course of obtaining the capital and the expertise, however, seem less committed to the future careers of their less fortunate covillagers and more concerned with carving out a point of entry for themselves into the established system. The best examples of this are the once-peasant parvenu construction team bosses (*gongtou*), who gather their fellow locals into a team and lead them to worksites in the city, but whose own time in the city is spent cultivating urban influentials. Also, since a great deal of floating migration is essentially seasonal sojourning,[3] the communities themselves tend to be stable, while the individuals who make them up are often on the move, whether back to the villages, to other cities, or to other work or dwelling sites within the same city.[4]

Third is the issue of family strategies, which has several dimensions here. The overwhelming proportion of the transients is male—as high as 87 percent in Beijing and dropping only to 74 percent in Wuhan, according to figures supplied by the Ministry of Construction. Whether they are single or married, this has several implications: since the family, if any, is left in the village, any savings that are garnered are remitted home and do not go toward building an urban future.

Moreover, these men, if single, find it difficult to find mates in the city and so are forced to marry rural women, reducing their commitment to integration into city life. This unbalanced sex ratio, far more skewed than the male-biased ratios that usually issue from the sex selectivity of migration in other societies, obviously makes for uncommon sorts of migrant communities at the place of destination.[5] Men on their own can and will do little to become part of the regular urban scene.

Other features of the floaters that are family related concern their children. Those brought along end up more often than not as helpers to their fathers in their handicraft trades or businesses, while those who come by themselves have been dispatched by poor rural parents, sometimes after only a few years of primary school, and are sent to toil in joint-venture enterprises under conditions so unsavory and with pay so poor (several sources claim half that given to adults for similar work)[6] that comparisons with nineteenth-century Britain readily leap to mind, if reportage literature out of Guangdong and Shanghai is to be believed.

Also on the subject of offspring, there are allegedly either 10 million or 20 million "black babies" populating the cities. These are those "illegitimate" children born outside the plan whose mothers escaped to the cities to deliver them away from the watchful eyes of village cadres. Born floating, their urban lives are bound to be marked as those of outcasts, unless, of course, they or their parents manage to buy or connect their way into the privileges of the settled.

Ethnicity, the fourth trait, takes on a particular connotation among Chinese migrants, given that the great majority of them are, after all, Han like most of the general population (see Honig 1992). The signs of ethnicity in racially disparate societies include language, dress/costume, custom, facial features, foods, religious practices, and skin color. But "ethnic" division in the eyes of the localistic—and, in response even to their fellow nonlocal Chinese, one might go so far as to say xenophobic—Chinese is chiefly defined by place of origin. In these terms certainly extraprovincialites but even rural people from the same province are viewed as foreign.

With respect to Chinese on the move, local snobbishness may single out the tasteless garb of the bumpkin or the peasant's sun-darkened skin and, as one urban woman in Wuhan depicted it, his or her "flavor of muddiness." In addition, I was assured by my stylish Harbin host in 1991 (working in the foreign affairs office of the provincial social science academy) that women native to that city were the best dressed in all China and that she could therefore tell at a glance a person from outside.[7] But in China language is the most significant source of difference where integration and mobility are concerned. Since many regions of China boast their own dialects, the language barrier people face when transporting themselves to new locales can segregate and subordinate them in relation to their host communities.[8]

This sense of ethnicity is also apparent in the tendency of migrants to dwell separately in the cities, just as sojourners did in Chinese urban places historically, by provincial (or county or village) origin, and sometimes by occupation as well. Scattered journal reports in the past few years and conversations with Chinese people in 1991 and 1992 attested to the presence within many major cities of an array of "villages," such as a "Zhejiang village," a "Jiangsu village," and so forth. Some sources claim that each of these communities is governed by its own special "coethnic" chiefs, who mediate the negotiations between their confreres and the local authorities.[9] This segmentation of the city, perhaps a part of a new spatial specialization, fragments the migrants as well as cutting them off from the stable urban population. It is thus a force that obstructs integration, and possibly mobility too, for the ex-peasant residents of cities.

The fifth migrant trait is intention to remain in the city. According to one migration specialist, whether or not a sojourner eventually does stay on in town, his or her belief that he or she will return to the countryside has a major impact on all sorts of urban behavior, much of it relevant to his or her ultimate prospects for mobility (Nelson 1976, 721–757).[10] The person expecting to commit to the urban setting will try to form relevant skills and to build up a reputation, credentials, and contacts there. The reverse, of course, is the case for those who see themselves as only passing through. And in dozens of interviews with floaters I repeatedly encountered either a sense of total aimlessness about the future or else a plan to return home within a short, specified period of time, after accumulating enough cash to build a house or marry in the village. As one young shoe repairman from Zhejiang working in Tianjin told me flippantly when asked about his intentions, *"Huo yitian, suan yitian"* (Live a day, write off a day).

In general, then, migrants who plan to sink roots at the destination make choices that improve the life chances both of themselves and of their offspring. It is the settled, not the roaming or seasonal migrant, who fits these conditions,[11] but scattered reports offer no clear indication of which of these or what proportion of these may be the better endowed as against those who work from a lack of means.[12] Once having made the decision to stay, for those who do so, however, the prospects for integration and mobility should increase somewhat, unless the barriers identified here (and those addressed in the next section) are just too rigid.

The last of our six traits of the migrants is their own subculture. We cannot generalize about these people themselves; indeed, there must be more than one subculture among them. To begin with their underclass, several sources, both oral and documentary, have attested to the docility, obedience, and hardworking habits of many of them, characteristics that link them with other undocumented and migrant laborers around the world (Solinger 1993).

But this may be just an initial stance, according to a Harbin scholar, replaced with time by feelings of dissatisfaction, small acts of disobedience, and work slowdowns, once the transients have learned of their comparative disadvantage. Such behavior matches the model of the "migrant subculture" depicted by a Harvard psychiatrist, based on data collected in migrant labor camps. In this model, filthy and debilitating conditions, combined with social isolation, extreme poverty, cultural deprivation, and social fragmentation, produce a mood of fatalism and antisocial behavior and result in deliberate wastefulness and the abuse of equipment (Cohen 1987, 196–204). Indeed, some of the migrants I visited living on the outskirts of Wuhan and Tianjin were residing in unheated, tentlike shacks without running water or electricity or five to six in a room equipped with nothing but two or three beds and several sewing machines at which the occupants labored night and day. That such people have become dispirited should not be surprising.

But, despite the strikes at foreign-funded firms in the Pearl river delta, such dissatisfaction may not generally find open expression among these transients. Many sources have noted the vulnerable position of such workers and their proclivity either to keep silent, engaging in only covert styles of dissent, or to petition quietly.[13] Surely the allegedly high rates of criminality (much of which may actually substitute for more conventional forms of political association and protest, which Elizabeth Perry's (1995) findings on the lack of unionization for temporary workers and their consequent reliance on criminal gangs suggest) among the transients must bear some relation to such moods of discontent.[14] Whether docile or dissident, these people, who must belong to the unendowed, are not likely to find easy access to the world of the settled urban elite.

Still, this is not the whole picture. Those earning well and building on their *guanxi* (personal relationships) to squeeze into this same world are doubtless cocky and satisfied. But whether they invest their rewards in positive acts to help them become a more permanent part of city society or return home to bask in the prestige their winnings have gained for them is still an open question.

In summary, migrants reach the cities equipped with a range of resources, strategies, traits, and attitudes. I have presented the plight of these people, where necessary differentiating between the minority, who hold or soon acquire the wherewithal to penetrate the realm of privilege, and the bulk of the floaters, who must scrape about the dregs in order to survive. While the odds for integration and then mobility are certainly much greater for the first group, given individuals must still choose whether to draw on those odds for the sake of an urban future. Their decision is no doubt colored in part by the factors of the receiving society, described below.

FEATURES OF THE RECEIVING SOCIETY

The literature on migration analyzes not just the migrants themselves in attempting to account for the life chances of these people in their destinations. The quality of the community they enter is also determining. Two authors of a recent volume on immigration into America speak of this element under the label *contexts of reception* (Portes and Rumbaut 1990, 85). Under this heading these scholars include the policies of the receiving government, the conditions of the host labor market, and the characteristics of the migrants' own ethnic communities in the new setting. In the Chinese case, government policies play an inordinately large role in shaping the entire context in all its aspects.

My choice of features of the receiving society most applicable to today's migrants in Chinese cities, in the context of reception, has been shaped by the comparative literature on migration. They are as follows: the nature of the class structure in the city (clearly a function of state policy in the Chinese case); the pattern of property ownership; the type of labor market; the political system; the patronage networks available to the migrants; the urban education system and access to it; housing opportunities in the cities; and the attitudes of the receiving community. I will also supply some material on the modes of adaptation that the transients assume in the cities. True, these features have all come under some degree of assault and have been steadily losing a portion of their power since the reform era got under way. But it is still safe to say that through the early 1990s not a single one of them had become undermined to the point that it ceased to affect in basic ways the options of the newcomers to the towns.

Just as in Latin American cities, in China a closed class structure impedes social mobility for newcomers. The class order of China, however, is clearly a function of government policy, as it is still most fundamentally determined by the state-imposed *hukou* system. Indeed, Chinese people are still subject to a finely graded ranking order, which classifies those with a *hukou* in the greatest metropolises at the top and those with small, isolated rural-township *hukou* at the bottom. It is the urban *hukou* that provides the basis for all the perquisites that urbanites—and only urbanites—enjoy.[15]

Many people with money or the proper sort of *guanxi* can exist rather well without a *hukou*. Still, in July 1991 I was told that the price of procuring a *hukou* in Harbin was as high as 3,000 yuan; in June 1992 friends in Wuhan and a Beijing cab driver agreed that combined with proper *guanxi* it could run at least as high as 20,000 yuan in Beijing. And journal articles speak of both black-market and official prices with the amounts varying with the prestige of the city. As the *Peasant Daily* noted in mid-1989, "People go on a 'black road' to get an urban *hukou;* those with power use power, those with money buy it; those with neither write, [and] run back and forth" (*Nongmin ribao,* 11 May 1989).

The essentially closed character of this class order is illustrated by the difficulty of marrying across its boundaries, as mentioned briefly above. For the most part city folk are not disposed to wed a "peasant," even a newly urban-based one. Even the official press admits this, quoting a female "peasant" textile worker in a city, who says, "My biggest worry is whether I can become a full-time worker and get an urban residence permit; if I can't, I'll have to find a boyfriend in the countryside and live apart." In the same paper on the same day a commentator states, "Rural workers find it difficult to get to know local young men, let alone marry them" (*China Daily,* 24 June 1991, 6). In the typical words of one interviewee in Tianjin, "We wouldn't [*buhuide*] accept them as regular urban people. . . . People look down on them as peasants. . . . Tianjin people don't want to marry outsiders."[16]

Researchers tell a plaintive tale of female peasant contract labor in the textile plants of Zhengzhou who "want to find an urban husband, but realize they don't possess the qualifications for this; it's hard to make friends with someone of a higher social position, so the pressure of the marriage problem gets greater and greater" (Li and Hu 1991, 345). Inquiring of my transient respondents whether they hoped to marry an urbanite, I was met not infrequently with expressions of incredulity or embarrassed laughter.

The role of the pattern of ownership is manifest in the status superiority of the state-owned firms. Their greater prestige was evident into the early 1990s in the preference of many urban youths for remaining unemployed rather than working in non-state-sector jobs. It is well-known that some 40 percent of the state-owned factories operate at a loss and will soon be forced to lay off workers. Nonetheless, the politicoeconomic order in China not only protects them, it accords them priority treatment. An entire bureaucratic apparatus operates to ensure their survival, with the result that those working in the "private" or "individual" economies may fear that their businesses exist under a cloud of uncertainty. For this reason, it is generally those who have nurtured adequate connections—whether through bribery or otherwise—who feel most confident about their chances of surviving and succeeding as private entrepreneurs to the point of accumulating capital for upward mobility.

The ownership structure also favors the permanent, urban, regular (*guding*) workers in many ways, while housing, eating, and finding a mate become bitter problems for contract labor brought in from the countryside. For instance, an official report on one of Zhengzhou's less profitable textile mills tells of two young peasant girls who had to be sent 20 to 30 yuan each month by their parents because they received insufficient help with living expenses, not to mention welfare benefits, from the plants that employed them (Li and Hu 1991, 344).

The fringe benefits that go with work in the state firms offer security only for the regular workers. This is a security for which contract and temporary workers cried out in the Cultural Revolution; their absence cannot be less painful today. Of all the different types of transients, only peasant contract laborers in profitable state or foreign-funded firms were getting some welfare benefits as of 1992, according to interviews in factories and at labor and textile bureaus in Wuhan and Tianjin in May and June 1992. This variable treatment bolsters Perry's (1995) findings of the continuing (but, taking into account the floaters, one should probably say the exacerbated) fragmentation of the labor force in today's China.

The third feature of the receiving community, the urban labor market, holds both advantages and disadvantages for the floating population. Most obviously, there is still enough unmechanized, casual, informal, unskilled labor in the cities to provide a special niche for the transients. Much of such work—in construction and in the textile, chemical, building materials, sanitation, packaging and hauling, and repair trades—is harsh, filthy, and exhausting. It has been disdained by urban young people eligible for more prestigious jobs in the foreign-trade sector.

At least in the short run, taking a position in these lines of occupation can have deleterious consequences for assimilation and mobility, they believe. These kinds of jobs as a rule provide no advancement and shunt the transients off into marginality. Consequently, being employed in this way precludes the possibility of achieving what a scholar of the Irish immigration into England of the 1840s called *work-day integration* (Finnegan 1982, 98). Like the displaced Irish of that time, many floaters labor in gangs of their fellow villagers or operate on their own. Another negative aspect of this special niche is its suitability for child labor.

One more question about the labor market concerns its degree of competitiveness and the effects this may have on life opportunities for the migrants. The urban Chinese labor market is above all highly segmented. As in all developing countries, there is a dual labor market, with immigrants working in the second, informal sector. Competition for the migrants exists just in the second sector among unskilled workers, and in most cases this means with members of other migrant/minority ethnic groups.

Several journal articles have commented on the saturation of segments of the second sector in China—in the urban construction market and, in some places, the crafts labor market as well. The result of this is not hard to guess. As in old Hankow, the unskilled labor market in today's Chinese cities is sectioned off by localized labor gangs, each with its own boss and turf, and brawls over economic opportunity are serious or frequent enough to be treated in the literature.[17]

New "spontaneous labor markets" for unskilled labor sprang up in the 1980s, having no fixed site, involving negotiation in the streets, following no regular procedures, and offering no guarantees. At one I visited as many as two hundred men and women of varying ages were lolling about in mid-afternoon hoping to find employment as nurses, restaurant workers, or painters. Aside from their irregularity and uncertainty, such institutions may sometimes prey on the naïveté of newcomers and encourage criminal and exploitative activities, according to Chinese sociologists who have studied them (Huang, Liu, and Peng 1988, 15–17; Wang, Wu, and Jiang 1990, 3).

With no way to enter the unions of regular labor, migrants in China cannot dream, at least not under present conditions, of the steady integration into the workforce enjoyed by the Irish earlier in this century in London. Only those who through *guanxi* manage to permeate their way into the workplaces of the permanent can begin to upgrade their life chances.

The political system, the fourth feature of the system confronting the cityward sojourner, denies these people any civic, legal, or political status. Even those who have registered as *temporary city dwellers* still lack the urban *hukou* and so remain disenfranchised. Moreover, as noted above, like others of their type around the world, these people are disinclined to protest openly, to organize, mobilize, aggregate demands, or even to lobby; such reticence saps them of political relevance.

In China's authoritarian, one-party system, in the absence of any competitive political parties or of legitimate representation for social groups (especially for those on the fringes of the system, such as our floaters), politics is useless. If an outsider could somehow build a bridge that led to Party membership, that person could become political in the Chinese context. But such an avenue must be blocked for the masses of migrants. Moreover, these people seem unlikely to have access to the type of alliances with state leaders that Perry's (1995) regular workers can call on.

Fifth is the nature of the patronage networks open to the transients. The issue here is the relation of migrants to the structures of power, status, occupation, and wealth. In this case people with means and those without are clearly demarcated. Migration theory emphasizes the importance for integration and economic success of "ethnic networks." Looking at other societies that do not have the types of barriers erected by the Chinese socialist system, scholars have found that in-migrants may be able to flourish if they can build links to already settled coethnics in their new communities who are situated in business or other professional circles or if they can participate in the community organizations formed by previously settled coethnics. Unlike the residents of some other towns, our floaters are not apt to be welcome to participate in the types of varied, popular associations that may be found among the permanent residents.

In China, since there are no political parties whose leaders might want migrants' votes or legal associations these people can join, brokers become all-important. But the brokers who serve the underclass are typically tied to the status quo, well aware that any alleviation of the lifestyle difficulties of their charges would only undermine their own power. It is often such brokers, bosses, or community chiefs in Chinese cities who bribe their way into some status for themselves; for their communities their efforts go toward sustaining their people's rights to continue with illicit practices.

The urban education system is the sixth feature of the municipal environment with which the floating people must cope. The formal prohibition on outsiders attending city schools has led to informal purchase prices for entry for floating children, varying by quality of school and city, as I learned in interviews in Guangzhou, Wuhan, and Tianjin in May and June 1992. A telling piece in a Guangdong journal of reportage literature recounts the inaccessibility of city schools for most of the transients' youngsters (Huang 1989, 20–21). Here are stories of truant twelve-year-olds collecting junk, a carpenter teaching his son his own trade rather than leaving him in the village to go to school, and a bean-sprout grower who worried that policy changes might force him and his kind out of the city and therefore did not want to invest his small pot of capital in bribing the teachers. A son helping the "scrap boss" earns 100 yuan a month: "If he went to school his family would lose that source of income and would have to pay school fees besides. School is for the boss's family," explains the author.

The same article also carries the tale of a construction work team leader who could afford whatever the managers of the school of his choice desired as the price for accepting his children; he must be in the minority. The worried writer muses that "shack-village residents will in the future become a 'structure' the large cities 'can't pull down'"; and "After them, we will have one or several 50 million appearing in the cities [of these] low-quality people." Surely the connection between educational opportunity and upward mobility must be one of the best known in any theory of achievement.

Access to housing was "crucial to any social improvement" in the nineteenth-century urbanization of Europe (Hohenberg and Lees 1985, 310). Given the extraordinary crowding and cramping that even regular city residents suffer in China, one must despair for the fate of the outsiders. Despite "commercialization" of urban housing in the current reforms, the purchase of most apartments still depends on hefty contributions from one's state-owned unit (or on help from wealthy overseas relatives). Therefore, with no real housing market, almost all urban dwellings being state allocated and enterprise owned, newcomers to the city who lack means are forced to live in a wide range of more or less desperate dwellings.

According to Rutkowski (1991, v), about 40 percent live in residents' homes (which must refer to those who have come to join or camp out in family members' apartments as well as those renting space in peasants' huts along the outskirts of the city).[18] Another 20 percent are in collective unit shelters (this would relate mainly to workers in factory dormitories but might include those in temporary work shacks at construction sites as well). A further 20 percent stay in hotels (including the many private inns and "underground hotels" that have cropped up everywhere in China today, many of which make ideal residences for peddlers and others in town for relatively brief commercial sojourns), hostels, or hospitals.

The remaining 20 percent are in "various other places." According to my research, these "other" places include a wide array of miserable hovels, such as squatter settlements, train stations, on the streets, under the eaves, under bridges, in free markets (a common practice for vegetable and egg peddlers is to lie on a plank under plastic sheeting inside their marketplace), on boats or wharves, in bathhouses, in public toilet stalls, in garbage dumps, on dormitory stairs, or along the river banks.[19]

According to this breakdown some 80 percent of the migrants do have a roof over their heads. But, except those residing with family, none of them is situated to become a part of regular city life. Presumably those in the residual category, as well as members of construction teams, are frequently on the move. Even if their housing were more normal, the geographic mobility dictated by looking for work would limit integration. Only those holed up in proper homes and those who are "kings" of the outdoor or construction-team communities have a hope of melting into the mainstream mold.

Localism and xenophobia that shade into overt discrimination, prejudice, and open hostility are the eighth feature of the urban setting that confronts the floaters. As one writer explained: "The floating population sometimes surpass the local people's tolerance level. . . . [T]hey can't buy transportation tickets, transportation is crowded to the point of *luan* [chaos], amusement areas are crammed, the price of local goods goes up. They often resentfully cry, 'Everything is spoiled by outsiders.' . . . In brawls, local people get more supporters among the onlookers; there are few dissuaders. The contradiction between local and outside people has now become a social contradiction. . . . They treat outsiders as second-class citizens and see them as the snatchers of local people's interests" (Zhang 1987, 25). Similarly, a public security officer in Beijing is actually said to have pronounced, "These out-of-towners are no better than animals" (*South China Morning Post,* 9 October 1991, 10). These sorts of attitudes among the "host" community cannot but color the reception these transients encounter now and the opportunities they find for social mobility in the near term. Moreover, these attitudes might affect all the migrants alike since even the successful outsiders could well be a target for resentment among the less fortunate legal urban residents who in their own eyes properly "belong" in the city.

All told, the environment the floaters face runs from chilly to frigid. Granted, many of them may not mind the harsh living conditions if their only motive is to scrape together capital to send back to the farm (either for themselves or for their families). But some untold proportion is camping down in the cities with some measure of permanence, and, for them, the closed class order, the biased ownership structure, the irregular labor market, the Party-dominated political system, the flimsy patronage networks, the elitist education system, the barren housing market, and the snobbish urban citizenry are bound to rankle. Even should some of these "foreign" folk manage to crash through or circumvent these several impediments, they too cannot fail to resent the effort called for.

CONCLUSION

This analysis of the fate of China's transients has laid out the paltry attributes they bear to a grim milieu. What does the presence of peasants in the cities—this new, reurbanization of China—help us to see about processes of class and community formation and the potential for a shift in social structure for outsiders in the wake of this country's market reforms? And what does it allow us to conclude about the progress of the market itself in China's reform era and its influence in this arena?

A new two-class structure has been emerging in the cities of China: on the one side, those for whom jobs, housing, education, cheap food, and medical care are an entitlement and, on the other, those who must scramble for these goods or do without. As this chapter has suggested, however, this breakdown is primarily, but not entirely, a matter of urban-*hukou* holders versus those with a rural registration. More precisely, those with an urban *hukou* can command the peak of the status hierarchy and the whole panoply of perquisites.[20]

In addition to them, though, is that minority of rural "outsiders" who lack the *hukou* but who have somehow managed to acquire either the funds or the social connections to enjoy entrée to at least some of the benefits it provides. One finding of this chapter is that, given all the barriers erected by the socialist system in China, this privileged group among the migrants is small relative to analogous groups in other countries.

On the other side of the divide are those transients who inhabit the cities lacking not only an urban *hukou* but also the material and social wherewithal that could substitute for its absence.[21] For our first un-*hukou*'d group, the prospects are reasonably good for climbing the newly modified status hierarchy that now shapes Chinese urban social life; for the second group, that procedure promises to be lengthy and tortuous. In fact, the current opportunity structure for most of these folk away from home reflects the class order forged over decades by the Communist system: for the most part, peasants newly resident in the cities retain their old status even as they radically alter their ways of life.

What about the transition from plan to market? If the state is receding, are economic modes of making good replacing mandatory and hereditary statuses? The answer to these queries, simply, is no. There has not yet been a full "withdrawal of the state" in this domain (if in any other). What we are witnessing is at once the promise of the market—a force for freedom, for geographic, and perhaps for social mobility—but at the same time a process that very much bears the stamp of the prior state socialist order. That residue of the old state with its passive weight may be distinguished from the measures taken by the active, living, intentional state of today. This present state may be less powerful in keeping the floaters out of the cities than are the remnants of the class order long in place in limiting the assimilation and integration of these peoples into current city life.

That old state cannot simply "withdraw" without a trace. For, despite the shrinkage of the plan and the drop in the prestige of the Party, the institutions and regulations of the state, along with the social relations these structures and rules have fashioned, still linger. Indeed, even those most able to circumvent these institutions and rules must adopt modes of circumvention that themselves are marked by the old system. This refers to the continuing need to develop connections—*guanxi*—with Party members and other gatekeepers in order to mediate the acquisition of capital, education, and other essentials necessary for upward mobility. Assimilation and later chances for mobility for all can occur only to the extent that, not just market forces overcome and replace these state-defined blockades, but a new political system, accompanied by new class and civic orders, can evolve. What is required is a most complex transformation involving fundamental alterations on several fronts simultaneously.

To judge from the data available, for the majority of the floaters, the probability of real integration and assimilation, based both on what they themselves can bring to bear and on the challenges they face in the urban setting, is not high. Thus, for the "peasant" population drifting into the cities' spaces and floating around them, there has not yet been an essential switch to marketization. Neither has there been any elemental decline in the ability of the Communist structure and its social system to sustain their old barriers against these new urban outcasts.

POPULAR CULTURE: ROCK AND ROLL

Popular culture takes many forms in today's China. With the growth of a middle class and the existence of a two-day weekend for students and urban workers, people have more time and resources for the pursuit of leisure than at any time since well before 1949. The wealthy have always enjoyed hobbies and connoisseurship of many sorts, from opera to poetry to calligraphy to tea drinking, and the poor have found ways to amuse themselves at festivals, temple celebrations, markets, and various holiday celebrations. Rural teenagers sang songs from mountaintop to mountaintop; swimming in the heat of the summer was not unknown if we are to believe Shen Congwen as he recounts his tales from childhood in Hunan (1982). China had the world's largest and most abundant cities for millennia, and those cities were filled with tempting opportunities to pursue pleasure, foremost among them food and drink. Since 1949 the state has controlled much cultural production in the service of ideology and morality, with state-sponsored song-and-dance troupes and ballet companies, professional writers employed by government programs, and so forth. But, since the 1980s, a noteworthy increase in popular culture has occurred, along with a remarkable—although not complete—relaxation in censorship and control.

Food in China must be mentioned, although we have not included a section on this topic. K. C. Chang (1977) claimed that the Chinese are the most food preoccupied of all peoples. (He acknowledges that the French and Italians might be worthy competitors.) Without attempting to evaluate this claim with scientific rigor, we believe that it is certainly true that food permeates all social life in China and that the amount of care, resources, time, and land devoted to the cultivation and preparation of food is astonishing. One of China's mythical culture heroes, Lord Millet, exemplified the concern with agriculture and people's livelihood that has been a significant part of Chinese life from the earliest records. With the flourishing of agriculture since the Reforms of the late 1970s, restaurants, tea houses, coffee shops, fast food, gourmet food, street food, and markets have all spread at an astonishing rate. Every important occasion is celebrated with the sharing or exchange of food.

Although food obviously serves to nourish the body, it also functions as a form of artistic expression and entertainment.

Literature in a wide array of forms has also increased. Highbrow literary fiction and essays coexist with martial arts novels and experimental avant-garde fiction. Bookstalls and magazine windows are found on every street, and newspapers are read with gusto. Poetry is no longer possessed solely by the elite, and various salons for the reading and performing of poetry can be found in most cities.

Television and movies also flourish. While few people possessed television sets twenty years ago, almost every home with electricity now has one. Popular television series are often melodramatic family romances set in the imperial past, with a dramatic assortment of setbacks and triumphs. Martial arts shows, like martial arts films, are among the most popular of offerings. Families often watch together, but the shows tend to provide simply background to the other activities of the household. A form of video player, the VCD, similar to the DVD, has allowed people to watch movies easily at home.

Travel is part of the popular culture activity of today's Chinese person of means. Domestic tourism is a huge part of the economy, and provinces such as Yunnan derive much of their income from it. There are certain preferred destinations: Beijing, Guilin, Xi'an, Dali, Xishuangbanna, and now Shanghai are probably foremost. At each destination can be found certain places that attract almost every tourist, from museums to gardens to buildings that are photogenic backdrops for the requisite memento. Many newlyweds opt to have a traveling honeymoon and see some of the country. Only a small percentage of the population flies, however; most people travel by train or bus.

The visual arts are also alive in China, with a range of offerings from small souvenirs for tourists to monumental sculpture and painting. Arts academies train professional artists, and modest paintings are commonly exchanged as gifts. Dance and theater are also vibrant now, both new, outside styles and more traditional forms.

It is in this context that we must understand rock and roll (*yaogun*). Music of a variety of genres—syrupy *tongsu* songs, classical orchestral music, traditional opera, karaoke, and so forth—is heard throughout the country. One variety is rock and roll, some of which is imported directly from the West. A far greater percentage comes from other Asian societies such as Hong Kong and Japan, where the influence of Western popular forms has been tempered by the inclusion of more indigenous musical elements. As in the 1960s and 1970s in the West, the older generation in China today does not necessarily appreciate this new musical form. Precisely this break with the older generation is desired by a small, hip sector among urban young people in today's China.—Eds.

ANDREW F. JONES

15
The Politics of Popular Music
in Post-Tiananmen China

We have included this article by Andrew Jones because it provides a glimpse
into the politics and economics of popular culture in contemporary China.
Jones draws a contrast between state-sponsored *tongsu yinyue* (popular music)
and *yaogun yinyue* (rock music) and shows how musical forms and musical
support derive meaning largely from the social context in which they are
found. While rock music in China looks to Western music for its inspiration, for
its musical details, and even for its themes, it is not identical to rock music in
the West because it is rebelling against a different type of oppression. Many
rock musicians, such as Cui Jian, contend that they are merely providing a kind
of symbolic or spiritual protest, that they have no political agenda. This may
be genuine or dissembling, but, despite such protestations, many listeners,
including the Party, have taken their music to be an expression of political
protest. Still, even for a short time after the Tiananmen massacre of 4 June
1989, the government permitted Cui Jian to perform—in order to raise money
to pay for the Asian Games. Finally, when it was realized that audiences were
using his concerts as a way to rally and express opposition to the government,
his concerts, which were held in Beijing in the summer of 1990, were halted.
He and other rock musicians do continue to perform (indeed, in 1997, Cui was
permitted to conduct a restricted-dates national tour of the United States),
but they are occasionally—especially on anniversaries of the 4 June massacre—
prevented from doing so.

Recordings of rock music compete in a market that already contains
many popular artists from Hong Kong and Taiwan; ironically, many of the
most avant-garde musicians in China are recorded and supported by companies from those two regions, yet their recordings are sold in the state-run as
well as private music stores. And, after rock's beginnings in China in the cosmopolitan embrace of foreign forms, rock has since the Tiananmen massacre
been more consciously nativist—whether for ideological or for commercial
reasons is hard to say. Moreover, the rapidly growing popularity of musical figures like Cui Jian, He Dong, and Tang Dynasty has stirred the Communist

Party's interest in profiting from the rock music phenomenon by controlling the wider distribution of recordings. Such cunning, profit-driven counterhegemony is what Jones ironically refers to as *serving the people's money.*

This short article shows how complex the interpretation of well-described events can be. Even after interviewing a number of participants in the contemporary rock scene in Beijing, Jones cannot be entirely sure about their motives or about all the causes of the contemporary form of popular music in China. It should be evident how quickly changes can occur in popular culture, in terms of both its manifestations and its reception, depending on the political, economic, cultural, and social circumstances that converge at any given moment. And, as we have seen in previous readings, even at their points of closest convergence—commerce and music—the cultures of China and the West remain distinctive.—Eds.

Popular music as propaganda—be it in support of resistance to Japanese aggression in the 1930s, anti-imperialism in the 1940s, Maoism during the Cultural Revolution, or economic modernization in the 1980s—has long been a fixture of modern Chinese political culture.[1] The extent to which popular music became a vehicle for popular protest during the Tiananmen movement of 1989, however, was unprecedented. Throughout the movement, popular music—and in particular the rock music (*yaogun yinyue*) that emerged in Beijing in the late 1980s as an "underground" alternative to state-run popular music (*tongsu yinyue*)—served as a powerful means for the public expression of political and cultural dissent. Cui Jian's "I Have Nothing" ("Yiwu suoyou") was adopted by students and workers as a marching anthem, several rock bands performed for hunger-striking students on the square, and satires of government corruption set to popular melodies were regularly broadcast over makeshift public address systems throughout Beijing. On a less overtly political level, the rock subculture's embrace of Westernization, antitraditionalism, and individualism had much to do with informing the sensibilities (and, ultimately, the political behavior) of the students and workers who participated in the protests.[2] In the months after the crackdown, despite the suppression of rock music on the part of the Chinese Communist Party (CCP) and a barrage of *tongsu* songs intended to drown out any dissonance that might have lingered in the wake of the movement's demise, rock music performances continued to provide one of the few forums in which popular dissent could be safely enacted.

In the more than ten years that have elapsed since the crackdown, however, the politics of popular music have changed in ways that throw fascinating and complex light on the current political situation in China. Rock music, although it remains on the margins of state-sanctioned culture, can no longer be characterized as an unambiguously counterhegemonic form. Instead, rock music's gradual absorption into China's burgeoning market economy has defused much of its politically oppositional potential while allowing for the music to extend its cultural influence well beyond the narrow confines of the Beijing subculture from which it originally arose. At the same time, the ideological agenda of rock music has increasingly less to do with its earlier advocacy of cultural and political democratization than with an (inherently problematic) embrace of market economics and nativist politics. In the work of youth cultural icons, such as the heavy metal rock band Tang Dynasty and the pop-rock singer Ai Jing, we see the beginnings of a kind of "commodity nativism" that—rather than providing a vehicle for popular protest—is in many ways complicit with the CCP's headlong rush toward the combination of economic liberalization and political authoritarianism that Nicholas Kristof (1993) has recently dubbed *market Leninism*.

ROCK MUSIC AS SUBCULTURE

The emergence of a rock music subculture in China is, of course, a relatively recent phenomenon. Indeed, it could be argued that, between 1949 and 1978, popular music as such simply did not exist in Mainland China. In the years after the CCP's ascension to power, the mass-mediated popular music produced in the prewar years in urban centers like Shanghai was suppressed in favor of officially sanctioned mass music (*qunzhong yinyue*) and revolutionary song (*geming gequ*) that had less to do with commerce and popular leisure than with the marriage of the CCP's ideological imperatives with its bureaucratic control of the mass media. With the institution of Deng Xiaoping's sweeping program of economic reform and "opening to the outside world" in the early 1980s, however, popular music in China underwent a remarkable renaissance. In the early 1980s, China began to import popular music from Taiwan and Hong Kong. By the mid-1980s, China had begun to develop its own state-run popular music industry in response to this influx. At the same time, the state-run song and dance troupes (*gewutuan*), record companies, and television studios responsible for producing and disseminating what has come to be called *tongsu* music began to be weaned from their reliance on state subsidies. Inevitably, the monolithic dominance of ideological concerns began to be challenged by the imperatives of the market; the fledgling industry began to engage not just in "serving the people" (*wei renmin fuwu*) with propagandistic paeans to the socialist modernization plans but also in "serving the people's money" (*wei renminbi fuwu*) with love songs and dance music based on foreign models (*Yinyue yanjiu* 1988, 23). By 1988, the industry had grown strong enough to challenge the dominance of imports from Taiwan and Hong Kong with a new and wildly popular style called *the northwest wind* (*xibei feng*) that grafted a combination of Chinese folk music and disco with lyrical meditations on traditional Chinese culture and the dilemmas posed by China's new era of rapid modernization.

At the same time, a rock music subculture had begun to emerge in Beijing outside of the confines of the mainstream popular music industry.

Excluded from the state-controlled mass media, and subject to periodic suppression on the part of the CCP, rock musicians like Cui Jian had by 1988 nevertheless managed to establish a significant following among college students, intellectuals, and private entrepreneurs in Beijing, largely by virtue of an underground network of privately owned performance venues and foreign investors. In the liberal political climate of the months before the outbreak of the Tiananmen movement, rock music was allowed to make limited incursions into a wider public realm. Cui Jian's seminal first album, *New Long March Rock* (*Xin changzheng lushang de yaogun*), was released by a state-run record company in March of that year and went on to serve as a kind of soundtrack for the Tiananmen movement.

The Tiananmen movement marked a major turning point in the development of rock music in China. Despite a government crackdown on rock music (itself precipitated by the active role many rock musicians had played in the movement), the number of rock bands active in Beijing increased exponentially. Cui Jian, in part because of the countercultural cachet conferred on him by the association of his music with the student protest, found himself elevated to the status of a youth cultural icon. His fame was further increased by a 1990 national tour, underwritten by the CCP as a means of raising funds for the eleventh Asian Games in Beijing, and canceled in midcourse when officials discovered that his performances had become volatile occasions for the direct expression of political dissent on the part of his predominantly college-aged fans.

Despite Cui Jian's widespread popularity, the rock scene as a whole remained an essentially subcultural phenomenon as of 1990, one similar in many ways to those common in industrialized Western states as well as Eastern Europe before the upheavals of 1989. Rock musicians and other participants in the rock scene formed a closely knit group of no more than several hundred people who shared a common commitment to the production, consumption, and discussion of music and identified themselves to each other and society at large through distinctive clothing styles, hairstyles, slang, and types of behavior (drug use, sexual activity) that deliberately transgress social norms.

In the view of most theorists of subcultural phenomena, this sort of rebellion against established norms is largely of a "symbolic" nature (Hebdige 1987, 92). Subcultural groups arise in order to confront socioeconomic problems faced by their participants. Their solutions to these problems, however, are largely of an expressive and symbolic nature; subcultures "provide a pool of available symbolic resources which particular individuals or groups can draw on in their attempt to make sense of their own specific situation and create a viable identity." Rather than engaging in political activism, subcultures wage "semiotic guerrilla warfare" at the level of music and fashion: their "rebellion seldom reaches [the level of] articulated oppositions" (Brake 1985, 27, 8).

The rock subculture in Beijing differed from this theoretical model in one important respect.[3] While rock musicians in Beijing disavowed the notion that their music constituted a form of political activism, their activities hinged on a clearly articulated, self-consciously held ideology of *cultural* opposition. The central concern of participants in the rock subculture—as expressed in song lyrics and in a series of interviews I conducted—was the need to rebel against "oppression" (*yayi*). *Yayi* was conceived of as a cultural problem, as the stifling of individual expression, liberty, and creativity brought about by what was seen as an authoritarian, conformist, and "feudal" cultural tradition. This repudiation of a (however imperfectly understood) Chinese "feudalism," of course, involved a concomitant embrace of nominally "Western" values. Accordingly, Gao Qi, a heavy metal guitarist, framed his discussion of rock music in terms of intergenerational conflict and the struggle of young people to create "viable identities" in an era of rapid modernization and social change:

> *Tongsu* music is written for an older audience. Rock is youth music. . . . Young people need to express themselves. They are in the process of developing their opinions, their identities. . . . In China, we have several thousand years of feudalism that makes people's thinking all alike, conformist, without individualism. Now, after reform and liberalization, you have a generation of youth that are familiar with all sorts of Western things and Western literature . . . and this has resulted in a complete cultural transformation. . . . The younger you are, the greater the Western influence. . . . The changes have been so fast that the generation gap is like leaping over thousands of years. And rock belongs to this younger generation. (Interview with Gao Qi, 20 July 1990)

Gao Qi's emphasis on an antitraditionalist individualism (and its non-Chinese origins) was echoed by Zhu Xiaomin, lead singer of the (now defunct) Thump Band (Tutu yuedui): "Rock has become an international phenomenon because it's a direct expression of basic human desires, of our unlimited capacities as human beings. Human personality is the same everywhere. Everyone needs to express themselves. . . . I don't like Chinese folk songs or *tongsu* music that's based on Chinese folk. All it can express is a closed [*fengbi*], parochial nationalism. If you're singing about China, you can't sing about yourself, about your basic human desires" (interview with Zhu Xiaomin, 19 July 1990).

This sort of faith in individualism informed every aspect of the rock subculture. The sheer physicality of rock music (itself a form borrowed from the West) was seen as a means of effecting a visceral liberation from cultural norms and of asserting individuality (Ping and Ma 1990, 6). Rock lyrics also echo this theme: many songs recount a kind of archetypal narrative in which the singers confront and ultimately deliver themselves from the oppression, hypocrisy, and alienation that characterize daily life to a new world of freedom and authenticity. Wei Hua's "Don't Try to Stop Me Again" ("Bie zai shitu zulan wo") is a typical example:

> Don't try to stop me again
> Don't use lies to trick me
> Don't try to hide the truth from me again
> I'll struggle free of these fetters in the end
> I don't need your promises, time would go by too slowly
> Even if I've suffered, the sun's rays will shine on me in the end.[4]

The rock performance, in turn, was conceived of as a space in which—in Cui Jian's words—rock fans could "feel real freedom" as they came together to enact a collective ritual of resistance against the "oppression" brought to bear on them by society at large. These performances, which by 1990 took place nearly every weekend in bars, hotels, and restaurants throughout Beijing, afforded rock musicians and fans an opportunity to derive a sense of effective empowerment in symbolic defiance of the "oppression" of the quotidian social world in which they were embedded.

ROCK MUSIC AND YOUTH CULTURE

This emphasis on rock music as a culturally oppositional subculture, however, is misleading in several different respects. First, in a social and cultural context as heavily politicized as that of modern China, distinctions between "symbolic," cultural activism and overt political activism tend to blur. Cui Jian's claim that he is essentially an apolitical figure, for instance, may strike many observers as disingenuous. Second, rock music has reached and influenced the political behavior of a far larger audience than its limited subcultural provenance might indicate.

The popularity of rock music (and particularly of Cui Jian) outside of its subcultural milieu has been inextricably linked with a larger youth culture centered around college campuses and the urban private sector.[5] When rock music has been allowed to be featured at large-scale concerts (as with both Cui Jian's Asian Games Tour and the Modern Music Festival held in Beijing in March 1990), audiences have been composed largely of students and private entrepreneurs (*getihu*)—some of whom were instrumental in promoting and financing the music in its earliest stages. Cui Jian has performed repeatedly at schools like Beijing University, and students often explore the bars and restaurants where rock performances take place. Such excursions became one component of the intellectual ferment of college life in the years before the Tiananmen uprising, as the student leader Shen Tong observes: "The 1980s were probably the years when the Chinese people enjoyed the most intellectual freedom they had had since the founding of the People's Republic of China in 1949. I became more aware of this when I entered Beida [Beijing University] and discovered that Western influences were everywhere. . . .

When my friends and I went out to various bars in the city, we heard new bands experimenting with rock-and-roll" (Shen and Ye 1990, 113).

These kinds of contacts exercised considerable influence on the development of student activism (as well as the emergence of what Geremie Barmé has termed *"liumang" culture*) in the late 1980s.[6] Indeed, the sensibilities and concerns of rock musicians and student activists involved in the Tiananmen democracy movement not only dovetail but are expressed through an almost identical rhetoric, one that takes as its focus the critique of feudalism in Chinese culture. This is strikingly apparent in a speech delivered by one of the most prominent student organizers of the Tiananmen demonstrations, Wuer Kaixi, on the cultural background of the 1989 movement. His statements serve to illustrate the way in which students both used rock songs, such as Cui Jian's "I Have Nothing," as a focal point for their own affective investments and incorporated the insights into their condition gained from the experience of listening to rock into their rhetoric (and, in the case of Tiananmen, into their political activity):

> Chinese culture is feudalistic, despotic, closed [*fengbi*]; it negates the individual, and it has lasted for 5,000 years. . . . After 1949 and during the Cultural Revolution this feudalistic culture developed to such an extreme that it now absolutely and completely negates individuality. With reform and the open door policy, and liberalism in thought and culture under Deng Xiaoping, resistance [to feudalism] erupted with full force. . . . In recent years, Chinese college students have been stressing the individual, the self, and rebelling against all sorts of authority . . . but this idealism and the sense of the individual are contradictory to the reality of present society [so] young people have been left lost and disoriented. The people who are most influential among young people are not [the prominent dissidents] Fang Lizhi and Wei Jingsheng, but . . . singers such as Cui Jian. His "I Have Nothing" . . . serves to reflect the sense of loss and the disorientation of Chinese youth. ("Chinese Writers under Fire" 1989, 19)

This set of ideas appears to be nearly identical to those expressed by the keyboard player of the Breathing Band, Dong Dong:

> China is afflicted by feudalism, by conservatism and close-mindedness [*fengbi*]. The feudal powers [*fengjian shili*] oppose rock music. Feudal power comes out of blind obedience to Confucian ideals, and relationships between people in society. The open door policy is one way to solve this, but it has been only superficial. People have learned some foreign technologies, but they're still psychologically feudal, and their social circles are still feudal. Even some of the rock musicians' long hair is a sign of this superficial approach to Westernization. We don't want to change the world, but we do want to challenge feudalism with a kind of spiritual liberalization [*jingshen shang de kaifang*], to help each individual solve these problems on a psychological level, through individual freedoms. (Interview with Dong Dong, Beijing, 21 June 1990)

Clearly, there is only a fine line between the rhetoric of Dong Dong's brand of cultural activism and the more explicitly politicized objectives of student activists. The political goals of student activists who took part in planning the Tiananmen movement echo the cultural critique of rock musicians and, especially, the sense of intergenerational conflict expressed previously by Gao Qi. Shen Tong relates a discussion held by a group of student activists several months before the outbreak of the Tiananmen movement that sheds light on this point: "China doesn't need a movement for national salvation. . . . [W]hat China needs now is personal liberation. What our generation needs to do is push for individual freedom" (Shen and Ye 1990, 150).

What, then, accounts for the similarity of the individualist, antifeudalist rhetoric shared by rock devotees and college students? One important link between the two groups is the mass media. College students and rock musicians have listened to the same *tongsu* music, watched the same films, and read many of the same books, magazines, and newspapers. Each group acknowledges the influence of Western popular music, literature, and art on the development of their generation's sensibilities. Perhaps the single most important link, however, was Su Xiaokang and Wang Luxiang's influential television miniseries *Heshang* (River elegy), which presented an attack on the despotism and conservatism of Chinese culture through a "deconstruction" of cherished national symbols—like the Great Wall—to a nationwide audience in 1988 (De Jong 1989–1990). Su posits the Yellow river as a symbol of a culture that has died young, arguing that China must abandon an irretrievably flawed tradition (embodied by the landlocked loess plains of northwest China at the source of the river) and turn its attention outward to the economically vibrant, "seafaring" southeast coast and, by extension, the modern West. The final scene of the series presents an image of the Yellow river pouring out into the sea, as a narrator advocates continued economic reform, cultural openness, and political democratization (Su and Wang 1988, 109–111).

Many analysts draw attention to the impact that *River Elegy* had on the protesters in 1989. Dru Gladney has even argued, quite persuasively, that the film's celebration of student activism, and its implicit advocacy of a political democracy characterized by dialogue and "transparency," had a formative influence on the way in which the Tiananmen movement unfolded (Gladney 1990).[7]

The influence of *River Elegy* on the ideological positions of rock musicians was considerably less direct. Fittingly, *River Elegy* engaged the imagination of rock musicians not as a political agenda but as a way in which to understand and discuss the ostensible "feudalism" of Chinese culture and rock's own antifeudalist stance. Rock musicians often speak of their music in terms of the temporal and geographic axes (from feudal Chinese tradition to Western modernity, from the stagnant northwestern plains to the vibrant southeastern coast and the ocean) along which the writers of *River Elegy* structured their critique of Chinese culture. When asked, "How would you define Chinese rock?" several interviewees unhesitatingly prefaced their responses with, "China has a five-thousand-year-old tradition of feudalism" (interviews with Cui Jian, Dong Dong, Gao Qi, and Zhu Xiaomin, Beijing, June–July 1990). Each interviewee went on to interpret rock music as a manifestation of a conflict between feudalism and modernity. Again, their language echoed that of *River Elegy:* Feudal culture is "landlocked/closed" (*fengbi*), while rock music is "liberalized/open" (*kaifang*). Cui Jian's own assessment of the cultural function and value of rock music, for instance, relies on a metaphor that quite obviously derives from the film: "Chinese history and Chinese culture are very long and very rich. But right now our culture is like a river without an exit, without a way out to the ocean. The river's moving, but we don't know where it's heading. What we want to do is find a way to release this river, to find an outlet for it, to let it flow into the ocean, and join with the world outside China. We want to create a new culture, a culture that isn't parochial and closed in on itself" (Cui Jian, as interviewed in the television documentary *China Rocks* 1991).

Many rock musicians did actively support both this "culturalist" agenda and the more explicitly political objectives of the student activists with whom they shared a common rhetoric through their participation in the Tiananmen movement. Even so, it is important to remember that their role in the protests remained peripheral. Rock musicians did not necessarily share the commitment of student activists to engage in direct political action. Some—including several members of the heavy metal bands Tang Dynasty and Black Panther—claim to have been either indifferent or opposed to the movement (interviews with Zhang Ju and Li Tong, Beijing, 3, 12 June 1992). Cui Jian claims that rock is a means to make people "feel real freedom," not to institute political reform (BBC-TV interview with Cui Jian). The distinction is important, even when the realms of cultural and political activism did overlap, as when musicians like Cui Jian and the punk rocker He Yong performed protest anthems at Tiananmen Square to hunger-striking students.[8]

POLITICAL USES OF ROCK

Meaning in popular music is mercurial. The ideological agenda of rock musicians, although certainly an important factor in shaping both the ways commentators have discussed the significance of the rock scene and the ways audiences have responded to it, can hardly be said to be decisive. Audiences are free to (mis)interpret, enjoy, and make use (political or otherwise) of a pop song in any number of different ways, regardless of authorial intent. Rock songs and rock performances have been utilized by students and other fans both as a means for affective empowerment, for cultural critique, and as a conduit for explicitly political protest.

Cui Jian's aforementioned "I Have Nothing" is a salient example, for it is the most popular song to have emerged from the rock subculture into a wider youth cultural realm. The song's lyrics are as follows:

> I've asked tirelessly, when will you go with me?
> But you just always laugh at my having nothing
> I've given you my dreams, given you my freedom
> But you always just laugh at my having nothing
>
> Oh! When will you go with me?
> Oh! When will you go with me?
>
> The earth under my feet is on the move,
> The water by my side is flowing on,
> But you always just laugh at my having nothing
> Why haven't you laughed your fill?
> Why will I always search?
> Could it be that before you I will always have nothing?
>
> Oh! When will you go with me?
> Oh! When will you go with me?
>
> The earth under my feet is on the move
> The water by my side is flowing on
>
> I'm telling you I've waited a long time
> I'm telling you my very last demand
> I need to grab both your hands
> Only then will you go with me
> That's when your hands will tremble
> That's when your tears will flow
> Can it be that you're telling me you love my having nothing?
>
> Oh, only then will you go with me
> Oh, only then will you go with me.
>
> (Cui Jian, *Xin changzheng lushang de yaogun* [1989])

"I Have Nothing," as with rock music in general, primarily works for its fans "on the affective level of [their] everyday lives, at the level of the strategies [they] use to gain some control over that affective life, to find new forms of pleasure and excitement, or to cope with new forms of pain, frustration, and boredom" (Grossberg 1987, 186). One college student at Cui Jian's Asian Games Tour concert in Xi'an expressed the song's power in this way: "When you sing it over and over again, you will learn how to be confident despite hard times, how to awaken yourself from stagnation. You will realize your self-worth after having followed a difficult road." Another concertgoer relates that, "When we sing this song, we don't feel ashamed of having nothing anymore" (Ping and Ma 1990, 6). This sort of reaction, of course, tallies with what rock musicians characterized as the central aim of their music.

The intensity of listeners' reactions to "I Have Nothing," however, often had less to do with individual empowerment than with political protest. Interpretations of the lyrics, of course, inevitably vary from listener to listener. A Beijing city official may see the song as a mystifying and subversive denial of the benefits conferred on China's youth by socialism. Others might hear the story of a love affair between a poverty-stricken young man and a snobbish, rich woman. Despite this ambiguity, or perhaps because of it, many listeners and critics read the text in terms of political allegory. Tim Brace has suggested that readers of the song lyrics try a simple test: for every *I* substitute a *we*, and for every *you* think of the Communist Party (Brace 1991, 63). Read in this light, the song becomes an ironic response to the Chinese lyrics of the "Internationale" ("Guoji ge"), a socialist anthem whose ubiquity in Chinese everyday life is second only to that of the national anthem:

Slaves rise up, rise up!
We cannot say that we have nothing [*yiwu suoyou*]
We will be masters of all under heavens.[9]

The substitution of *we* for *I* makes implicit sense both in terms of the politicization that has surrounded Chinese popular music since its inception and in the way in which we enjoy pop music. Much of the pleasure of listening to popular music results from identifying our own passions with those of the singer. This identification, of course, links us not only with the performer but also with the other members of the audience—with a community of shared feeling. The singer's *I* becomes our *I*. Our *I*, in turn, merges with a collective *we*. Cui Jian denies that the song addresses the government, that "I Have Nothing" is equivalent to "we have no freedom and democracy." On the streets of Beijing and Hong Kong, however, the use of the song as a marching chant in the spring of 1989 demonstrated that his objections may well have been beside the point.

In the months after the crackdown, moreover, rock music continued to serve as a rallying point for participants in China's urban youth culture. Audiences, cognizant of the music's oppositional cultural stance and its association with the democracy movement, often utilized rock concerts as an opportunity to publicly and vocally show their discontent with the regime. The following description of Cui Jian's 1990 Asian Games benefit show in Beijing, written by an anonymous rock music fan, is both a testament to the sense of political empowerment that fans derive from rock music performances and revealing of the political volatility that led the CCP to cancel Cui's tour. Much of the poignance of this particular performance lay in the fact that it took place only months after the crackdown at Tiananmen Square:

In order to raise money for the 11th Asian Games, even this guy has been allowed to give a performance. Nowadays his songs are full of a kind of decadent mood, and he has been prevented from giving many concerts. But yesterday he challenged the authorities again. He sang a forbidden song when the audience encouraged him with passionate applause. He tied a red cloth over his eyes, and his guitarist gagged himself with a red cloth as well. What did this mean? Of course, everyone in Beijing knew exactly what it meant! Most of the audience of 15,000 people rose to their feet. It was so exciting, just like that other unbelievable day and night [i.e., 3–4 June 1989]. (Personal communication, "off the record" comments, March 1990)

ROCK AFTER TIANANMEN

From 1989 to 1994, and periodically thereafter, Chinese rock musicians have been engaged in a sort of ideological cat-and-mouse game with CCP authorities. Rock music remains largely excluded from television and radio. Restrictions on performance remain tight, especially in Beijing, where rock shows have been banned for the entire month of June every year since 1990, presumably because officials fear that they will provide audiences with an opportunity to commemorate the anniversary of the 4 June 1989 massacre. Even so, rock music cassettes (almost all of which have been produced by Hong Kong and Taiwanese record companies because of a lack of domestic support) are openly sold at state-run audiovisual outlets, largely because domestic record industry officials are eager to "serve the people's money" and capitalize on the market potential of the form. In addition, rock is increasingly disseminated throughout the provinces through media over which the authorities have little or no control. Rock music videos, produced by foreign investors, air on the Hong Kong–based Star TV cable network, to which many urban households have access, through either satellite dishes or bootleg videotapes. Bootleg cassettes have also become common. Many rock bands, finally, have taken to circumventing performance restrictions in the capital by simply playing in provincial cities in which officials are less wont to enforce government sanctions against the music.

Perhaps the most significant change that has occurred, though, involves what Geremie Barmé has termed the *compradorization* of the Chinese avant-garde (Barmé 1992a). In order to make a living and achieve commercial success in a restrictive and sometimes hostile domestic climate, rock musicians have been forced to rely almost exclusively on the financial support of off-shore investors from Hong Kong and Taiwan. As a result, Mainland rock music is both "imported home" by way of Star TV and companies like Taiwan's Rock Records and exported abroad to Hong Kong and Taiwan. Ironically, though, the music's principal market is abroad, largely because the domestic market is saturated by Hong Kong and Taiwanese imports. In 1989, for instance, nine of the ten top-selling records in Shanghai were imported from Hong Kong and Taiwan. These economic circumstances, as I argue later, have had much to do with the gradual abandonment of an oppositional cultural politics on the part of many rock musicians in Beijing.

Subcultural expressions of dissent of the sort I outlined in the preceding sections do continue to play an important role in rock music. *Beijing Rock* (*Yaogun Beijing*), a domestic compilation of rock music released in the summer of 1993, is a case in point: it was produced and distributed by Tianjin Audio-Visual Company, a state-run record company. Many of the values espoused by rock musicians in 1990 are in prominent evidence here: singers like Wei Hua, the Women's Band (Nüzi dui), and Black Panther (Heibao) rebelliously call for individual liberty, attack hypocrisy, and sing of the virtues of authentic self-expression. Wang Yong, formerly a Cui Jian collaborator, contributes a song, "Requiem March" ("Anhun jinxingqu"), that is a thinly veiled tribute to the victims of the democracy movement:

> . . . Tears of terror streamed from your frightened eyes
> Future ideals rang from your lips
> Now dead souls sing, awaiting your arrival
> And the living grieve as they see you off
> Rest in peace, come back to life. . . .
>
> (Music and lyrics by Wang Yong)

COMMODITY NATIVISM

The packaging notes for the cassette, however, reflect a new awareness of rock's status as a commodity pitted in direct competition with a massive influx of Hong Kong and Taiwanese imports. Its attempt to frame how consumers should react to the product at hand also reflects the ongoing commoditization of the music: rather than emphasizing the potentially volatile realm of performance that was once the focal point of the rock subculture, the copywriter dwells on the pleasures of private consumption: "[This tape] will also answer a question you've probably never thought about before— where can I find music that fuses artistry, intelligence, and commercial potential and that's been created and produced by we Mainland Chinese [*dalu ziji chuangzao, ziji zhizuo*]? Flip open your tape player, and let the forceful sound of rock music reverberate through your personal space [*ni de kongjian*]." This assertion of nativist sentiment ("we Mainland Chinese")— itself quite foreign to the kind of internationalist, individualist sensibility routinely voiced by rock musicians in 1990—is echoed by several of the songs included on the tape, in terms of both lyrics and musical style. Several songs incorporate traditional Chinese instruments into arrangements that in all other respects mirror those of their Anglo-American counterparts. Wang Yong's "Requiem March" concludes with a Buddhist chant recited by a local monk. The heavy metal band Again sets a Song dynasty song lyric (*ci*) by Xin Qiji to wailing electric guitars. Gao Qi, fronting a new band called Overload (Chaozai), sings a paean to peasant revolt called "Ancestors."

These nods to traditional culture are part of a larger effort on the part of many rock musicians in Beijing to create "rock and roll with Chinese characteristics" (*you Zhongguo tese de yaogun yue*). This effort was one of the primary concerns of many of the rock musicians (including Tang Dynasty and Dou Wei of the band Dreaming) I spoke with in Beijing in June 1992. The phrase itself is in common usage among rock musicians in Beijing and derives from the official CCP injunction that China must build a "modern socialist civilization with Chinese characteristics." The rock subculture is closely knit and characterized by a remarkably high degree of intellectual self-consciousness. Musicians frequently discuss and debate the nature and function of the "cultural phenomenon" that their music represents. Over the course of a month I spent researching the rock scene in Beijing in June 1992, those informal debates repeatedly and urgently returned to the vexed question of how (and whether) rock musicians could convey a distinctly Chinese sensibility by way of a foreign musical form. Often, these discussions were framed in terms reminiscent of the late Qing reformer Zhang Zhidong's argument that China must pair *ti* (Chinese essence) with *yong* (Western practices) in order to regain parity with the West: "A few years ago, everybody [in the scene] was excited by rock music, just by the form [*xingshi*] itself. But now we need to discover how to use the form to create something of our own. We're moving from form to content [*neirong*]. Instead of just borrowing a Western form, we need to make music that's based on Chinese life" (interview with Dou Wei, 8 June 1992). These debates were undergirded by the notion that Chinese culture and Western culture are fundamentally and intractably different. Lao Wu, lead guitarist for Tang Dynasty, explains the band's use of traditional Chinese instruments and imagery in terms of cultural essentialism: "Rock is based on the blues, and we can never play the blues as well as an American. It's just not in our blood. We can imitate it, but eventually we'll have to go back to the music we grew up with, to traditional Chinese music, to folk music" (interview with Lao Wu, 3 June 1992).

In some cases, finally, the desire to reclaim Chinese tradition was expressed in terms of a nativist cultural agenda that represents nothing less than a negation of the *River Elegy*–esque rhetoric current in 1989. Although the rhetorical vehemence with which Yang Jun, lyricist and artistic director for Tang Dynasty, advocates a nativist return to traditional roots is atypical, his ideas are instructive as to the kinds of dilemmas faced by Chinese rock musicians as a whole:

> I've been Westernized almost my whole life. I spent twenty years absorbing anything Western that I could get my hands on. I never knew anything about my own tradition. And now I really hate anything from the West. I resent its influence. . . . [M]odern Chinese culture has never lived up to the tradition because it's been ruined by all the Western influence. We have to get back to our roots, "back to the Tang dynasty" [quoting from a song by Tang Dynasty]. That's the only way we can revitalize our nation and our culture. That's what the mission of this cultural phenomenon [rock music] should be all about. (Interview with Yang Jun, He Yong, and Li Tong, 12 June 1992)

Yang Jun's comments, of course, reveal many of the paradoxes inherent to any such "mission." Chinese rock musicians are, almost by definition, a creation of "Western influence," and Chinese rock is necessarily a hybrid form.

The rationale behind having named the band Tang Dynasty—as explained to me by Zhang Ju, the band's bass player—is itself an effort to reconcile these paradoxes symbolically. On the one hand, the Tang dynasty represents the apex of traditional Chinese civilization. On the other, its capital, Chang'an, was characterized by its cosmopolitanism and openness to cultural influences (and particularly exotic new forms of popular music) arriving from Central Asia and the Middle East. These themes shape much of the band's work: its eponymous domestic debut fuses heavy metal, Xinjiangese folk harmony, and traditional Chinese instrumentation. In songs like "A Dream Return to the Tang Dynasty" ("Meng hui Tangchao"), nativist sentiments are conveyed through lyrics written in a pastiche of ersatz classical and modern Chinese:

> Chrysanthemum, ancient sword, and wine
> Percolate like coffee into the hubbub of the courtyard
> The stranger from abroad pays homage to the moon at the Altar of the Sun
> The splendor of the ancients enchants us
>
> Wind—cannot blow away our grievances
> Flowers—cannot color over our longing for home
> Snow—cannot reflect the mountain stream
> Moon—cannot fulfill the ancient dream
>
> Following the patterns on my palm
> Branded there by fate
> Following fate I fall into a trance
> In dream I return to the Tang dynasty.
> (Music and lyrics by Tang Dynasty, trans. Kaiser Kuo)

Here, the geographic axes of the *River Elegy* argument are reversed. Rather than a flawed and peripheral nation that must flow out to the sea in order to redeem itself, we are presented with a "central kingdom" to which foreigners "pay homage." This fantastic vision of Chinese dominance, however, is inevitably disrupted by the specter of China's debasement at the hands of contemporary reality. The "splendor" of Tang times is only a dream, and the dreamer is left with only "grievances" and "longing."

Although "A Dream Return to the Tang Dynasty" can hardly be characterized as a coherent ideological message, the presence of nativist discourse in contemporary Chinese music may well indicate the emergence of, in Edward Friedman's phrase, "strong shoots of a new nationalism . . . breaking up out of the old discredited [anti-imperialist nationalism], producing a new identity holding the promise of a better future for all Chinese, though not necessarily a democratic future" (Friedman 1993, 1–2; chap. 3, this volume).

The final point is an important one, for, while the band strongly disclaims that their music has anything to do with politics, its cultural agenda is in many ways complicit with the CCP's post-Tiananmen market-oriented authoritarianism. As many commentators have noted, in the absence of the

Maoist ideological glue that once supported the regime, the CCP has increasingly sought to mobilize the nationalistic sentiments of its citizenry in an effort to maintain a measure of legitimacy. This trend is perhaps most vividly exemplified by the massive propaganda campaigns and barrages of nationalist rhetoric accompanying both China's sponsorship of the Asian Games in 1990 and its (unsuccessful) campaign to win for itself the honor of hosting the 2000 Olympics in Beijing.

The extent to which commerce and nativism are intertwined in the work of Tang Dynasty is also emblematic of the politics of China's increasingly market-driven, export-oriented economy. The band is an avowedly commercial venture, and, in this light, its nativism (displayed visually through videos filmed in traditional settings, cover art featuring traditional calligraphy, and even band members' penchant for wearing topknots and Tibetan jewelry onstage) is perhaps less an ideological stance than a marketing device, one designed to differentiate the band from its slick, eminently contemporary Hong Kong and Taiwanese competition both at home and abroad.[10] This interpretation is shored up by the kind of commercial discourse that has come to surround rock music in recent years. Barmé, for instance, cites a 1991 *China Youth News* article that implores the government to tolerate rock music, if only because it alone can prevent the inundation of the Mainland market by Hong Kong and Cantonese pop (Barmé 1992b, 20). There is not just a little irony here: an oppositional subculture based on an Anglo-American musical form that originally sprang from a repudiation of traditional Chinese culture is nationalistically invoked in the official press as a domestic alternative to foreign products.

TOWARD 1997

I want to close with a song that in many ways provides a complex summation of the politics of popular music in post-Tiananmen China. Ai Jing's "My 1997" was perhaps the most popular song to emerge from the rock subculture in 1993, selling well over fifty thousand copies in the Mainland alone within a month of having been released. The song—like Cui Jian's "I Have Nothing" before it—is a remarkable example of the way in which popular music fuses individual desires and national concerns and, in doing so, provides its listeners with opportunities for affective empowerment and (if only symbolic) political protest. Ai Jing's song, though, is less a tale about having nothing than about wanting everything. Ai Jing's personal narrative—set to chiming, folksy guitars and the pluck of a three-stringed Chinese lute (*sanxian*)—is an ambiguous political act, one that both subtly impugns Chinese communism and satirically embraces Chinese nationalism as it (quite literally) maps the contours of a new China transfigured by rapid political change and commodity economics:

My music teacher was my papa
He's been working in a state-run factory for twenty years now
My mother used to sing northern style opera
She always sighs that she never saw good times
When I was little I won prizes for singing
My two sisters wanted to be just like me
When I was seventeen I left my hometown Shenyang
Because I sensed that I wouldn't find my dreams there
I came all alone to the unfamiliar city of Beijing
And joined the famous Eastern Song and Dance Troupe led by Wang Hun
Really, I loved those days in art school best of all
But my teachers probably don't feel that way

Making a living with my voice wasn't so bad
I sang my way down to the Shanghai Bund
And from Shanghai, I sang my way down to the south for which I had
        longed
I spent a long time in Guangzhou
Because my boyfriend lives in Hong Kong

When will I get to go to Hong Kong? What are people like in Hong Kong?
He can come to Shenyang, but I can't go to Hong Kong

Hong Kong, Hong Kong, Hong Kong, Xiao Hou says I should check it out
Hong Kong, Hong Kong, what's so fragrant about the fragrant harbor?
I hear that it's Cui Jian's biggest market
Let me go see that brilliant world, put a big red stamp on my passport

Come quick 1997! What's it really like to shop at Yaohan?
Come quick 1997! Then I can go to Hong Kong!
Come quick 1997! Let me stand on the stage of Hunghom Auditorium!
Come quick 1997! He'll take me to the night markets!
Come quick 1997! What kind of clothes do they sell at Yaohan?
Come quick 1997! Then I can go to Hong Kong. . . .[11]

In closing, it is worth noting two things that illustrate how quickly artistic themes can be overtaken by events in contemporary China: Yaohan Department Store has recently opened branches in Beijing and Shanghai, and the cover art that accompanies Ai Jing's recording shows the singer enjoying the sights of Hong Kong's Lam Kwai Fong district. Life imitates art, the art, not of revolution, but of commerce. Such is the state of rock and roll under market Leninism.

SPIRITUAL LIFE

Historically, the Chinese have been what Westerners would regard as a religious people. Although because such religion as they practice is inextricably intertwined with the rhythms of daily life, it is largely invisible and, consequently, not very well represented. The Chinese Revolution may have modified the character of this religiosity, but it did not eliminate it. Certainly, one of the most prominent features of the nation's postmodern present is the wide popularity of religion.

Owing to the international outrage over the government's treatment of Falun Gong, the spiritual life of the Chinese people is a topic of which foreigners have developed an awareness. There is little depth of understanding to this awareness beyond the instinctive denunciation of the government's violent repression of the cult. However, such an awareness of Chinese religious activity provides a point of departure for an exploration of contemporary spiritual life.

Just to set the record straight, the constitution of the People's Republic of China explicitly affirms the freedom of religion, specifically within the context of established and, most important, officially acknowledged religions. Presently, there are five official religions in China that nominally enjoy the government's toleration: Islam, Catholicism, Protestantism, Buddhism, and Daoism. These are all liturgical traditions, with elaborately articulated rites and well-defined ecclesiastical authorities. By the government's own estimates, hundreds of millions of Chinese are counted among the faithful of these traditions: 15–20 million Muslims; 10–30 million Protestants; 8–10 million Catholics; fifty thousand Daoists; and seventy thousand Buddhists. Anyone would be justified in questioning the accuracy of these figures, especially the small numbers of Daoists and Buddhists, which, by the government's admission, represent the acknowledged members of their clergies. Most Chinese, especially those living in the countryside, are more than passively familiar with both Buddhism and Daoism. Indeed, as Edward Davis (2001) has recently demonstrated, these official religious traditions are thoroughly enmeshed with the unofficial, popular religions according to which most Chinese live and that lie far outside the radar of official government acknowledgment.

Yet it is the unofficial religion—that of spirit possession and shamanism, the twin pillars of the enduring edifice of popular cults, particularly ancestor worship—that has seen the greatest resurgence since the mid-1980s. At the same time as those in rural areas have participated in this popular religious revival, residents of China's cities have turned increasingly to matters of faith in addressing the attendant anomie of rapid modernization. *Qigong*, along with many other physical cultivation and meditation practices, provides a welcome spiritual alternative to the aggressive acquisitive demands of China's cash nexus. Falun Gong, a New Age product of China's postmodern morass, may be an "evil cult," according to the government's denunciation, but it is a religion of the alienated, the dispossessed, the middle class, the entrepreneur, the upwardly mobile, and the Party member. It is perhaps for this reason that so much of what we know about China's contemporary spiritual life comes from the press surrounding this misbegotten cult and why we, as well as the Chinese government, know precious little about the vibrant and expanding unofficial religion of China's masses.—Eds.

16
Magic, Science, and *Qigong* in Contemporary China

In this final section of the book, we consider religion and spirituality, long prominent among Chinese but since the Revolution actively discouraged by the Communist Party. Today, the government of China officially recognizes five religions: Buddhism, Islam, Daoism, Roman Catholicism (under the aegis of the "Chinese Catholic Patriotic Association"), and Protestantism. Religious freedom is explicitly defended in Article 36 of the revised state constitution of 1982. In the two decades since this last promulgation, and particularly in the 1990s, participation in officially sanctioned religion has grown substantially: there are in China today 15–20 million Muslims, 8–10 million Catholics, 10–30 million Protestants, and uncounted millions of Buddhists and Daoists.

While these officially sanctioned religions are tolerated (although with notable exceptions, as Jensen points out in the afterword), they are distinguished from superstition (*mixin*), which can be prosecuted by the state. Religious and spiritual activity other than that registered with the state under the five principal categories is technically *mixin* and potentially illegal. Forms of divination, lineage temples, cults to local earth, mountain, and water deities, geomancy, and ancestor worship lie beyond the official designation of religion, but they are so widespread and increasingly popular that they are tolerated as features of local custom. *Qigong* (various exercises, meditation practices, and more fantastic demonstrations of the ability to control *qi*, "vital energy"), like these local customs, eludes designation within the official rubrics, and it, too, has grown in popularity and in an accelerated fashion in urban centers since the 1989 Tiananmen massacre. There are centers for *qigong* instruction and a welter of books on the salubrious effects of the techniques learned from the few masters of the teaching.

Eric Karchmer, a cultural and medical anthropologist, takes on the question of how *qigong* is viewed in contemporary, post-Mao China (implicitly Beijing), asking from where it draws its legitimacy. He concludes that these "ancient" practices, formerly considered mystical and superstitious, have largely been purged of those overtones and are now seen as "scientific"— using vocabulary from both traditional Chinese medicine (TCM) and Western biomedicine to explain their miraculous efficacy. His work distinguishes ana-lytically between "preventive" and "curative" *qigong,* with the former much allied with medicine and the latter allied both with astounding feats of power and with healing. Concerned to expose charlatans and frauds, the govern-ment has sponsored scientific investigations into *qigong,* demonstrating a "scientific basis" for some of its claims and the fraudulence of others.

Karchmer is ultimately concerned with the centrality of science in con-temporary China, where even traditional practices, claiming a five-thousand-year-long past, are subject to scrutiny by the scientific method. Chinese fol-lowers of the practice, along with the author, understand that one way in which *qigong* may be reconciled with official Communist taxonomy is by dis-tinguishing it from religion and also from *mixin,* by certifying through empiri-cal demonstration its status as science. Through this reconstruction of the the-oretical and practical debates concerning the character of *qigong,* we may discern the complexities underwriting the Chinese government's ongoing struggle with Falun Gong, a cult whose spiritual calisthenics is grounded in preventive and curative claims very similar to those of *qigong.* An unregistered religion is in this instance far more threatening than a spiritual practice of dubious scientific merit, and herein lies the unwritten limits of toleration and the battle lines of a new resistance.—Eds.

There are hundreds of millions of people out in the fresh air everyday and have been for twenty-four centuries, with the belief that, if they do these exercises [*qigong*], that is how they will maximize their health. So the ques-tion to Western science is, Are they right? Or are they all just deluded?

David Eisenberg, in Bill Moyers' PBS program
Healing and the Mind (1993)

Since the early 1980s, millions of enthusiasts seeking health benefits, miracle cures, and sometimes supernatural powers have made a system of deep-breathing exercises, known as *qigong,* one of the most popular activities in China (*Concise English-Chinese Chinese-English Dictionary* 1990). By the late 1980s, the local media was calling this enthusiasm for *qigong* a craze (*qigong re*), and some sources reported that there may have been as many as 200 mil-lion adherents in China (Perry and Fuller 1991, 675). The *qigong* craze was not an isolated phenomenon. Numerous observers have pointed to the revival of other "traditional cultural practices" in the post-Mao era, such as in religious practices, ritual observances, lineage halls, shamanic practices, divination, and Book of Changes hobbyism (Siu 1989; Smith 1991; Dean 1993; Kipnis 1997; Judith Farquhar, personal communication). These cultural "revivals" might be seen as acts of resistance to the rapid pace of modernization in post-Mao China, a time when that country has made greater strides toward the "opening of markets," the "liberation of productive forces," and "moderniza-tion" than in any previous era. But most *qigong* practitioners go to great lengths to make precisely the opposite point: *qigong* is a modern, and, more important, a scientific, practice. This chapter examines the role that these discourses on the modern, scientific nature of *qigong* have played in shaping its colorful history during China's reform era.

The central concept in *qigong* practice is the manipulation of *qi,* a term that often refers to "breath," "air," "vapor," and "vital energy."[1] It should be noted that, in all the classic discussions of *qi* that predate this century, the energetic notion of *qi* is radically different than the concept of *energy* as taught in the modern sciences. *Qigong* is the modern Chinese term for a wide variety of meditative exercises that focus on breath/energy control. These exercises have had a long historical association with medical (especially techniques of health preservation), religious, and martial arts practices in China.[2] As the short history of *qigong* presented below will demonstrate, there may be significant differences between the current styles of *qigong* practice and their historical antecedents.

In modern China, "traditional" cultural practices, such as *qigong,* have been subject to intense political scrutiny. The state has often promoted "good traditions" (usually involving physical exercise or cultural entertainment, such as the Spring Festival, the Dragon Boat Festival, and the Mid-Autumn Festival) as compatible with the goals of the modern socialist state and reflecting "Chineseness" while repressing "bad tradition" (including festivals for local gods, ghost festivals, spirit possession, divination, and so on) as superstitious and detrimental to the achievement of these goals (Feuchtwang and Wang 1991). Uncomfortably straddling this division between good and bad tradition—promoting physical health but by superstitious means—*qigong* has always had a volatile relation with the state. The inherent instability of this relation could be seen in the voluminous literature on *qigong* produced in the late 1980s, which, despite the immense and growing popularity of *qigong,* was pervaded by a sense of crisis. Beside long discussions of the principles, techniques, benefits, and even dangers of *qigong,* nearly all authors seem eager to assure their readers that *qigong* is a "good tradition" (although there was never such an explicit statement of the stakes). The key rhetorical device in this anxious struggle for legitimacy has been to assert the scientific nature of *qigong.* With varying degrees of explicitness, these texts all reiterate the sentiments of Zhan Wentao, former director of the State Administration of Traditional Chinese Medicine: "Science is the life source of *qigong.* Without science, *qigong* will perish" (Wang 1991, 8).

In the reality of everyday social life, legitimacy is most often thought to be the province of politicians and political scientists concerned with the justification of specific forms of state rule. In academe, few discussions of this topic can avoid reference to Max Weber's (1978) seminal analysis of the three ideal-types of legitimate rule—traditional, rational-legal, and charismatic. But, in the case of *qigong,* the legitimating discourses in question are concerned, not with state rule, but with constituting a position for a certain social practice within the Chinese national social formation, determined both by state goals of modernization and by the discourses of a modern nation-state in which average citizens also participate. The precarious status of *qigong* in Chinese society contrasts with that of traditional Chinese medicine (TCM), which, as a result of massive reform efforts in the 1950s under the auspices of the Communist government, overcame a similar crisis of legitimacy to become an important branch of the Chinese health-care system.[3] *Qigong*, however, has never enjoyed such a nurturing relation with the state. According to the official historiography, *qigong* was "discovered" by Liu Guizhen in the 1950s, when he was apprenticed to a local teacher of *neiyanggong* (literally translated, "internal nourishing exercises"), a practice of Buddhist origins. When his chronic stomach ulcers were soon cured, Liu Guizhen decided to break with the traditional master-to-disciple ethics of transmission and make these exercises available to the general public. With state support, he purged the exercises of their "superstitious dross" by expunging their religious content and strictly limiting their use to medical purposes. He called the exercises "*qigong,*" which later became the general term for *qi*-based styles of exercises. In 1956, Liu Guizhen was named the head of the nation's first *qigong* convalescence center in Beidaihe, a seaside resort (Zhang n.d., 8). But, during the Cultural Revolution, Liu Guizhen's *neiyanggong* and other forms of *qigong* were officially condemned as "sorcery" and prohibited. In the post-Mao era, the state once again permits *qigong* practice but ambivalently so, upholding *qigong* as a valuable cultural tradition that can improve the health of the people while criticizing its "superstitious" content and suppressing masters who have large devoted followings.

With such a history, it is not surprising that proponents of *qigong* are eager to secure the prestige of Western science for their legitimating project. But this stratagem has potential costs as well as benefits. In the remainder of the chapter, I will examine these costs by considering two fundamentally different approaches to the practice of *qigong* that have emerged as part of this debate. For lack of more appropriate terms, I call them preventive "*qigong*" and curative "*qigong.*"[4] The former approach emphasizes the prevention of illness through the personal maintenance of one's health in daily exercise regimens. The latter emphasizes the curing of ailments, often serious disabilities and terminal illnesses, by master practitioners. The former advocates meditative exercises that cultivate "internal *qi*"; the latter focuses on the development of "external *qi*" (the master's ability to externally emit internal *qi*) and associated supernatural powers. I will argue that the scientific discourses on the legitimacy of preventive and curative *qigong* in contemporary China operate by an exclusionary logic that cannot contend with the powers cultivated in either type of *qigong* practice. Scientific inquiry necessarily asks certain questions and precludes others, thereby creating a specific framework through which to view its object of study. When science is adopted as the ultimate arbiter of "truth" for the study of *qigong,* whose foundational concepts, such as *qi,* cannot be neatly accommodated by scientific categories of analysis, the answers to these questions can only confirm the unscientific nature of *qigong* and its inherent falsehood. As I argue below, scientific discourse not only fails to enhance the legitimacy of *qigong* but also, in fact, subtly undermines it. It becomes difficult to view *qigong* through anything other than the disparaging ethnocentric lenses provided by David Eisenberg[5] in this chapter's epigraph: *qigong* is either a romanticized, mythical fountain of New Age wisdom ("twenty-four centuries" old), or it is simply a superstitious ("deluded") practice. In short, the economy of Western scientific discourse is such that it can only reproduce itself or create its other, magic.

QIGONG AS NEW AGE MYSTICISM

Perhaps the best and most cogently argued statement of the principles of what I call preventive *qigong* is *A Thousand Questions about Traditional Chinese Medicine: The Qigong Volume* (1991), by Zhang Honglin and Hu Weiguo of the Chinese Academy of Traditional Chinese Medicine.[6] The authors open with the question, "What is *qigong*?" and respond by emphasizing its historical connection to traditional technologies of health preservation (*yangsheng*) and the principles of TCM:

> *Qigong* has a long history in our country. In ancient times, related practices were called *tuna, daoyin, xingqi, fuqi, liandan, xiudao, zouchan*, etc. . . . Traditional Chinese medicine considers *qigong* a skill for training the true *qi* [*zhenqi*] of the human body by cultivating *qi*, accumulating *jing*, and completing *shen*.[7] . . . If true *qi* is abundant, life flourishes; if true *qi* is deficient, the human body weakens and falls ill; if true *qi* is exhausted, life ceases. Practicing *qigong* is a method for cultivating this type of internal force. . . . We can summarize the above in one sentence: *Qigong* is a personal mind-body therapy with Chinese national and cultural characteristics. . . . It is unique to the Chinese people, a practical activity that is centrally guided by the traditional Chinese medicine entity of "*qi*." (Zhang and Hu 1991, 1–2)

The explicit connection made in this passage (as well as in the book's title itself) between *qigong* and the theory of TCM is quite typical of the claims made by the proponents of preventive *qigong*. Having mobilized the TCM entity of *qi* as the guiding principle of *qigong* practice, it would seem that the authors have also made a categorical rejection of Western science as the legitimate epistemological ground on which *qigong* practice is based. Yet, in the very next sentence, the authors make clear that no such act of resistance is intended: "Following the progress of science, we can use a knowledge of the appropriate modern sciences to understand *qigong*. This will deepen our substantive knowledge of *qigong*" (Zhang and Hu 1991, 2).

Throughout the book, explanations based in the theory of TCM operate side-by-side with those based in Western science. The authors' response to the question, "Why is it said that *qigong* is a method of personal mind-body training?" provides an example of the latter:

> 1. *Qigong* is rich in psychological training. . . . One important aspect of *qigong* training is to make one's consciousness enter a state of quietude such that one is "half asleep, half awake." This process of actively altering one's consciousness from a state of alertness to one of quietude is the embodiment of personal mind-body training. . . .
> 2. *Qigong's* training of the body is realized by two methods. The first method is the direct training of the body. . . . The second method is indirect. It begins with the psychological activity induced by practicing *qigong*. Psychological changes operate via the neural and neuroendocrine systems to produce changes in physiological function. Changes in physiological function then bring about morphological changes. [In short], the effects are realized through the psychological-physiological-morphological response system. (Zhang and Hu 1991, 5)

Here, the "Chinese national and cultural characteristics" of TCM are forsaken for the universal principles of biomedicine. Points 1 and 2, the psychological and physical aspects of *qigong* training, faithfully reproduce the mind-body split so emblematic of Western procedures of knowledge. But mapping *qigong* training over the biomedical mind-body divide presents the authors with a new problem: namely, how an exercise involving relatively little bodily movement can produce the dramatic physical health benefits claimed by so many practitioners. The solution advanced by the authors is to make the human psyche the agent of therapeutic change and the "psychological-physiological-morphological response system" its mechanism of operation. Their solution does not, however, succeed completely in demonstrating *qigong's* consistency with the principles of biomedicine because it inverts the standard relation of mind to body in biomedicine, where the mind is treated as incidental to the real health concerns of the body. This inversion of the mind-body dualism of biomedicine explains why the proponents of the preventive style of *qigong* also frequently make comparison to and seek legitimation from "alternative" health practices in West, such as faith healing, biofeedback, and hypnosis. These scholars have correctly perceived that these alternative practices also assert the primacy of the mind over the body, although they have failed to realize that such associations are likely only to distance them further from the mainstream scientific community, whose acceptance they so urgently seek.

The psychological-physiological-morphological response system performs another important rhetorical function. It makes it possible scientifically to explain away the more magical and superstitious aspects of *qigong* practice, such as when masters claim to have paranormal abilities or the ability to heal patients by emitting "external *qi*." Using the explanatory device of the psychological-physiological-morphological response system, the authors argue that patients are mistaken when they attribute physical sensations, such as warmth, numbness, or the sensation of electricity, to the master's healing *qi*. If the treatment conditions—the master's manipulation of authority, words, gestures, movements, eye contact, and facial expression—are controlled, these sensations cease and the therapy fails. This fact is supposed to demonstrate that the patient's experience is produced by "psychological suggestion," the effects of which are realized via the psychological-physiological-morphological response system (see Zhang and Hu 1991, 155–157).

In the curative style of *qigong*, the effects of this response system are cleverly concealed by the illusion of "external *qi*." The mechanism by which both styles achieve their health benefits is the same, and the results are anything but miraculous. The authors cautiously suggest that, in diseases like gastric ulcers, high blood pressure, coronary heart disease, neurasthenia, and cancer, where stress is an important factor in the disease pathology, *qigong* can play an adjunctive, supplementary role in the healing process by improving relaxation and overall physical harmony (see Zhang and Hu 1991, 27–28, 138–149). It should not, however, be used to take the place of drug treatments and other recognized therapies. The "superhuman powers" of certain *qigong* masters and their "miracle cures" are, in fact, just superstitious beliefs: the artifact of deceptive performances, untruthful boasts, media sensationalization, and the patient's attribution to the master of powers that really lie in one's self.

These two passages from *One Thousand Questions*—one steeped in the language of TCM, the other in that of biomedicine—lay out the very ambitious project of the authors: to create a modern practice of *qigong* that is faithful to its historical roots in Chinese technologies of health but at the same time suitable to the demands of a modern nation, to create a practice that is both traditional and scientific, culturally unique but with global aspirations. In trying to constitute this paradoxical position for preventive *qigong*, the legitimating discourses of the authors reveal an obsession with theory, both in traditional and in scientific idiom. Although these two theoretical systems are given relatively equal space in the text, they are not given equal weight. The task of the authors is to construct a legitimate place for *qigong* in the modern Chinese nation; and, therefore, their real theoretical labors are in the realm of science, translating the traditional idiom of *qigong* into modern scientific terms and delimiting its new scientific boundaries. The result of this work is to diminish the centrality of the theory of TCM (despite the authors' claims) to *qigong* practice, if not make it outright expendable except as a marker of cultural and national identity. If pursued to its logical conclusion, this sort of argumentation leads to an Eisenberg-like trivialization of *qigong*, transforming it into just another form of exercise, like jogging or step aerobics, but attractively packaged in a wondrous New Age wrapping of Chinese mysticism.

Discourses on the legitimacy of curative *qigong* reflect very different concerns than do those on preventive *qigong*, focusing on the individual accumulation of *qi* and power in the bodies of the masters and practitioners. In the late 1980s, two important means of legitimating these accumulations emerged: public demonstrations and scientific experiments.

Public demonstrations of the powers of *qigong* masters are often credited with fanning the craze for *qigong*. The authors of *Exposing the Deceptions of the "Great Qigong Masters"* (Zhang et al. 1991), a book dedicated to debunking curative *qigong*, provide a short and satirical list of the most commonly seen types of performances:

> The *qigong* master clutches a live electrical wire in his bare hand. A light bulb is touched to the master's body. It glows brightly as the master smiles.

> The flesh-and-bones body of the *qigong* master bears the weight of an enormous slab of stone. The violent swings of a sledge hammer smash the stone, but the master remains unscathed.

> The bare torso of the master is bound by a heavy metal chain. With a loud shout, he snaps the metal chain in two.

> The sharp tip of a spear is pressed into the master's throat. The shaft of the spear bends to the point of breaking, but the master is not hurt in the slightest.

> The master lies on a bed of nails, walks barefoot over glass shards and hot coals, breaks bricks and tablets over his head, and is beaten with clubs and hacked by knives, as if he must suffer the punishments of all nine levels of purgatory. The spectators look on aghast, but in each instance the *qigong* master appears calm and composed. (Zhang et al. 1991, 107, 191; Li Zhiyong 1988, 423)

The venues for such performances have ranged from sidewalks to the most widely watched of nationally televised programs, such as the 1988 CCTV Spring Festival program. Although these demonstrations have a potent "seeing is believing" credibility and may be a great boost to a master's reputation, they have not been sufficient to legitimate curative *qigong* alone.

It is not possible to fully grasp the importance of the public *qigong* demonstration without introducing the contemporaneous paranormal functions (*teyi gongneng*) phenomena, which also achieved a great deal of media attention in the 1980s. Just as *qigong* was becoming a nationwide fad in the 1980s, individuals with *teyi gongneng,* such as extrasensory perception, clairvoyance, telepathy, and psychokinesis, were being discovered around the nation. The discovery of such individuals began in 1979 when the *Sichuan Daily* reported that a young boy from Dazu county in Sichuan could "read" written symbols (characters, numbers, diagrams, etc.), not by using his eyes, but by touching the piece of paper (folded to conceal the text) to his ear (Zhu and Zhu 1987). Less than a year later, approximately two thousand scientists, medical specialists, journalists, and other leading intellectuals were watching fourteen individuals with *teyi gongneng* (significantly all but one were children ranging in age from nine to fifteen) perform similar paranormal feats at the Human Paranormal Science Conference in Shanghai. The journal *Ziran zazhi* (Nature magazine), which had hosted the conference, declared that it had conclusively demonstrated the authenticity of these extrasensory "reading" abilities in these children (vol. 3, no. 3 [1980], 221). *Teyi gongneng* soon found support in China's scientific community, where eminent scholars, such as Qian Xuesen, the man credited with single-handedly creating China's rocket and missile programs, were championing it as the harbinger of a new scientific revolution—the "human sciences" (*renti kexue*)—that would explore the depths of human potential.

In the vision of Qian Xuesen, TCM, *qigong,* and *teyi gongneng* form a "system." Paranormal functions may be possessed innately, by, for example, the young *teyi gongneng* children, or they may be acquired, by, for example, the *qigong* master. In the latter case, Qian argued that the theory of TCM guides the *qigong* practitioner (Qian et al. 1988, 8). Taken together, the three "harbor the most basic principles of the human sciences [*renti kexue*]. They are not superstitious, but rather on the cutting edge of modern science and technology" (19). But, by the early 1990s, public interest in *teyi gongneng* was waning, and many of the early coterie of *teyi gongneng* children were moving on to other activities (Xiong Jic, personal communication, 1991).[8] Scientists had made little theoretical progress despite considerable investment in research, and the emergence of frauds had allowed skeptics to dismiss the phenomena as clever magic tricks. It was at just this moment that the powers of the *qigong* masters were reaching their magical and sensational zenith. Although the intellectual community had lost faith, *qigong* enthusiasts had never been more enthralled by the *teyi gongneng*–like demonstrations of the *qigong* masters, which became the sine qua non for attracting followers. But proponents realized that curative *qigong,* like *teyi gongneng,* could not sustain itself solely through performance. They also claimed to have made major scientific discoveries.

The most important area of scientific research concerning curative *qigong* has been on "external *qi,*" the notion that "internal *qi* can be externally emitted" (*neiqi waifang*). Proponents and critics cite it as the crucial premise on which curative *qigong,* its magical powers, and its potential legitimacy stand (Zhang et al. 1991, 191). There have been two basic types of scientific experiments concerning "external *qi.*" The first seeks to demonstrate its "material basis." The original and most influential of such experiments, conducted in 1979 by Gu Hansen of the Shanghai Nuclear Research Institute, measured the electromagnetic spectrum of the "external *qi*" emitted by the master Lin Housheng. Gu Hansen's investigation showed that "external *qi*" consisted of "low-frequency modulated infrared radiation" (Li Zhiyong 1988, 423). Supplementary studies later revealed that "static electricity," other "electromagnetic waves," and certain types of "particle streams" also make up the material basis of "external *qi*" (Lin 1988, 212; Zhang et al. 1991, 199). These discoveries made possible new advances in the bionics industry, with the development of *"qigong* information (*xinxi*) therapy devices" that imitated the electromagnetic waves of "external *qi.*" Lin Housheng reports that, in clinical tests, these devices were found to be as effective as the *qigong* masters, if not more so because they did not exhaust the "true *qi*" (*zhenqi*) of the master (Lin 1988, 218–219).[9] The authors of *Exposing the Deceptions* have questioned both the reliability (whether they can be repeated) and the validity (whether they measure anything more than normal low-level human emissions of light, heat, and electromagnetic waves) of these experiments (Zhang et al. 1991, 200).[10]

The second type of experiment seeks to demonstrate the material effects of external *qi*. The most influential of such experiments was featured prominently on the front page of the 24 January 1987 edition of the *Guangming ribao*. The article reports that Lu Zuyin and Li Shengping of the Qinghua University Joint *Qigong* Scientific Research Group had demonstrated that, from a distance of more than two thousand kilometers, the *qigong* master Yan Xin was able to use his external *qi* to alter the molecular structure of various substances (tap water, 0.9 percent saline, 50 percent glucose solution, and 1.5 milligram/milliliter medemycine) that had all been sealed in bottles and placed in darkened rooms (Zhang et al. 1991, 193–195).[11] A second and almost equally influential experiment, conducted at the General Naval Hospital by a group of researchers under the direction of Assistant Hospital Director Feng Lida, demonstrated that one master was able to stimulate and inhibit bacteria growth, according to his intentions at the time of external *qi* emission (Zhang et al. 1991, 198).

The authors of *Exposing the Deceptions* have challenged these and all other external *qi* experiments on the basis of their lack of methodological rigor. In the case of molecular alteration by external *qi,* the authors point out that the two experimenters, Lu and Li, published their results against the wishes of a third collaborator, Professor Zhao Nanming, the head of the Qinghua University Biology Department, who insisted that the results may not be reliable (i.e., repeatable). Professor Zhao noted there may have been problems in solution preparation, that temperature control of the laboratory rooms could not be as rigorous as the experimenters claimed (since Qinghua University does not have laboratories of that caliber), and that neither of the experimenters knew how to operate the laser Raman spectrometer (used for detecting molecular changes in the solutions) and required the assistance of a graduate student, who also later questioned the accuracy of the results. In the case of bacterial growth modified by external *qi,* the authors repeated the experiment with the assistance of a microbiologist from the Chinese Academy of Traditional Chinese Medicine. They enlisted the same *qigong* master who participated in the original experiment but were unable to duplicate the results. The *qigong* master also confessed that he did not recall intending the growth or inhibition of bacteria in the original experiment. Similar attacks on external *qi* and proponents of curative *qigong* also appeared in the Ministry of Health's *Health News* (a daily newspaper widely read by Chinese medical professionals) and other nationally distributed newspapers. Together, this investigative work played a significant role in debunking the claims of the country's most prestigious *qigong* masters.

This debate on the existence of external *qi* should not, however, be dismissed as simply an example of bad science that fanned a nationwide exercise craze. Nor should we leap to Eisenberg-like conclusions that millions of practitioners of *qigong* who believe in external *qi* are all "deluded." Even the myth-smashing authors of *Exposing the Deceptions* were not out to destroy *qigong*. Indeed, two of the seven contributors were the authors of *One Thousand Questions,* ardent proponents of preventive *qigong*. Instead, I would like to draw attention to the inadvertent results of this grand debate on the nature of *qi,* which has for both parties represented the apotheosis of the scientific experimentation as the ultimate judge of the epistemological "truth" of *qigong*. The most magical entity in this debate has been, not external *qi,* but the fetishized scientific experiment, which has been granted powers far in excess of anything claimed by proponents of external *qi*. Godlike, with the power to create, the scientific experiment has been granted the power to determine the fate of curative *qigong* in modern China.

The ironic use of the scientific experiment—to make the apparently magical entity of external *qi* real—has also inadvertently exposed another deception—that of the scientific experiment. The sociologists of science Bruno Latour and Steve Woolgar have shown, not only that extensive labor must be invested in the production of objective, scientific facts, but also that this labor must be concealed. Latour and Woolgar argue that true objectivity cannot exist since all observers are socially and historically positioned actors. The scientific facts that they record achieve their real, objective, "out there" quality only when the long and difficult process of transforming matter into a written form of representation—a process that can never be divorced from the social and historical contingencies during which it takes place—is forgotten as that representation stands in for and is taken to be equivalent to the original matter (Latour and Woolgar 1986, 64). "Scientific facts are formulated in the denial and obliteration of their own historicity" (277).

Thus, objectivity—the view from nowhere, the ultimate decontextualization of the observer, and the mode of seeing intrinsic to Western science—is, not a "natural" worldview, but the product of a certain concealed labor of seeing. The external *qi* experiments remind us how meticulous and rule bound this labor is. Each experiment cited above was challenged as methodologically weak in spite of the fact that the researchers claimed to adhere to standardized research protocols. In fact, these experiments suggest that, if the rules of the experiment are altered just slightly, we could be living in a very different cosmos filled with radically different entities. The danger of strange entities populating the scientific cosmos requires a constant policing of the boundary between the "real" and the "magical." It is in this act of exclusion, where the magical other and the scientific self are simultaneously defined against each other, that science reveals its ironic dependence on magic. In constituting itself, science must also create the very thing that it rejects.

CONCLUSION

If the scientific discourses on the legitimacy of *qigong* achieve their goal, there can be no doubt that it will be a costly and violent victory. But, as long as the state project of modernization and the development of science and technology remain the dominant social issues of the day, this violence will be inevitable. In the exclusionary logic of Western science, there is no way to contend with the powers and potential inherent in *qigong* practice. In the postcolonial obsession of legitimating indigenous practices according to the criteria of Western science, the investigation of the important experiences of the practitioners and patients who have been healed and made powerful by *qigong* will have to be abandoned as meaningless. In the end, we can realistically look forward to only two possible outcomes to the current crisis of *qigong:* the trivialization of *qigong* as a simple form of exercise or its outright rejection as a mere collection of magic tricks and superstitious beliefs.

17
The Spirits of Reform

The Power of Belief in Northern China

Like Eric Karchmer, the anthropologist Diane Dorfman is interested in looking at the role of beliefs about rationality, modernization, and power in the contemporary People's Republic especially as these coalesce around complexes of faith. Her article examines the ubiquitous belief in *mixin*, superstition, on the part of north China *nongmin* (peasants). Although all *nongmin* sometimes profess belief in animal spirits, they do not do so at all times. Discussing these "multiple, shifting subjectivities," Dorfman shows the many ways in which beliefs interplay with economic and political circumstances. The village in a rural county west of Beijing where she conducted her field research was visited by four animal spirits—the weasel, fox, snake, and hedgehog—each of which created different kinds of mischief and demanded different kinds of recompense. When villagers were seen to suffer from ailments, medical doctors would either treat them or refer them to specialists in spirit healing. These healers cannot demand payment but may accept offerings, showing that they are moral and selfless.

Morality is superimposed on political and economic tendencies, with an especially stark contrast drawn between the moral Mao era (before the mid-1970s) and the relatively immoral Deng Xiaoping, postreform era (since the mid-1980s). *The Reforms* refers to economic restructuring begun in 1985, which restored a degree of autonomy to producers and began the dismantling of the planned, redistributive economy in favor of a limited free-market economy. The social consequences of this dismantling have been dramatic, with great numbers of workers in township enterprises laid off, male household heads leaving the land for semiskilled work in the cities, and care of the domestic rural economy in the hands of wives, mothers, and able-bodied children. The disarray of the rural social order has yielded conditions of fear and uncertainty that are particularly amenable to the resurgence of folk religious ideology and practice.

In a fascinating explanation that reflects the curious fusion of Communist politics and spirit possession, villagers claim that Mao was virtuous, poor, and like them and that, since he himself was a powerful spirit (a turtle), he had succeeded in banishing the animal spirits. But, with the ascendance of Deng's capitalist reform program and its continued national elaboration under Jiang Zemin, corruption and wealth have arrived in rural China, and the animal spirits have returned, as a kind of emanation from the center. The intersection of competing and supporting discourses of power, value, health, and identity may all be seen here in this intriguing case of animal spirit possession in rural north China, a parable of the persistence of religion alongside revolution.—Eds.

When Sun Xiulan's son began having periodic convulsions (*choufeng*) she called on a spirit healer. The healer traveled from his home in the mountains west of Beijing to Wulin, Sun's suburban county.[1] He checked the walled yard fronting her house and told Sun that a yellow weasel spirit (*huangshulang*) had taken up residence there. The yard was littered with old tools, building materials, broken furniture, torn straw mats, and farming implements. In one corner stood a disused toilet: a pit surrounded on three sides by a low stone wall. The healer explained that the piles of junk were a perfect home for the weasel, who claimed the territory, in part, by imprinting its influence on her son; the deaths of Sun's mother- and sister-in-law within the last year were also a sign of the spirit's curse on the family. He agreed to try to exorcise the possessing spirit using incense, spells, spirit money, and food offerings and "patting of the hands" (*pai shou*). To coax the spirit to leave, the yard had to be cleaned—carefully, so as not to suddenly anger the weasel—and a roof had to be built over the toilet to contain the weasel's power.

When I met Sun Xiulan in the winter of 1990, she told me what the healer had said. She knew I had heard about her son's illness because villagers often gossiped about it. She knew the villagers gossiped that her son still suffered convulsions, that her yard was still full of junk, and that her family was poor and ill fated. Sun stayed at home taking care of her son and, until the woman's death, her mother-in-law. With only her husband's income, the family was poor in comparison with many villagers who had prospered under the Reforms and were building new brick homes. Neighbors said the healer would have to be called again, but Sun told me she was sure the weasel had left.

People in Wulin frequently discussed the Four Animal Spirits or Four Sacred Animals (*sidaxian* or *sidamen*), of which the yellow weasel is one, and their ability to possess humans and cause illnesses (*nao suihuo*). They sometimes referred to the spirits by the Party-state's term for them, *mixin* (superstition), but they used this term largely when eschewing belief in the existence of the spirits.[2] When Wu San, a group leader in a collective seedling nursery, dismissed the spirits as superstition, he explained to me that the Chinese Communist Party opposed superstition and did not allow people to believe in or practice it: "We *nongmin* [peasants] used to believe in [*xin*] *mixin,* but now the state forbids it [*guojia bu rang xin*]." Later, during the long summer break after lunch, Wu San chatted with two women in his group. Lin Sao recounted how her neighbor's son had been possessed by a vengeful snake a few days before and a healer had cured him. Wu San nodded in agreement and said his cousin had been healed a couple of years previously. The young man had begun babbling and had developed a rash. "The healer said it was a weasel that wanted money. He negotiated with it and told my uncle to burn spirit money; then my cousin got well and didn't remember a thing," said Wu San. Lin Sao then noticed me sitting a few feet from her and said, laughing, "This is *mixin*. You Americans don't have *mixin*, do you?"[3] I said there were many forms of spirit healing in the United States, and she seemed to decide that the spirits might not be dismissed as *mixin* by the anthropologist from the "modern, scientifically advanced" United States. She said, "We *nongmin* all believe in the animal spirits."

From this and subsequent conversations, and from attendance at healing sessions, I learned that "*nongmin* believe in the spirits" and recognize that the state (*guojia*) names their belief *mixin*. What is named *mixin* is prohibited and antithetical to the modern, rational China that the economic reforms and the Four Modernizations are building. The name *mixin* may operate as what Ann Anagnost argues is the symbolic language the Party-state deploys in its attempt to reinscribe "local landscapes with its totalizing order." In Wulin, naming the spirits *mixin* may be a sign of the incomplete reinscription of local practice or of multiple processes of inscription. While Wu San has learned the Party's "narrative of progress" (Anagnost 1994, 222), equating superstition with a failure to modernize, he also transgresses it by affirming his belief. Yet belief echoes the narrative of progress when it embraces censure for the messy, poor, decidedly unmodern Sun.

Nongmin is the term people in Wulin used to name themselves as individuals and as a group. *Nongmin* names the people who identified themselves as such and discussed the spirits with me. Identification with belief in the spirits was embodied in *nongmin*. I use *nongmin*, leaving the word usually translated "peasant" in pinyin romanization because it imparts somewhat the depth with which people seemed to embody this identity.[4]

Nongmin is also an official identity assigned to the majority of Wulin residents as part of their *hukou* (residence registration).[5] *Nongmin* thus represents both *hukou* and self-naming and so reveals the articulation in the construction of categories of the "official" and "local" that are usually held apart.

For *nongmin*, images and knowledges of themselves and the state must be held apart to be meaningful. They construct and bind the categories because their identities are at stake in distinguishing what they perceive as the contents of the categories. The contents of the categories include power and powerlessness. *Nongmin* name themselves as those who have no power, those who are *niuma* (beasts of burden) or *bin* (slaves) in relation to the state, in which power, by definition, resides. Power is not understood only in terms of the power to condemn the spirits by naming them *mixin*. Power is linked to particular forms of wealth. Corruption and abuse of power to gain wealth pervade the construction of categories. People in Wulin echoed charges made by students in the 1989 demonstrations but focused on issues within the county. Corruption was prevalent in Wulin; the head of the county had been charged with bribery and replaced in 1987. People were not convinced that such a public move had changed much and often discussed what they saw as an example of how local officials willfully abused their positions: the officials' control over year-end distributions of agricultural and industrial collective profits, which constitute the bulk of collective wages, allowed work-unit heads to claim disproportionately large sums for their own allotments. In 1991 an anonymous big-character poster condemned one factory head for extorting money (*louqian*) and stated that lower-level staff had been given unbelievably and unjustly small sums.

Nongmin claim they earn wealth through labor and thus are poor and moral; officials abuse their power to obtain wealth through corruption and thus are rich and immoral. A woman who contracted land defined herself as follows: "I'm a *nongmin; nongmin* just work [*ganhuor,* 'physical labor'] and then eat." Laboring *nongmin* are contrasted with officials who do not *ganhuor* but *shangban* (go to work at the office); the reward of a full belly also contrasts with the privileges and wealth officials are perceived to accumulate.

Issues surrounding wealth are embodied in the animal spirits and in people who construct themselves as *nongmin.* Constructing themselves, they create the subjects they name *nongmin.* The contradiction between *nongmin* defining opposed, reactive entities and their active involvement in constructing both the entities and the imagined separation between them is the basis on which I argue that *nongmin* participate in producing power.

Wealth is an important component in the persons *nongmin* want to become; it is embedded in the discourses through which *nongmin* become distinct from the state. How people and wealth should interact versus the ways they do interact is being constructed within the bounds of the identities *nongmin* oppose.

Recognizing that the Reforms have meant transformation, that new practices, ideas, and relations are coming into being, need not lead to the Reforms becoming a reified causal entity. I am interested in the appearance of the animal spirits in the context of economic reforms, newly accessible wealth, and changes in sociopolitical organization, but defining my project of learning about the spirits as one that evaluates "the impact of reforms" or "local responses" to them cleaves to an inhibiting analytic vocabulary. My time in Wulin followed the violent repression of demonstrations in Tiananmen Square by six months. People in Wulin were openly critical of Deng Xiaoping, the Party, and officials, denouncing corruption, the abuse of power, and cadres enriching themselves at the expense of industrial, agricultural, and commercial development. Their denunciations are the context in which the animals appear as surely as *the Reforms, post-Mao liberalization,* or any periodizing trope is. Their denunciations become another act of constructing the state as a coherent entity defined by corruption and brutality and as distinct from *nongmin.* Historical context is a discernible thread interweaving *nongmin* ideas about and their construction of spirits and power, but it is not determinative of them. I argue that spirits produce the Reforms as much as the Reforms produce the spirits.

I am not writing *nongmin* into being as generic agents but exploring their multiple, shifting subjectivities. Wu San's remarks are important not because I can "catch" him believing in the spirits after he repudiates them. He moves from a nonbelieving subject of the Party to a believing *nongmin* and reveals how situated, contingent, and shifting subjectivities are. *Nongmin* is a multivalent term, a signifier with a continuously expanding and contracting range of signifieds. This is an additional reason why I continue to use the word *nongmin*. It is the fixed sign people deploy in much the same way social theorists deploy *state and society;* the word is fixed, while people and power relations shift around and evolve within it.

Before continuing to explore these issues, I must return to the spirits. Discussing them in greater detail, I present them as a site on which we can see the articulation of categories, the production of persons and power.

THE FOUR ANIMAL SPIRITS

The animals that possess humans and cause strange illnesses (*xiebing* or *yibing*) are the snake, fox, weasel, and hedgehog, all of which are commonly seen in the villages. They are locally referred to as the Four Animal Spirits. The fox, snake, and other animals are recognized as spirits in other parts of China, but this particular group of four seems unique to this area. A woman who had married into Wulin from a northern suburb said that the rabbit was a fifth spirit in her home village; she found it odd that there were only four spirits in Wulin.[6]

The four animals attain the status of fairies (*jing*) or celestial beings (*xian*) by passing through trials (*guoguan*). Unlike gods or apotheosized humans, they are not granted their powers by the heavenly ruler, the Jade Emperor (Yuhuang Dadi), but must pass trials or work to achieve them. Trials often involve danger to the animal: avoiding a car when crossing a road or surviving being teased by young boys (whose youth protects them from the spirits' vengeance) advances the animal to greater powers. The physical appearance of an animal that has attained the status of a spirit does not change, but its powers enable it to possess humans. Chen Jie, a woman whose niece had battled an illness caused by a fox, told me that before 1949 her parents had kept a pen in the yard to raise hedgehogs. "They are gods of wealth [*cai shen*], and my parents hoped one would take up residence in our yard to improve our fortunes. When we moved we didn't take it; it caused my grandfather to get ill [*nao*] until we built a pen [for it] in our new place."

The animals' spirits usually seek weak or sickly persons to possess and make ill. One young man said the spirits were analogous to hooligans (*liumang*) "preying on those least likely to fight back." Although the symptoms of possession vary, people feel ill; they babble incoherently, laugh or cry at frequent intervals, or sleep for long periods. Some develop indiscriminate rashes, swelling, or blotches. The spirits demand offerings of spirit money and require specialist healers, who must themselves be possessed with the power of another spirit, to cure the ill person. I return to a discussion of healers and their practices below.

Possessing: The Spirits' Power

Emily Martin (Ahern) argues that belief in temple gods is largely reaffirmed by continual experience of the efficacy of the gods' powers to affect humans (Ahern 1981). So it is with the animal spirits. Possessions relentlessly signal the spirits' efficacy and were what people pointed to when they explained why the spirits were "real" and not *mixin*.[7] Throughout my stay in Wulin, I spoke with a broad range of people who claimed to believe in the spirits: rich, poor, young, old, Party members, and contracting cultivators. Some people, like Wu San, claimed they did not believe in the spirits. Many of the unbelievers were also like Wu San in simultaneously inhabiting the dismissive, modern, scientific subject of the Party-state and the believing *nongmin*. Shifting from unbeliever to believer was not only a tactic for dealing with the fear that I might be a dismissive, modern American. It also points to shifting, multiple identities and their continual production and reproduction. We may also see in people who disavow belief in the spirits a rewriting of the identity *nongmin* (as unbeliever) or perhaps a distancing from the identity. I return to this in my discussion of how the coherence of what *nongmin* names unravels.

Even professed unbelievers told me about each animal's distinct character. The weasel is feared and despised because it possesses people only to cause trouble or get spirit money burned to persuade it to leave. A healer told me weasels seek weak humans to possess so that they can profit from the spirit money burned to exorcise them. Another healer said weasels do not want money; they just enjoy causing trouble. Both conclusions were borne out in accounts of possessions. A woman was chatting with an elderly male visitor when he glanced out into the courtyard, saw a weasel, and asked why she was keeping such a thing. The woman told me, "You can't speak of them; they don't like you to notice them. The old man got up to leave and was dead before he got home." In the case of Wu San's cousin, burning spirit-money offerings took care of the weasel.

Snakes are well-known seekers of revenge. They possess in order to exact revenge on those who have accidentally or purposely harmed them. A man who hit one while hoeing became spotted and listless, signs that the snake had possessed him as punishment. A brigade official who tossed a snake out of his office nearly died. A weasel may be placated with money, but the process of healing a snake possession is more complex, requiring specialist healers to negotiate with the snake.

Fox possessions are also perilous, and I twice heard of a fox working with a ghost. A fox may work with the ghost of a deceased family member who has grievances with the living over an untended grave or other domestic disputes.[8] Healers are also able to negotiate with ghosts, but all their powers depend on the spirits who heal through them.[9]

The Power to Heal

Some families of possessed people consulted medical doctors but told me the symptoms of spirit possession disappeared when the patient arrived at a clinic. Doctors either found no illness or admitted that the patient had a "spirit sickness" (*xiebing*) and required a specialist healer.[10] The family then called in a spirit healer.

The fox and the snake both can possess the body of a human they deem worthy and through him or her heal people stricken by spirit sicknesses. Healers are in communication with their spirits throughout the healing session, following their spirits' instructions. They speak with the malevolent spirit, find out why it is angry, and negotiate the release of the stricken person. At each curing session, healers burn spirit money offerings to their healing spirits. They light incense, then jab or pat the patient after blowing on their fingers or waving them in the incense smoke. At the end of these sessions, one healer drew spells on tea leaves and told his patients to brew and drink the tea daily.

Patients and healers say healers must be moral, compassionate, and benevolent. One healer was described as a self-sacrificing daughter-in-law who carried her invalid mother-in-law to the clinic on her back. Another told me he had been a selfless production-team leader who had been called by a fox to heal after he retired. Spirits heal only through mortals whom they have sought out, and they seek only those they determine are virtuous. A virtuous healer is more critically distinguished by the fact that he or she must never ask for any remuneration. They may accept the gifts, cash, and offerings patients proffer, but, if they suggest any compensation, their spirits will abandon them, and they will lose their powers.

A snake spirit had sought out Du Shifu (Master Du), a popular local healer. Du had studied under his maternal uncle, also a healer. The demand for Du's services is high; he was called to heal most evenings, sometimes twice in one night. His virtue requires that he abjure reward, yet becoming a healer establishes an identity that dictates forms of behavior that afford what are broadly recognized as privileges. For the healing session, Du requires patients to arrange for his transportation to their homes by car. The ability to ride in a car is still a mark of luxury and power throughout rural China; it is a privilege usually only powerful Party cadres enjoy. The healer's other terms were that people must believe in him and prepare the incense and tea leaves he uses to heal. At all jobs he was greeted with tea and imported cigarettes, both of which he consumed in copious amounts throughout the evening. He explained to me that the snake spirit used both to build its healing powers.

Patients and their families begged the healer to stay for a meal with meat and liquor. He did stay unless, as was common, he had to be off to another patient.

People offered the healer a sum of money after the cure was completed. Some said they wanted to give the amount they would have been charged by a doctor, who would have collected a fee but been unable to provide a cure. The amount was usually in the tens or hundreds of yuan. Du said his snake spirit told him which families were too poor to accept money from. At the Lunar New Year former patients visit healers with offerings of foodstuffs, liquor, tea leaves, and cigarettes for the healers' spirits. Du made weekly offerings to the snake spirit and said much of what he received for healing was used to purchase the offerings.

Although healers may not ask for gifts or money and no one spoke of paying or receiving a fee for the service of healing, they do expect to receive something.[11] I use the terms *gift* or *offering* because, as David Aberle found in his study of Navaho religion, rather than being part of an isolated transaction involving payment for a service, gifts to healers were part of an encompassing system of reciprocity. Aberle argues that the offering of a gift for spirit healing was an extension of the cosmic reciprocity between gods, humans, and the earth, in which all Navaho interacted. The healer "must be given something, or the ceremony will not be efficacious" (Aberle 1982, 46). Chinese healers told me it was possible that a person who failed to offer a promised amount, or an amount in keeping with his or her ability to pay, might become ill again.[12]

Reciprocal exchanges are obligatory, but demanding a fee turns healing into a commoditized market transaction that transgresses the boundaries of the moral. The tension between gift and market exchange is not structurally consistent with an opposition between moral and immoral—moral *nongmin* accumulate wealth, not corruption, from the market—but involves the mutually constitutive processes of evolving subjectivity and accumulating wealth. Both processes draw issues surrounding moral persons and moral wealth into the realm in which persons and power are produced.

POWER, WEALTH, AND MORALITY: ARTICULATION

Immoral Authorities: The Current Regime

Nongmin oppose the present with the past and weave power into history by opposing the eras of Deng and Mao. They join the spirits' activities with a chain of signs linking the present with Deng, the Reforms, wealth, and corruption. We have seen that *nongmin* discourse on the reform-era present recalls the national conversation on official corruption emblematic of pre- and post-Tiananmen China. I often heard people discussing Wulin officials who gave coveted jobs in collective industrial enterprises only to those who could offer sufficient gifts or favors in return. Several people referred to the ascendancy of a form of *guanxi* (social relations/connections) through which Wulin officials exchanged wealth and privilege among themselves; power and privilege are the conditions by which one may participate and are also the reward for participation in this form of *guanxi,* which is a corrupt exchange.[13]

Recall that an identifying characteristic of *nongmin* is powerlessness, and we see that *nongmin* are excluded from the wealth and power accessible to participants in corrupt exchanges. Among *nongmin* this exclusion expands discursively and imaginatively to bar them from access to all wealth. A number of people who contracted land said that they would gladly give up the tiring, dirty labor; the rising fees for seeds, fertilizers, and tools; and the insecure income dependent on weather, timing, and markets. "But," a woman said, "I have no *guanxi.* How could I get a factory job? *Nongmin ganhuor.*"[14] She perceives her desire for wealth and position to be thwarted by the triumph of power over hard work; this becomes another means to locate one more absolute distinction from the state. Contractors of land claim that the situation confronting them is enabled by Deng's regime, in which high officials' involvement in corruption sanctions corrupt *guanxi* at every subsequent level of the official hierarchy. They blame Deng for allowing and enabling corruption and abuse of power, erecting him as an archetype of amoral leadership.

This corrupt present is also the moment in which *nongmin* experience a rise in the incidence of spirit possessions. In their view, the lack of a moral leader, corruption, and the disregard for social ties fueling individuals' pursuit of profit combine to create conditions in which the spirits feel free to act. A healer said: "During the Cultural Revolution all the ghosts and spirits hid. Now they are everywhere; if they have a chance to attack you, they will. It's their time now to do as they wish; just like being an official, if you have a shady opportunity, you can get a privileged position too. So spirits look for people to take over and get a free ride."

People explained that the spirits are active because they do not recognize the power of Deng. *Just like an official* becomes the most salient analogy for the spirits' opportunism and self-promotion and interweaves the meaning of the spirits with what is usually cordoned off as the political realm. It is Deng's lack of power over them that enables the spirits. The spirits' power to possess and heal can be transferred into an official idiom when meanings articulate at will, particularly when pervasive corruption allows officials to offer such apposite models for possessing spirits. The spirits go beyond representing to indict the corrupt present as that present is woven into the meaning of the spirits.

Moral Authority: Mao

Corruption and abuse of power are documented and experienced daily in China, but conceptions of Deng and the cosmological judgment spirit activities represent are not simply products of contemporary experiences.[15] Historical imaginations also are involved, constructing an idealized past that constitutes an other that can be opposed to Deng's amorality. Histories generate memories of Mao as an antithesis of amoral rule and contrast the corruption of today with what is envisaged as the moral authority of the past.

According to people in Wulin, Mao developed a model of the good person who would lead the transformation to communism, and he lived it. He called on all Chinese to serve the people and went to villages to learn from the masses. A retired production-team leader told me Mao never had servants, had never taken any amount of money over his Central Committee salary, and had forgone meat to eat the coarse grains *nongmin* were making do with during the famines of the early 1960s.[16] Moreover, Mao's virtue founded a morality that suffused society. A former collective leader spoke nostalgically of the days when no one thought of monetary rewards for work and a populist spirit held sway. He claimed that all Chinese were inspired by Mao's unwavering devotion to the people and his principles of morality and virtue.[17] "Cadres used to work in the fields alongside commune members; they walked to meetings miles away and took along a couple of steamed buns—they never had the cars or banquets today's cadres do." Power was embodied in moral models. A middle-aged couple who contracted land together told me that Mao instructed the people to follow the principles of virtue he demanded of Party members through "thought work" (*sixiang gongzuo*), stressing honesty and selflessness. They blamed the current lack of thought work for corruption and lazy youth who would rather steal than work.

Critically, Mao awarded social status and mobility to those who conformed to his standard of socialist ethics and revolutionary fervor. The poor were well situated to "live the example" of the moral models and achieved a moral stature unattainable by those who owned wealth, who were by definition amoral. To the predominantly poor-peasant population of the dry, marginal agricultural area encompassing Wulin, this was a previously unknown valorization of the self, and they embraced the model conflating poor and moral. They drew strength as well as self-esteem from the maintenance of moral selves. It appears that it was not only the morality of Mao's authority that legitimated his leadership; legitimation was effected in the moralizing influence Mao's leadership had on the population as a whole. People could remake themselves in an intelligible image that was recognized as socially superior. *Nongmin* could be like walking, bun-eating cadres, who were like them. The mutual influences of moral leaders and the moral poor twine another thread in the articulated whole that produced *nongmin* as subjects.

The historical memory of Mao engages the meanings of the animal spirits. Memory is fostered by the animal spirits' activities, as the spirits' activities are made meaningful by memories. The current rise in possessions stands in contrast with what people described as a cessation of spirit activity from 1949 through the rule of Mao. "The animal spirits will only act tough until a figure of authority that they fear and respect commands the scene," Du explained. They fled after 1949 because they recognized a superior moral authority in

Mao. During Mao's campaigns against superstition, the spirits had no choice but to heed his call for the eradication of spirits and flee. A middle-aged woman who worked with one of the healers explained, "When Mao said, 'Away with all demons and monsters' [*sao chu niugui sheshen*], they fled. You didn't see any of the animal spirits around here then." Several people told me that Mao's formidable power emanated from his own spiritual essence, contending that Mao was a turtle spirit, which is of an order higher than the four animal spirits. Mao was said to have known this himself, but he did not like to divulge the information. According to Liu Ge, a young man who hoped to develop spiritual powers, Mao and current top leaders kept the books revealing magical secrets for themselves. "They [top officials] know if we got ahold of the books we'd believe in the magic and not in them. They all believe in it, and Mao was a master of it," he explained. A collective accountant asked me how I thought Mao could command so many followers, human and spiritual. "All that he said was incantations [*zhouyu*]," she explained. Mao's spiritual essence also points to a blurring of boundaries and permeability across categories, which I discuss below.

Mao's morality and Deng's corruption anchor a binary opposition between what are actually mutually constitutive, continuously evolving images emanating from the cosmic realm, folk beliefs, Maoist propaganda, and ancient as well as recent histories. People drew the Jade Emperor, Yue Fei,[18] and Confucius into discussions of moral authority and its subversion. Mao and Deng emerge as the central opposition undoubtedly because their authority was experienced by a large majority of Wulin residents and they presided over what were significant changes in people's lives—the Revolution, collectivization, and decollectivization.[19] But I reiterate that I am not suggesting that people were presenting comprehensive or virtual models and memories. The opposition between Mao and Deng eclipsed most other figures because it was connected to the chain of binary signs opposing moral to immoral, past to present, poverty to wealth, honesty to corruption, and fleeing to possessing spirits. Mao's morality is constructed in the present through attempts to perceive, evaluate, and finally condemn Deng; representations of Deng as corrupt enable the remembering of Mao as an idealized, moral leader.[20]

Mao is constructed as a turtle and Deng as an archetype of corruption; perhaps less visibly, *nongmin* also come into being in the meanings of the spirits. *Nongmin* become possible because of the interweaving of meanings that produces Mao and Deng. Below I look first at how this interweaving enables a rethinking of state and society as opposed entities. I then look at how this interweaving produces *nongmin,* how it folds into itself, and how the coherence of *nongmin* collapses into it.

The Power of the Spirits

The meaning of the spirits is inextricably bound to Mao and Deng, the past and present, discourses on moral wealth and market reforms. Identifying

Mao as a turtle spirit may appear to be *nongmin* obeying a cosmological hegemony that absorbs historical transformations into static moral categories. But to read the animal spirits as an enduring body of beliefs into which *nongmin* have incorporated the changes of the past forty years essentializes peasant traditionalism and posits a traditional obscurantism that leaves the state free to act at will.

A traditionalist argument also denies the pivotal transformations occurring in the meanings of the spirits. People in Wulin incorporated changes in the conception of the official to understand the mass-line-based power of Mao and changes in the substance of the crucial means of evaluating moral leadership: cadres who labored alongside *nongmin* and workers, economic asceticism, and a ruler who championed the poor and politically dispossessed. Yet these images cannot be read as imposed by the Party-state. *Nongmin* were part of the project of making such images meaningful, which they accomplished partly through making Mao a turtle, partly through transformations in themselves. They made themselves poor *and* moral and now are making themselves *rich* and moral by incorporating in the spirits and in the *nongmin* identity categories of wealth, such as are represented by privileges offered healers. I discuss the ways wealth is incorporated and represented below. At this point I recall that the Maoist morality lauded in a spirit-free past is founded on the exalted status poor *nongmin* (*pinnong*) attained. Mao fused poverty with morality and fastened both to *nongmin*. Deng's reforms have led to the refashioning of wealth as acceptable and desirable, negating and transforming its Maoist associations with exploitation, capitalism, and oppression.

Yet Deng has rescued wealth from Mao's capitalist purgatory only to immerse it in corruption and resurrect unequal access, the ascendancy of private accumulation over human relationships, and the equation of official position with corruption and disregard for the people. The challenge *nongmin* face is to detach wealth from Maoist economic asceticism to make it accessible to moral persons while maintaining the tie between morality and *nongmin*. They engage the contradiction inherent in the official promotion of honest wealth and the ubiquity of official corruption. They draw on morality, wealth, and corrupt officials to fashion an identity that is not unequivocally prescribed by any leader.

This challenge *nongmin* face incorporates into their identity both Mao's morality and Deng's promotion of wealth. *Nongmin* claim that the activities of the animal spirits represent cosmological accord with their view of Deng as an illegitimate ruler. According to Romeyn Taylor's work on imperial folk beliefs, spirits are allies to local groups and stand with them against an oppressive regime (Taylor 1990). The animal spirits stand as cosmic support for denunciation of Deng and may be read as empowering the dispossessed by affirming a legitimate cosmological authority that they can claim supersedes Deng's corrupt regime. Cosmic authorities prescribe moral rule to leaders and moral obedience to subjects. The spirits potently exemplify the weight of those prescriptions. Deng's immorality is punished through discursive representations and through the spirits' active intervention in the bodies of mortals.

Nongmin see the spirits' power, not as opposing their leaders, but as dependent on or even derived from them. Spirits flee Mao's morality and resurface under Deng's corruption. *Nongmin* at no point read in the spirits any suggestion of an alliance in fighting oppressive rulers. The spirits' response to Deng's oppressive regime is to invade the bodies of *nongmin,* not Deng. Mao himself *is* a spirit.

The Multiple Sources of Coherent *Nongmin*

The meanings embedded in the spirits weave together power, history, wealth, and persons. Embedded in the spirits is a code that contains and produces the meanings that define persons and impose limits to subjectivities. These meanings contain the identities of "moral *nongmin*" and their other: "immoral officials." Morality is represented in an idiom of wealth through the spirits' powers, healers, and offerings and is based on a cosmic reciprocity that privileges the moral being. The code negotiates the relation between morality, wealth, and persons critical to the construction of moral, wealthy *nongmin.* While reform policy promotes a market and rational economic persons to go along with it, enduring questions surrounding the meaning of wealth, the desire for it, and the means of acquiring it confront individual worthiness. This confrontation is played out and to some extent resolved in the tensions among gifts, markets, moral wealth, and persons represented in the spirits and in the imagined state.

The moral being no longer must eschew wealth, as people did under Mao, but in fact is the only one deserving of it (see Anagnost 1989; Brokaw 1991). This being distinguishes the (moral) wealth of *nongmin* from the (immoral) wealth of officials by working for it and subordinating it to social ties to create the antithesis of corrupt *guanxi*'s goal of private accumulation. In spirit healing, exchanges of wealth privilege the creation of social ties and social obligations over the possession of the object; offerings to healers and healers' offerings to their spirits are part of an encompassing cosmic reciprocity. Healers offer services and receive a reciprocal return of wealth from patients who receive the healing power. Healers make a moral offering with no thought of reward. They are selfless givers who then receive wealth—the offerings, meals, cigarettes, and money grateful patients give—that they in turn offer to their spirits. Patients can also exemplify the moral giver: to be deserving of the gift of healing they must offer gifts, meals, offerings to the healer's spirit, and cash in exchange. The spirits represent the investment of labor that entitles one to reward: they pass trials or work to achieve their powers.

Believing in the spirits, people construct moral *nongmin* from these images. They learn that to be deserving of wealth they must work to achieve it and offer it with no thought of return. Those who receive are reminded that they must reciprocate. Thus *nongmin* can be wealthy and sustain the image that is their legacy from Mao. Believing in the spirits, people pass on and produce tales of possession that simultaneously tell them how to be *nongmin*. People believe in or subscribe to meanings of persons while simultaneously constructing the meanings and the persons they name.

The meanings of wealth embedded in the spirits weave together with those associated with Mao and Deng. Memories of mutual aid and voluntary labor intersect with norms of reciprocity in healers and patients. Morality must now recognize the necessity of maintaining a rejection of the individual accumulation of wealth as an end while guaranteeing that correct acts will be rewarded with wealth.[21] Those who give represent a Maoist repudiation of private accumulation because they share their wealth; it is a fiction of repudiation that enables givers to be deserving of owning wealth.

The logic of the market intervenes in the morality of reciprocity in the incorporation of Deng. He provides the archetype of corruption against which *nongmin* contrast moral, earned wealth. In the spiritual idiom, against the critiques of official corruption we can read a mandate for a moral market that involves offering moral wealth—wealth that is earned, not derived through corruption. *Nongmin* identify themselves with that market because their money is deserved. *Nongmin* must accumulate wealth through narrowly defined market transactions—sale of their labor and/or crops; entrepreneurial activities; or salaried employment—so that it can be distinguished from wealth tainted by corruption. The gifts and cash passing through healers' and patients' hands represent earned wealth, conspicuously displayed; people exhibit fine foods, imported cigarettes, and cars and drivers as the fruits of their labors and signs of their success in the market. They give and receive what they condemn officials for appropriating but render it discrete because it is the product of what the spirits define as a moral transaction. With the proper place of wealth in human relationships secured to *nongmin* through the images and practices of spirit healing, the identity of officials is wholly allied with corruption and wholly distinguished from that of the *nongmin*. But *nongmin* sketch a distance between themselves and corrupt officials only by the necessary move of collapsing that distance in referring to their other as they construct themselves.

Blurred Borders

The spirits represent a site around which boundaries blur. The categories of Mao, Deng, and *nongmin* are all constructed on this site, but the powerful and powerless, moral and immoral, also entwine. Spirits prey on the weak and powerless yet also seek good people and endow them with the power to heal the possessed. Weak people get sick; strong and moral people heal. Perhaps more critically, any distinction between the spirits and officials is blurred: both embody the immoral power that preys on the weak and the moral as well as the moral power to serve the people. At a personal level, the fact that corruption in Deng's regime disrupts the social body by renouncing what *nongmin* term *legitimate* social and political relations leads to the disruption of individual bodies by the spirits. The return of the spirits—like the departure of Mao—abandons the powerless to the scavenging of the powerful. On the cosmic level, the spirits also embody virtues and norms of reciprocity that recall Maoist morality. Both Mao and the spirits are a standard by which to distinguish and denounce the present regime.

Healers' identities also blur into those of scorned officials. Healers hold power. They serve the people as an official should, and they enjoy the illicit privileges officials do—they are driven in cars and feasted. The reciprocity represented by good healers, who offer their services and receive patients' offerings of wealth and privileges, mirrors that of corrupt officials, who receive gifts and privileges in return for their services too. Healers are also like officials in that they do not make explicit requests for goods; but, if goods are not offered, requests are rarely granted.

From the categories' mutual permeability Mao emerges as a turtle spirit. He is remade in the *nongmin* image, his power translated into an alternative, localized language. He transcends the bounds of the official—moral or immoral—to inhabit the cosmic realm, but only because he can be identified with poor *nongmin*. Mao is situated in the most distant, lofty realm from which power is imposed on mere *nongmin* mortals and brought into the villages as the most prosaic model for the moral masses' transformation. *Nongmin* remade themselves in Mao's image as revolutionary heroes and remade Mao in their image as a turtle. The multivalency and ambivalence that is embodied in Mao is exemplified by Du's memory of his maternal grandfather, a powerful healer who equated his powers with Mao's. "The old man pointed to Mao's portrait and said, 'When I go, you go; we're equal,' and a few months after the old man died, Mao died. Mao was a *shen* [spirit]," said Du. Liu Ge's belief that the nation's leaders are masters of magical powers conveys a similar message that might be termed a *projected articulation;* people are saying not only that their beliefs are held by officials but that the latter's power and authority in politics extends to the spiritual realm as well.

While I have no evidence that Mao or any of the current leaders were masters of the spiritual arts, I learned from Liu Ge and the accountant who told me Mao ruled through incantations that the distance between *nongmin* as believers in the spirits and "corrupt officials" collapses. The power to name and to call Mao a turtle spirit positions *nongmin* constructions within realms in which the Party-state is imagined. Mao's power emanated, not from Mao himself, from his armies, or from his control of the press alone, but from diverse, complexly intersecting social relations. Mao must become a turtle to command the people of Wulin. They make him a turtle and thus their ruler. Deng is opposed by the spirits; as a mere mortal he will never command the total submission of *nongmin,* who will not produce his power.

Making Multiple *Nongmin:*
Divisions of Class and Gender

Healing exchanges inscribe selfless generosity that is rewarded into the behavior of patients and their families, compelling them to give wealth to others. The healers' expectations of offerings of wealth oblige patients to provide them with privileges such as being driven in cars, feasted, and offered cigarettes, good tea, and fine liquor. *Nongmin* may develop as moral members of the community only if they fulfill their obligations as generous hosts and gift givers. To accumulate and hold private wealth they must first instantiate themselves within the community by showing they have the economic power to give.

The power to impose codes introduces into the villages the hierarchy *nongmin* would situate between themselves and corrupt officials. When boundaries blur, hierarchy and immorality are no longer outside; when they move into *nongmin,* the divisions that people impose on each other are most evident along class and gender lines. Sun Xiulan represents a widening divide between rich and poor. It is not that only the poor become possessed but rather that the spirits provide the discursive means to restrict their identities from the moral realm. The gossip about Sun reveals that one can no longer be moral and poor; not only are people being called on to earn wealth through a market and not corruption, but they also are being called on to achieve a standard of living that approaches the urban, consumer-oriented standard. They must not only give but *have* wealth or be unworthy. The poor must compete with rising expectations and increasingly ubiquitous consumption or be excluded from the reciprocal exchanges that instantiate one in the moral and deserving community. If Sun had a new brick home, color television, mattress, and carpet, there might be more sympathy for her son's illness.

The healer becomes an imposing elite figure that forces even the poorer residents of Wulin to purchase and offer goods on a variety of occasions: weddings and holidays as well as healing sessions. Bride wealth and dowry are also—and have been historically—arenas for the display of wealth and the struggle to be recognized among the elite.

Wealth disrupts the *nongmin* identity in other ways as well. A well-known wealthy villager, the head of a Wulin factory, often talked about the *nongmin* among whom he lived: "a backward [*luohou*] lot" who would never get ahead in the new competitive system. He laughed at "their" spirits. When we were discussing pervasive corruption and the ever-degenerating Communist Party, he declared that he was just a *nongmin* and powerless to fight the state. He restored the powerless, even "backward" identity that could never be misconstrued with *corrupt official.* He allows himself—and his *hukou* allows him—to return to a *nongmin* identity because he is secured to the wealth that eclipses what he disparages in *nongmin.* The "poor" aspect of the honest *nongmin* identity that is offered along with powerlessness as the signal proof of distance from corrupt, wealthy officials is simultaneously the aspect most readily discarded.

The gendering of *nongmin* is also manifest and repressive. Women healers' service to others is defined and restricted, which limits the persons women can be. Their service is more personalized and quotidian than male healers'. A woman was sought by a spirit to heal because of her faithful, "privatized" service as a daughter-in-law; a man was chosen because of his "public" service as a production-team leader. A woman healer I was told about had gained a name by caring for sick children, which is understood as more typically feminine work. This gendering of healers' identities extends to the positions they can claim and the offerings they are given. The two women healers I knew worked in and around their villages; neighbors came to their homes, or the women made house calls. No one sent cars for them or gave them the lavish meals and imported cigarettes given men. This may imply a restriction of women's access to wealth to their relationships with men, who, as healers, and as the vast majority of managers, heads, and officials, have more direct access.

Finally, lack of belief in the spirits cracks the seamless *nongmin*. Professions of disbelief may be a sign of the reclassifying of *nongmin* in the post-reform society that brought an American anthropologist wandering into their villages and images of American science and technology onto their televisions. Some unbelievers may have been attempting to reassign the meanings constituting the identity *nongmin* to embrace the scientific and modern. But the reassignment of meaning should not be interpreted as the successful imposition of Party discourses on modernity. My reading is that it may be the insertion of *nongmin* into the democratic society promoted most recently during the occupation of Tiananmen Square. A more "scientific" *nongmin* would be able to act with students rather than being acted on by them. But this is an issue requiring further study, and it cannot be fully answered here because the boundary between believer and unbeliever is also blurred.

CONCLUSION

Through the spirits, *nongmin* are involved in creating the terms and practices concerned with the confrontation between morality and wealth as it is played out in the struggle over accumulation in market and gift exchanges. The animal spirits and the healing practices associated with them signal that *nongmin* are producing meanings that engage the contradiction inherent in the official promotion of honest wealth and the ubiquity of official corruption. Their discourses echo those of their rulers when moral wealth and power embrace individual hard work and honesty—practices involved in the most depersonalized forms of production and market exchange. They reassert moral principles by imposing regimes of knowledge and practice on themselves. They work with meanings of market and gift to assert an identity that is morally distinct from a corrupt-official identity. They also reclaim the gift exchange from corrupt officials for the redeployment of individual market earnings in personalized nonmarket exchanges. The offering of gifts to animal spirits and spirit healers not only facilitates the inscription of moral/amoral in subjectivities but also provides the space in which *nongmin* can effect moral exchanges in practice. And it is in this practice that the moral divide breaks down.

Identities, subjectivities, moralities, and definitions of wealth are being constructed by people who name themselves *nongmin,* but it is in the act of distinguishing themselves from a state that we see that their very being is intimately connected with those who occupy formal positions of power. Mao and Deng, Party and Reform discourse, all figure in the beings who become *nongmin.* Officials are not distanced in practice—in creating *nongmin* as wealthy, moral people—as they are in the discourse that represents discrete entities.

The historical specificity of the issues concerning people in Wulin affirms that the spirits are "of the Reforms"; but the complex configuration of social relations involving various hierarchies (gender, class, bureaucratic) enveloping and producing *nongmin* attests that the Reforms do not produce the spirits. Powers developing among *nongmin* through their spirits and Reform-era wealth place *nongmin* in the position to redefine their identities, but their power also suggests that the position *nongmin* now occupy in the field of subjectification is not newly carved but has existed alongside central authorities before. Their power allows us to comprehend the more centralized power of historic and contemporary Chinese governments as a product of patterns developing on myriad sites throughout Chinese society. It also allows us to map the forms of power produced within every perceivable social group—both within China and migrating across the globe as workers, students, and immigrants—and follow the complex ways in which these groups relate to each other rather than continually opposing two entities: state and society.

Afterword

Centers and Peripheries, Nation and World

If we have realized the chief objective of the course from which this interpretive anthology was drawn—familiarizing students with contemporary Chinese life through a combination of critical readings and active engagement in the everyday—then the reader of these pages may be disturbed. Disgruntlement appeared early in the reactions of our students to the incongruous details of life in southwest China, yielding a range of questions that reflected an elemental confusion: Why do so many Chinese eat with spoons instead of chopsticks? Why do people live in the partially completed upper floors of high-rise construction sites? Why are many city streets unpaved? Why are horse carts the most common means of transporting heavy loads? Why don't modern Chinese residential compounds have at least a bathroom on each floor? Why are the Communist Party and the People's Liberation Army barely visible in the city? Why is the government tearing down old stone and mortar dwellings? Why is the government relocating Muslim Chinese? Why is China a class society? Why are so many elderly people working in the street picking up trash to sell for recycling? Why do men dance with men and women dance with women? Why are Chinese unafraid of criticizing their officials and the law? Why do so many Chinese believe in magic? Why are Chinese so concerned about hygiene but apparently ignorant of the germ theory of disease? Why are there so many homeless people? Why are some school-age children not in school? Where is the socialism in China? A number of these queries have been answered for the reader in the selections presented above and were answered by the reading and local observation for our students, but their asking revealed a critical chasm between textbook knowledge and experience, thus the consequent disgruntlement.

Some of the students had traveled within the United States. A few had been abroad. And some had never left Colorado; thus, a flight around the world should have proved disorienting. But it was not especially, for they had read widely about the places to which they would travel and steeped themselves in works on Chinese culture, history, politics, and society. In our era of globalism—or at least our era of heightened popular consciousness of it—a journey of twelve thousand miles is actually not much. However, as we have learned in the preceding chapters, it is not the getting to China but the traveling within it that is startling. Here, on the local ground of the nation's 1 million villages, 100,000 townships and urban wards, and outside the standard national portrait, the distance between what one knows of China and what actually transpires there trebles. Caught in this space, it is sometimes difficult to reconcile text-based perceptions with experienced reality.

And, of course, there are always contradictions, as when our students encountered the partially razed grounds and shattered stele of a mosque dating from the fourteenth century that yet bore placards from the municipal Communist Party committee certifying the Party's political and financial support for Islam and its defense of ethnic diversity. Strategically located in the rear of the provincial capital's department store (*baihuo dalou*), the mosque, central courtyard, imam's residence, acolytes' quarters, and classrooms, all four centuries' old, stood astride the path of the department store's inevitable expansion. One day (indeed, merely a day before the students visited), a group of young men appeared and torched the classrooms and acolytes' quarters, stopping long enough to take a sledgehammer to three stone stele commemorating imperial honors bestowed on the mosque by the Wanli (1573–1619), Kangxi (1662–1722), and Guangxu (1875–1908) emperors. Several acolytes who had acted in defense of the imam were badly beaten and taken to jail. Among the myriad stone fragments and dust and the charred classroom remains, the imam assured our students that the compound would be rebuilt and the stele restored, even though, as one student observed, the main gate to the compound had been closed, blocked by the temporary green metal fencing peculiar to construction sites all over the country. In a society undergoing such a vast transformation, there are tensions, but this particular eruption made little sense in terms of the China that the students knew, a China where ethnic groups were constitutionally protected and, more important, were the ample source (as was the mosque) of tourist dollars. It was only when they drew this moment into dialogue with their own experience and knowledge of Western history—the Holocaust, "ethnic cleansing" in Bosnia-Herzegovina, American slavery—that they accounted for the contradiction.

In much the same way, the contemporary Chinese ground traversed in these chapters reveals a place unfamiliar yet comprehensible; it is this combination of strangeness and familiarity that says much about the end of the Middle Kingdom syndrome, China's place within the converging economic, cultural, and political relations of the globe, and the unique perspective of the new millennium's students. New information conveyed about sexuality, identity, homelessness, ethnic and political pluralism, gender relations, religious belief, and popular music undermines the "knowledge" that the student takes for granted. Nevertheless, it does not leave her bewildered; instead, these disclosures provoke reconsideration of the student's default knowledge and a corresponding effort to re-cognize China. For example, one does not think of ethnic diversity in general or Muslim fundamentalism in particular when thinking of China; however, from a growing awareness of the place of Islam in today's international politics in nations like Iran, Afghanistan, India, Indonesia, Turkey, and Pakistan, one can easily infer such an "ethnoreligious resurgence" in China's northwest of the sort described by Dru Gladney (chap. 6).

In other words, the initial revelation of the strange occurs against the backdrop of the common portrait of a "centered," uniform post-Communist state, whereas the familiarizing adjustment is made through comparison with global political phenomena. The Middle Kingdom stereotype of China, one abetted by the Chinese government (as pointed out by Sydney White [chap. 7], Susan Blum [chap. 8], and Mary Erbaugh [chap. 10]) and the U.S. media alike, is slowly giving way to a more nuanced, if not more accurate, portrait of a diverse cultural ecology of contradictory politics wherein the much vaunted political center (as explained by Liu Binyan [chap. 2]) exerts negligible influence over a vast, contentious, and increasingly self-determining periphery.

Today China, at least in the minds of its educated urban residents, is in a distinctive moment—*houxin shiqi,* "post–new age"—and so it has joined the chorus of global culture. China is postmodern, and it has the information revolution to show it. In greeting someone, it is as common to ask, "Are you hooked up?" as it is to inquire, "Have you eaten yet?" (Barmé and Ye 1997, 140). The urban streetscape of China's cities is dotted with the icons of global capital: Microsoft, Nike, Reebok, Johnny Walker Red, Dunhill Cigarettes, Starbucks, McDonalds, Shiseido, each peddling products some buy and most only long for, but all carrying with them a certain cachet. The planet's interconnections are immense and growing, and one might presume that the chances for finding mystery in and misunderstanding China have declined. Perhaps it is ironic that more information about life in China has not sufficiently diminished ignorance, a fault of our own and of the Chinese government. It is seductive to think of a postmodern China of Internet service providers with citizens in Nikes slouching uncomfortably around Starbucks tables laden with lattés, for it makes China our twin and lessens barriers to understanding. We would urge the reader to resist the temptation of postmodern similarity and remember that perhaps 4 percent of Chinese families own a computer, that 72 percent of the population lives in the countryside, and that an astonishing number of Chinese have never used a telephone. Apparent analogues of experience measured by common commercial placements actually facilitate cultural misunderstanding; such is the problematic allure of "globalism."

The diverse panorama of experience, life, and language collectively exhibited in these contributions is, then, the most salient and enduring feature of Chinese life. The challenge of bringing this to the undergraduate student whose awareness of China has grown in recent years is that of overcoming stereotypes, those reproduced in the U.S. media and conventional textbooks and those accentuated by the Chinese government. China's human diversity is fatal to the uniform national biography of the state and, therefore, represents a central problem of the contemporary government. This is most evident in the last five chapters, especially Dorothy Solinger's portrait of a people on the move (see chap. 14) and in a Chinese scholar's calculation that, at any given New Year celebration, more than 25 million Chinese are in transit (Li 1997). With the disclosures of forced relocation in Kosovo, where up to 1 million Muslim refugees moved into the neighboring states of Macedonia, Albania, Bosnia, and Montenegro, the student has perhaps a sense of the remarkable volume of human transit in contemporary China. It is a nation in flux, moving rapidly from what it once was, but not altogether certain of where it is going.

Owing to the power of apparent analogy to weaken the student's critical faculties, we insist here at the end that attention to the details of local experience must be tempered with awareness of the changing politics of the "center." The student must draw her gaze up from the obliterating detail of the everyday to see how the weight of its challenge to the state has been felt in recent years. The diversity of China's periphery represented in this collection is more than a snapshot of an inner world rarely seen in the West; it is as well testimony to the changes within the politics and outlook of the Chinese Communist Party. To offer a spectral representation of the formerly unrepresented is especially possible now in the wake of the government's recognition of the significance of yielding to local impulses toward democracy—village elections, geographic mobility, economic freedom, and the modest expansion of civil control of the military and public security forces. Indeed, these rudimentary gestures toward political reform will be difficult to reverse and inevitably will complicate our picture of China, just as China complicates its own singular national representation. Moreover, the subtle, and perhaps too deliberate, move toward greater civilian participation in government defended by rule of law should honor and protect the diversity that it reveals while bringing China into line with the growing democratization of the Asia-Pacific region. Indeed, this may be one of the most significant consequences of closer relations between Taiwan and China as well as Beijing's hosting of the 2008 summer Olympic games and China's recent entrance into the World Trade Organization.

As U.S. students of the Chinese experience, our perspective on this transformation is a "view from afar," yet we always see in China what it means for us or what we find intelligible in it. So this view is at the same time a close-at-hand reckoning of sameness and difference wherein far more has been assumed than known. China and the contiguous forty-eight American states are roughly equal in geographic area (9,572,900 and 9,327,614 square kilometers, respectively). This near equivalence is worth noting because, to most Western observers, China is larger—very much larger—than the United States; that it is not should make us reconsider, as we have throughout this volume, the "facticity" of the China that we "know." The fact that China is divided into thirty-one provinces all administered according to a northern vernacular by a political party from offices in Beijing encourages us to presume that it is like the United States with its fifty-state federal system administered from Washington, D.C.: a politically coherent, administratively integrated, national entity. However, awareness of the profound linguistic differences inherent in the soil of the many regions singularly construed as *China* or of the regional and local limits of U.S. national sovereignty forces us to consider the status of these nations as ideas.

Administrative integrity and political coherence are always measured from the center outward and begin from an assumption of national unity as conveyed in the ideological sentiments "the American people" and *women Zhongguoren,* "we Chinese." Uniformity of this sort is an ideological artifact of the great idea of nationhood that weakens any popular inclination—American or Chinese—to query the fit of a vast, diverse periphery and a political center. Looking back over these chapters, one gets a glimpse of a nation and a people, not so much in transition, as in transformation, the outcomes of which are ambiguous. Yet, armed with an uncommon but more representative knowledge of China "off center," any student, anyone, may venture an educated guess of the direction of change for self and society at the margins and at the center of what little remains of the idea of the "Middle Kingdom."

Notes

Part I. The Center and the Noncenter

Chapter 3. Symbols of Southern Identity

1. There are even claims of a genetic boundary around the Yangzi river (*Proceedings* 1988).

2. For the importance of museums to national identity formation, see Anderson ([1989] 1991).

3. This north-south peasant opposition is captured in Siu (1990).

4. In contrast, Kang Youwei saw Chu people as having become Han Chinese in ancient times, as Manchu supposedly had in modern times (Duara 1992, 25).

5. The book *Wu Yue wenhua* (Wu Yue culture) (1991) depicts the independent power of the Wu people in the Yangzi valley going back to 1100 B.C.E., including a major influence from exchanges with non-Chinese peoples. In contrast to this narrative of the dynamic, open, and commercial south of Chu and Wu Yue, the Han dynasty historian Sima Qian characterized the region as a "large territory sparsely populated where people eat rice and drink fish soup . . . where people enjoy self-sufficiency without commerce. The place is fertile and suffers neither famine nor hunger. Hence the people are lazy and poor and do not bother to accumulate wealth" (Young 1988, 42).

6. "A provincial official of a northeastern province informed the author that during previous student demonstrations some student traders had openly said that Manchuria would have developed faster if it had remained under Japanese rule" (Ch'i 1991, 320).

7. Likewise, Taiwanese national identity includes the notion, rejected by Jiang's anti-imperialist heirs, that Taiwan has done so well, in part, because of the Japanese and would have done better yet had the Japanese stayed and the anti-imperialist Chinese never come.

8. In general, "newly acquired financial power has caused them [regional leaders] to identify themselves more and more with local interests." In particular, the regional military has had to cooperate with these interests to make military enterprises profitable. "Another reason why the military has sought to improve its ties with local administrations is that demobilized servicemen have to rely on local governments to obtain employment" (Fu 1992, 82, 78).

9. The next two paragraphs draw on White and Cheng (1993).

Chapter 5. Chinese Turkestan

1. The term *Hanyu* is what local officials used to contrast this language—that of the Han Chinese—to that of other ethnic groups. "Hanyu" is essentially the same language as Putonghua. [*Editors' note.*]

2. Which is written.

3. Reviewing my notes on my interviews with Xinjiang Education Commission officials, I am uncertain whether the four thousand figure they gave me included both Han Chinese students from Xinjiang and local minority students, but I believe it did include both.

4. In the three years following my 1988 visit, the dramatic collapse of communism in both Eastern Europe and the Soviet Union changed the situation in fundamental ways. Initially, Beijing was seriously concerned, and in some respects alarmed, by these developments. However, the Chinese government continued to try to strengthen relations with the government in the Soviet Union during 1989–1991, and trade expanded. Then, after the dissolution of the Soviet Union, China rapidly established ties with all the successor states. But there was continuing concern that there could be chaos in the Soviet Union, which could have unpredictable effects across the border in northwest China.

*Chapter 6. Ethnoreligious Resurgence in
a Northwestern Sufi Community*

1. Najiahu, which I translate "Na Homestead," is a brigade (*dadui*) belonging to Yanghe commune (*gongshe*). Now that Yanghe has become a township (*xiang*), Na Homestead can be considered a large village, comprising eleven teams (*xiaodui*).

2. A 1964 report collected by the county "United Front Office" (Tongzhanbu) claimed that, in 1954, over two hundred were worshiping at the mosque five times daily, 9.5 percent of the total Hui population, whereas present participation stands at only eighty worshipers, 4.7 percent. The population of the village has almost doubled since that time.

3. As elsewhere in Central Asia, in Hui villages any elder who possesses advanced Islamic knowledge (*Ahlin*) or who can read the Qur'an is generally recognized as an *ahong* (imam). Among the traditional non-*menhuan* Gedimu or Khufiyya, the "teaching" (*kaixue*) *ahong* is recognized as the preacher (*woerzu*) and responsible for delivering the main Friday sermon (*hutubai*). The mosque is generally administered by a committee (*siguan weiyuanhui*) that replaced the traditional "three-leader system" (*sandaozhi* or *zhangjiao zhidu*) in 1958, after the Democratic Reform Campaign (*minzhu gaige*)—among the Jahriyya, the term *zhangjiao ahong,* for the teaching *ahong,* is preserved. The assistant to the teaching *ahong* is now known as the *zhangxue ahong;* the mosque administrator in charge of daily affairs is the *si shifu* or *si guan zhuren.* The teaching *ahong* among the Gedimu and Yihewani is often transferred (*sanxue*) to another mosque after an average of three years. An elder with minimal Islamic knowledge is known as a "second *ahong*" (*er ahong*) or even "primary school *ahong*" (*xiaoxue ahong*).

4. The largest mosque in Ningxia, located in Tongxin, dates from the late sixteenth century. It was spared destruction by Red Guards during the Cultural Revolution because it was the site where Chairman Mao Zedong declared the first

Hui autonomous county on 20 December 1936. Weizhou was the site of the oldest and largest mosque in Ningxia, but it was destroyed in 1966. It was under reconstruction in 1985, but the former Islamic architecture is not being restored.

5. The only available figures on Ningxia for the average wage of workers in state-owned units was 936 yuan per year and in collective owned units 646 yuan per year in 1982. This does not reflect typical rural income, which averaged about 400 yuan according to most areas I surveyed.

6. The study revealed that individual giving among six households in a Gedimu village averaged 7.52 percent, among six households in a Jahriyya village 11.99 percent, and among five households in a Yihewani village 9.34 percent.

7. A rather new development is the sending of Hui *manla* to mosques in Xinjiang, where Arabic-language study is much more advanced due to the influence of the Arabic script in Uighur and the proximity to Pakistan with its recently opened Karakoram highway. In September 1987, while visiting a mosque in Kashgar, I met a Hui *manla* from Hezhou who was studying there for six years for precisely those reasons. He mentioned his desire to travel to Mecca through Pakistan and how much more inexpensive and convenient the hajj had become since the opening of the road. He served at the only Hui mosque among the 160 Uighur mosques in the city.

8. Hui women's head coverings veil the hair, forehead, and neck but leave the face exposed. In heavily populated Hui areas, particularly among communities influenced by the Yihewani, such as Linxia, Gansu province, and Xining, Qinghai province, almost all women over twelve years of age wear them. While it is not a consistent practice in every area, young unmarried women often wear green, married women tend to wear black, and older women white, generally after their husbands die or their grandchildren are born.

9. I heard of at least three other cases of elderly party members becoming *ahong* in Pingluo, north of Yinchuan.

10. The question of the unbelief of committed believers, and the seemingly unproblematic acceptance of that apparent contradiction among Taiwanese folk religionists, is addressed in detail by Jordan and Overmeyer (1986, 173–180, 270).

11. The freedom-of-religion policy is stated in Article 36 of the "Draft of the Revised Constitution of the PRC" and is summarized in an editorial in *Hongqi* (Red flag) (16 June 1982).

[Religious policy has remained a work in progress. A 1997 white paper on the subject, "Freedom of Religious Belief in China," can be found at http://china-embassy.org/eng/7129.html. (*Editors' note.*)]

12. In response to the effort to distinguish clearly between Islam and Hui ethnic identity, northwest Hui authors have recently produced numerous articles arguing the inseparable interrelation of Islam with the historical formulation of Hui identity and customs.

13. This legend is also recorded in a *Shaanxi Gazetteer*. Note as well in this legend the failure to mention the Han covillagers in Teams 1 and 11. See also Rossabi (1981) and Armijo-Hussein (1989).

Chapter 7. Town and Village Naxi Identities in the Lijiang Basin

This chapter was extracted from White (1993) and represents part of a chapter in my *Narratives of Modernity in Socialist China: Naxi Identities, Medical Practices, and the State in the Lijiang Basin, 1949–1990*, the manuscript of which is still in progress. It is based on fieldwork that was conducted over a twenty-month period in the Lijiang basin, primarily in 1989 and 1990. For research support, I am indebted to the former Committee on Scholarly Communication with the People's Republic of China, the Wenner-Gren Foundation for Anthropological Research, Sigma Xi, a University of California, Berkeley, Humanities Grant, a University of California, Berkeley, Department of Anthropology Lowie Scholarship, and a grant from the Temple University Center for East Asian Studies. Special thanks to my China sponsor, the Kunming Institute of Botany, and to the many others who have provided support for and feedback on my research. Special thanks also to Lionel Jensen and Susan Blum for their excellent editing.

1. My discussion in this chapter is specifically concerned with Naxi of the town and village contexts of the Lijiang basin (Lijiang bazi), not with Naxi of the much more remote areas to the north and northwest of the basin. With the important exception of Naxi who live in such relatively low-lying (elevation approximately four thousand feet) fertile areas along the Jinsha river (Jiangbian) as Shigu and Judian (who have been considerably influenced by Han culture), Naxi who reside in the mountainous areas (*shanqu*) to the north and northwest of the basin have been much less influenced by Han Chinese culture than have Lijiang basin Naxi. (See Mueggler 1991; McKhann 1992; White 1993; Rees 1994.)

2. There is an awareness among both town and village basin Naxi residents that an increase in the number of loanwords (*jieci*) from Hanhua (Chinese) has occurred over the last few decades. While the ability to speak Hanhua is a marker of education, and while the ability to speak Kunminghua (the Kunming dialect of Mandarin) had a spate of fashionability among "hip" Dayanzhen youth in the early 1990s, Naxihua is still unquestionably the prevailing language of the basin. On language in Kunming, see Blum (chap. 8 in this volume).

3. There are a variety of interpretations of how the term *gaituguiliu* should be translated. I am using June Teufel Dreyer's translation and definition "to change from native to regular administration" (1976, 11, 284). It should be noted that the implementation of this system involved economic as well as government transformations since ownership and sales of land were involved, especially to incoming Han.

4. This stereotype of "the Naxi" as "matriarchal" has its origins in the fact that the Mosuo people of Lugu lake, to the northwest of the Lijiang basin, are also formally labeled as *Naxi* by the Chinese state. The Mosuo are classified by Chinese ethnologists, most of whom adhere to the nineteenth-century Morganian/Engelsian social evolutionary scheme, as still being in the *matriarchal social evolutionary stage*. Most Lijiang basin Naxi are emphatic about distinguishing themselves from the Mosuo, who practice matrilineal descent and "walking marriage" (*zouhun*). In Chinese popular media, however, this association of images of "matriarchy" is made with the Naxi in general and has been avidly adopted by foreign travelers in the area through their misinformed guidebooks (not just those in English, but undoubtedly those in other Western languages as well). (See Shih 1993; Blum 2001.)

5. This indistinguishability of Han and minority cultures recalls the judgment of David Wu (chap. 9 in this volume) that the Bai and the Han are so similar as to be identical.

6. These "vegetable peasants" (*cainong*), like those adjacent to most towns and cities in China, are in a particularly good position to become prosperous in

post-Mao China since they can sell most of their vegetables for tidy (cash) profits to city residents and do not have to worry about either producing grain or paying part of it to the government in taxes. (Like city residents, they receive grain coupons from the government that allow them to buy a set amount of rice or other grain at reduced rates.)

7. It is not clear what the proportion of Han to Naxi and residents of other "nationalities" is since the census survey has no breakdown by ethnicity.

8. In an urban parallel to the collectivization that was implemented throughout rural China in the late 1950s, the vast majority of residents in town and city contexts of the PRC (such as Dayanzhen) were organized into "work units" (*danwei*) during this first decade after the Chinese Communist Revolution. The bifurcated structure of state (*guojia*) versus collective (*jiti*) work units is a legacy of this period.

9. Susan Blum (2001, and chap. 8 in this volume) discusses this phenomenon of modal classification of minority traits by Han.

10. The seven natural villages of Tiger Springs have both Chinese names (which are the same as those used prior to 1949) and Naxi names.

11. The application of class labels was common in Lijiang and throughout China's southwest in the land reform period, 1950–1953.

12. There were also, of course, a number of suicides during various Maoist period political movements among members of these families who succumbed to the relentless pressure. Potter and Potter (1990) have demonstrated the consequences of class labeling in the 1950s, detailing its psychological excesses.

13. I have argued elsewhere (White 1997, 1998, 2001) that basin Naxi have appropriated stated-framed minority nationality categories and discourses, strategically employing them in locally distinctive ways. This has been the case particularly with respect to how basin Naxi fashion gender identity, and it is observed in their relation to the state, to other Naxi and minorities, as well as to Han in the basin and larger Naxi area.

Chapter 8. Ethnic and Linguistic Diversity in Kunming

Research for this chapter was supported by the Committee on Scholarly Communication with the People's Republic of China. In Kunming, my host institution was Yunnan University, where I was housed by both the Department of Chinese, under Professor Li Zhaotong, and the Department of History, under Professor Lin Chaomin. I am grateful to both teachers for their guidance, although mistakes and shortcomings in the product of my research are my own responsibility. This chapter derives in part from my *Portraits of "Primitives"* (2001).

1. A fascinating book challenges the veracity of Marco Polo's claim to have visited the capital in China during the Yuan dynasty (1271–1368) (see Wood 1996).

2. *Backward* is used in the spirit of Chinese usage, whereby there is an absolute scale from *backward* to *advanced* or *modern,* measured by such things as new buildings, availability of indoor plumbing and electricity, types of conveyances, wide, paved streets, and so on.

3. Fruit is ideologically peripheral, being a snack food and not part of meals. People often eat enormous amounts of it. I am grateful to Stevan Harrell for refining my ideas on this point.

4. For a fascinating and relevant discussion of the use of statistics for the forging of modern Basque identity, see Urla (1993).

5. Although in this chapter I treat the construction of identity only in the PRC, many areas of similarity might be pointed out in Taiwan. PRC policies are in many ways a result of the Guomindang legacy (see Pye 1975; Dreyer 1976; Deal 1979), but the situation that the Guomindang faced in Taiwan was quite different from that on the Mainland. In Taiwan, the principal tension was between Han who migrated before the twentieth century, known (in Mandarin) as *benshengren* (natives), and those who arrived in 1949, the *waishengren* (outsiders). For a history of the 28 February incident, the most violent confrontation between the two groups, see Lai, Myers, and Wou (1991).

6. Minority languages must be standardized before a single script can be devised for them. This often involves arbitrarily selecting the dialect of one group, thus excluding others. For a discussion of how this process worked in parts of Africa, see Irvine (1996).

7. There is also evidence of growing prestige of non-Mandarin varieties, as the economic standing of areas where such languages are spoken increases. Erbaugh (1995) has written of this increasing power. In the summer of 1996, a conference on "written Taiwanese" (*taibun*) was held at the University of British Columbia.

8. These terms are used quite imprecisely in Kunming, by all but linguists. Just as English speakers use *accent* to describe linguistic differences generally, so do ordinary people tend to speak of, for example, *kouqiang* or *Baoshanqiang,* reserving *fangyan* for more technical discussions.

9. Glazer and Moynihan (1975, 8) pointed out that, in the 1970s in the United States, an increase in ethnic awareness was accompanied by a decrease in actual difference between ethnic groups. In the 1990s, ethnic awareness is accompanied by separatism and insistence on recovery of a putative "authentic" tradition, even if that tradition must be (re)constructed. See the description in Clifford (1988) of the "predicament of culture" wherein identity is lost but claimed nonetheless. I am grateful to Lucien Miller for this point. For consideration of the evidence as to whether cultural differences are being eradicated, see Hannerz (1992). There is some evidence that these differences may be growing, despite a belief that the world is becoming more homogeneous.

Chapter 9. The Construction of Chinese and Non-Chinese Identities

I gratefully acknowledge the useful comments of Tu Wei-ming, Wang Gungwu, Cho-yun Hsü, Mark Elvin, Wang Ling-chi, and other participants at the October 1990 conference, part of the Dialogue of Civilizations Project, at the East-West Center in Hawai'i.

1. This holiday, celebrated principally in Taiwan, commemorates the end of imperial China on 10 October 1911. [*Editors' note.*]

2. Many Chinese communities, for lack of an alternative Chinese word, still call themselves *huaqiao* to this day.

Chapter 10. The Secret History of the Hakkas

I thank Dick Kraus for innumerable critical suggestions and also Cynthia Brokaw, Ruth Dunnell, Sue Glover, Michael Nylan, and Zhan Kaidi. The National Endowment for the Humanities and the Center for Chinese Studies at the University of California, Berkeley, provided support.

1. Another three heroes are Hunan natives from the Xiang subethnic group of Han Chinese: Mao Zedong (Xiangtan county), Peng Dehuai (Xiangtan county), and Liu Shaoqi (Ningxiang county). The non-Hakka, non-Hunan heroes are Li Dazhao (Leting, Hebei), Qu Qiubai (Changzhou, Jiangsu), Zhou Enlai (Huai'an, Jiangsu), and Dong Biwu (Huang'an, Hubei).

2. Hakka sources also claim Yang Shangkun as a Hakka.

3. This villager also described how the British had used ethnicity to divide and conquer. Japanese imperialists manipulated Hakka-Cantonese animosities as well.

4. Luo ([1993] 1973, 15) cites a copy of a partial family tree supplied by Sun's older sister. But he also relies, bizarrely, on Sun's English monolingual biographer's romanization of Sun's ancestral village (Linebarger 1925, 37). Luo, unable to find anything corresponding to a "Kung Kun" on the East river, argues that Sun followed a traditional Hakka taboo on identifying one's ancestral village to outsiders and so referred to the village by a nickname. Yang (1988, 160) also claims Sun as a Hakka. Details on Sun come from Restarick (1931, 5), Schiffrin (1980, 22), Moser (1985, 247), and Schinz (1989, 369).

5. The southeast coast subsystem includes the Hakka homeland, including northeast Guangdong and western Fujian. The Lingnan mountain subsystem has Hakkas scattered throughout Guangdong. But they are especially concentrated in the northern uplands of the Lingnan mountains and the rockier coastal areas, including Hong Kong. The middle Yangzi subsystem includes Hakkas who live on the Fujian-Jiangxi border. In the upper Yangzi subsystem, Hakka settlements are southeast of Chongqing. In the northwest subsystem, Hakka settlements ring Chengdu and are scattered about the mountains on the Shaanxi border.

6. Until this century, Meixian was called Jiaying (Kiaying), and Changting was called Tingzhou. Hakkas are also called *newcomers* (*xin ren*) or *arrivals* (*lai ren*). They are often called *Cantonese,* especially in Taiwan, Hunan, and Sichuan. The Hakka dialect is also called *dirt Cantonese* (*tu Guangdonghua*), *newcomer talk* (*xin min hua*), or *rough border talk* (*ma jie hua*) (see Cui 1985, 10). Japanese imperialists referred to Hakkas as *Cantonese* even when writing ethnography or developing a Hakka writing system using kana. English readers may be further perplexed by references to the Hoklos, who are not Hakka at all but people of southern Fujian ancestry living in Guangdong. (*Hoklo* is the Cantonese pronunciation of *Fu lao,* from "Fujian" and *lao,* "fellow" [Blake 1981, 72].)

7. After the 1989 Beijing massacre, outraged Chongqing students who were fellow natives of Deng Xiaoping's home village rushed to the Deng family graveyard to dig up the graves. They found two military detachments already in place to arrest them (Chan and Unger 1991, 117).

8. Mandarin is the native language of 70 percent of Mainlanders and some 10 percent of Taiwanese. Some 9 percent of Mainlanders speak the Wu dialect of Shanghai and Zhejiang. About 5 percent speak Yue, called *Cantonese* in English, and 5 percent speak Xiang, native to most of Hunan. Mao Zedong retained his almost impenetrable Xiang accent to the end of his days. About 3 percent speak Gan, mostly within Jiangxi province. The Min dialects of Fujian are native to 2 percent. Northern Min is not mutually intelligible with the Southern Min spoken around Xiamen (Amoy) and by 80 percent of the Taiwanese. (See Norman 1988, 119–228; Ramsey 1987, 87–111; *Yuyan wenzi* 1988, 89–93, 112–115, 237–242, 292–297, 408–411, 421–423, 500–504; and Ramsey, chap. 4 in this volume.)

9. Arif Dirlik (personal communication, 18 September 1990) refers to Ming Chan's work on labor history (see, e.g., Chan 1981).

10. Capitals included Changting (Tingzhou) for Fujian, Ningdu for Jiangxi, Jianning for Fujian-Jiangxi, Huichang for Guangdong-Jiangxi, Hengfeng for northeastern Jiangxi, Lianhua for western Jiangxi, and Hongxin for the Hunan-Jiangxi border.

11. Others among the 11 Hakkas and probable Hakkas in the 105 top leaders for 1989 include Liu Ren, the second Beijing Party secretary; Zeng Xianlin, an engineer; Song Renqiong, who did underground work, followed Zhang Guotao on the Long March, later edited *Hong qi*, and chaired the Party's Central Organization Committee; Peng Peiyun, prominent in higher education and one of only two women above the *buzhang* minister level; and Cai Cheng, a security official.

12. This information was obtained when I visited the plant, and spoke with its manager, Liu Guifa, on 11 March 1989.

Part III. Social and Cultural Margins

Chapter 12. The Cut Sleeve Revisited

1. The "cut sleeve" (*duan xiu*) tradition stems from the Han emperor Ai (Aidi), who, rather than disturb his sleeping (male) partner, cut off his sleeve and thus started a courtly revolution in fashion signaling one's sexual preference.

2. This is a pseudonym for the interviewee, suggested by a mutual friend. Sadly, the subject of this report passed away in February 1991, of nephropathy and related complications. The article is dedicated to "G.I. Joe" posthumously.

3. Explaining the gap between official presumptions and actual sexual practices and lifestyles is the object of sexual ethnographic study. In qualitative interviewing, the ethnographer discerns the forces that shape the person's sex life, the kinds of relationships chosen, the rationales and decisions that are made and actions taken. In the political culture system that is China, these personal options are seldom negotiated outright, nor are they ever accommodated without tensions.

4. Ruan and Bullough (1989) give accounts of catamites (young boys who serve as sex partners for adult men) existing in the courts from the time of the "Yellow Emperor" (Huang Di, 2490–2413 B.C.E.) forward. Official dynastic histories show that, for example, in the Western Han dynasty alone, all ten male emperors either had homosexual lovers or accepted homosexuality. The controversy over whether Puyi, the "last emperor," was actually homosexual is well documented by Ch'en (1965), who leans toward accepting accounts of those close to Puyi that both before and after his political demise he engaged in homosexual acts.

5. As examples, several presenters at the First Sino-American Management of HIV Disease Symposium (Beijing, 7–8 November 1990) made statements about homosexuality while treating the broader topic of their papers:

> Zhu Qi (Associate Professor, National Health Education Institute, Beijing): "The root cause of AIDS's swift spread is unhealthy lifestyles, such as homosexuality, drug addiction, and nonmarital sexual relations." "The strong points of our health education are to arouse and intensify people's responsibility for personal sexual behavior . . . to condemn nonmarital sexual behavior and homosexuality . . . "

Wang Xiaodao (Vice Dean, Department of Medical Psychology, Beijing Medical University, Chair, Chinese Sex[ual] Science Committee): "Unrestrained and unnormal [sic] sex conducts (including homosexual, bisexual, illegal sex, multiple sex partners, commercial sex workers, and sex tours); drug taking; uncivilized and unhealthy lifestyle(s); are the social behavior bases that cause the prevalence of AIDS."

Yang Shangchi (Public Health Office, South Fujian Province): "AIDS is mainly transmitted by sexual intercourse, with the highest incident among sexual promiscuity such as illicit prostitutes, whore mongrels [sic], and homosexuals."

6. At most dance clubs, and particularly in those situated at hotels, guards are posted to ensure the appropriate behavior of dancers. Acting like Western "bouncers," these individuals will ensure that appropriate conduct is maintained by dancers; that the prescribed physical distance is kept between participants; that no rowdiness be allowed or alcoholic beverage brought in. In some clubs, provincial rules do not allow foreigners, except expatriate Chinese, to enter dance clubs; guards allegedly preserve the legal environment of clubs. In actuality, guards act more as figureheads and often look the other way when confronted with socially compromising situations.

7. Until 1992 foreign-exchange coupons or certificates (FEC) were legal tender for tourists but not allowed as mediums of exchange for Chinese themselves. Most side jobs in clubs, such as those of singers, are paid in FEC as an added bonus to the worker. FEC are the legal tender in tourist shops and in many cases command a percentage higher exchange rate than "people's money" (renminbi) or the yuan. In the early 1990s, for example, renminbi commanded a 6:1 exchange with the U.S. dollar, while the FEC was valued at 8:1. To be paid in FEC was considered a sign of cachet, a status symbol itself.

8. The poetic euphemism split peaches (fentao) has a long-standing tradition of representing homosexual love. Begun during the Zhou dynasty (Hinsch 1990), it now represents sharing "delicious" love or sharing a sexual moment. Aptly, G.I. Joe applies this "sharing of moments" to the impersonal but highly charged erotosexual interactions of some who frequent toilets.

9. TCM, or traditional Chinese medicine, is based on interventions that use herbal medicines. Diagnoses are undertaken from the point of view of numeral pathology, febrile or consumptive diseases. (All are diagnostic categories under TCM. In addition, TCM also uses acupuncture, acupressure, and other traditionally based mediations.)

Chapter 14. The Floating Population in the Cities

I acknowledge the Committee on Scholarly Communication with the People's Republic of China and the United States Information Agency for support that made possible two research trips to China (one to Harbin in July 1991 and one to Guangzhou, Nanjing, Wuhan, and Tianjin in May and June 1992). Much of the information in this chapter comes from material collected during those visits. I also wish to thank the Social Science Academies of Heilongjiang, Guangdong, Wuhan, and Tianjin, especially Zhou Lu, Hao Maishou, and Huang Hongyun; the Wuhan City Foreign Affairs Office, especially Yin Guilan; the Johns Hopkins–Nanjing University Center for Chinese and American Studies; and unaffiliated friends who helped me in Wuhan and Nanjing, including (but not limited to) Bernadine Chee, Lu Gang, Lu An, and Shen Yingquan. I was a research associate at the East Asian Institute at Columbia University when I prepared the first draft of this essay, and I appreciate technical assistance I received there and John Smollen's photocopying services. Barry Naughton's and Rick Baum's editorial suggestions were also very useful.

1. These numbers derive from sample surveys that count as members of the floating population anyone away from home on the day on which and at the time at which the survey was conducted. The majority of the movers are probably moving within the countryside and to medium and small cities and towns. This chapter, by contrast, concentrates on their lives in the big cities, where they often account for one-fifth to one-fourth of the total population.

2. Li and Hu (1991, 119) present this data. There is, however, some notable regional variation in this regard, even among the major metropolises. On p. 155 of their book the figures for these categories among Shanghai's transients are, respectively, 43.9, 24.2, and 11.1 percent; on p. 167 it is stated that in Wuhan those with junior high school and primary school education together represent 67 percent while illiterates amount to 9.3 percent; and in Guangzhou 19.67 percent have gone to primary school, 68.7 percent to either junior or senior high school, and only 2.96 percent are illiterate.

3. According to one source, 12 million peasants work in the cities the year around. If this is true, there must be tens of millions of others coming and going. This is reported in FBIS (1991, 65), which is quoting an article in the Shanghai journal *Shehui* (Society). Gu (1990, 8) claims that in the late 1980s more than 700,000 peasant workers were permanently living in Beijing, of whom 650,000 were laboring, 60,000 were in commercial work, and 20,000 were nursemaids.

4. In cities to the far north, such as Harbin, or in the far west, such as Urumqi, there is a great deal of what has been termed *migratory bird* migration. I learned about this in interviews in Harbin in July 1991 and in Yuan and Tang (1990). See Sha (1990, 10–12); and "Rural Workers Thrive" (1991), which explains how peasants return to the countryside in the agricultural busy season.

On the other hand, according to Rutkowski (1991, 10), one-third stay in the cities they have reached for more than one year. Li and Hu (1991, 9) cite an average figure across eight cities of 28.67 percent on this. As early as 1985 scholars writing about Shanghai maintained that seasonality was decreasing among floaters, as "the slack season [for migration] is no longer slack and the busy season is busier" (Zheng et al. 1985, 4). Also, a writer on Beijing recently said that more and more are tending toward a longer stay there (*China Daily,* 18 June 1992, 3).

5. Nelson (1976, 727) contains a table showing ratios of males to females in major cities of Latin America, Africa, and South and East Asia. In Santiago, Bogotá, Mexico City, Lima, and Caracas males numbered less than 50 percent of migrants; in Nairobi, Tunis, and Cairo the proportion was between 50 and 60 percent; and only in Bombay and Calcutta did it rise to between 66 and 75 percent in the 1960s. See also Lees (1979, 48), which states that the sex ratio was unbalanced among Irish immigrants into London in the late nineteenth century but on p. 50 mentions that family groups constituted a large segment of the migrants.

6. The Chinese government has recently admitted to the presence of 4 million child laborers, according to *Zhengming* (Contend) (Hong Kong) 171 (January 1992): 15–16. A circular issued by the Ministry of Labor in November 1991 even

revealed that the children involved were sometimes younger than twelve, worked up to fourteen hours a day, and were paid just half the adult wage (ibid.).

7. Siu (1990, 63) lists the same marks of "foreignness" in a small southeastern China town.

8. According to Kirkby (1985, 53 n. 62), "Migrants to other areas are unable to speak the local dialect even after decades."

9. According to Zeng (1988, 24–25), there are gangs or factions (*bang, pai*) among trash collectors, from Zhejiang, Subei (North Jiangsu), Anhui, and Shandong, each with their own leaders. The leaders, unlike their subordinate gang members, do not live in the trash heaps.

10. In particular, the migrant committed to the city will put his or her savings into constructing an urban future, may try to upgrade his or her city dwelling, and may form or join associations that fight to satisfy urban needs.

11. Rutkowski (1991, ii) puts forward the notion of "two different and increasingly separated pools of floaters: those who stay long, enter the labor market and in terms of way of life become similar to permanent urban residents with a *hukou,* and those who move for various purposes for a short time, usually without changing their labor market status." See also Kirkby (1985, 32), who speaks of the transients as "part settled and part floating." See also Woon (1991, 31), who states, "It is the capitalistic entrepreneurs, not the exploited proletarians, who roam in search of opportunity."

12. Although Woon (1991) claims that it is the wealthy, successful migrants who are on the move, untold ranks of the beggars and stragglers remain at large in the country; Tang and Chen (1989, 19) attest to ten thousand persons' collecting garbage in Shanghai. Also McGregor (1991, 5) maintains that "up to three million peasants roam the country in search of work." Thanks to June Dreyer for sending me this last article.

13. Cornelius (1974), Perlman (1976, 187, 243), DeWind, Seidl, and Shenk (1979), and West and Moore (1989, 5), among many others, speak of the preference for either quiescence or pursuing legitimate channels in making demands among those so placed.

14. As in all other societies where numbers of outsiders are climbing, Chinese authorities have found that over a third of the criminal cases, and up to 40 percent of the arrests, especially in the big cases, involve migrants. Rutkowski (1991, vii) was told that 10 percent of all the migrants were arrested for criminal acts in 1987, a share ten times higher than that among permanent workers. As always, one must question such figures since the propensity of the police to target and blame outsiders must be high. I discuss this in Solinger (1993).

15. The benefits afforded by the possession of an urban *hukou* are discussed in *Nongmin ribao* (Peasant daily), 23 November 1988, 3, and 11 May 1989. Thanks to Tom Bernstein for showing me these articles. There is also a discussion of the deprivations experienced by those lacking the urban *hukou* (the inability to receive education, to gain employment, to receive health care, to participate in elections, to serve in the army, or to marry, plus ineligibility for state-allocated housing and grain) in Zhang (1988, 8).

16. Interview with a scholar on 8 June 1992. Similarly, on 16 June, an official from the city's Labor Bureau told me, "Tianjin people wouldn't look for a man without a *hukou* to marry." On the other hand, many scholars interviewed in Guangzhou thought good-looking peasant women had a pretty good chance of

marrying a local man in the growing middle-sized, export-oriented, foreign-invested Pearl river delta cities and sometimes in Guangzhou as well. In general, Guangzhou seems more open to allowing outsiders to assimilate than did the other cities I visited.

17. See, for example, Wang, Wu, and Jiang (1990, 2–3). I was also told about this problem in an interview in Harbin with a social science researcher on 25 July 1991.

18. Li and Hu (1991, 17) found that 57.45 percent of the floaters of Beijing lived in the cities near suburbs; for Shanghai the figure was 55.66 percent. Some of these must be in peasant homes, some squatting.

19. Huang, Liu, and Peng (1988, 16) list some of these less savory sites. I spoke with a young girl in Nanjing working in a restaurant seventeen hours a day and sleeping on a chair there at night; other restaurant workers I met in Wuhan's outskirts slept on their restaurant's second story, on the floor.

20. Given the growing problem of unemployment ("waiting for employment") among urban youths, however, it is no longer strictly accurate to claim that all those with urban registrations receive all the benefits that classification once provided. When state-owned enterprises have laid off all unnecessary workers, the problems for urban residents will be compounded.

21. This group has yet one more distinction: this is the difference between those registered as temporary urban dwellers (they hold a *zhanzhusheng,* or temporary living certificate) and those who dare to brave the odds and live unprotected without any proper legal label at all. This last group verges on the brink of illegality since its members "violate regulations" (*bu fuhe guiding*) and so are the most vulnerable of all.

Chapter 15. The Politics of Popular Music in Post-Tiananmen China

1. By *popular music,* I indicate music that is disseminated through the mass media, is sold as a commodity, and has its roots in the acculturation of Western musical forms.

2. The student leader Wuer Kaixi claims that Cui Jian's influence on the students participating in the movement far outstripped that of political dissidents like Fang Lizhi ("Chinese Writers under Fire" 1989, 15).

3. The following conclusions are based on a series of more than twenty interviews I conducted with participants in the Beijing rock scene in the summer of 1990.

4. Wei Hua, lead singer of Breathing (Huxi yuedui), is notable for the fact that she became a rock singer after having been fired from her post as an English-language newscaster at CCTV after having reported sympathetically on the student movement in 1989. Lyrics by Wei Hua and Gao Qi, included on Wei Hua, *Taiyang sheng* (The sun rises), RCA/BMG Pacific 8-280048 (1990). For more examples of rock lyrics, see Jones (1992, 155–163).

5. By *youth culture,* I indicate the sensibilities and leisure patterns (consumption of music, literature, etc.) of young people who have not distanced themselves from the mainstream in terms of their institutional affiliations, lifestyles, or aspirations. *Subculture* is distinct from *youth culture* in that its participants have largely divorced themselves from the mainstream. See Gold (1989).

6. *Liumang* literally means "hoodlum" but is used by Geremie Barmé as a kind of rubric for the culture of China's urban, bohemian fringe (artists, unem-

ployed youth, private entrepreneurs, rebellious students, etc.). See Barmé (1992c).

7. *River Elegy* included footage of the epochal 4 May 1919 student movement as well as shots of the student demonstrations for democracy that swept across many major Chinese cities in the winter of 1986–1987. In addition, the film included a short segment on the use of hunger strikes as a political weapon—a method that, before Tiananmen, had never been employed by activists in China.

8. He Yong's most notorious song, "Garbage Dump" ("Laji chang") likens Chinese culture to a garbage dump and a slaughterhouse and urges listeners to "tear it down!" Cui Jian performed a song called "Opportunists" ("Toujifenzi") that was written on the occasion of the outbreak of the student movement and urges young people to "show our strength" and "voice our desires." Interestingly, one English-language article quotes a source suggesting that Cui Jian was "used as a pawn by student leaders" and abruptly cut short his performance at Tiananmen because he was disgusted "by all the bullshit that was going down" (Ebert 1991).

9. "Guoji ge," as performed by the China Broadcast Arts Troupe Symphony Orchestra, on *Zhonghua renmin gongheguo guoge, guoji ge* (The national anthem of the People's Republic of China and the Internationale) (Zhongguo changpian gongsi HL-314, 1984).

10. This is seemingly not an isolated trend but a consciously adopted marketing policy on the part of Rock Records. A recent compilation of Chinese rock—intended primarily for the Taiwan market—capitalizes on nativist images by billing itself as *China Fire* and featuring guitar-wielding Chinese swordsmen in traditional livery galloping across the cover.

11. From Ai Jing, "Wode 1997" (My 1997), lyrics by Ai Jing, music by Ai Jing and Eddie Ramdriampionana (Taipei: Rock Records RD 1187, 1992).

Chapter 16. Magic, Science, and Qigong in Contemporary China

1. The concept of *qi* is central, not only to the practice of *qigong,* but also to traditional Chinese medicine and all the traditional Chinese sciences. But it often proves quite slippery to Western readers and, as this chapter will demonstrate, even to modern-day Chinese. In his discussion of this concept, Nathan Sivin (1987, 47) points out that the complementarity of distinct matter and energy in modern physics should not be confused with *qi* as an energetic entity. The energy of *qi* can never be divorced from its material substrate. Manfred Porkert (1974, 168) has formulated the most concise definition: *qi* is both "'configurational energy'—i.e., energy of a definite direction in space, of a definite arrangement, quality, or structure—and 'energetic configuration.'"

2. Like the practice itself, definitions of *qigong* are highly contentious and politically charged. More commonly seen examples can be found in Zhang and Chang (1989) and Song (1989, 60).

3. During the Republican era, the state viewed TCM as an obstacle to the development of a modern medical system and passed legislation to abolish it in 1929. This legislation was soon overturned in the wake of massive protests by TCM practitioners, although official prejudice persisted. Today, many TCM physicians believe that Mao's statement of support in 1958—"traditional Chinese medicine is a great treasure"—marked an important turning point in official attitudes (see Farquhar 1993; and Sivin 1987).

4. There are countless styles of *qigong* practiced today in China, many of which might not fit neatly into this division of preventive and curative *qigong*. Indeed, the two approaches may comfortably coexist in the same style of *qigong* practice, as some students pursue more prosaic health goals while others seeks to cultivate more extraordinary powers. There are also other schools of *qigong*, such as "hard" (*ying*) *qigong* found in martial arts, which do not claim to have therapeutic benefits. Nonetheless, the somewhat artificial division between preventive and curative *qigong* serves to illustrate the discursive strategies so important to *qigong* practice.

5. David Eisenberg—a graduate of Harvard Medical School—comments more extensively on his observations of *qigong* practitioners in his *Encounters with Qi* (1985). Today, he is a leader in the field of alternative medicine research in the United States.

6. Although first published in 1991, this book is now in its fourth edition, with over 250,000 copies published. It has also been serialized in its entirety in two different newspapers.

7. *Jing, qi,* and *shen* are foundational concepts in TCM. In the basic theory textbook now used in institutes of TCM, the first chapter is devoted to *jing, qi, shen* theory.

8. Xiong Jie, a participant in the 1980 *Ziran zazhi* conference, told me: "Why should I still perform when no one cares any more?"

9. Although *qigong* information therapy devices never developed into important commodities, the invention of similar devices has spawned the emergence of some of China's largest private enterprises. Today, Zhoulin Biospectrum, which produces devices that innocently look like infrared space heaters but in fact are supposed to mimic precisely the spectrum of electromagnetic waves emitted by the body, ranks as one of China's top twenty-five medical equipment producers.

10. It is interesting to note, however, that Zhang et al. (1991) do not challenge the premise of these experiments—the notion that external *qi* has a material basis—perhaps because of their own personal commitments to Marxist historical materialism. According to classic understandings of *qi*, the energy of *qi* is always embedded in its material substrate and should not be convertible into other energetic forms (electromagnetic waves etc.) independent of that substrate.

11. This experiment has now been translated into English and can be viewed at the following website: http://www.interlog.com/~yuan/yanwat.html.

Chapter 17. The Spirit of Reform

Funding for the fieldwork on which this article is based was supplied by a grant from the Department of Anthropology, Johns Hopkins University. An earlier version of this work was presented at the April 1994 Association for Asian Studies meeting, and it has benefited from comments by Gillian Feeley-Harnik, Lian Shaoming, Emily Martin, Melissa Wright, and three anonymous *positions* reviewers.

1. Wulin, other place-names, and all personal names are fictitious. I conducted ethnographic fieldwork in this rural county west of Beijing from 1989 to 1991. I was initially assigned to a collective nursery by the administrators who "oversaw" my research, but I soon began living and working in three villages nearby. The people with whom I worked asked that I maintain their own and their home's anonymity. Wulin is a predominantly vegetable-producing former

commune. Though most of the land was contracted out to individual cultivators, some collective production was reinstituted in the mid-1980s, ostensibly to ensure supplies to capital markets. A number of collective industries launched over the past twenty years have diversified the local economy and absorbed some of the surplus labor.

2. For discussions of the ambiguity surrounding official policy on and definitions of *mixin*, see Feuchtwang and Wang (1991), MacInnis (1989), and Anagnost (1994). The declared position of the Chinese government, according to Feuchtwang and Wang, is that *mixin* involves "an evil power that makes people attribute their fate to 'supernatural and mysterious forces' instead of to the Party's leadership and hence is regarded as something running counter to the general principles laid down in the PRC's Constitutional Law. . . . Nonetheless the focus of legal discussion in fact is not on the 'ignorant' and 'disorganized' aspects of popular religion, but rather the organized aspects of popular ritual activities which may lead popular ritual to run out of the control of official administrative and security organizations. . . . In the PRC [People's Republic of China] Criminal Law (1979) some popular religious practices are prohibited on the grounds that . . . people may use them to 'make rumors' (*zao yao*) and 'cheat people for money and property' (*zaqu qiancai*)" (1991, 262). *Mixin*, Anagnost argues, is never fixed and serves as a catch-all "other" against which the modern and/or scientific can be presented.

3. Here we see *mixin* being used in the sense the Party uses it, to describe something false or "backward"; what people in Wulin believe in they say is "real" (*zhende*), and they do not name it *mixin*.

4. The translation of *nongmin* is peasant or peasantry. Sometimes *farmer* is used, but the latter conveys a sense of land ownership to Western readers that is not relevant to socialist (or in many cases presocialist) Chinese. I am not using *peasant* either; there is an enormous anthropological literature surrounding the definition and deployment of the term *peasant*. To avoid the analytic baggage not pertinent here, I use the word people used with me: *nongmin*.

5. For a detailed discussion of *hukou*, see Potter (1983).

6. Animal spirits are found throughout China, geographically and historically. Literary descriptions of the spirits include Pu Songling's well-known *Liao zhai* (Strange tales). For Song dynasty accounts of officials' battles with spirits and gods, see Boltz (1993). In the 1940s, Li Wei-tzu conducted ethnographic research on the spirits in Wulin and several other counties encircling Beijing. His is an invaluable source, and I thank Emily Martin for bringing it to my attention. See Li (1948).

7. See n. 3 above.

8. A fox possessed a woman, causing her arm to grow numb. A healer negotiating with the fox to release the woman found that it was working with the ghost of the woman's deceased first husband. The ghost was angry because the woman was giving money to her second husband's children, who, he was sure, would not take care of her when she grew old.

9. The critical differences between animal spirit and ghost possessions are beyond the scope of this essay. For a discussion that includes both types of possession, see Boltz (1993).

10. According to people of Wulin, the doctors in the county clinic have only recently begun to admit that a patient has a spirit illness that requires a specialist healer.

11. None of the healers I met or was told about relied on healing as a sole source of income. All had full-time jobs in factories or agricultural collectives. Du was an accountant in a local factory.

12. Du told me his uncle had been promised 3,000 yuan by a man who sought him as a last resort to cure his cancer. Following treatment by Du's uncle, who had found a vengeful snake causing the illness, tests at the clinic certified that the man had recovered. "The man gave my uncle about 200 yuan, which naturally made him pretty angry; so he called the snake back, and the man died a month later," explained Du.

13. *Guanxi* is often used to describe corrupt exchanges or the use of a personal tie to gain some privilege or position. It also refers to relations between friends, relatives, and business and political associates for which no taint of corruption is implied, but such relations are considered a legitimate basis for exchanging favors, services, and privileges.

14. Factory work was considered superior by a majority of Wulin residents because it is cleaner, is less tiring, and provides a steadier and potentially larger income. Profitable factories distributed large sums (from 3,000 to 6,000 yuan in 1990) at the graded year-end distribution of collective profits. A growing number of people, particularly younger people with middle school educations, are finding jobs in county factories, but lack of *guanxi* forecloses higher-paid managerial positions and confines them to low-paying positions.

15. Articles in the Chinese press (e.g., "Zhichi dang de jiben luxian" 1990) document cases of officials convicted of embezzlement or extortion. Rocca (1993) and Yang (1989) offer anthropological analyses of the pervasiveness of corruption at all levels of Chinese society. As I write this article in 1995, Jiang Zemin is launching a new and vigorous battle against corruption, although it is believed to be a strategy of removing opposition to his claim to post-Deng power.

16. People throughout China, including those in Wulin, had difficulty obtaining even coarse grains during the famines. Estimates of the number of starvation victims climb into the hundreds of thousands, if not millions. The fact that Mao's own policy blunders during the Great Leap Forward were a major contributor to the famines was only hinted at by people in Wulin. They laid the blame on the Soviets, explaining that, after relations between the two nations deteriorated, the Soviets demanded that China repay the debts incurred from aid given throughout the 1950s. A lack of hard currency forced the Chinese to meet these demands with food, which the famine-stricken country could ill afford to give away. Rapacious Soviets serve as another historical foil against which Mao's righteousness is imaged.

17. Stuart Schram notes that in Mao's early writings his criteria for the quintessential Communist Party member were primarily concerned with moral qualities such as loyalty, a spirit of sacrifice and hard work, and the disparagement of riches (Schram 1984). Susan Shirk argues that Mao attempted to consolidate state control in the postrevolutionary period by instituting a "virtuocracy," believing "the responsibility of the Communist Party was to lead people toward virtue" (Shirk 1984, 56).

18. Yue Fei was a Song dynasty military commander who fought to restore the empire after defeat by the Jin forced the Song to the south. He was executed by the Song ruler chosen to replace the emperor captured by the Jin for fear his military might would threaten the successor's power. He is a hero of socialist

China; tales of his life, his patriotism, and the injustice of his death were common fare in the media and at schools.

19. Only Zhou Enlai received a comparable appraisal. He was linked to Mao as a model of legitimate authority and in discussions of the past that often began with the phrase "Zhuzi he zongli zai de shihou . . ." (In the time of the chairman and premier . . .).

20. In discussing Foucault's critique of historicism, Robert Young offers an apt description of the way the historical memory of the *nongmin* "enables the expropriation and control of the past according to the perspective and truth of the present" (1990, 80).

21. David Arkush's work on rural proverbs and folk operas shows the historical pervasiveness of the idea that material reward must be linked and even subsumed to hard work and integrity. See Arkush (1984, 1990). Cynthia Brokaw shows these links to have been crucial to a neo-Confucian rebellion against a late Ming deterioration of social hierarchies and their displacement by categories defined by merchants' wealth. See Brokaw (1991).

Bibliography

Aberle, David. 1982. The Navaho singer's "fee": Payment or prestation? In *Studies in southwestern ethnolinguistics,* ed. Dell Hymes and William Bittle. The Hague: Mouton.

Ahern, Emily Martin. 1981. *Chinese ritual and politics.* Cambridge: Cambridge University Press.

Alley, Rewi. 1977. Meixian, the great Hakka center. *Eastern Horizon* 16, no. 5: 16–30.

———. 1980. Guang'an, birthplace of Deng Xiaoping. *Eastern Horizon* 19, no. 8:7–13.

Anagnost, Ann. 1989. Prosperity and counterprosperity: The moral discourse on wealth in post-Mao China. In *Marxism and the Chinese experience: Issues in contemporary Chinese socialism,* ed. Arif Dirlik and Maurice Meisner. Armonk, N.Y.: M. E. Sharpe.

———. 1994. The politics of ritual displacement. In *Asian visions of authority: Religion and the modern states of East and Southeast Asia,* ed. Charles F. Keyes, Laurel Kendall, and Helen Hardacre. Honolulu: University of Hawai'i Press.

———. 1997. *National past-times: Narrative, representation, and power in modern China.* Durham, N.C.: Duke University Press.

Anderson, Benedict. [1989] 1991. *Imagined communities: Reflections on the origin and spread of nationalism.* Rev. ed. London: Verso.

Andrew, G. Findlay. 1921. *The crescent in north-west China.* London: China Inland Mission.

Anthems of defeat: Crackdown in Hunan province, 1989–1992. 1992. New York: Asia Watch.

Arkush, David. 1984. If man works hard the land will not be lazy: Entrepreneurial values in north China peasant proverbs. *Modern China* 10:461–480.

———. 1990. The moral world of Hebei village opera. In *Ideas across cultures: Essays on Chinese thought in honor of Benjamin I. Schwartz,* ed. Paul A. Cohen and Merle Goldman. Cambridge, Mass.: Harvard University, Council on East Asian Studies.

Armijo-Hussein, Jacqueline. 1989. The sinicization and Confucianization in Chinese and Western historiography of a Muslim from Bukhara serving under the Mongols in China. In *The legacy of Islam in China: An international symposium in memory of Joseph F. Fletcher,* ed. Dru C. Gladney. Cambridge, Mass.: The Center.

Averill, Stephen C. 1983. The shed people and the opening of the Yangzi highlands. *Modern China* 9, no. 1: 84–126.

———. 1987. Party, society, and local elite in the Jiangxi Communist movement. *Journal of Asian Studies* 46, no. 2: 279–303.

Baixing (Hong Kong). 1 March 1992. Translated in *Inside China Mainland*, vol. 14, no. 5 (May 1992).

Banister, Judith. 1987. *China's changing population*. Stanford, Calif.: Stanford University Press.

Barmé, Geremie. 1992a. The greying of Chinese culture. In *China Review, 1992*, ed. Kuan Hsin-chi and Maurice Brosseau. Hong Kong: Chinese University Press.

———. 1992b. Official bad boys or true rebels? *Human Rights Tribune*, vol. 3, no. 4.

———. 1992c. Wang Shuo and *liumang* ("hooligan") culture. *Australian Journal of Chinese Affairs*, no. 28 (July): 23–64.

Barmé, Geremie, and Linda Jaivin, eds. 1992. *New ghosts, old dreams*. New York: Random House.

Barmé, Geremie, and Sang Ye. 1997. The great firewall of China. *Wired* 5, no. 6 (June): 138–151, 182.

Barnett, A. Doak. 1993. *China's far west: Four decades of change*. Boulder, Colo.: Westview.

Barth, Fredrik. 1969. Introduction to *Ethnic groups and boundaries: The social organization of cultural difference*, ed. Fredrik Barth. Boston: Little, Brown.

Befu, Harumi, ed. 1993. *Cultural nationalism in East Asia: Representation and identity*. Berkeley: University of California, Berkeley, Institute of East Asian Studies.

Bell, A. P., and M. S. Weinberg. 1978. *Homosexualities*. New York: Simon & Schuster.

Bennett, Gordon A., and Ronald N. Montaperto. 1972. *Red Guard: The political biography of Dai Hsiao-Ai*. Garden City, N.Y.: Doubleday.

Benton, Gregor B. 1989. Communist guerrilla bases in southeast China after the start of the Long March. In *Single sparks: China's rural revolutions*, ed. Kathleen Hartford and Steven M. Goldstein. Armonk, N.Y.: M. E. Sharpe.

Berninghausen, John, and Ted Huters. 1976. The development of revolutionary literature in China. *Bulletin of Concerned Asian Scholars* 8, no. 1 (January–March): 2–12.

Bernstein, Richard, and Ross H. Munro. 1997. *The coming conflict with China*. New York: Knopf.

Blake, C. Fred. 1981. *Ethnic groups and social change in a Chinese market town*. Honolulu: University of Hawai'i Press.

Blum, Susan D. 1992. Ethnic diversity in southwest China: Perceptions of self and other. *Ethnic Groups* 9:267–279.

———. 1994. Han and the Chinese other: The language of identity and difference in southwest China. Ph.D. diss., University of Michigan, Department of Anthropology.

———. 1998. Pearls on the string of the Chinese nation: Pronouns, plurals, and prototypes in talk about identities. *Michigan Discussions in Anthropology* 13:207–237.

———. 2001. *Portraits of "primitives": Ordering human kinds in the Chinese nation*. Lanham, Md.: Rowman & Littlefield.

Bockman, Harald. 1987. Naxi studies in China: A research report. University of Oslo, Norway. Typescript.

Bodman, Richard W., and Pin P. Wan, eds. and trans. 1991. *Deathsong of the river: A reader's guide to the Chinese TV series "Heshang."* Ithaca, N.Y.: Cornell University, East Asia Program.

Boltz, Judith Magee. 1993. Not by the seal of office alone: New weapons in battles with the supernatural. In *Religion and society in T'ang and Sung China,* ed. Patricia B. Ebrey and Peter N. Gregory. Honolulu: University of Hawai'i Press.

Boorman, Howard, and Richard C. Howard, eds. 1967. *Biographical dictionary of republican China.* New York: Columbia University Press.

Bourdieu, Pierre. 1982. *Ce que parler veut dire.* Paris: Fayard.

Bourdieu, Pierre, and Jean-Claude Passeron. [1970] 1990. *Reproduction in education, society, and culture.* Translated by Richard Nice. London: Sage.

Brace, Tim. 1991. Popular music in contemporary Beijing: Modernism and cultural identity. *Asian Music* 22, no. 2 (spring/summer): 43–66.

Bradley, David. 1987. Language planning for China's minorities: The Yi Branch. In *Pacific linguistics, C-100, a world of language: Papers presented to Professor S. A. Wurm on his 65th birthday,* ed. Donald C. Laycock and Werner Winter, 81–89. Canberra: Australian National University, Research School of Pacific Studies.

Brake, Michael. 1985. *Comparative youth culture: The sociology of youth culture and youth subcultures in America, Britain, and Canada.* London: Routledge & Kegan Paul.

Brokaw, Cynthia. 1991. *The ledgers of merit and demerit.* Princeton, N.J.: Princeton University Press.

Butterfield, Fox. 1982. *China: Alive in the bitter sea.* New York: Bantam/*New York Times* Books.

Cable, Mildred, with Francesca French. [1942] 1987. *The Gobi desert.* Reprint. Boston: Beacon.

Caimao Jingji. 11 March 1990. Translated in Joint Publication Research Services CAR 90 049, 11 July 1990.

Cen Kailun. 1988. *Xingfu hua* (Flower of happiness). Wuhan: Changjiang Wenyi chubanshe.

Chan, Anita, and Jonathan Unger. 1991. Voices from the protest movement, Chongqing, Sichuan. In *Pro-democracy protests in China: Reports from the provinces,* ed. Jonathan Unger. Armonk, N.Y.: M. E. Sharpe.

Chan, Ming K. 1981. *Historiography of the Chinese labor movement, 1895–1949: A critical survey and bibliography of selected Chinese source materials at the Hoover Institution.* Stanford, Calif.: Hoover Institution Press.

Chang, K. C. 1977. Introduction to *Food in Chinese culture: Anthropological and historical perspectives,* ed. K. C. Chang, 3–21. New Haven, Conn.: Yale University Press.

Chang Kuo-t'ao [Zhang Guotao]. 1971. *The rise of the Chinese Communist Party, 1921–1927.* Lawrence: University of Kansas Press.

Chao, Emily. 1990. Suicide, ritual, and gender transformation among the Naxi. *Michigan Discussions in Anthropology* 9:61–74.

———. 1995. Depictions of difference: History, gender, ritual, and state discourse among the Naxi of southwest China. Ph.D. diss., University of Michigan, Department of Anthropology.

———. 1996. Hegemony, agency, and re-presenting the past: The invention of Dongba culture among the Naxi of southwest China. In *Negotiating ethnicities in China and Taiwan,* ed. Melissa J. Brown, 208–239. Berkeley: University of California, Center for Chinese Studies and Institute of East Asian Studies.

Chao, Emily, and Sydney D. White. 1990. Saving sisterhoods: Naxi *huo cuo*. Paper presented at the annual meeting of the American Anthropological Association, December 1990, New Orleans.

Chen Changfeng. 1958. With Chairman Mao on the Long March. In *Stories of the Long March*, ed. Liu Po-ch'eng et al. Peking: Foreign Languages Press.

———. [1959] 1972. *On the Long March with Chairman Mao*. Peking: Foreign Languages Press.

Ch'en, J. 1965. The last emperor of China. *Bulletin of the School of Oriental and African Studies* 28, no. 3: 336–355.

Chen, Kuiyuan. 1991. Study Marxist nationality theory and correctly understand national issues in the new period. *Shijian,* 1 October. Translated in Joint Publication Research Services CAR 92 021, 16 April 1992.

Cheng Tiejun. 1988. Xibu zai yimin (There is a migration to the West). Ph.D. diss., State University of New York at Binghamton, Sociology Department.

Ch'i, Hsi-sheng. 1991. *Politics of disillusionment.* Armonk, N.Y.: M. E. Sharpe.

Chiang, William W. 1995. *"We two know the script; we have become good friends": Linguistic and social aspects of the women's script literacy in southern Hunan, China.* Lanham, Md.: University Press of America.

China Islamic Association [Zhongguo Yisilanjiao Xiehui]. 1981. *The religious life of Chinese Muslims.* Beijing: Foreign Languages Press.

China Rocks: The long march of Cui Jian. 1991. Directed by Greg Lanning. BBC-TV.

Chinese oil workers in Iraq. 1986. *Beijing Review* 12:37.

Chinese writers under fire: The struggle for human rights in China. 1989. *PEN American Center Newsletter,* no. 70 (December).

Ci hai (Sea of words). 1979. 2 vols. Shanghai: Shanghai cishu chubanshe.

Clifford, James. 1988. *The predicament of culture: Twentieth-century ethnography, literature, and art.* Cambridge, Mass.: Harvard University Press.

Cohen, Anthony P. 1993. *Self consciousness: An alternative anthropology of identity.* London: Routledge.

Cohen, Myron L. 1968. The Hakka or guest people: Dialect as a sociocultural variable in southeastern China. *Ethnohistory* 15, no. 3:237–292.

———. 1991. Being Chinese: The peripheralization of traditional identity. *Daedalus* 120, no. 2 (spring): 113–134.

Cohen, Robin. 1987. *The new helots: Migrants in the international division of labor.* Aldershot: Avebury.

Concise English-Chinese Chinese-English dictionary. 1990. Beijing: Commercial Press.

Conner, Walker. 1984. *The national question in Marxist-Leninist theory and strategy.* Princeton, N.J.: Princeton University Press.

Constable, Nicole. 1994. *Christian souls and Chinese spirits: A Hakka community in Hong Kong.* Berkeley and Los Angeles: University of California Press.

———. ed. 1996. *Guest people: Hakka identity in China and abroad.* Seattle: University of Washington Press.

Cornelius, Wayne. 1974. Urbanization and political demand making: Political participation among the migrant poor in Latin American cities. *American Political Science Review* 68, no. 2:1125–1146.

Crossley, Pamela Kyle. 1990. *Orphan warriors: Three Manchu generations and the end of the Qing world.* Princeton, N.J.: Princeton University Press.

Cui Rongchang. 1985. Sichuan fangyan de biandiao xianxiang (The making of the Sichuan dialects). *Fangyan* (Chinese dialects), vol. 1.

Das Gupta, Jyotirindra. 1975. Ethnicity, language demands, and national development in India. In *Ethnicity: Theory and experience,* ed. Nathan Glazer and Daniel P. Moynihan, with Corinne Saposs Schelling, 466–488. Cambridge, Mass.: Harvard University Press

Dautcher, Jay. 2000. Protests, popular culture, and the politics of religion on China's western frontier. In *China beyond the headlines,* ed. Timothy B. Weston and Lionel M. Jensen, 273–294. Lanham, Md.: Rowman & Littlefield.

Davis, Edward L. 2001. *Society and the supernatural in Song China.* Honolulu: University of Hawai'i Press.

Deal, David M. 1979. Policy toward ethnic minorities in southwest China, 1927–1965. In *Nationalism and the crises of ethnic minorities in Asia* (Contributions in Sociology, no. 34), ed. Tai S. Kang, 33–40. Westport, Conn.: Greenwood.

Dean, Kenneth. 1993. *Taoist ritual and popular cults of southeast China.* Princeton, N.J.: Princeton University Press.

De Crespigny, R. R. C. 1991. Patterns of nature and man. In *The Chinese: Adapting the past, facing the future,* ed. Robert F. Dernberger, Kenneth J. DeWoskin, Steven M. Goldstein, Rhoads Murphey, and Martin K. Whyte, 114–123. Ann Arbor: University of Michigan, Center for Chinese Studies.

DeFrancis, John. 1950. *Nationalism and language reform in China.* Princeton, N.J.: Princeton University Press.

———. 1984. *The Chinese language: Fact and fantasy.* Honolulu: University of Hawai'i Press.

———. 1989. *Visible speech: The diverse oneness of writing systems.* Honolulu: University of Hawai'i Press.

De Jong, Alice. 1989–1990. The demise of the dragon: Backgrounds to the Chinese film *River elegy. China Information* 4, no. 3 (winter): 28–43.

Deng Xiaoping. 1985. *Build socialism with Chinese characteristics.* Beijing: Foreign Languages Press.

Despres, Leo A. 1984. Ethnicity: What data and theory portend for plural societies. In *The prospects for plural societies,* ed. David Maybury-Lewis, 7–29. Washington, D.C.: American Ethnological Society.

DeWind, Josh, Tom Seidl, and Janet Shenk. 1979. Contract labor in U.S. agriculture: The West Indian cane cutters in Florida. In *Peasants and proletarians: The struggles of Third World workers,* ed. Robin Cohen, Peter C. W. Gutkind, and Phyllis Brazier, 380–396. New York: *Monthly Review* Press.

Diamond, Norma. 1988. The Miao and poison: Interactions on China's southwest frontier. *Ethnology* 27, no. 1 (January): 1–25.

Dikötter, Frank. 1992. *The discourse of race in modern China.* Stanford, Calif.: Stanford University Press.

Dillon, Michael. 1996. *China's Muslims.* Hong Kong: Oxford University Press.

Dreyer, June. 1976. *China's forty millions: Minority nationalities and national integration in the People's Republic of China.* Cambridge, Mass.: Harvard University Press.

Duara, Prasenjit. 1992. *Rescuing history from the nation: Questioning narratives of modern China.* Chicago: University of Chicago Press.

Duke, Michael. 1989. Reinventing China. *Issues and Studies* 25, no. 8 (August): 29–53.

———. 1990. *The iron house.* Clayton, Utah: Peregrine Smith.

———. 1993. Thoughts on politics and critical paradigms in modern Chinese literature studies. *Modern China* 19, no. 1 (January): 41–70.

Ebert, Hans. 1991. Cui Jian's rock resonates in hearts of China's youth. *Billboard,* 9 May.

Ebrey, Patricia Buckley. 1991. Shifts in marriage finance from the sixth to the thirteenth century. In *Marriage and inequality in Chinese society,* ed. Rubie S. Watson and Patricia Buckley Ebrey, 97–132. Berkeley and Los Angeles: University of California Press.

Edwards, John. 1994. *Multilingualism.* London: Penguin.

———, ed. 1984. *Linguistic minorities, policies, and pluralism.* London: Academic.

Eisenberg, David. 1985. *Encounters with qi.* New York: Norton.

Ekvall, Robert. 1939. *Cultural relations on the Kansu-Tibetan border.* Chicago: University of Chicago Press.

Elegant, Robert S. 1968. *The center of the world: Communism and the mind of China.* 2d ed. New York: Funk & Wagnalls.

Erbaugh, Mary S. 1995. Southern Chinese dialects as a medium for reconciliation within greater China. *Language in Society* 23, no. 1 (spring): 79–94.

Esherick, Joseph. 1972. Harvard on China: The apologetics of imperialism. *Bulletin of Concerned Asian Scholars* 4, no. 4 (December): 9–16.

Evans, Harriet. 2000. Marketing femininity: Images of the modern Chinese woman. In *China beyond the headlines,* ed. Timothy B. Weston and Lionel M. Jensen, 217–244. Lanham, Md.: Rowman & Littlefield.

Fabian, Johannes. 1981. Six theses regarding the anthropology of African religious movements. *Religion* 11 (April): 109–126.

———. 1986. *Language and colonial power: The appropriation of Swahili in the former Belgian Congo, 1880–1938.* Berkeley and Los Angeles: University of California Press.

Farquhar, Judith. 1993. *Knowing practice: The clinical encounter of Chinese medicine.* Boulder, Colo.: Westview.

Fei Xiaotong. 1980. Ethnic identification in China. *Social Science in China* 1:94–107.

Feuchtwang, Stephan, and Mingming Wang. 1991. The politics of culture; or, A contest of histories: Representations of Chinese popular religion. *Dialectical Anthropology* 16, nos. 3–4:251–272.

Finnegan, Frances. 1982. *Poverty and prejudice: A study of Irish immigrants in York, 1840–1875.* Cork: Cork University Press.

Fishman, Joshua. 1966. *Language loyalty in the United States: The maintenance and perpetuation of non-English mother tongues by American ethnic and religious groups.* The Hague: Mouton.

Fishman, Joshua A., Charles A. Ferguson, and Jyotirindra Das Gupta, eds. 1968. *Language problems of developing nations.* New York: Wiley.

Fitzgerald, C. P. 1972. *The southern expansion of the Chinese people.* Canberra: Australian National University Press.

Fitzgerald, John. 1994. "Reports of my death have been greatly exaggerated": The history of the death of China. In *China deconstructs: Politics, trade, and regionalism,* ed. David S. G. Goodman and Gerald Segal, 21–58. London: Routledge.

Foreign Broadcast Information Service (FBIS). 1990. State issues 1990 census communique no. 3. *China Daily Report* FBIS-CHI-90-223 (19 November): 29.

———. 1991. Farmers move to urban areas for "better life." FBIS-CHI-91-165 (26 August): 64–65.

Foster, George M. 1967. Peasant society and the image of the limited good. In *Peasant society: A reader,* ed. Jack M. Potter, May N. Diaz, and George M. Foster, 300–323. Boston: Little, Brown.

Foucault, Michel. [1976–1984] 1978–1986. *The history of sexuality.* Translated by Robert Hurley. 3 vols. New York: Vintage.

Franz, Uli. 1988. *Deng Xiaoping.* Boston: Harcourt Brace Jovanovich.

Friedman, Edward. 1993. A failed Chinese modernity. *Daedalus* 122, no. 2 (spring): 1–17.

Friedman, Edward, Paul Pickowicz, and Mark Selden. 1991. *Chinese village, socialist state.* New Haven, Conn.: Yale University Press.

Frolic, Michael. 1980. *Mao's people.* Cambridge, Mass.: Harvard University Press.

Fu, Feng-Cheng. 1992. The decentralization of Peking's economic management and its impact on foreign investment. *Issues and Studies* 28, no. 2 (February): 67–83.

Galbiati, Fernando. 1985. *P'eng P'ai and the Hai-Lu-Feng Soviet.* Stanford, Calif.: Stanford University Press.

Gao, Michael Ying-Mao. 1973. *The People's Liberation Army and China's nation building.* White Plains, N.Y.: International Arts and Sciences Press.

Gates, Hill. 1993. *China's motor: A thousand years of petty capitalism.* Ithaca, N.Y.: Cornell University Press.

Gellner, Ernest. 1983. *Nations and nationalism.* Ithaca, N.Y.: Cornell University Press.

Geographical Knowledge, no. 1. 1992. Republished in *People's Daily* (overseas ed.), 6 February 1992.

Gil, V. E. 1991. An ethnography of HIV/AIDS and sexuality in the People's Republic of China. *Journal of Sex Research* 28, no. 4:521–538.

Giles, Howard, and Bernard Saint-Jacques, eds. 1979. *Language and ethnic relations.* Oxford: Pergamon.

Gladney, Dru C. 1990. Tiananmen: Retrospection and mediation. Lecture presented to the New England China Seminar, Harvard University, 20 March.

———. 1996. *Muslim Chinese: Ethnic nationalism in the People's Republic.* 2d ed. Cambridge, Mass.: Harvard University, Council on East Asian Studies.

Glazer, Nathan, and Daniel P. Moynihan. 1975. Introduction to *Ethnicity: Theory and experience,* ed. Nathan Glazer and Daniel P. Moynihan, with Corinne Saposs Schelling, 1–26. Cambridge, Mass.: Harvard University Press.

Glunin, Vladimir, and Alexander Grigorev. 1991. A conception of China's recent history. *Far Eastern Affairs* (Moscow), no. 3:114–128.

Gold, Tom. 1989. Guerilla interviewing among the *Getihu.* In *Unofficial China: Popular culture and thought in the People's Republic,* ed. Perry Link, Richard Madsen, and Paul G. Pickowicz. Boulder, Colo.: Westview.

Goldwin, Robert A., Art Kaufman, and William A. Schambra, eds. 1989. *Forging unity out of diversity: The approaches of eight nations.* Washington, D.C.: American Enterprise Institute for Public Policy Research.

Goodman, Bryna. 1991. New culture, old habits, native-place organizations, and the May Fourth Movement. In *Shanghai sojourners,* ed. Frederic E. Wakeman Jr. and Wen-hsin Yeh, 76–107. Berkeley: University of California, Institute of East Asian Studies.

Goodman, David. 1981. *Beijing street voices: The poetry and politics of China's democracy movement.* London: Marion Boyars.

Goodman, David S. G., and Gerald Segal, eds. 1994. *China deconstructs: Politics, trade, and regionalism*. London: Routledge.

Goullart, Peter. 1955. *Forgotten kingdom*. London: John Murray.

Greenhalgh, Susan. 1993. The peasantization of the one-child policy in Shaanxi. In *Chinese families in the post-Mao era*, ed. Deborah Davis and Stevan Harrell, 219–250. Berkeley and Los Angeles: University of California Press.

———. 1994. Controlling births and bodies in village China. *American Ethnologist* 21, no. 1:3–30.

Grossberg, Lawrence. 1987. Rock and roll in search of an audience. In *Popular music and communication*, ed. James Lull. Newbury Park, Calif.: Sage.

Grunfeld, A. Tom. 1985. In search of equality: Relations between China's ethnic minorities and the majority Han. *Bulletin of Concerned Asian Scholars* 17, no. 1:54–67.

Gu Biling, Luo Rulan, and Zhou Ping'er. 1992. Gangtai qunxing shanyao Shenzhen: Liang di yanyi wenhua fengmo dalu (Hong Kong and Taiwan stars shine in the Mainland). *Zhongguo shibao zhoukan*, 16–22 February, 66–67.

Gu Chu. 1990. A look at the face of big cities' *"mangliu."* *Shehui*, vol. 1.

Guangming ribao (GMRB). 12 June 1990. Translated in JPRS CAR 90 049 (11 July 1990): 13–19.

Guldin, Gregory, ed. 1990. *Anthropology in China*. Armonk, N.Y.: M. E. Sharpe.

Gumperz, John J. 1982a. *Discourse strategies*. Cambridge: Cambridge University Press.

———, ed. 1982b. *Language and social identity*. Cambridge: Cambridge University Press.

Gunn, Anne. 1990. Tell the world about us. *Australian Journal of Chinese Affairs*, no. 24 (July).

Han Jinchun and Li Yifu. 1984. Hanwen *minzu* yi ci de chuxian jiqi chuqi shiyong qingkuang (The emergence of the term *minzu* in Han [Chinese] language and usage). *Minzu yanjiu* 2:36–43.

Han Suyin. 1965. *The crippled tree*. New York: Putnam's.

Hannerz, Ulf. 1992. *Cultural complexity: Studies in the social organization of meaning*. New York: Columbia University Press.

Harrell, Stevan. 1990a. Ethnicity, local interests, and the state: Yi communities in southwest China. *Comparative Studies in Society and History* 32, no. 3 (July): 515–548.

———. 1990b. Introduction to *Violence in China*, ed. Jonathan N. Lipman and Stevan Harrell, 1–25. Albany: State University of New York Press.

———. 1995a. Civilizing projects and the reaction to them. In *Cultural encounters on China's ethnic frontiers*, ed. Stevan Harrell, 3–36. Seattle: University of Washington Press.

———, ed. 1995b. *Cultural encounters on China's ethnic frontiers*. Seattle: University of Washington Press.

———. 1995c. A history of the history of the Yi. In *Cultural encounters on China's ethnic frontiers*, ed. Stevan Harrell, 63–91. Seattle: University of Washington Press.

Harrison, James Pinckney. 1972. *The long march to power: A history of the Chinese Communist Party, 1921–72*. New York: Praeger.

Hashimoto, Mantaro J. 1973. *The Hakka dialect: A linguistic study of its phonology, syntax, and lexicon*. Cambridge: Cambridge University Press.

He Bochuan. 1991. *China on the edge.* San Francisco: China Books and Periodicals.

He Liyi, with Claire Anne Chik. 1993. *Mr. China's son: A villager's life.* Boulder, Colo.: Westview.

Hebdige, Dick. 1987. *Subculture: The meaning of style.* London: Routledge.

Herdan, Innes. 1992. *The pen and the sword: Literature and revolution in modern China.* London: Zed.

Hinsch, Brett. 1990. *Passions of the cut sleeve: The male homosexual tradition in China.* Berkeley and Los Angeles: University of California Press.

Hinton, William. 1983. *Shenfan.* New York: Random House.

Hohenberg, Paul M., and Lynn Hollen Lees. 1985. *The making of urban Europe, 1000–1950.* Cambridge, Mass.: Harvard University Press.

Holmgren, Jennifer. 1990. Imperial marriage in the native Chinese and non-Han state, Han to Ming. In *Marriage and inequality in Chinese society,* ed. Rubie S. Watson and Patricia Buckley Ebrey, 58–96. Berkeley and Los Angeles: University of California Press.

Honig, Emily. 1992. *Creating Chinese ethnicity: Subei people in Shanghai, 1850–1980.* New Haven, Conn.: Yale University Press.

Horowitz, David. 1985. *Ethnic groups in conflict.* Berkeley and Los Angeles: University of California Press.

Hsin, Chi. 1978. *Teng Hsiao-ping [Deng Xiaoping]: A political biography.* Hong Kong: Cosmos.

Hsu, Francis L. K. 1963. *Under the ancestors' shadow.* Stanford, Calif.: Stanford University Press.

Hu Nai'an. 1964. *Zhongguo minzu zhi* (Chinese ethnography). Taipei: Shangwu.

Hu, Sheng. [1948] 1955. *Imperialism and Chinese politics.* Peking: Foreign Languages Press.

Huang Bicheng, Liu Yong, and Peng Shaoci. 1988. A report from Changsha's labor market. *Shehui,* vol. 3.

Huang Ruide. 1989. The next generation among the floaters. *Nanfeng chuang* (South wind window, Guangzhou), vol. 9.

Huters, Theodore. 1989. Between praxis and essence. In *Marxism and the Chinese experience: Issues in contemporary Chinese socialism,* ed. Arif Dirlik and Maurice Meisner, 316–337. Armonk, N.Y.: M. E. Sharpe.

Irvine, Judith. 1996. Sound politics: Speaking, writing, and printing in early Colonial Africa. Paper presented to the Ethnohistory Workshop, University of Pennsylvania, 18 April.

An Islamic investment corporation. 1986. *Beijing Review* 17:25.

Jackson, Anthony. 1979. *Na-Khi religion: An analytical appraisal of the Na-Khi ritual texts.* The Hague: Mouton.

Jensen, Lionel M. 1997. *Manufacturing Confucianism: Chinese traditions and universal civilization.* Durham, N.C.: Duke University Press.

Johnson, Elizabeth. 1984. Great-Aunt Yeung: A Hakka wage-laborer. In *Lives: Chinese working women,* ed. Mary Sheridan and Janet W. Salaff, 76–91. Bloomington: Indiana University Press.

———. 1988. Grieving for the dead, grieving for the living: Funeral laments of Hakka women. In *Death ritual in late imperial and modern China,* ed. James L. Watson and Evelyn S. Rawski, 135–164. Berkeley and Los Angeles: University of California Press.

Jones, Andrew F. 1992. *Like a knife: Ideology and genre in contemporary Chinese popular music.* Ithaca, N.Y.: Cornell University, East Asia Program.

Jordan, David K., and Daniel L. Overmeyer. 1986. *The flying phoenix: Aspects of Chinese sectarianism in Taiwan.* Princeton, N.J.: Princeton University Press.

Jun shi (The military). 1989. Vol. 32 of *Zhongguo da baike quanshu* (The great Chinese encyclopedia). Beijing: Zhongguo da baike quanshu chubanshe.

Kao, Michael Y. M., ed. 1975. *The Lin Biao affair.* Armonk, N.Y.: M. E. Sharpe.

Kinsey, A. C., W. B. Pomeroy, and C. E. Martin. 1948. *Sexual behavior in the human male.* Philadelphia: W. B. Saunders.

Kipnis, Andrew B. 1997. *Producing Guanxi: Sentiment, self, and subculture in a north Chinese village.* Durham, N.C.: Duke University Press.

Kirkby, R. J. R. 1985. *Urbanisation in China: Town and country in a developing economy, 1949-2000.* London: Croom Helm.

Kleeman, Terry F. 1998. *Great perfection: Religion and ethnicity in a Chinese millennial kingdom.* Honolulu: University of Hawai'i Press.

Klein, Donald W., and Anne B. Clark. 1971. *Biographical dictionary of Chinese communism, 1921-1965.* Cambridge, Mass.: Harvard University Press.

Kristof, Nicholas. 1993. China dumping communism in headlong pursuit of profit. *San Francisco Chronicle,* 7 September.

Kuo, Warren. 1970. *Analytical history of the Chinese Communist Party.* Taipei: Institute of International Relations.

Labov, William. [1966] 1972. Hypercorrection by the lower middle class as a factor in linguistic change. In *Sociolinguistic patterns,* 122-142. Philadelphia: University of Pennsylvania Press.

Lai, Tse-han, Ramon H. Myers, and Wei Wou. 1991. *A tragic beginning: The Taiwan Uprising of February 28, 1947.* Stanford, Calif.: Stanford University Press.

Lambert, Wallace. 1972. Evaluational reactions to spoken languages. In *Language, psychology, and culture: Essays by Wallace E. Lambert.* Stanford, Calif.: Stanford University Press.

Lampton, David M., with Yeung Saicheung. 1986. *Paths to power: Elite mobility in contemporary China.* Ann Arbor: University of Michigan, Center for Chinese Studies.

Larson, Wendy, and Richard Kraus. 1989. China's writers, the Nobel Prize, and the international politics of literature. *Australian Journal of Chinese Affairs,* no. 21 (January): 143-160.

Latour, Bruno, and Steve Woolgar. 1986. *Laboratory life.* Princeton, N.J.: Princeton University Press.

Lattimore, Owen. 1929. *The desert road to Turkestan.* Boston: Little, Brown.

——. 1940. *Inner Asian frontiers of China.* New York: American Geographical Society.

Lau, M. P., and M. L. Ng. 1989. Homosexuality in Chinese culture. *Culture, Medicine, and Psychiatry* 12:465-488.

Lawrence, Anthony. 1986. *China: The long march.* London: Merhurst.

Lawton, Thomas, ed. 1991. *New perspectives on Chu culture during the Eastern Zhou period.* Princeton, N.J.: Princeton University Press.

Leach, E. R. 1954. *Political systems of highland Burma.* Boston: Beacon.

Lee, Leo Ou-Fan. 1991. On the margins of the Chinese discourse. *Daedalus* 120, no. 2 (spring): 207-225.

Leeming, Frank. 1993. *The changing geography of China.* Oxford: Blackwell.

Lees, Lynn Hollen. 1979. *Exiles of Erin: Irish migrants in Victorian London.* Ithaca, N.Y.: Cornell University Press.

Lehmann, Winfred P., ed. 1975. *Language and linguistics in the People's Republic of China.* Austin: University of Texas Press.

Leong, S. T. 1985. The Hakka Chinese of Lingnan: Ethnicity and social change in modern times. In *Ideal and reality: Social and political change in modern China, 1860–1949,* ed. David Pong and Edmund S. K. Fung. Lanham, Md.: University Press of America.

Leung, John K., and Michael Y. M. Kau, eds. 1992. *The writings of Mao Zedong, 1949–1976.* Vol. 2. Armonk, N.Y.: M. E. Sharpe.

Li, Cheng. 1997. *Rediscovering China: Dynamics and dilemmas of reform.* Lanham, Md.: Rowman & Littlefield.

Li Gucheng. 1988. *Zhonggong zui gao lingdaoceng* (China's highest leaders). Hong Kong: Mingbao.

Li Jiequan. 1990. Dui dangzhi ji danghua jiaoyu de pipan (Criticism of Party rule and Party education). *Mingbao yuekan,* September, 34–37.

Li Lin-Ts'an. 1984. *Moso yanjiu lunwen ji* (Collected research essays on the Moso). Taipei: National Palace Museum.

Li Lugeng and Zhang Luhong, eds. 1987. *Zhongguo lishi ditu tianchong lianxi ce: Zhongguo lishi: Di san ce* ("Fill in the blanks" map workbook for Chinese history: Chinese history series: Workbook 3). 2d ed. Beijing: Renmin jiaoyu chubanshe.

Li Mengbai and Hu Xin, eds. 1991. *Liudong renkou dui da chengshi fazhan di yingxiang ji duice* (The influence of the floating population on big cities' development and countermeasures). Beijing: *Jingji ribao* chubanshe (*Economic Daily Publishing Co.*).

Li Wei-tzu. 1948. On the cult of the four sacred animals (*szu ta men*) in the neighborhood of Peking. *Folklore* 7:1–94.

Li Zhiyong, ed. 1988. *Zhongguo qigong shi* (The history of Chinese *qigong*). Henan: Henan Science and Technology Publishing Co.

Liang Maochun. 1988. Dui woguo liuxing yinyue lishi sikao (Reflections on the history of Chinese popular music). *Renmin yinyue,* vol. 7.

Lin Housheng, ed. 1988. *Qigongxue* (The study of *qigong*). Qingdao: Qingdao Publishing Co.

Lin, Yih-Tang, comp. N.d. *What they say: A collection of current Chinese underground publications.* Taipei: Institute of Current Chinese Studies.

Lindqvist, Cecilia. 1991. *China: Empire of living symbols.* Translated by Joan Tate. Reading, Mass.: Addison-Wesley.

Linebarger, Paul. 1925. *Sun Yat Sen and the Chinese Republic.* New York: Century.

Ling, Ken. 1972. *The revenge of heaven: Journal of a young Chinese.* New York: Putnam's.

Liu Binyan. [1956] 1980. At the bridge construction site. Translated by Philip Robyn. In *Literature of the People's Republic of China,* ed. Kai-yu Hsu, 212–228. Bloomington: Indiana University Press.

———. [1979] 1983. People or monsters? Translated by James V. Feinerman with Perry Link. In *People or monsters? and other stories and reportage from China after Mao,* ed. Perry Link, 11–68. Bloomington: Indiana University Press.

Liu Su. 1987. Keep rural girls in school. *China Daily,* 17 April, 1.

Liu, Tao Tao, and David Faure, eds. 1996. *Unity and diversity: Local cultures and identities in China.* Hong Kong: Hong Kong University Press.

Liu Xiaobin. 1991. *Dian wenhua shi* (A history of Dian culture). Kunming: Yunnan Renmin Chubanshe.

Lu Xueyi. 1991. Several problems in the study of current rural social strata. *Gaige,* no. 6 (20 November): 157–163. Translated in JPRS CAR 92 093 (24 April 1992).

Luo Xianglin. [1933] 1973. *Kejia yanjiu daolun* (An introduction to the study of the Hakka: Ethnicity, history, and culture). Taipei: Shijie keshu di er ci keqin dahui.

Luo, Zi-ping. 1990. *A generation lost.* New York: Avon.

Ma Yin, ed. 1989. *China's minority nationalities.* Beijing: Foreign Languages Press.

MacInnis, Donald E. 1989. *Religion in China today: Policy and practice.* Maryknoll, N.Y.: Orbis.

Mackerras, Colin. 1994. *China's minorities: Integration and modernization in the twentieth century.* Hong Kong: Oxford University Press.

———. 1995. *China's minority cultures: Identities and integration since 1912.* New York: St. Martin's.

Mair, Victor H. 1991. What is a Chinese "dialect/topolect"? Reflections on some key Sino-English linguistic terms. *Sino-Platonic Papers* 29 (September): 1–31.

Mao Dun. [1978] 1979. Writing reform takes another big stride forward. In *Language reform in China,* ed. Peter J. Seybolt and Gregory Kuei-ke Chiang, 380–382. White Plains, N.Y.: M. E. Sharpe.

Mao Tse-tung [Mao Zedong]. [1927] 1967. Investigation of the peasant movement in Hunan. In *Selected works of Mao Tse-tung,* vol. 1. Peking: Foreign Languages Press.

———. 1969a. On correcting mistaken ideas in the Party. In *Selected works of Mao Zedong,* 1:105–116. Beijing: Foreign Languages Press.

———. 1969b. The Struggle in the Chingkang [Jinggang] mountains. In *Selected works of Mao Zedong,* vol. 1. Beijing: Foreign Languages Press.

———. 1990. *Report from Xunwu.* Translated, with an introduction and notes, by Roger R. Thompson. Stanford, Calif.: Stanford University Press.

Mason, Isaac. 1929. The Mohammedans of China: When, and how, they first came. *Journal of the North China Branch of the Royal Asiatic Society* 60:1–54.

Mauss, Marcel. [1925] 1967. *The gift: Forms and functions of exchange in archaic societies.* Translated by Ian Cunnison. New York: Norton.

McGregor, James. 1991. Growing millions of jobless peasants swarm through China, rousing fears of rural unrest. *Asian Wall Street Journal Weekly,* 6 May.

McKhann, Charles F. 1989. Fleshing out the bones: The cosmic and social dimensions of space in Naxi architecture. In *Ethnicity and ethnic groups in China,* ed. Chien Chiao and Nicholas Tapp, 157–178. Hong Kong: Chinese University of Hong Kong, New Asia College.

———. 1992. Fleshing out the bones: Kinship and cosmology in Naqxi religion. Vol. 1. Ph.D. diss., University of Chicago, Department of Anthropology.

———. 1995. The Naxi and the nationalities question. In *Cultural encounters on China's ethnic frontiers,* ed. Stevan Harrell, 39–62. Seattle: University of Washington Press.

Meeting praising the services of Islam in building the Four Modernizations. 1984. *China Daily,* 17 November.

Middle East trade links sought by Ningxia. 1984. *China Daily,* 14 November, 2.

Morawska, Ewa. 1990. The sociology and historiography of immigration. In *Immigration reconsidered: History, sociology, and politics,* ed. Virginia Yans-McLaughlin. New York: Oxford University Press.

Moseley, George V. H., III. 1973. *The consolidation of the south China frontier.* Berkeley: University of California Press.

Moser, Leo J. 1985. *The Chinese mosaic: The peoples and provinces of China.* Boulder, Colo.: Westview.

Mueggler, Erik. 1991. Money, the mountain, and the state: Power in a Naxi village. *Modern China* 17, no. 2:188–226.

———. 2001. *The age of wild ghosts: Memory, violence, and place in southwest China.* Berkeley and Los Angeles: University of California Press.

Naughton, Barry. 1989. The Third Front: Defense industrialization in the Chinese interior. *China Quarterly,* no. 115 (September): 351–386.

Nelson, Joan M. 1976. Sojourners versus new urbanites: Causes and consequences of temporary versus permanent cityward migration in developing countries. *Economic Development and Cultural Change* 24, no. 4 (July): 721–757.

Newell, William H. 1962. *Treacherous river: A study of rural Chinese in north Malaya.* Kuala Lumpur: University of Malaya Press.

1978 National College Entrance Examination of the People's Republic of China, The. 1979. Washington, D.C.: U.S. Department of Health, Education and Welfare, Office of Education.

Norman, Jerry. 1988. *Chinese.* Cambridge: Cambridge University Press.

Olsen, John. 1993. Archeology in China today. *China Exchange News* 20, no. 2 (summer): 3–6.

Ono Kazuko, with Joshua A. Fogel, eds. 1989. *Chinese women in a century of revolution, 1850–1950.* Stanford, Calif.: Stanford University Press.

Ortner, Sherry B. 1974. Is female to male as nature is to culture? In *Woman, culture, and society,* ed. Michelle Zimbalist Rosaldo and Louise Lamphere, 67–87. Stanford, Calif.: Stanford University Press.

The overseas Chinese: A driving force. 1992. *Economist,* 18 July, 21–24.

Overseas investors sought for Ningxia. 1984. *China Daily,* 20 June, 2.

Pan, K. T. [1947] 1970. Causes of homosexuality in Chinese documents and literature. In *Psychology of sex,* ed. Havelock Ellis, 351–354. Taipei: Cactus.

Pan, S. 1990. Manual, oral, anal, and homosexual behavior today in Chinese civil peoples. Paper presented at the First Sino-American Management of HIV Disease Symposium, Beijing, 7–8 November.

Pan, Suiming, Zongjian Wu, and Vincent E. Gil. 1995. Homosexual behaviors in contemporary China. *Journal of Psychology and Human Sexuality,* vol. 7, no. 4.

Perlman, Janice E. 1976. *The myth of marginality: Urban poverty and politics in Rio de Janeiro.* Berkeley: University of California Press.

Perry, Elizabeth. 1992. State and society in contemporary China. *World Politics,* vol. 41, no. 4 (July).

———. 1995. Labor's battle for political space: The role of worker associations in contemporary China. In *Urban spaces in contemporary China: The potential for autonomy and community in post-Mao China,* ed. Deborah S. Davis, Richard Kraus, Barry Naughton, and Elizabeth J. Perry, 302–325. Washington, D.C.: Woodrow Wilson Center Press/Cambridge University Press.

Perry, Elizabeth, and Ellen Fuller. 1991. China's long march to democracy. *World Policy Journal* (World Policy Institute, New York) 8, no. 4 (fall): 663–685.

Ping Fang and Ma Mu. 1990. Yiwu suoyou: Zhongguo yaogun gexing Cui Jian (I have nothing: Chinese rock star Cui Jian). *Xiju shijie,* vols. 3–4.

Polachek, James M. 1983. The moral economy of the Kiangsi Soviet (1928–1934). *Journal of Asian Studies* 42, no. 4:805–829.

Polo, Marco. 1958. *The travels.* Translated, with an introduction, by Ronald Latham. Harmondsworth: Penguin.

Porkert, Manfred. 1974. *The theoretical foundations of Chinese medicine.* Cambridge, Mass.: MIT Press.

Portes, Alejandro. 1990. From south of the border: Hispanic minorities in the United States. In *Immigration reconsidered: History, sociology, and politics,* ed. Virginia Yans-McLaughlin. New York: Oxford University Press.

Portes, Alejandro, and Ruben G. Rumbaut. 1990. *Immigrant America: A portrait.* Berkeley and Los Angeles: University of California Press.

Potter, Sulamith Heins. 1983. The position of peasants in modern Chinese social order. *Modern China* 9 (April): 465–499.

Potter, Sulamith Heins, and Jack M. Potter. 1990. *China's peasants: The anthropology of a revolution.* Cambridge: Cambridge University Press.

Price, Don C. 1990. Nation as family: Revolution for the ancestors. Paper presented at the annual meeting of the Association for Asian Studies, Los Angeles, 25–28 March.

Proceedings of the National Academy of Sciences. 1988. 85:6002–6006.

Pruitt, Ida. 1945. *A daughter of Han: The autobiography of a Chinese working woman.* Stanford, Calif.: Stanford University Press.

Pye, Lucian W. 1975. China: Ethnic minorities and national security. In *Ethnicity: Theory and experience,* ed. Nathan Glazer and Daniel P. Moynihan, with Corinne Saposs Schelling, 489–512. Cambridge, Mass.: Harvard University Press.

Qian, Jiaoju. 1986. *Qishi niande jingji* (The experience of seventy years). Hong Kong: Post Cultural Enterprises.

Qian Xuesen et al. 1988. *Lun renti kexue* (On the human sciences). Beijing: Renmin Junyi Chubanshe.

Qiao Huantian. 1987. What were the effects on modern Chinese society of the invasion of the Western powers? *Renmin ribao,* 26 June.

Ramsey, S. Robert. 1987. *The languages of China.* Princeton, N.J.: Princeton University Press.

Rees, Helen Margaret. 1994. A musical chameleon: A Chinese repertoire in Naxi territory (Taoism, Buddhism, Confucianism). Ph.D. diss., University of Pittsburgh.

Remnick, David. 1992. Defending the faith. *New York Review of Books,* 14 May, 44–51.

Restarick, Harry Bond. 1931. *Sun Yatsen, liberator of China.* New Haven, Conn.: Yale University Press.

Rocca, Jean Louis. 1992. Corruption and its shadow: An anthropological view of corruption in China. *China Quarterly* 130, no. 130 (June): 402–416.

Rock, Joseph Francis. 1947. *The ancient Na-khi kingdom of southwest China.* 2 vols. Cambridge, Mass.: Harvard University Press.

———. 1963. *The land and culture of the Na-khi tribe of the China-Tibet borderland.* Wiesbaden: Franz Steiner.

Rossabi, Morris. 1970. The tea and horse trade with Inner Asia during the Ming. *Journal of Asian History* (Wiesbaden) 4, no. 2:135–168.

———. 1981. *China and Inner Asia from 1368 to the present day.* London: Thames & Hudson.

Roy, David Tod. 1971. *Kuo Mo-jo [Guo Muoruo]: The early years.* Cambridge, Mass.: Harvard University Press.

Ruan, F., and V. L. Bullough. 1989. Sex in China. *Medical Aspects of Human Sexuality* 23:59–62.

Ruan, F., and Y. Tsai. 1987. Male homosexuality in the traditional Chinese literature. *Journal of Homosexuality* 14:21–33.

———. 1988. Male homosexuality in contemporary Mainland China. *Archives of Sexual Behavior* 17, no. 2:189–199.

Ruan, Ming. 1992. The political and economic situation in China after the June 4th massacre of 1989. *Changing China,* vol. 2, no. 3 (summer).

Rural workers thrive in urban workplace. 1991. *China Daily,* 24 July.

Rutkowski, Michal. 1991. China's floating population and the labor market reforms. Preliminary draft report. Washington, D.C.: World Bank, December.

Sage, Steven F. 1992. *Ancient Sichuan and the unification of China.* Albany: State University of New York Press.

Salisbury, Harrison. 1985. *The Long March: The untold story.* New York: Harper & Row.

———. 1992. *The new emperors.* Boston: Little Brown.

Schell, Orville. 1988. *Discos and democracy.* New York: Pantheon.

Schiffman, Harold. 1996. *Linguistic culture and language policy.* London: Routledge.

Schiffrin, Harold Z. 1980. *Sun Yat-sen: Reluctant revolutionary.* Boston: Little, Brown.

Schinz, Alfred. 1989. *Cities in China.* Berlin: Gebruder Borntraeger.

Schneider, Laurence. 1976. National essence and the new intelligentsia. In *The limits of change: Essays on conservative alternatives in republican China,* ed. Charlotte Furth, 57–89. Cambridge, Mass.: Harvard University Press.

Schram, Stuart. 1966. Mao Tse-tung [Mao Zedong] and secret societies. *China Quarterly* 27, no. 1:1–13.

———. 1984. Classes old and new in Mao Zedong's thought, 1949–1976. In *Class and social stratification in post-Revolution China,* ed. James Watson. Cambridge: Cambridge University Press.

Schwarcz, Vera. 1986–1987. Behind a partially open door. *Pacific Affairs* 59, no. 4 (winter): 577–604.

———. 1992. Memory and commemoration. In *Popular protest and political culture in modern China,* ed. Jeffrey Wasserstrom and Elizabeth Perry. Boulder, Colo.: Westview.

Seagrave, Sterling. 1985. *The Soong dynasty.* New York: Harper & Row.

Seybolt, Peter J., and Gregory Kuei-ke Chiang. 1979. *Language reform in China: Documents and commentary.* White Plains, N.Y.: M. E. Sharpe.

Seymour, James, ed. 1980. *The Fifth Modernization: China's human rights movement, 1978–79.* Scanfordville, N.Y.: Human Rights.

Sha Song. 1990. An analysis of the characteristics of robbers who come to Shanghai from outside. *Shehui*, vol. 10.

Shaffer, Lynda. 1982. *Mao and the workers: The Hunan labor movement, 1920–1923.* Armonk, N.Y.: M. E. Sharpe.

Shen Congwen. 1982. *Recollections of West Hunan.* Translated by Gladys Yang. Beijing: Panda.

Shen Tong and Marianne Ye. 1990. *Almost a revolution.* Boston: Houghton Mifflin.

Sherard, Michael. 1972. Shanghai phonology. Ph.D. diss., Cornell University.

Shih, Chuan-Kang. 1993. The Yongning Moso: Sexual union, household organization, gender, and ethnicity in a matrilineal duolocal society in southwest China. Ph.D. diss., Stanford University, Department of Anthropology.

Shih, Vincent Y. C. 1967. *The Taiping ideology: Its sources, interpretations, and influences.* Seattle: University of Washington Press.

Shirk, Susan. 1984. The decline of virtuocracy in China. In *Class and social stratification in post-Revolution China,* ed. James Watson. Cambridge: Cambridge University Press.

Silverstein, C. 1981. *Man to man: Gay couples in America.* New York: Morrow.

Siu, Helen F. 1989. *Agents and victims in south China: Accomplices in rural revolution.* New Haven, Conn.: Yale University Press.

———. 1990. The politics of migration in a market town. In *Chinese society on the eve of Tiananmen: The impact of reform,* ed. Deborah Davis and Ezra F. Vogel. Cambridge, Mass.: Council on East Asian Studies/Harvard University Press.

———, ed. 1990. *Furrows: Peasants, intellectuals, and the state: Stories and histories from modern China.* Stanford, Calif.: Stanford University Press.

Sivin, Nathan. 1987. *Traditional medicine in contemporary China.* Ann Arbor: University of Michigan Press.

Skinner, G. William. 1977a. Cities and the hierarchy of local systems. In *The city in late imperial China,* ed. G. William Skinner. Stanford, Calif.: Stanford University Press.

———. 1977b. Regional urbanization in nineteenth-century China. In *The city in late imperial China,* ed. G. William Skinner. Stanford, Calif.: Stanford University Press.

Smedley, Agnes. 1956. *The great road: The life and times of Chu Te [Zhu De].* New York: *Monthly Review* Press.

Smith, Michael Peter, Bernadette Tarallo, and George Kagiwada. 1990. Coloring California: New Asian immigrant households, social networks, and the local state. Paper presented at the annual meeting of the American Political Science Association, San Francisco, August.

Smith, Richard. 1991. *Fortune tellers and philosophers: Divination in traditional Chinese society.* Boulder, Colo.: Westview.

Snow, Edgar. 1984. *Red star over China.* New York: Vintage.

Solinger, Dorothy J. 1993. Chinese transients and the state: A form of civil society? *Politics and Society* 21, no. 1 (March): 91–122.

———. 1999. *Contesting citizenship in urban China: Peasant migrants, the state, and the logic of the market.* Berkeley and Los Angeles: University of California Press.

Song Sichang. 1985. Kunming ji qi shijiao zongjiao chubu diaocha (Preliminary research on religion in Kunming and environs). In *Kunming minzu minsu he zongjiao diaocha* (Research on Kunming nationalities, customs, and religion), ed. Yunnan Editorial Group, 122–148. Kunming: Yunnan minzu chubanshe.

Song Tianbin. 1989. Qigongxue de jiben gainian yu fazhan jianshi (The basic concepts and brief history of development of *qigong* studies). *Beijing TCM Journal*, vol. 1.

Spence, Jonathan D. 1978. *The death of Woman Wang*. New York: Penguin.

Stafford, P. 1967. *Sexual behavior in the Communist world*. New York: Julian.

Stockard, Janice E. 1989. *Daughters of the Canton delta: Marriage patterns and economic strategies in south China, 1860–1930*. Stanford, Calif.: Stanford University Press.

Su Xiaokang. 1991. *Death song of the river: A reader's guide to the Chinese TV series "Heshang."* Edited and translated by Richard W. Bodman and Pin P. Wan. Ithaca, N.Y.: Cornell University, East Asia Program.

Su Xiaokang and Wang Luxiang. 1988. *Heshang*. Hong Kong: Joint Publishing Co.

Sun Lung-kee. 1992. Social psychology in the late Qing period. *Modern China* 15, no. 3 (July): 235–262.

Sun Shaozhen. 1991. Fangyan wenhua he zhengzhi beijing de guanxi (The connection between ethnolinguistic subculture and the political alliances). *Xin Wan Bao* (The new evening post, Hong Kong), 22 May.

Suryadinata, Leo. 1988. Government policy and national integration in Indonesia. *Southeast Asian Journal of Social Science* 12, no. 2:111–131.

Tan, Chee-Beng. 1982. Peranakan Chinese in northeast Kelantan with special reference to Chinese religion. *Journal of the Malaysian Branch of the Royal Asiatic Society* 55, pt. 1:26–52.

———. 1988. *The Baba of Melaka*. Petaling Jaya: Pelanduk.

Tan liuxing yinyue (Discussing popular music). 1988. *Yinyue yanjiu*, vol. 2.

Tang Xiaotian and Chen Donghu. 1989. Forced residence and urban society criminals. *Shehui*, vol. 9.

Tao Yunkui. 1943. Lun biandi hanren ji qi yu piajiang jianshe zhi guanxi (On the relation between frontier Han Chinese and the development of frontier land). *Bianzheng gonglun* 2, nos. 1–2:28–34.

Taylor, Romeyn. 1990. Official and popular religion and the political organization of Chinese society in the Ming. In *Orthodoxy in late imperial China*, ed. K. C. Liu. Berkeley and Los Angeles: University of California Press.

Thorp, Robert. 1992. "Let the past serve the present": The ideological claims of cultural relics work. *China Exchange News* 20, no. 2 (summer): 16–19.

Thrasher, Alan R. 1990. *La-Li-Luo dance-songs of the Chuxiong Yi, Yunnan province, China*. Danbury, Conn.: World Music.

Tilly, Charles. 1990. Transplanted networks. In *Immigration reconsidered: History, sociology, and politics*, ed. Virginia Yans-McLaughlin. New York: Oxford University Press.

Times Atlas of China. 1974. New York: Quadrangle.

Tu, Wei-ming. 1991a. Cultural China: The periphery as the center. *Daedalus* 120, no. 2 (spring): 1–32.

———. 1991b. Heshang: Whither Chinese culture? In *Deathsong of the river: A reader's guide to the Chinese TV series "Heshang,"* ed. and trans. Richard Bodman and Pin P. Wan. Ithaca, N.Y.: Cornell University, East Asia Program.

Tyson, James, and Ann Tyson. 1995. *Chinese awakenings: Life stories from the unofficial China*. Boulder, Colo.: Westview.

Urla, Jacqueline. 1993. Cultural politics in an age of statistics: Numbers, nations, and the making of Basque identity. *American Ethnologist* 20, no. 4:818–843.

———. 1996. Basque hip-hop? Language, popular music, and cultural identity. Paper presented to the Ethnohistory Workshop, University of Pennsylvania, 28 March.

van Gulick, R. H. 1961. *Sexual life in ancient China.* Leiden: E. J. Brill.

Vogel, Ezra F. 1989. *One step ahead in China: Guangdong under reform.* Cambridge, Mass.: Harvard University Press.

Wang Gungwu. 1988. The study of Chinese identities in Southeast Asia. In *Changing identities of the Southeast Asian Chinese since World War II,* ed. Jennifer W. Cushman and Wang Gungwu, 1–22. Hong Kong: Hong Kong University Press.

Wang Meizhi. 1991. *Qigong xiulian zhinan* (*Qigong* training guide). Beijing: Zhishi.

Wang, X. 1990. AIDS, the punishment from God to sex liberty. Paper presented at the First Sino-American Management of HIV Disease Symposium, Beijing, 7–8 November.

Wang Yanling, Wu Yekang, and Jiang Jianping. 1990. Get enlightenment from a bloody lesson. *Shehui,* vol. 8.

Ward, Barbara. 1965. Varieties of the conscious model: The fishing people of south China. In *The relevance of models for social anthropology,* ed. Michael Banton, 113–137. London: Tavistock.

Watson, James L., ed. 1997. *Golden arches east: McDonald's in East Asia.* Stanford, Calif.: Stanford University Press.

Watson, Rubie S. 1991. Wives, concubines, and maids: Servitude and kinship in the Hong Kong region, 1900–1940. In *Marriage and inequality in Chinese society,* ed. Rubie S. Watson and Patricia Buckley Ebrey, 231–255. Berkeley and Los Angeles: University of California Press.

Weber, Max. 1978. The types of legitimate domination. In *Economy and society: An outline of interpretive sociology,* ed. Guenther Roth and Claus Wittich, 212–301. Berkeley and Los Angeles: University of California Press.

Weinberg, M. S., and A. P. Bell. 1972. *Homosexuality: An annotated bibliography.* New York: Harper & Row.

West, Martin, and Erin Moore. 1989. Undocumented workers in the United States and South Africa: A comparative study of changing control. *Human Organization* 48, no. 1 (spring): 1–10.

Weston, Timothy B. 2000. China's labor woes: Will the workers crash the Party? In *China beyond the headlines,* ed. Timothy B. Weston and Lionel M. Jensen, 245–271. Lanham, Md.: Rowman & Littlefield.

White, Lynn, and Li Cheng. 1993. China coastal identities. In *China's quest for national identity,* ed. Lowell Dittmer and Samuel Kim, 154–193. Ithaca, N.Y.: Cornell University Press.

White, Sydney D. 1993. Medical discourses, Naxi identities, and the state: Transformations in socialist China. Ph.D. diss., University of California, Berkeley, Department of Anthropology.

———. 1997. Fame and sacrifice: The gendered construction of Naxi identities. *Modern China* 23, no. 3:298–327.

———. 1998. State discourses, minority policies, and the politics of identity in the Lijiang Naxi people's autonomous county. *Nationalism and Ethnic Politics* 4, nos. 1–2:9–27.

———. 2001. Medicines and modernities in socialist China: Medical pluralism, Naxi identities, and the state in the Lijiang basin. In *Healing powers: Traditional medicine, shamanism, and science in contemporary Asia,* ed. Linda H. Connor and Geoffrey Samuel, 171–194. Westport, Conn.: Bergin & Garvey.

Whitson, William W., with Chen-hsia Huang. 1973. *The Chinese high command: A history of Communist military politics, 1927–71.* New York: Praeger.

Womack, Brantley. 1992. Where Mao went wrong: Epistemology and ideology in Mao's leftist politics. *Australian Journal of Chinese Affairs,* no. 28 (July): 23–40.

Wood, Frances. 1996. *Did Marco Polo go to China?* Boulder, Colo.: Westview.

Woolard, Kathryn A. 1983. The politics of language and ethnicity in Barcelona, Spain. Ph.D. diss., University of California, Berkeley.

———. 1989. *Double talk: Bilingualism and the politics of ethnicity in Catalonia.* Stanford, Calif.: Stanford University Press.

Woon, Yuen-fong. 1991. Rural migrants and regional development in the People's Republic of China: The case of Kaiping county in the Pearl river delta region. Paper presented at the fiftieth-anniversary meeting of the Association for Asian Studies, New Orleans, 5–8 April.

Wu, David Y. H. 1974a. Adaptation and change: The Chinese in Papua New Guinea. Ph.D. diss., Australian National University.

———. 1974b. Ethnicity and adaptation. *Southeast Asian Journal of Social Science* 5, nos. 1–2:95.

———. 1982. *The Chinese in Papua New Guinea.* Hong Kong: Chinese University Press.

———. 1989a. Culture change and ethnic identity among minorities in China. In *Ethnicity and ethnic groups in China,* ed. Chien Chiao and Nicholas Tapp, 11–22. Hong Kong: New Asia College.

———. 1989b. Zulei yishi zhi chuangzao yu zaichuangzao (The construction and reconstruction of ethnic identity). Paper presented at the Conference of Ethnic Relation and Regional Development, Academia Sinica, Taipei, 1 September.

———. 1990a. Chinese minority policy and the meaning of minority culture: The example of Bai in Yunnan, China. *Human Organization* 49, no. 1 (March): 1–13.

———. 1990b. Ethnicity and culture change. In *Proceedings of the Second International Conference of Sinology.* Taipei: Academia Sinica.

———. 1991. The construction of Chinese and non-Chinese identities. *Daedalus* 120. no. 2 (spring): 159–179.

Wu Yue wenhua (Wu Yue culture). 1991. Shenyang: Liaoning Education Publishing House.

WuDunn, Sheryl. 1990. A deputy culture minister is removed by Beijing. *New York Times,* 13 June.

———. 1991. Deng shuns hometown, but still it's a magnet. *New York Times,* 13 May.

Xu Ye, Wang Qinghua, and Duan Dingzhou. 1987. *Nanfang lushang sichou lu* (The southern Silk Road). Kunming: Yunnan minzu chubanshe.

Yang, Benjamin. 1990. *From revolution to politics: Chinese Communists on the Long March.* Boulder, Colo.: Westview.

Yang Huandian, Liang Zhenshi, Li Puying, and Liu Cunhan. 1985. Guangxi de hanyu fangyan (gao) (Distribution of dialects in Guangxi [draft]). *Fangyan* (Chinese dialects), vol. 3.

Yang, Mayfair. 1989. The gift economy and state power in China. *Comparative Studies in Society and History* 31, no. 1 (January): 25–54.

Yang, S. 1990. Public opinion poll on AIDS in south Fujian. Paper presented at the First Sino-American Management of HIV Disease Symposium, Beijing, 7–8 November.

Yang Zhongmei. 1988. *Hu Yaobang: A Chinese biography*. Translated by William A. Wycoff. Edited by Timothy Cheek. Armonk, N.Y.: M. E. Sharpe.

Yin Meng. 1958. Weishenme ba Kejiahua dangzuo shaoshu minzu yuyan? (Why should Hakka be considered a minority language?). *Zhongguo yuwen* (Languages of China), vol. 74, endpaper.

Young, Crawford. 1976. *The politics of cultural pluralism*. Madison: University of Wisconsin Press.

———, ed. 1993. *The rising tide of cultural pluralism: The nation-state at bay*. Madison: University of Wisconsin Press.

Young, Lung-chang. 1988. Regional stereotypes in China. *Chinese Studies in History* 21, no. 4 (summer): 32–57.

Young, Robert. 1990. *White mythologies: Writing history and the West*. London: Routledge.

Yu, Xinyan. 1991. *Xuexi yu yanjiu* (Study and research), 9 May. Translated in JPRS CAR 91 052 (23 September 1991).

Yuan Jiahua, et. al. 1960. *Hanyu fangyan gaiyao* (An outline of the Chinese Dialects). Bejing: Wenzi gaige chubanshe.

Yuan Xin and Tang Mingda. 1990. A preliminary investigation of Xinjiang's floating population. *Renkou yu jingji* (Population and economy) 3:46–52.

Yuyan wenzi (Languages and writing systems). 1988. Vol. 19 of *Zhongguo da baike quanshu* (The great Chinese encyclopedia). Beijing: Zhongguo da baike quanshu chubanshe.

Zeng Jingwei. 1988. Big cities' "trash collectors." *Nanfeng chuang* (South wind window, Guangzhou), vol. 1.

Zhang Honglin. N.d. *Qigong yi ci ji qi neihan yanbian de kaoxi* (*Qigong* and analysis of its inner evolution). Chinese Academy of Traditional Chinese Medicine, Beijing. Typescript.

Zhang Honglin and Hu Weiguo. 1991. *Zhongyi yi qian wen: Qigong pian* (A thousand questions about traditional Chinese medicine: The *qigong* volume). Shanghai: Shanghai Science and Technology Publishing Co.

Zhang Jie. 1987. What's wrong with him? *Renditions* 27–28 (spring–autumn): 141–157.

Zhang Qingwu. 1988. Basic facts on the household registration system. *Chinese Economic Studies* 22, no. 1:3–106.

Zhang, Tianxin. 1993. Review of *Diplomatic history of the late Qing dynasty*, by Yang Gongsu (in Chinese). *China Daily*, 20 September.

Zhang Tongji and Zhang Yongqing. 1986. A study and analysis of the "dual functions" of Islam in Xiji district (Ningxia province) and their relation to building a spiritual civilization. *Ningxia Social Sciences*, vol. 2. A translation appears in D. MacInnis, *Religion in China today* (Maryknoll, N.Y.: Orbis, 1989), 256–257.

Zhang Wenjiang and Chang Jin, eds. 1989. *Zhongguo chuantong qigongxue cidian* (Dictionary of traditional Chinese *qigong*). Taiyuan: Shanxi People's Publishing Co.

Zhang Xianliang. 1986. *Half of man is woman*. Translated by Martha Avery. New York: Ballantine.

Zhang Yanghou et al. 1991. *"Da qigongshi" pianshu jiemi* (Exposing the deceptions of the "great *qigong* masters"). N.p.: Falu Chubanshe.

Zhang Youren. 1987. Respecting outsiders should become social public morality. *Shehui,* vol. 6.

Zhang Zhengming, ed. 1987. *Chu wen-hua shi* (History of Chu culture). Shanghai: Shanghai People's Publishing House.

Zheng Guizhen, Guo Shenyang, Zhang Yunfan, and Wang Jufen. 1985. A preliminary investigation of Shanghai's city district's floating population problem. *Renkou yanjiu* (Population research), vol. 3.

Zhichi dang de jiben luxian zhengqie chuli jingjiao nongcun fazhan de jige wenti (Support the Party's basic line and correctly handle problems in suburban rural development). 1990. *Beijing ribao,* 7 April, 3.

Zhongguo gong-nong hong jun Chang Zheng tu (A map of the Long March of China's workers, peasants, and Red Army). 1979. In *Ci hai* (Sea of words). Shanghai: Shanghai cishu chubanshe.

Zhonghua renmin gongheguo fen sheng dituji (Province-by-province maps of the People's Republic of China). 1977. Beijing: Ditu chubanshe.

Zhou Enlai. 1958. Dangqian wenzi gaige de renwu. *Wenzi gaige,* February, 1–6.

Zhu De. 1981. Muqin de huiyi (Remembering my mother). *Wen xuan* (Literary selections [of Zhu De]), vol. 1. Beijing: Beijing yuyan xueyuan.

Zhu Huaxin and Cao Huanrong. 1987. The historical position of China's reform. *Renmin ribao,* 6, 7 October. Translated in JPRS CAR 87 056 (9 November 1987).

Zhu, Q. 1990. HIV is nothing, healthy behavior is everything. Paper presented at the First Sino-American Management of HIV Disease Symposium, Beijing, 7–8 November.

Zhu Yiyi and Zhu Runlong. 1987. *Zhongguo de chaoren* (China's supermen). Shanghai: Shanghai Wenhua Publishing Co.

Contributors

A. Doak Barnett, late of the Department of Chinese Studies, Johns Hopkins School for Advanced International Studies, and the Brookings Institution.

Susan D. Blum, Department of Anthropology, University of Notre Dame.

Diane Dorfman, Northwest Regional Educational Laboratory, Portland, Oregon.

Prasenjit Duara, Department of History, University of Chicago.

Mary S. Erbaugh, a linguist in Eugene, Oregon.

Edward Friedman, Department of Political Science, University of Wisconsin–Madison.

Vincent E. Gil, Department of Anthropology-Sociology, Vanguard University of Southern California.

Dru C. Gladney, Department of Asian Studies, University of Hawai'i at Mānoa, and Research Fellow in the Program for Cultural Studies at the East-West Center.

Erwin J. Haeberle, Robert Koch Institute, Archive for Sexology, Berlin.

Lionel M. Jensen, Department of East Asian Languages and Literatures, University of Notre Dame.

Andrew F. Jones, Department of East Asian Languages and Cultures, University of California, Berkeley.

Eric Karchmer, Department of Anthropology, University of North Carolina, Chapel Hill.

Liu Binyan, Princeton China Initiative.

Dalin Liu, Shanghai Sex Sociology Research Center, Shanghai University.

Man Lun Ng, Hong Kong Sex Education Association.

S. Robert Ramsey, Department of Hebrew and East Asian Languages and Literatures, University of Maryland.

Dorothy J. Solinger, Department of Politics and Society of the School of Social Sciences, University of California, Irvine.

James and Ann Tyson, Correspondents, *Christian Science Monitor.*

Sydney D. White, Department of Anthropology, Temple University.

David Yen-ho Wu, Department of Anthropology, Chinese University of Hong Kong.

Li Ping Zhou, Shanghai Sex Sociology Research Center, Shanghai University.

Index

Chu culture, 31–32, 37, 41, 347n.4; national interest in, 35–36

class struggle, after Cultural Revolution, 258–259; and the "floating population," 273–274, 277, 279, 281, 286. *See also* ethnicity

commodity nativism, 6, 291–293, 302–307, 359n.10. *See also* rock and roll music

common language (*putonghua*). *See* Mandarin

Communist Revolution, role of Hakka, 200–205; suppression of homosexuality, 240; Tiger Springs, 142. *See also* Chinese Communist Party; Mao Zedong

Confucianism, 8, 10; familism and rejection of homosexuality, 240; importance of male progeny, 266; and modern Chinese "feudalism," 297; peasant morality and, 333; traditional roles of women, 253, 266, 268

contraception, attitudes towards, 234; knowledge of, 234; use of, 234. *See also* family planning; health; sexuality

crime, 25–29; "black societies," 28, 29; "floating population," 280, 284, 357n.9, 14; labor gangs and worker exploitation, 284, 357n.9; market reform's effect on, 265; religion and, 116; sex offenses, 227

Cui Jian (rock musician), 16; and "commodity nativism," 6; icon of political dissent, 294, 296–297, 301–302; "I Have Nothing," 297, 299–301; influenced by *River Elegy*, 299; influence on youth, 294, 296–297, 299–301, 306, 358n.2, 359n.8; music as expression of political and cultural rebellion, 291–292, 301, 294, 296, 299–300, 306; repression by CCP, 291, 294, 301; Tiananmen movement, 292, 294. *See also* rock and roll music

cultural assimilation, *bun tong*, 180–181; Hakka, 192–193; ideal of cultural unity, 193–194; importance of *hukou*, 357n.16; language and, 178–181, 279; Malay culture, 179–180; of minority groups, 170, 174–175, 177–178, 192–193; of peasants in urban areas, 357n.16;

peranakanization, 178–180; wealth and, 180–181. *See also* cultural chauvinism; ethnicity; Han; Han chauvinism

cultural chauvinism, 190; Hakka and Han ideal, 193–194; Han, 168–170, 172, 174, 177–178, 181; history of, 169–170, 177–178; state-sponsored, 343–345. *See also* cultural assimilation; cultural unity; ethnicity; Han; Han chauvinism

Cultural Revolution, 38, 91, 94; "class struggle," 258–259; effect on women, 258–259; Liu Guizhen, 314; negation of individuality, 297; role of Hakka, 206–208; suppression of *qigong*, 314; suppression of religion, 259, 331; weakening of CCP, 116. *See also* Chinese Communist Party; Mao Zedong; modernization

cultural unity, GMD's nationalist propaganda, 171–173; Han chauvinism, 168–170, 172, 174, 177–178, 181; *huaqiao* and, 169; importance in China, 168. *See also* "Chineseness;" cultural assimilation; Han

D

dance clubs, meeting place for homosexuals, 241–245; state supervision of, 355n.6

Daoism, number of adherents, 309, 311; status as official religion, 309. *See also* religion

dating, 235. *See also* marriage; sexuality; youth

Dayanzhen ("vegetable peasants"), as domain of modern socialist state, 136; economy, 137; gender roles, 138; history, 135, 351n.8; urban/rural distinction, 140; "vegetable peasants," 136, 350n.6. *See also* Chinese Communist Party; *nongmin*; rural life

Democracy (*minzhu*), 37, 42, 44, 344; advocacy of in rock music, 291–293; student activism, 297; Tiananmen Movement, 291–292, 297. *See also* student activism; Tiananmen Movement

People's Republic of; Chinese Communist Party; Communist Revolution; Cultural Revolution; Great Leap Forward

marriage, 15, 68; arranged marriage, 220, 232–233, 251, 253, 259, 267; divorce and extramarital affairs, 227, 236, 240; domestic abuse, 254–255, 264–266; endogamous marriage, 121–122; finding a spouse, 232; "floating population," 278; gender inequality, 249, 253, 265; of homosexuals, 238; Hui, 121; Hui-Han intermarriage, 121; Islamic, 122; love, 235; Naxi, 133; poverty and dissatisfaction, 224; pre-marital sex, 227, 229, 231–232; quality of, 224; rural family dynamic, 254, 260, 267–268; sale of brides, 249, 251, 254, 265–266; sex, 223, 227, 235; social class and, 357n.16; societal attitudes, 222; state policies and, 240; Tiger Springs, 141. *See also* dating; family planning; gender; sexuality; women

Marxism, and Hakka, 200–201. *See also* Chinese Communist Party

Mauss, Marcel, on gift-giving, 109

media, spread of electronic media, 100–102

medicine, abortion, 227, 232; AIDS epidemic, 221–222, 227; contraception, 257; *qigong* 313, 359nn.2, 4; *qigong*, TCM and biomedicine, 311–312, 316–317; in rural areas, 261; scientific testing of *qigong*, 312, 314–315; sex research, 221; sexually transmitted disease, 221–222, 227; sexual problems, 226; spirit healer-patient relationship, 330, 335; spirit healing, 323–324, 327–330, 335, 361n.8, 362n.12. *See also* biomedicine; health; *qigong*; sexually transmitted disease; spirit healing; Traditional Chinese Medicine

military, People's Liberation Army, 103; provincial armies, 29; women in, 258. *See also* Chinese Communist Party

millenarianism, Hakka participation, 199; Older Brother Society, 199; Society of God Worshipers, 185, 198; Taiping

Rebellion, 185. *See also* Taiping Rebellion

minorities. *See* ethnic minorities

mixin. See superstition

modernization, 9–10, 77–80, 82–83, 91, 93, 97, 99, 102, 151; cultural revival as rejection of, 312; kazakhs, 82–83; Kunming, 151, 351n.1; music, 293, 299; of TCM, 314. *See also* Cultural Revolution; economic reform

money, foreign-exchange certificates, 355n.7

Mongolians (Meng), 52, 149. *See also* ethnicity; ethnic minorities

music, 217; mass music (*qunzhong yinyue*), 293; the northwest wind (*xibei feng*), 293; politicization of popular music, 292–293, 295, 301; popular music (*tongsu yinyue*), 292–295; revolutionary music (*geming gequ*), 293; rock music, 291–296. *See also* Ai Jing; Cui Jian; popular music; rock and roll music

N

Nanjing Massacre of 1937, 255

Nanzhao Kingdom, 175–176. *See also* Bai

national identity, 16, 41–44, 347n.2; acculturation and, 178; as *hanren*, 173–174; historical identity, 181–182; of *huaqiao*, 167–169, 171–172, 182; Minjia, 175; nationalist education and propaganda, 170, 171, 182; of *peranakans*, 178; social classes, 182; Zhang Taiyan, 169–170; *zhongguoren*, 169–170; *zhonghua minzu*, 169–170. *See also* cultural chauvinism; cultural unity; ethnicity; Han; Han chauvinism

nationalism, xv, 31–44, 182; anti-imperialism and, 34, 37–38, 42–43; commodity nativism and, 304–305; and creation of China-oriented identity for *huaqiao*, 171; opposed to individualism, 295; popular music and, 292–293, 295, 301; promotion by CCP, 306. *See also* "Chineseness;" commod-ity nativism; Han Chauvinism; national identity; patriotism

Nationalist government. *See* China, Republic of; Guomindang

national security, North China, 52; South China, 52; strategic industrial planning, 208

nativism. *See* commodity nativism; "Chineseness;" cultural chauvinism

Naxi people, 131–132, early religious influences, 133; economy, 134, 137, 143, 146; education, 138, 142; gender roles, 137–139, 143; identity construction, 146–147, 351n.13; influence of CCP, 146; language, 133, 350n.2; Lijiang basin, 132, 146, 350n.1; marriage and kinship systems, 133; political views, 134; status of women, 134, 143, 350n.4; women's *huo cuo* organizations, 145–146. *See also* ethnicity; ethnic minorities; *Dayanzhen*; Tiger Springs

New Guinea, Chinese living in, 171–173; Chinese patriotism, 172–173; GMD and Taiwan, 172–173; GMD influence, 172–173; *peranakan* and *totok* ethnicities, 173, 178. See also *huaqiao; peranakans*

nongmin (peasants), attitudes towards Deng Xiaoping and Reforms, 326, 330–331, 333–337, 339–340; belief in spirits, 323–325, 327–328, 332–333, 339–340; Dayanzhen ("vegetable peasants"), 136, 350n.6; gift economy, 329–330, 335–337, 339–340; idealization of Mao, 323, 332–335, 337; identity of, 325–326, 328, 333–334, 336, 338–340; lack of knowledge about sex, 228; migration to urban areas, 249, 251, 257, 262–263, 271–274, 278, 323; opposition to government corruption, 325–326, 331; political and economic powerlessness, 326, 331, 334; role of spirit healers, 329–330, 335, 338; urban assimilation of, 357n.16; wealth and morality, 326, 334–336, 338. *See also* rural life; spirit healing; superstition

North China, 47; geography, 47–50; identity, 32–38, 40–43; language, 49–55; security, 52. *See also* China, People's Republic of

O

"overseas Chinese." See *huaqiao*

P

patriotism, of New Guinea Chinese, 172–173. *See also* national identity; nationalism

peasants. See *nongmin*

Peng Pai (CCP revolutionary), 200–201. *See also* Chinese Communist Party; Guomindang

People's Liberation Army (PLA), 103; Hakka prominence in, 206. *See also* Chinese Communist Party; military

peranakans, 180; identity and perception as Chinese, 173, 178. *See also* New Guinea

politics, 35, 39, 42–44, 89–90, 95–96, 99, 102; ethnic minorities, 95–97; government corruption, 27–30, 325–326, 330–331, 335, 362n.15; *guanxi*, 330–331; involvement of women, 258, 260; in Kunming, 151; Naxi, 134; political consciousness, 37; popular music and, 292–293, 295, 301; of poverty, 332, 334; powerlessness of peasantry, 326, 331, 334; reform, 106. *See also* Chinese Communist Party; Cultural Revolution; Great Leap Forward; Mao Zedong; Naxi people

popular music (*tongsu yinyue*), development of state-run industry, 293–294; as political propaganda, 292–293, 295, 301. *See also* Chinese Communist Party; music

popular religon. See superstition

pornography, CCP campaign against, 227, 229; increase, 227. *See also* sexuality; women

poverty, arranged marriage, 232–233; economic reforms and, 261–262; "floating population," 280–281, 285; Hakka, 197, 208–209; Maoist morality, 332, 334; peasant identity and, 325–326, 334; peasant morality and, 332, 334, 338; sale of women and, 249, 254; south and southeast China, 183,

357n.12. *See also* economic reform; *nongmin*; rural life

pregnancy, premarital sex, 227, 232; unregistered children, 278. *See also* abortion; family planning; health; sexuality; women

prostitution, blamed for AIDS epidemic, 354n.5; increase, 222, 227, 273. *See also* HIV/AIDS; sexuality; sexually transmitted disease; women

public bathrooms (as trysting places), 239, 244. *See also* homosexuality; sexuality

putonghua (common language). *See* Mandarin

Q

qi. See qigong

qigong, 17, 359nn.2, 4; becoming more scientific, 311–312; CCP scrutiny of, 312–313; contrasted with biomedicine, 316–317; devices, 360n.9; growth in popularity, 311–313; inadequacy of science to adjudge, 314–315; internal support for scientific testing of, 314, 316–317; methodology, 313; number of practitioners, 312; "preventive" and "curative" distinction, 314; *qi*, 359n.1, 360n.10; scientific explanation of, 316–317; scientific scrutiny of, 312, 316–317; styles of, 359n.4. *See also* Liu Guizhen; medicine; superstition

Qin dynasty (221–210 B.C.E.), 40, 44

R

"receiving society," 281–287. *See also* "floating population"

Reforms, The. *See* economic reform

religion, 11, 14, 17, 68, 91; Bai, 176–177; CCP and, 106, 309, 311; Communist Revolution and, 309; crime and, 116; Cultural revolution, 259; economic reform and, 323–324, 326, 340; flexibility of, 179–180; folk religion, 309–310, 323–325, 327–330, 361n.2; Malayan Chinese, 179–180; Naxi, 133; officially sanctioned religions, 309, 311;

official repression, 106, 259, 309, 342, 361n.2; popularity of, 309; religious freedom, 311; resurgence of popular religion, 12, 106–126, 312, 323–324, 326, 331, 334, 340; spirit possession, 327–328; women in, 177; worship of Mao, 260. *See also* Buddhism; Christianity; Daoism; Islam; superstition

"River Elegy" (*Heshang*), 9, 359n.7, critique of government, 298; influence on rock and roll musicians, 299, 305; inspiration to Tiananmen movement, 298. *See also* Cui Jian; democracy; rock and roll music; Tiananmen movement

rock and roll music (*yaogun yinyue*), 217–218, 290; in Beijing, 295–296; CCP suppression, 219–292, 302; as commodity, 303; "commodity nativism," 293, 303–305, 359n.10; construction of youth identity, 295–296, 300, 306; as cultural opposition, 295, 298–299; democratic agenda, 291–293; economic reform and, 292–293; growth of, 293–294; international support, 302; as rebellion against political oppression, 291–292, 294–296, 299, 301, 306; student activism, 297, 298–299, 358n.2, 359n.8; Tiananmen movement and, 291–292, 299, 302; Western influence, 290–292. *See also* Ai Jing; Cui Jian; music; student activism; Tiananmen Movement

rural life, 86; arranged marriage, 220; class divisions, 338; economic reforms and, 323; family dynamic, 253–254, 257–258, 260, 263, 267–268; famine, 257–258; folk religion, 323–325, 327–330; lack of sexual knowledge, 228; marriage, 249, 251, 253, 259–260, 265, 267; medicine, 261; political and economic powerlessness, 326, 331, 334; prejudice against women, 251–252, 256–258, 263, 265–267; raising children, 261–262; religion, 253, 323–324, 325–326, 331; resurgence of folk religion, 323–324, 325–326, 331; sexuality, 220, 257–258; spirit healing, 323–324, 327–329; suicide rates, 250; women, 251, 256–257, 260,

262–263, 339; women in agriculture, 251, 256–257, 260, 262–263; worker migration, 249, 251, 257, 262–263, 272, 323; work ethic and morality, 363n.21. *See also* Dayanzhen; *nongmin*; poverty; spirit healing; Zhao Xinlan